The Audubon Society Master Guide to Birding

A Chanticleer Press Edition

Consultants
Davis W. Finch
Paul Lehman

Authors
Robert Arbib
George Archibald
Henry T. Armistead
Frank C. Bellrose
Louis R. Bevier
Clait E. Braun
Peter F. Cannell
Thomas H. Davis
Kim R. Eckert
David L. Evans
John Farrand, Jr.
Davis W. Finch
Kimball L. Garrett
Daniel D. Gibson
Joseph A. Grzybowski
Gordon W. Gullion
Harold J. Harju
Dan Clark Holliman
Paul A. Johnsgard
Kenn Kaufman
Stuart Keith
Paul Lehman
Ron Naveen
John C. Ogden
Kenneth C. Parkes
Wayne R. Petersen
H. Douglas Pratt
John T. Ratti

William L. Robinson
Walter Rosene
Richard W. Stallcup
Paul W. Sykes, Jr.
Scott B. Terrill
Theodore G. Tobish Jr.
Peter D. Vickery
Terence Wahl
Robert B. Weeden
Claudia Wilds

The Audubon Society Master Guide to Birding

1 Loons to Sandpipers

John Farrand, Jr.,
Editor

Alfred A. Knopf, New York

This is a Borzoi Book
Published by Alfred A. Knopf, Inc.

Prepared and produced by
Chanticleer Press, Inc., New York.

Color reproductions by Nievergelt Repro AG, Zurich, Switzerland.
Type set in Century Expanded by Dix Type Inc., Syracuse,
New York. Printed and bound by Dai Nippon Printing Co., Ltd.,
Tokyo, Japan.

First Printing

Library of Congress Catalog Number: 83-47945
ISBN: 0-394-53382-8

Contents

Acknowledgments

This book was written not only for the birders of North America but by them. While preparing these guides even my non-birding associates at Chanticleer Press became converts. I was gratified when an enthusiastic group turned out recently in the early morning for a staff bird walk in Central Park. I wish to celebrate the spirit of my colleagues and to thank them for their good will and their professional help.

I am deeply grateful to the authors of the species accounts, both for their expert prose and for suggestions on what photographs and artwork were necessary to accompany their text, and for numerous suggestions and advice. Without their enthusiastic and industrious cooperation, this book would not have been possible. I am equally thankful to the authors of the special text sections, whose contributions have expanded the scope of the book.

Davis W. Finch, Paul Lehman, and J. V. Remsen served as consultants and read all or some of the species accounts. Their careful perusal of the text resulted in many improvements, and the authors and editors are indebted to them.

In addition to the authors and consultants, thanks are due to many other birders and ornithologists for suggestions, advice, encouragement, and additional tangible assistance in the preparation of this series. I would like to make special mention of John Bull of the American Museum of Natural History for his frequent advice on nomenclature and distribution. Others who have assisted the authors and editors are Dennis J. Abbott, Paul Adamus, C. Wesley Biggs, Paul A. Buckley, William S. Clark, Elaine Cook, Betty Darling Cotrille, Robert H. Day, Joseph DiCostanzo, Matthew P. Drennan, Jon Dunn, R. Michael Erwin, Norm Famous, Frank B. Gill, Sharon Goldwasser, Delphine Haley, John P. Hubbard, George L. Hunt, Jr., Ned K. Johnson, Lars Jonsson, Ivy Kuspit, Mary LeCroy, Lori Leonardi, Trevor Lloyd-Evans, Fred E. Lohrer, Frederick C. Mish, Burt L. Monroe, Jr., Gale Monson, Joe Morlan, J. P. Myers, John P. O'Neill, Dennis R. Paulson, Roger Tory Peterson, William C. Russell, Lawrence A. Ryel, Gary D. Schnell, Fred C. Sibley, Kenneth K. Tate, Michael H. Tove, Guy A. Tudor, Barbara Vickery, Peter Warshall, Bret Whitney, Janet Witzeman, and Alan Wormington.

I am deeply indebted to Arnold Small, Kenneth Fink, Herbert Clarke, and the 203 other photographers whose work forms the bulk of the color illustrations in these volumes. I would like to thank Thomas H. Davis, who helped to identify the difficult plumages of gulls, and Stephen A. Bailey for his assistance in selecting photographs of western *Empidonax* flycatchers. I appreciate the help of Robert Cardillo, Martine Culbertson, Alec Forbes-Watson, and Mark Robbins of VIREO, the growing library of bird photographs at the Academy of Natural Sciences in Philadelphia, for their hospitality and willingness to make their files available to me; to Charles Walcott and David Blanton of the Laboratory of Ornithology at Cornell University for permitting us to use their photograph collection for this project; and to Helen Kittinger of the Alabama Ornithological Society for generously sharing the photograph collections of that organization.

Of the many fine bird artists whose work so enhances this book, I am especially indebted to art editor Al Gilbert, who took on the task of assigning the paintings and drawings, coordinated the efforts of the team of artists he assembled, and executed many fine paintings himself, and to art consultant Guy A. Tudor, whose valuable advice was frequently sought and generously given. The other artists who have contributed their work to this book are James E. Coe, Michael DiGiorgio, Georges Dremeaux, Robert

Gillmor, H. Jon Janosik, Michel Kleinbaum, Lawrence B. McQueen, John P. O'Neill, John C. Yrizarry, and Dale A. Zimmerman. All of these artists have been inspired by the late George M. Sutton, and many have benefited from his direct tutelage in the art of bird painting. "Doc" Sutton would surely have been proud of the illustrations herein—of their lifelike quality and the careful attention to proper habitat. The artists would like to dedicate their work in these volumes to the memory of George M. Sutton— ornithologist, teacher, friend, and one of America's greatest painters of bird life.

Special thanks are due to the authorities of several museums for making specimens available to the artists and authors: Lester L. Short and his staff at the American Museum of Natural History; Ralph W. Schreiber and Kimball L. Garrett of the Los Angeles County Museum of Natural History; J. V. Remsen and John P. O'Neill of the Louisiana State University Museum of Zoology; and Stephen M. Russell of the Department of Ecology and Evolutionary Biology at the University of Arizona.

To Les Line, Editor-in-Chief of Audubon magazine, I am indebted for his early endorsement of the idea of this work, and for his constant encouragement during its preparation.

I am very grateful to Massimo Vignelli, who translated the concept of the book into an effective and workable design.

At Chanticleer Press, I owe a debt of gratitude to Paul Steiner for his energetic and wholehearted enthusiasm for the project since its earliest stages; to Gudrun Buettner for the original conception of the book and for her spirited assistance in solving editorial and graphic problems during the preparation of the series; to Susan Costello, whose encouragement and problem-solving abilities have done much to make this book what it is; to Ann Whitman for her assistance in editing and coordinating the manuscript in its various stages and her seemingly tireless attention to editorial details; to Mary Beth Brewer for her invaluable help in editing the special essays and organizing the material to enable us to meet our deadlines; to Carol Nehring, for the knowledge and expertise she brought to bear on the layouts, and her assistants Ayn Svoboda and Karen Wollman; to Helga Lose and Amy Roche, for their expert efforts in ensuring the accuracy of color reproductions and shepherding the project through its intricate production stages; to Edward Douglas for his assistance in gathering and selecting the tens of thousands of photographs that were reviewed during the preparation of this book; and to Karel Birnbaum, Katherine Booz, Lori Renn, and Susan Van Pelt for their assistance in editorial matters.

At Alfred A. Knopf, Inc., I wish to extend my appreciation to Robert Gottlieb and Anthony M. Schulte, whose sponsorship of the project and confidence in it made this ambitious work possible; to Charles Elliott for his unwavering support and help in shaping the editorial content of the work; to Angus Cameron for his far-ranging knowledge of natural history; and to Barbara Bristol, who should be commended for her competent stewardship of the guides.

John Farrand, Jr.

The Audubon Society

The National Audubon Society is among the oldest and largest
private conservation organizations in the world. With over 500,000
members and more than 480 local chapters across the country,
the Society works in behalf of our natural heritage through
environmental education and conservation action. It protects wildlife
in more than 70 sanctuaries from coast to coast. It also operates
outdoor education centers and ecology workshops and publishes the
prizewinning *Audubon* magazine, *American Birds* magazine,
newsletters, films, and other educational materials. For further
information regarding membership in the Society, write to the
National Audubon Society, 950 Third Avenue, New York, New
York 10022.

Preface

For years the birding community has been waiting for an advanced field guide, one that would include the increasingly sophisticated and subtle clues to bird identification discovered in recent decades. These have been brought to light by birders whose expertise may lie with a particular group of birds, the birds of a specific habitat or region, or a single species. The new information resulting from these field studies has validated our assumption that it is impossible for an individual birder to know everything about all the species on our continent.

For this reason we have tried to prepare the most complete, up-to-date, and useful field identification guide ever devised. We began by assembling a distinguished panel of expert authors from all parts of the continent, from Florida to Alaska and California to Maine. The 61 authors contributed 835 species accounts in their areas of concentration or wrote special essays; consultants with a special understanding of both the eastern and the western regions reviewed the text. In addition, we asked the authors to advise us on photographs required to illustrate each species. In some instances a single photograph was sufficient; in others up to six pictures were required. We invited the most accomplished bird photographers to submit their work. From the tens of thousands of transparencies that we reviewed, we selected those that best show the diagnostic field marks of each bird. To illustrate those rare or elusive species that are infrequently photographed, we commissioned nine well-known artists to paint portraits of the birds in their habitats. Artists also provided the hundreds of black-and-white drawings, many of them flight diagrams, to supplement the field marks shown in the color photographs and paintings.

While these guides have been designed to satisfy the demands of advanced birders, we have also supplied beginners with what they need to know to start an absorbing hobby that can last a lifetime. To provide the vital information required during the few seconds a bird may be visible, we list key field marks for each color illustration. For further clarification, those features that can be easily seen are shown with arrows and numbers on the illustrations. Maps that illustrate the range descriptions are also given. Of interest to birders of all levels are the special essays that expand the scope of the guide by explaining how to find and identify birds, how to understand modern scientific classification and nomenclature, and other subjects.

Rather than present all of this material in a single massive volume, we decided to divide it into three volumes, each of which may be conveniently carried into the field. We have arranged the species according to the latest classification of North American birds adopted by the American Ornithologists' Union in 1982. Accidental species are placed in an appendix of the volume that covers birds related to it.

We hope these guides, with their contributions from many experts, will be what they are intended to be: a master guide to birding.

Part One

Introduction

Bird identification has today almost become a science. Using color, pattern, shape, size, voice, habitat, and behavior, birders are continually finding new ways to distinguish similar species. The journals *American Birds* and *Birding* frequently publish articles on field identification, while at the annual meetings of the American Birding Association, birders attend seminars on how to identify such puzzling groups as storm-petrels, immature gulls, the small sandpipers known as "peeps," and diurnal birds of prey. Birders have spent long hours in the field working out subtle but useful distinctions, such as the differences in the head shapes of gulls, in the wing- and tail-flicking of *Empidonax* flycatchers, and the flight characteristics of storm-petrels. There are now specialists in the identification of shorebirds, gulls, storm-petrels, shearwaters, and hawks. Clues are being found that allow us to differentiate birds that have long been considered indistinguishable.

Birding has come a long way during its history, and the term "birder" itself, in the evolution of its meaning, reflects the change in our attitude toward birds. For centuries a birder was someone who killed birds, usually for sport or for food; Shakespeare used the term in this sense. The modern meaning of the term arose in the 1940s, as birding became an increasingly popular pastime. Today's birders, armed with binoculars, telescopes, and cameras, and aided by the great collections made by the bird students of the 19th century, are vastly more sophisticated than their counterparts of decades ago.

Ludlow Griscom

Born in New York City in 1890, Ludlow Griscom may justly be called the father of modern field identification. He began attending meetings of the Linnaean Society of New York at an early age. Entirely on his own, he set out to learn the birds of the northeastern United States. Later in his life he wrote:

"At a meeting of the Linnaean Society of New York when a school boy, I reported having seen Bicknell's Thrush [a form of the Gray-cheeked Thrush], my identification being based on the erroneous supposition that its call-note was diagnostic. The resultant storm of criticism rendered me practically speechless. Then and there I planned to become a reliable observer and to investigate the scientific possibilities of sight identification."

The results of this determination were not long in coming. Although his prowess in field identification was doubted by many of his colleagues, Griscom developed an ability to identify birds in the field better than anyone else in his time. To prove his point, he finally took one of his friends, a doubting Thomas, into the field. When Griscom identified a small bird high in the trees overhead as a female Cape May Warbler, his friend was skeptical but prepared. Having brought along his shotgun, he collected the bird. When the specimen was retrieved from the ground, they found it was, as Griscom had said, a female Cape May Warbler. After a few more incidents of this kind, the idea that birds were identifiable while still alive and in the field began to gain ground.

The 19th Century

The practice of shooting birds rather than just looking at them was standard among serious ornithologists in North America before Griscom's time. The main method of study for men like Alexander Wilson, John James Audubon, and Thomas Nuttall was to shoot the birds they encountered and then identify them in the hand.

Most birders were men of leisure or professional collectors, and their attention was devoted to discovering new species of birds and documenting, with specimens, the ranges of these species. Although these pioneering ornithologists learned much about the habits of birds, as an examination of Wilson's nine-volume *American Ornithology* or Audubon's five-volume *Ornithological Biography* will attest, there was only one way to enter the field of ornithology— armed with a shotgun.

Gaining a knowledge of birds in the first half of the 19th century was a long and arduous task, the work of a lifetime. North American birds were still poorly understood; many species had not yet been discovered, and males and females of a single bird were sometimes considered separate species. Throughout much of the 19th century, for instance, there were thought to be three species of waterthrushes, rather than two. Moreover, the differences between species that had been discovered were sometimes unappreciated; it was not until 1811, for example, that Alexander Wilson established that the Common Nighthawk and the Whip-poor-will, two abundant eastern birds, are two separate species. A student of birds during this period faced enormous difficulties; communication between ornithologists was poor, and there was no reliable book on the bird life of North America until 1808, when the first volume of Wilson's *American Ornithology* appeared.

A major ornithological work in its day was Elliott Coues' two-volume *Key to North American Birds*, published in 1872 and still in print in the early 20th century. This monumental book began with a 58-page section entitled "Field Ornithology: being a manual for the collecting, preparing, and preserving of birds." In counseling beginning ornithologists, Coues stated: "The Double-barrelled Shot Gun is your main reliance."

The only bird records that were accepted were those accompanied by a specimen. This attitude is succinctly stated in an expression common among ornithologists of the day: "What's hit is history; what's missed is mystery." Private collectors assembled large cabinets of bird specimens, just as entomologists do today. These specimens eventually found their way into public institutions and now form the core of the collections of many museums.

Toward the end of the 19th century, the shotgun began to give way to binoculars and telescopes. By then nearly all North American bird species had been discovered and their ranges established with collected specimens; the sequence of their molts and plumages was generally understood. This gradual change came about partly because ornithologists were turning their attention to the study of living birds in the field and partly, perhaps, because of the growing public distaste for killing birds that were not game birds or species thought to be harmful to crops and livestock. Books began to appear in which field identification was stressed. Foremost among these were Frank M. Chapman's *Handbook of Birds of Eastern North America*, published in 1895, and Florence Merriam Bailey's *Handbook of Birds of Western North America*, which appeared in 1902. Both of these books were less cumbersome than earlier bird books had been, and had briefer descriptions. But even Chapman's book included complicated "keys" intended for identification in the hand, and Chapman considered a shotgun an important piece of equipment in bird study.

Birding Today

The development of field identification techniques was gradual. As late as 1922 Ludlow Griscom himself had certain reservations that seem amusing today. He wrote, for example, that it was "practically impossible" to distinguish immature Forster's, Arctic, and Common terns, the two species of scaups, male Cooper's and female Sharp-shinned hawks, and immature Blackpoll and Bay-breasted warblers. He considered it "very difficult" to tell apart adult Great and Double-crested cormorants, female Common and Red-breasted mergansers, Snowy Egrets and immature Little Blue Herons,

Greater and Lesser yellowlegs, and Herring and Ring-billed gulls. Yet through the efforts of Griscom and the younger men he influenced, among them Allan D. Cruickshank, Joseph J. Hickey, and Roger Tory Peterson, field identification became respectable. At the same time on the West Coast, Ralph Hoffmann was writing *Birds of the Pacific States;* this ground-breaking book appeared in 1927 and was the first to use the term "field mark"—a term familiar to all birders today. Hoffmann italicized his field marks, just as present-day field guides do, and his descriptions were brief, concentrating on the points of distinction between species.

It was Roger Tory Peterson, a disciple of Griscom but like him largely self-taught, who put field identification on firm footing. His *Field Guide to the Birds* was published in 1934 and his *Field Guide to Western Birds* in 1941, and both have appeared in several editions. These were the first truly compact field guides, and with Peterson's own paintings, they resolved the distinctions between the "impossible" or "very difficult" species that Griscom had listed just a few years earlier. The guides gave field marks for all the species then known to occur regularly in North America. Bird identification was now within the reach of anyone willing to learn about it. No mention was made of shotguns; binoculars and telescopes were standard equipment for birders.

Today only a small number of museum ornithologists still require a specimen to verify an unusual sighting, and specimens have become very difficult to obtain. Federal and state permits are usually issued only to professional ornithologists and stipulate which species and how many specimens may be collected. Moreover, rarities usually turn up in parks, wildlife refuges, and bird sanctuaries—places where collecting is impossible. Birders today often document rarities with a camera and recognize them by using the many new field marks that have been found since Ludlow Griscom first made field identification an exacting and respected pursuit. Griscom once said that the secret to identifying birds in the field was to have as clear a mental image as possible of each species. The mental images of the modern birder are growing clearer every year.

John Farrand, Jr.

Head

1. *Malar streak/*
   Mustache
2. *Throat*
3. *Chin*
4. *Lower mandible*
5. *Upper mandible*
6. *Lores*
7. *Forehead*
8. *Median crown stripe*
9. *Crown*
10. *Eyebrow*
11. *Eye-ring*
12. *Nape*
13. *Ear coverts*

Body

1. *Breast*
2. *Lesser wing coverts/*
   Shoulder
3. *Median wing coverts*
4. *Greater wing coverts*
5. *Belly*
6. *Flanks*
7. *Back*
8. *Scapulars*
9. *Wing bars*
10. *Tertials*
11. *Rump*
12. *Secondaries*
13. *Uppertail coverts*
14. *Outer tail feathers*
15. *Undertail coverts*
16. *Primaries*
17. *Leg/Tarsus*

Upperwing Surface

1. *Primaries*
2. *Primary coverts*
3. *Alula*
4. *Wrist*
5. *Lesser wing coverts*
6. *Median wing coverts*
7. *Scapulars*
8. *Greater wing coverts*
9. *Tertials*
10. *Secondaries*

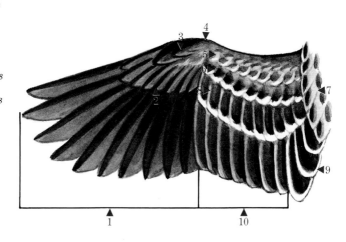

How to Use This Guide

Experienced birders will already know how to use this guide. In each volume the families and species are arranged according to the latest classification of the American Ornithologists' Union, adopted in 1982; this new sequence is followed by professional ornithologists. In all, the three volumes treat 68 families and 835 species. All but the rarest birds—116 accidental or casual species that have been recorded in North America only a few times—are treated in full; these rare birds are discussed in an appendix of the volume that contains their close relatives. If you are familiar with the new A.O.U. sequence, you can quickly refer to the proper volume and page. You can also locate a particular species by consulting the index; each volume has an index to its contents, and Volume III has a comprehensive index to all three volumes.

If you are a beginning birder, take some time to familiarize yourself with the birds covered in these guides. Examine the color plates, and note the kinds of field marks that are useful in identifying a species and in distinguishing it from similar species. Read the family descriptions, which summarize the general appearance of the birds in each family. Note that many species occur in more than one plumage, depending on the season or on the age, sex, or geographical origin of the bird. Take a moment to see how a range map illustrates the range statement for each species; the map should tell you at a glance which species are likely to occur in your area.

Illustrations

In this guide, the color illustrations and text face each other for speedy reference. Each species may have from one to six color illustrations, arranged in an order that facilitates comparison with similar plumages of other species. Next to each color illustration is a small "plate key," that is, a black-and-white reproduction of the color plate. Superimposed on this plate key are numbered red arrows, corresponding to a numbered list of field marks. Beneath this list of numbered features, other field marks such as size, shape, behavior, voice, and habitat are given. Numerous black-and-white drawings, often bearing numbered arrows as well, supplement the color plates. These drawings generally depict the same plumage as that shown in the color plates; a drawing that illustrates a different plumage is accompanied by a label.

Each family of birds begins with a general description of the family and a list of all of the members of the family found in North America. Accidental species, which are treated in an appendix, appear in light-face type in this list.

Each text entry begins with the English and scientific names of the species. A typical species account goes on to discuss the bird's habitat, its behavioral characteristics, and other useful identification information, followed by the following sections:

Description

The description begins with the approximate length of the bird both in inches and in centimeters. The bird's shape, color, and pattern are described, and where necessary, several different plumages are discussed, along with other features that vary in importance, depending on the bird. (For example, bill color may clinch identification of one species, but be of only very minor interest in another.) Geographical forms that were once considered distinct species are included; many of these forms have widely used English names of their own; where these names are mentioned, they are given in quotation marks.

Voice

The voice is described for all species in which it is useful for identification. In general, only diagnostic songs and calls are given.

Similar Species

This section refers the reader to those species with which the bird is most likely to be confused; in many cases, a brief comparative description gives the most important differences between the two. In a few instances, a bird is so distinctive that no section on similar species is included. Accidental species are indicated by an asterisk.

Range

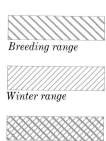

Breeding range

Winter range

Permanent range

The breeding range of a species is generally given first, followed by the winter range. Where only one range is outlined, it may be assumed that the bird is sedentary. A brief indication of the ranges of birds outside of North America is also given. Range maps accompany the range statements. The breeding range is indicated on the map by diagonal hatching. Where there is overlap between the breeding and winter ranges, or wherever a species occurs year-round, both ranges are superimposed. For consistency, the ranges are cut off at the Mexican border, even though the ranges of many species extend into Mexico or beyond. In the case of very rare species that occur in North America infrequently as well as those that have a very limited distribution, no range map is provided.

Other Features

This guide includes a number of features of interest to both beginning and advanced birders. In the front of each book, the orders of birds covered in that volume are described briefly. Drawings have been provided to show the parts of a bird, and special essays on How to Identify Birds and How to Find Birds have also been included. In the back of each volume, a glossary defines technical terms used in the text. Also in the back of each volume is a section that discusses the accidental species that fall within the scope of that volume. The section on accidentals includes brief descriptions and an indication of where these very rare species have occurred. While the guide follows the A.O.U. sequence and nomenclature, the accidentals included are those recognized in the *A.B.A. Checklist: Birds of Continental United States and Canada*, second edition, published in 1982 by the American Birding Association. Finally, a special section on classification and nomenclature has been provided.

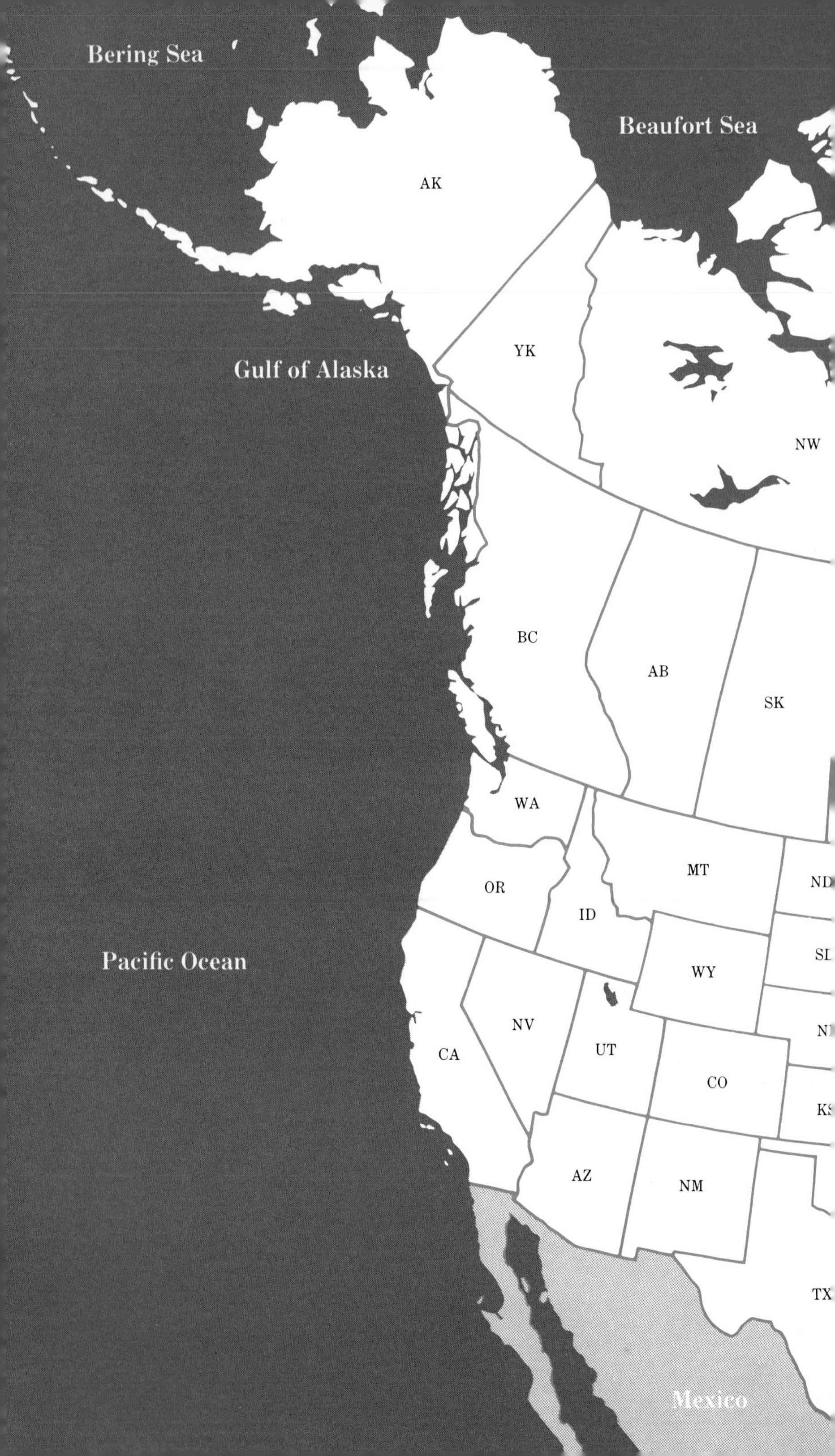
Bering Sea
Beaufort Sea
AK
YK
Gulf of Alaska
NW
BC
AB
SK
WA
MT
OR
ID
WY
Pacific Ocean
NV
UT
CA
CO
AZ
NM
TX
Mexico

How to Identify Birds

Beginning birders usually identify species by comparing birds they see with illustrations or descriptions. To identify birds correctly, novices normally must examine them slowly in detail under favorable conditions. Experts, on the other hand, do not have to look so carefully; they have a mental picture that is far more detailed than any illustration. Their identifications are based on a variety of clues, considered singly or in combination. Here are some of the most important ones.

Size

The size of a bird, although it may be difficult to determine when the bird is far away or by itself, is a useful clue in identifying it. As you learn to recognize birds, you will quickly become familiar with their size relative to other species. Select a series of common and widespread birds of different sizes, such as the House Sparrow, American Robin, Rock Dove, American Crow, Canada Goose, and Great Blue Heron, and use these to gauge the size of other birds you see. You will soon be able to judge whether an unfamiliar bird is smaller than a House Sparrow, about the size of an American Robin, or somewhat larger than a Rock Dove. Very often in a flock of shorebirds or waterfowl, a single bird will stand out because it is larger or smaller than the others. If you already know that the other members of the flock are Sanderlings, for example, you will have a head start in identifying the single, unfamiliar bird. In cases where you cannot judge the size of a bird, its shape is the next feature to consider.

Stocky build

Shape

Shape is one of the most readily observed characteristics of a bird and one of the most important in identification. Your impression of a bird's shape will be influenced by several features. The body may be compact and stocky, like that of a European Starling or a member of the auk family, or it may be slender, like a Yellow-billed Cuckoo's or Red-breasted Merganser's. The neck may be very long, as in herons and the Anhinga, or very short, as in many small sandpipers. The legs, too, may be very long, as in most herons, or very short, as in terns. The bill may be conical, like that of a House Sparrow; slender and pointed, like that of a warbler or kinglet; heavy and pointed, like that of a Belted Kingfisher or a heron; decurved, like that of a curlew or Long-billed Thrasher; or hooked, like the bill of the American Kestrel and Red-tailed Hawk. The wings may be long and pointed, like those of terns, swifts, and swallows, or distinctly rounded, like those of quails. Tails vary greatly in shape. Some birds, like European Starlings and nuthatches, have short tails, while others, like gnatcatchers, thrashers, and wagtails, have very long tails. A bird's tail may be squared at the tip, like a Cliff Swallow's; notched, like that of a House Finch or Tropical Kingbird; deeply forked, like the tail of a Common Tern or Barn Swallow; rounded, like a Blue Jay's; or pointed, like a Mourning Dove's. Posture is often an important aspect of a bird's shape. Plovers tend to stand in a more upright position, with the head held higher, than sandpipers of similar size. Flycatchers usually perch with the body held almost vertically, rather than in the horizontal posture of warblers, vireos, and kinglets. Even among closely related species, there may be differences in posture: Yellow-crowned Night-Herons often stand in a more upright posture than do Black-crowned Night-Herons, and Rough-legged Hawks often perch in a more horizontal posture than Red-tailed Hawks.

Slender build

Long legs

Many species can be identified by shape alone. For example, virtually all North American ducks have a distinctive head shape; when seen in profile, they can often be identified by this feature.

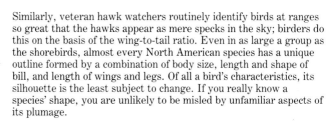

Similarly, veteran hawk watchers routinely identify birds at ranges so great that the hawks appear as mere specks in the sky; birders do this on the basis of the wing-to-tail ratio. Even in as large a group as the shorebirds, almost every North American species has a unique outline formed by a combination of body size, length and shape of bill, and length of wings and legs. Of all a bird's characteristics, its silhouette is the least subject to change. If you really know a species' shape, you are unlikely to be misled by unfamiliar aspects of its plumage.

Color and Pattern

Black-and-white wing pattern

Color and pattern are important, too. The brilliant red of a male Northern Cardinal is often one's first clue to the identity of this bird, visible before its conical bill can be seen and before one is familiar with its distinctive, tail-pumping flight. The solid blue of male Indigo Buntings and Mountain Bluebirds at once sets these birds apart from all others. In much of the continent, a flash of bright orange and black in the treetops can instantly be called a Northern Oriole. Before a beginning birder learns the distinctive shape and manner of flight of an American Kestrel, its colors—bluish-gray and rufous in the male, rufous-brown in the female—enable him to identify this small falcon. If you note that a distant goose is white with black wing tips, you have narrowed the possibilities to only two species, the Snow Goose and Ross' Goose. Among the spotted thrushes, a bird in which only the tail is rust-colored is a Hermit Thrush; one with rust on the head and back is a Wood Thrush; a bird whose upperparts are wholly tawny is a Veery; while a bird with no rust or tawny in the upperparts is either a Gray-cheeked or Swainson's thrush.

White outer tail feathers

Carefully noting the color and pattern of a bird is essential in identifying it. Watch for wing bars; vireos, for example, can be sorted into two groups, those with wing bars and those without. Other wing patterns can be helpful, too, especially if the bird is in flight. The black-and-white wing pattern of a flying Willet is diagnostic, as are the red shoulders of Red-winged and Tricolored blackbirds, and the flashes of white in the wings of White-winged Doves, Red-headed Woodpeckers, Northern Mockingbirds, shrikes, and male Phainopeplas. Watch for rump and tail patterns. A departing Northern Flicker can be identified at a glance by its white rump; the pale buff rump of a Cliff Swallow or Cave Swallow quickly eliminates all other swallows. A yellowish or greenish warbler with large yellow tail patches must be a Yellow Warbler, while one with large white tail patches and a yellow rump is likely to be a Magnolia. White outer tail feathers mark the juncos and a variety of open-country birds: meadowlarks, pipits, Horned Larks, and Vesper Sparrows. A large flycatcher with a white tail tip must be an Eastern Kingbird, while in the West, a kingbird with white outer tail feathers must be a Western.

Look carefully at the pattern of the head. Watch for eyebrows, eye-rings, eyelines, mustaches, or throat patches; note the color of the crown, ear coverts, and lores. Take special note of any unusual color pattern: the red head and yellow body of a male Western Tanager, the golden-buff nape of a male Bobolink, the white sides on the rump of a Violet-green Swallow, and the rufous rump of the gray Lucy's Warbler are all diagnostic. The pattern of many species makes them easy to identify. Flying waterfowl and many warblers usually can be recognized by pattern alone. When other features are all but invisible, particularly in poor light or at great distances, a bird's distinctive pattern can often be discerned.

White wing patches

Behavior

Many birds walk, swim, or fly in so characteristic a manner that behavior by itself can permit identification. Given an unlabeled specimen of a Water Pipit, most birders are not likely to recognize it at once, yet they can identify the living bird from hundreds of yards away by its bounding, stuttering flight or its habit of emphatically pumping its tail when on the ground. Some behavioral clues are obvious, like the big, splashy dives of Northern Gannets and Ospreys, the constant nodding of a yellowlegs, the head-bobbing motion of a swimming coot, the zigzag flight of a Common Snipe when it is flushed from a wet meadow, or the mothlike flight of a Common Poorwill. Others are subtle, such as the flight mannerisms of kittiwakes and the wing- and tail-flicks of flycatchers. Behavioral clues are almost unfailingly reliable and can help in identifying birds under a variety of circumstances. The differing flight styles of hawks, for example, or the various feeding postures of shorebirds can be used to identify them almost at the limit of visibility.

Conical bill

Vocal Clues

In many situations, it is easier to hear birds than to see them. Whether you are in the rain forest of the Northwest, the warbler-filled woods of New England, or the cypress swamps of the Carolinas, you are certain to hear many more birds than you see. The vocalizations of birds may be divided into two rough categories: songs and calls. Songs are usually given by adult males on territory during the nesting season, but may also be heard during migration and, in some species, during the winter as well. In certain species, such as the Rose-breasted Grosbeak and Northern Mockingbird, females as well as males may produce songs. Many songs are rather complex, like those of the Winter Wren and most wood warblers, but some are very simple, like the short, metallic *tslit* of Henslow's Sparrow. Calls, or call notes, are generally more simple, and are often given throughout the year under a variety of situations to express alarm, to maintain contact with other members of a flock, or during interactions with a mate or young.

Slender, pointed bill

Knowing the songs and calls of a region's birds will enable you to identify a far higher percentage than you could with binoculars alone. Identification by voice is almost always reliable. The shorebirds, for example, have flight calls, given at all times of the year, that are absolutely distinctive. Every shorebird native to North America, as well as vagrant species from the Old World, can be identified by these notes alone. Thus, if you are familiar with shorebird voices, you can identify the birds with certainty anywhere at any time of year, whether they are breeding in the Arctic, migrating through our latitudes, or wintering in South America. You can identify them even in darkness, and up to the limits of audibility. All North American songbirds, as well, have distinctive voices; in many cases, even their minor calls—lisps or chips—are recognizable. For example, of the large New World subfamily of wood warblers, about 50 fairly closely related species breed in North America. All have songs that can be learned readily; in fact, their songs differ more markedly than their plumages. Each song can be distinguished and mentally catalogued according to a variety of characteristics: pitch, cadence, duration, loudness, frequency of utterance, and quality. Although the song structure of a species may vary slightly from region to region, the quality of the song will almost always remain recognizable.

Heavy, pointed bill

Habitat and Range

Most people know that ducks and gulls are water birds and that thrushes are birds of the forest, but few beginning birders are aware of how specific most species are in their habitat requirements. Although these requirements may vary somewhat according to region and season, they are still quite rigid; experienced bird watchers expect to see certain birds in certain habitats. Warblers are as selective as any group: Tennessees breed in tamarack,

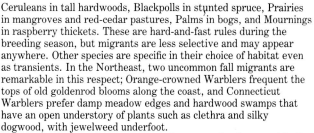

Ceruleans in tall hardwoods, Blackpolls in stunted spruce, Prairies in mangroves and red-cedar pastures, Palms in bogs, and Mournings in raspberry thickets. These are hard-and-fast rules during the breeding season, but migrants are less selective and may appear anywhere. Other species are specific in their choice of habitat even as transients. In the Northeast, two uncommon fall migrants are remarkable in this respect; Orange-crowned Warblers frequent the tops of old goldenrod blooms along the coast, and Connecticut Warblers prefer damp meadow edges and hardwood swamps that have an open understory of plants such as clethra and silky dogwood, with jewelweed underfoot.

Pointed tail

Knowing habitat preferences greatly increases the chances of finding particular birds; it can also limit what we expect to find. In many cases, habitat by itself helps us to identify species. For example, even if they can barely be seen or heard, blackbirds in northern bogs are almost certain to be Rusties. Finally, the range of most birds is determined in large part by the availability of a specific habitat. Although the ranges of most species are continuously expanding or contracting, they can nonetheless be geographically defined or mapped. Knowledge of range enters into virtually every identification, usually as a subconscious first consideration. So too does an awareness of the average arrival and departure dates of migratory species.

Becoming an Expert

To the uninitiated, the identifications made by experienced birders often seem to approach wizardry. Experts, rather than comparing the bird they have seen with illustrations in a field guide, weigh a number of attributes that together give the species a distinctive personality. The better you know a species, the more ways you have to identify it. Many North American birds have three or even more

Notched tail

identifiable plumages, which can be bewildering at first, until one realizes how many factors are invariable: shape, voice, behavior, and range.

Looking at Birds

There is no secret to becoming skilled in identifying birds: Just look and listen. Observation may seem simple at first, but you will progress faster if you look attentively and repeatedly, even at common species. For many beginners, examination stops and binoculars come down the moment the bird is identified. In fact, this is the time to start looking. Make the effort. Imagine, for example, that this is the last Downy Woodpecker you will see for a long time, or that you will soon be asked to describe or even draw it. If you have difficulty getting a firm grasp on a bird's appearance, first look

Forked tail

at its eye, and to force yourself to look closely, try to ascertain the color of the iris. Then study the size and shape of the bill and its length in relation to the distance separating its base from the center of the eye. Next, extend your study of the bird's proportions to the length of its legs and to the position of the folded wing tips in relation to the tip of the tail. From these observations, proceed to an examination of the bird's coloring and patterns. This deliberate approach might seem tedious, but birds lend themselves to careful observation, and you will almost certainly find it engrossing and rewarding. You will soon discover that you can memorize birds in much the same way you memorize human faces. It is possible to acquire a permanent familiarity with a seemingly limitless number of bird species, but to do so you must look carefully. Most expert bird watchers spend much time simply studying the appearance of birds, even familiar ones. This enjoyable exercise results in a far more detailed acquaintance than is required for simple identification, but it also makes one aware of the differences between species that superficially appear to be similar. Bear in mind that you can know what a bird looks like only by *looking* at it. This sort of bird study demands fairly close-range and leisurely observation, but do not pass up a chance to watch a distant bird—you may be surprised at how much you can see. With good light and good binoculars, you can identify distinctively patterned birds as small as warblers, in flight, even overhead, at a great distance, but you will not know this until you try it.

Looking at museum specimens or, better yet, at live birds trapped at a banding station, can also be extremely helpful. Side-by-side comparison of similar species can reveal differences that may help you in field identification. Juxtaposing and comparing eight or ten species of warblers, for example, will demonstrate as no field guide can the diversity that exists within this group. You will discover how much these species vary in size, bill shape, wing length, rictal bristles, or any number of small details. Studying specimens or captive birds will also help you to learn about the arrangement of feathers: which ones are involved in the wing bars, for instance, and how the tail feathers are shingled, with the central pair, or "deck feathers," on top and the outermost underneath. These insights will help you to understand what you see in the field.

Rounded wings

Listening to Birds

Learning bird songs may seem difficult at first, but we learn them much as we learn melodies, by attentive and repeated listening. You can be more or less energetic in acquiring this familiarity with bird voices, but you will progress faster if you make it a rule to track down every unfamiliar call. This may initially seem overwhelming, but your ear will soon become remarkably good at resolving a tangle of noise into recognizable voices, and a dawn chorus of bird song will become a delightful exercise in auditory discrimination. Try to attach a set of associations to each bird vocalization by describing it to yourself or comparing it with other sounds you know; make your mental description of sounds as detailed as possible. If you can whistle, try to copy the sound you are learning; to imitate it acceptably you will have to listen closely to the model. The more characteristic sounds of most North American birds are available on commercially produced recordings. Although listening to records or tapes removes the learning process one step from direct experience, it will at the very least make you sensitive to aspects of bird song that make the voices of each species distinctive and recognizable. Even the least expensive recording equipment can be helpful, too, since listening to your own tapes allows a comparative or analytical approach to the study of bird song. Moreover, playback of a reasonably good field recording will often attract the singing bird and enable you to observe it more closely.

Long, pointed wings

Conclusion

Bird watching has attracted an ever increasing number of devotees in North America. The science—some would say the art—of bird identification has been considerably advanced and refined in recent years. Field problems have been clarified or resolved, vocalizations studied, behavioral clues detected, and distinguishing characteristics isolated. As a result, bird watchers of today are immeasurably more sophisticated than those of only a few decades ago. Bird identification is now a field in which one can quickly achieve a high degree of competence, with all its attendant satisfactions. And bird watching—need it be said?—is a pursuit with many, many rewards.   *Davis W. Finch*

How to Find Birds

To become a successful birder, you may have to change the habits of a lifetime. The best birders rise before dawn, put on drab clothing, go out in all weathers, and learn to move carefully and quietly, keeping their ears open and their voices soft.

Clothing
Unless you have always been an outdoor person, you will find your wardrobe gradually transformed and your conversation increasingly filled with discussions of boots, rain gear, and long underwear. The most important rule is: Wear dull colors, preferably the natural ones, muted greens, browns, and grays. Steer clear of apparel that squeaks, rustles, or gets snagged easily. In the desert, birders need footgear that is thornproof; elsewhere, choose comfortable shoes that dry quickly or waterproof boots. Boots with rubber feet and leather tops are a widespread favorite, but as you track birds across mud flats and marshes you may want knee or hip boots as well. Since birding often requires standing around in sharp winds and icy temperatures, layers of protection against the cold are essential. However, soundproof ear coverings should be avoided, except perhaps on winter boat trips, one of the coldest of all birding situations.

The Clock
Songbirds are easiest to see during the three hours after dawn, when they feed most actively. The two hours before sunset can also be productive. During the rest of the day, most small birds are relatively sluggish and silent, especially on a warm afternoon. On the other hand, most kinds of water birds are easy to find throughout the day. Vultures, hawks, and eagles are most likely to be seen well after sunup; they hunt when visibility is best and soar on the thermal currents formed by sun-warmed air.

Dusk is the best time to scan winter fields and marshes for Short-eared Owls, cruise back roads for nightjars and displaying Woodcock, and visit summer marshes for spectacular flights of herons and ibis and glimpses of most of the rails.

Birders usually search for rails and owls at night and arm themselves with tape recordings of owl calls and strong flashlights. During spring migration and early in the nesting season, birders in the field at first light are treated to the auditory excitement of the dawn chorus; woodland species in particular join in a crescendo that gradually dies away after sunrise.

Regional Resources
Many states, provinces, and regions now have annotated checklists or bird-finding guides that indicate the time of year that each species is present and most common, as well as the locations and habitats where each might be found. Such a list or guide should be one of your first purchases. If your region has not yet produced this kind of guide, buy one for the area nearest you.

Local bird clubs schedule field trips to visit areas at the times of year that birds are most plentiful there or when seasonal specialties are present. If you cannot join a group expedition, try to visit the site within a week or two of a scheduled outing. Club newsletters or calendars often list other events of interest, like pelagic trips organized especially for viewing seabirds and marine mammals.

In many areas throughout the United States and Canada, recorded telephone messages are available to birders. Updated once or twice a week, they supply information about unusual sightings in the area as well as news of migration, birding sites, and field trips. Call the local Audubon Society chapter for the telephone number, or ask birders you meet in the field for it. These messages often provide directions to spots where rare birds have been found; these spots are often fruitful places for a visiting birder to look for common local species as well.

Weather
Every birder yearns to go afield on a beautiful spring or autumn day, but wind, rain, and extremes of temperature may keep you inside when some birds are most visible.

Although strong winds keep small birds out of sight, many water birds huddle close to the windward shore, in the lee of protecting banks, dunes, or vegetation. In autumn especially, a day or two after a cold front has passed through, northerly winds bring the best conditions for watching raptors migrating down mountain ridges or along the coasts. Onshore gales accompanying major coastal storms provide the best opportunities for observing seabirds of all kinds from land, and the first day after a hurricane many birders rush to the coast or to bays, rivers, and major lakes within a hundred miles or so of the sea.

Although bird-watching is virtually impossible in heavy rain, there is a lot of activity immediately after the rain stops. If you can keep your binoculars dry, a low ceiling and light drizzle can produce the best possible conditions for seeing migrating passerines. Songbirds are often forced down by nasty weather aloft; since they may occupy whatever cover they can find, you are likely to see a hedgerow, a clump of trees, or a brushy ravine alive with birds.

The hottest days of summer coincide with the peak migration time for southbound shorebirds. During the heat shimmer of late morning and early afternoon, go for a swim or hide in air-conditioned shelter, but take advantage of the long hours before and after the worst heat of the day.

Cold winter weather is good for birding snugly from your car, searching open country for raptors and visiting seedeaters such as longspurs and Snow Buntings. You may want to comb through stands of conifers for wintering owls, seek out patches of open water where waterfowl crowd together, or scan landfills, harbors, and beaches for rare gulls. If you notice a feeding station, check to see what species are visiting it.

Effective Behavior
The fundamental skills of birding are looking, listening, moving carefully, and concentrating on one bird at a time.

On foot, a birder is likely to cover less than one mile an hour. The point is to hear every chip note or rustle in the foliage and to spot every movement. Once you have heard a sound or seen a movement, your goal is to locate, identify, and observe the bird without frightening it away.

Although sharp eyes are partly a gift, the ability to pick up motion improves with practice. Always locate and relocate the bird first without binoculars. Keep your eyes on the motion while you move your binoculars in front of them. When you acquire a telescope, study the bird's surroundings through binoculars before you narrow your field of vision a second time by looking through the more powerful optical instrument.

Study an unfamiliar bird thoroughly before you turn to a field guide. If you cannot bear to take notes on its appearance and behavior before you try to identify it, at least tell yourself exactly what features you are seeing and hearing before you turn to a guide; if the bird flies away when your eyes are not on it, you will still have several features to check. If there are two of you, you can describe it to each other; one person can keep track of the bird while the other does the first round of research.

Looking for land birds requires a minimum of conversation and a maximum of attention to sounds. Speak only when you must, and then in a soft voice or whisper. Learning to recognize songs takes most of us much longer than visual identification, and learning all the chips, calls, and alarm notes is the task of a lifetime. Begin by tracking down and identifying every invisible singing bird you can. Try to verbalize the pattern you hear, and commit it to memory. Avoid abrupt movements: Shift position only if you have to, and then do so slowly and gently. Learn to refrain from pointing, or to point with your finger only, keeping your hand against your body. Better yet, practice describing where a bird is as economically as possible.

As you stalk a bird, learn to recognize its signs of alarm: a freeze in posture, a cocked head, a half-raising of the wings, and so on. If these clues tell you that you are getting too close, back off a little, or at least stop moving until the bird shows that it is used to your presence.

Try not to loom over a bird. Stay off the skyline if you can; on high ground, crouch or sit. The less conspicuous you are, the more birds you are likely to see.

Imitations of the Eastern Screech-Owl's call in the East or of the Northern Pygmy-Owl's in the West are enormously effective for attracting small birds. If you cannot master the screech-owl's tricky call, use a taped version; it works even better. Anybody can learn to "spish," that is, to make the sound "spshsh, spshsh, spshsh," which can draw quite a crowd of songbirds if you keep at it long enough. One responsive chickadee can pull in dozens of other birds if you keep it fussing at you. Most important, remember that overuse of these techniques quickly turns into harassment, and there is no excuse for seriously upsetting a bird, especially one that may be nesting.   *Claudia Wilds*

Orders

In zoological classification all birds are placed in the class Aves.
Classes are divided into orders, which are in turn divided into from
one to several related families. Discussed below are the orders of
birds covered in this volume.

Gaviiformes

The order Gaviiformes contains only one small, uniform family, the
Gaviidae, or loons. These foot-propelled, swimming and diving birds
(they are called divers in the Old World) generally come ashore only
to nest in marshes and on the borders of lakes and ponds; they spend
much of the year in coastal marine waters or deep inland lakes.
Loons are found only in the northern hemisphere; they nest in
boreal and Arctic regions, but winter farther south.
Although the sexes look quite similar, all species have distinct
breeding and winter plumages. In flight, the neck is held slightly
below the plane of the body, creating a hunchbacked appearance.
Important characteristics for differentiating species include the
dorsal and neck patterns, overall size, and head and bill shape.

Podicipediformes

This order consists of only one family, the Podicipedidae, or grebes.
These small to medium-size diving birds propel themselves with
their feet. They occur on fresh water and, during the nonbreeding
season, in marine waters near the shore. This family is nearly
worldwide in distribution; the more northerly species of North
America are highly migratory.
Grebes are long-necked and usually sharp-billed; all have lobed toes.
They are very awkward on land, and even their nests are usually
floating structures. The sexes look alike, but in many species the
winter and breeding plumages are distinct. Species differences
involve such features as size, head pattern, and head, crest, and bill
shape.

Procellariiformes

Collectively known as the "tubenoses," the Procellariiformes are the
most exclusively marine of North American birds; they are found
throughout the world's oceans but are most diverse in the southern
hemisphere. Of the four families, three occur in North America. All
tubenoses are web-footed and long-winged, with excellent powers of
flight; the nostrils are enclosed in tubes, and the bill is often
complexly plated. In size, they range from very large to very small:
the albatrosses (family Diomedeidae) are among the largest of the
flying birds; the shearwaters, fulmars, and petrels (family
Procellariidae) are medium-size; and the storm-petrels (family
Hydrobatidae) are small, sometimes as small as swallows.

Many tubenoses in North America undertake long migrations from
breeding grounds in the southern oceans. Since they may not attain
breeding age for several years, young tubenoses spend much time
in ocean waters well away from breeding colonies.
Tubenoses are often identified from boats, under conditions that
preclude feather-by-feather inspection. Differentiation is therefore
often based on the style of flight and on overall shape and size. Also
important are wing, back, and rump pattern, dorsal-ventral
contrast, and bill size, shape, and color. Except for the large
albatrosses, adults and immatures tend to look similar. Many
Procellariidae show two or more distinct color morphs.

Pelecaniformes

The pelicans and their allies form a diverse, worldwide group but
are found primarily in coastal and marine habitats. All six families in
the order occur in North America. Of these, three (the tropicbirds of

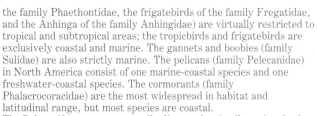

the family Phaethontidae, the frigatebirds of the family Fregatidae, and the Anhinga of the family Anhingidae) are virtually restricted to tropical and subtropical areas; the tropicbirds and frigatebirds are exclusively coastal and marine. The gannets and boobies (family Sulidae) are also strictly marine. The pelicans (family Pelecanidae) in North America consist of one marine-coastal species and one freshwater-coastal species. The cormorants (family Phalacrocoracidae) are the most widespread in habitat and latitudinal range, but most species are coastal.

The Pelecaniformes are outwardly diverse, but in all species the four toes are connected by webbing, a characteristic unique to this order. Almost all species are adapted for eating fish, which they catch by plunge-diving (gannets, boobies, tropicbirds, and the Brown Pelican), dipping (American White Pelican), underwater pursuit (cormorants), spearing (Anhinga), or surface dipping and piracy (frigatebirds).

The adult and immature plumages are distinct in most species; seasonal change is limited primarily to the colors of the soft parts, and to plumes and other adornments.

Ciconiiformes

In North America, the order Ciconiiformes contains three families of long-necked, long-legged wading birds. This order is worldwide in distribution, although poorly represented at high latitudes, and contains two additional small families.

Most diverse and familiar in North America are the herons (family Ardeidae), which are found in a variety of wetland habitats. The herons are the only family of this order to fold their necks in flight. Ibises and spoonbills (family Threskiornithidae) are structurally rather similar to the herons; they are characterized by specialized bills, which are decurved in the ibises and spatulate in the spoonbills. Of the storks (family Ciconiidae), only one species occurs regularly in North America; these birds are also long-necked and long-legged, with heavy bills and excellent powers of soaring flight. In this order, the sexes look generally alike, but adults and immatures may differ to varying degrees. A few species of herons have distinct color morphs. Seasonal change usually involves brightening of the color of the soft parts and the acquisition of long plumes.

Phoenicopteriformes

The small order Phoenicopteriformes contains only the flamingos (family Phoenicopteridae), which are restricted to South America, Africa, and the southernmost parts of Eurasia and North America. Only one species, the Greater Flamingo, occurs in North America. Flamingos are gregarious, long-legged, long-necked birds with unique, downward-bent bills. Plumage is predominantly pink or white with black flight feathers.

Anseriformes

In North America, the order Anseriformes contains the familiar ducks, geese, and swans of the family Anatidae; collectively, these birds are called waterfowl. The only other family in the order consists of the small, Neotropical screamers (family Anhimidae). Waterfowl are worldwide in distribution. Breeding species are least diverse in the tropics. Most species that breed at high latitudes are very migratory and gather in large flocks on wintering grounds. North American waterfowl have webbed feet and a variably flattened bill. They feed by diving in deep water, dabbling in shallow water, or grazing on land. Although male and female ducks usually differ markedly, this is not true of geese, swans, and whistling-ducks. Male ducks undergo a rapid, dull eclipse plumage phase after breeding season. A few species show marked geographic variation in pattern, and, in geese, size. Ducks are often identified in the field on the basis of flight pattern; head and bill shape is frequently important in distinguishing closely related species.

Falconiformes

Nearly all of the diurnal birds of prey of the order Falconiformes have a sharp, hooked beak and, except in many carrion-feeders, powerful talons. Most are highly skilled in pursuit and soaring flight. The order is worldwide in distribution; in North America, it contains three families. The family Cathartidae, or New World vultures, consists of large and very large carrion-feeders, probably only distantly related to the other falconiform groups. The family Accipitridae is a diverse one, containing the various hawks, eagles, harriers, and kites, as well as the Osprey. The family Falconidae includes both the pointed-winged falcons and the scavenging caracaras.

In most birds of prey, the sexes are similar in plumage; exceptions include the harriers, the Snail Kite, and some falcons. In most species, the females are larger than the males. Immatures usually differ from adults in plumage. Many species, such as some hawks of the genus *Buteo*, are extremely variable in plumage; identifications are consequently often based on size and shape, flight pattern, and silhouette. Many species are highly migratory.

Galliformes

The fowl-like birds of the order Galliformes are nearly worldwide in distribution. In North America, the order is represented by one species (the Plain Chachalaca) of the Neotropical family Cracidae (currasows, guans, and chachalacas) and by the diverse family Phasianidae, which contains several distinct groups; those native to North America are the Wild Turkey, grouse, and New World quail. Several Old World species have also been introduced into North America.

Members of this order are strong-legged, stout-billed, terrestrial or partly arboreal birds. In most groups, the males are considerably larger and more brightly colored than the females; the females almost always are cryptically colored. One group, the ptarmigans, shows marked seasonal variation in plumage. Many species are quite vocal, and some, primarily grouse, perform elaborate communal courtship displays.

Gruiformes

This diverse, worldwide order contains groups that variously resemble chickens, herons, ducks, and shorebirds. Many of the families are small and have limited tropical distribution. In North America, the order includes the large, widespread family of rails and coots (Rallidae), the cranes of the family Gruidae, and the family Aramidae which consists solely of the Limpkin.

Although this order is quite diverse, most North American species are found in marshes and other wet, vegetated areas. Some species, especially the coots, are primarily aquatic. The sexes look alike, but adults and immatures may differ greatly. Many rails are notoriously difficult to observe, so vocalizations are important in identifying them. Although many species in the Rallidae family are migratory, only the cranes routinely undertake long flights between roosting and feeding grounds.

Charadriiformes
Suborders Charadrii and Scolopaci

The large, diverse, worldwide order Charadriiformes contains several distinct adaptive lines. The suborders Charadrii and Scolopaci contain the groups variously known as the shorebirds or waders. In North America, the suborder Charadrii contains the major family Charadriidae (plovers) and the smaller families

Haematopodidae (oystercatchers), Recurvirostridae (stilts and avocets), and Burhinidae (the thick-knees, which are accidental in North America). The suborder Scolopaci includes the large and diverse family Scolopacidae (sandpipers) and the tropical family Jacanidae (the jacanas); one jacana species just enters North America.

Most birds of the order Charadriiformes occur near shores, marshes, mud flats, or fields, and use their variously adapted bills to probe or pick for food. Most are long-legged, and some in the family Scolopacidae have extremely long bills. The sexes look generally alike in plumage, although female phalaropes are noticeably brighter in color than males, and the breeding male Ruff (Scolopacidae) is spectacularly adorned, unlike the duller female. Although seasonal variation in plumage may be slight, it is marked in many plovers, the American Avocet, and many groups of sandpipers. In the first fall after hatching, juveniles may show plumage that is distinct from that of breeding or winter adults. Young jacanas retain throughout their first year a plumage very different from that of adults. Fine details of bill shape, feather pattern, and vocalization are important in distinguishing very similar species, especially some of the smaller members of the family Scolopacidae.

Most species within these suborders are at least partially migratory; many are Arctic nesters that undertake long-distance migrations. The timing of migration may vary between the sexes and among age groups. In a typical fall migration, adults (often males first) move south, overlapping narrowly or broadly with a later southward movement of juveniles.   *Kimball L. Garrett*

Part Two

Loons

(Family Gaviidae)
Loons are large, heavily built diving birds. Although they must run
across the water's surface to take flight, they are strong fliers.
When alighting on the water, loons may plane across the surface for
some distance with wings raised. They dive with a forward leap or a
slower roll, and sometimes simply "sink," expending a minimum of
effort. They are awkward on land and seldom come ashore except
when nesting. Loons in flight have a characteristic "hump-backed"
posture, with head and neck drooping in front, and legs trailing
behind a short tail. Sexes are alike; immatures are similar to
nonbreeding adults. Breeding plumages of the 4 species are
distinctive, but nonbreeding plumages are much more similar.
Nesting on the tundra and inland lakes, most loons winter along
ocean coasts and on large lakes. (World: 4 species. North
America: 4 species.)   *Terence Wahl*

Red-throated Loon

Gavia stellata
The Red-throated Loon occurs commonly in many types of marine
habitats, but is found most often along shorelines with shallow water
and in estuaries. While frequently only 1 or 2 birds may be seen
at a time, hundreds may congregate in loose flocks in prime feeding
areas, and large numbers are observed migrating past coastal
points. This species characteristically carries the bill pointed slightly
upward.

Description
24–27″ (61–68.5 cm). The red throat patch, black-and-white striped
nape pattern, pale gray head, and nearly plain back make birds in
breeding plumage unmistakable. Winter-plumage birds have a pale
appearance and a plain-looking face; the Red-throated's pale head
and neck lack the sharply defined contrast between dark upperparts
and white underparts seen in the Arctic Loon, helping to distinguish
the 2 species in flight. The Red-throated's overall paleness and the
fact that the head and neck seem to be about the same thickness
make it look more snakelike than other loons. The slender, uptilted
bill is a good mark in all seasons.

Voice
Wide variety of quacks, mews, shrieks, and other notes during
breeding season; most typical call a *gah-gah-gah-gah*, given by flying
birds. Rather vocal for a loon in late winter and spring before
leaving for breeding areas, giving a short, yelping wail.

Similar Species
See Arctic Loon. Yellow-billed Loon much larger, darker, has much
heavier, uptilted bill with yellow cast. Grebes slenderer, with
longer, thinner necks; most are smaller or show white wing patches
in flight.

Range
Breeds in tundra and along Arctic seacoasts around perimeter of
North America south to British Columbia and Quebec. Winters
along coast from Aleutians south to Baja California in Pacific, from
Newfoundland to Florida in Atlantic, along Gulf Coast, and on Great
Lakes. Also in Eurasia.   *Terence Wahl*

Red-throated Loon
Arctic Loon
Common Loon
Yellow-billed Loon

Breeding plumage
1. *Red throat.*
2. *Gray head.*
3. *Plain back.*

Winter plumage
1. *Slender, uptilted bill.*
2. *No strong contrast between upperparts and underparts.*

Arctic Loon

Gavia arctica
In winter, the Arctic Loon is more often seen in large, compact flocks than are other loons, and tends to occur in deeper waters and along exposed ocean coastlines. At this time it often forages in tidal fronts and turbulent channels. During migration, large numbers are commonly seen from headlands and jetties along the west coast of North America, with flocks passing by for hours.

Description
23–29″ (58.5–73.5 cm). Breeding-plumage birds have a shining silver-gray crown and nape, bold black-and-white back pattern, and white-striped black throat; they are easily identified at a great distance, both in flight and on the water. In nonbreeding-plumage birds the black head and hindneck contrast very sharply with the clear white throat and underparts; the dark feathering extends cleanly from the bill, below the eye and down the side of the neck, interrupted only by a white cheek area below and behind the eye. The back appears very dark and uniformly colored. The slender, darkish bill is normally held horizontally.

Voice
Wide variety of quacks, growls, and croaks as well as clear notes and wails on breeding grounds. Reportedly almost silent in winter.

Similar Species
Red-throated Loon in winter plumage pale, less contrasting; carries bill tilted upward. Common Loon larger, with more white around eye, less sharp definition between dark and light areas on head and neck; often with suggestion of collar on sides of neck and steeper forehead profile. Murres smaller, stockier.

Range
Breeds across much of Alaska and northern part of Canada east to Hudson Bay. Winters along Pacific Coast from Alaska to Baja California. Very rare on Atlantic Coast. Also in Eurasia.
Terence Wahl

Common Loon

Gavia immer
This familiar, widespread loon winters principally in protected bays, estuaries, and lakes; it is also seen in migration out to sea. It has slower wingbeats than the smaller Red-throated and Arctic loons.

Description
28–35″ (71–89 cm). In breeding plumage, the large Common Loon is black-headed, with a heavy, daggerlike black bill, a white necklace, prominent white checkers on the back, and white underparts. In nonbreeding and immature plumages, birds are essentially blackish above and whitish below (though lacking the sharp black-and-white contrast of the Arctic Loon), with some variation in the amount of white showing on the sides of the head. Dark traces of a collar are often visible on the sides of the neck. The bill in winter is whitish with a blue cast, and a variable dark line extends the length of the ridge of the upper mandible. It is normally held horizontally, though sometimes tilted slightly upward. Young birds have more prominent barring across the back. This species sometimes appears "crested."

Winter plumage
1. *Slender, horizontal bill.*
2. *Steep forehead.*
3. *Strong contrast between upperparts and underparts.*

   Often in flocks.

Breeding plumage
1. *Silvery-gray crown and nape.*
2. *Large spots forming bold patches on back.*

Breeding plumage
1. *Heavy, black bill.*
2. *Black head.*
3. *Back densely checkered with small spots.*
4. *White necklace.*

Voice
Loud, distinctive, yodeling call in breeding areas and also in wintering areas in late winter and early spring.

Similar Species
Winter Yellow-billed Loon browner above, whiter on face; heavy, consistently uptilted bill has yellow cast. Arctic Loon smaller, with sharply marked black-and-white contrast on head and neck, no trace of collar, and more sloping forehead profile. Feet of Red-throated and Arctic loons smaller, less conspicuous in flight.

Range
Breeds across much of Alaska, Canada (except north-central Arctic), New York, and New England; in past across northern tier of contiguous United States. Winters principally along coast from Aleutian Islands south to California, from Newfoundland south to Gulf Coast, and on lakes and bays near coasts. Migrates through much of continent. Also in Eurasia.   *Terence Wahl*

Yellow-billed Loon

Gavia adamsii
Nesting on the tundra, the very large Yellow-billed Loon has the most northerly breeding range of all the loons. It is a rare to uncommon winter visitor to marine waters of western North America, and occurs casually on inland lakes. This species is similar in appearance and behavior to the Common Loon; only in recent years has knowledge of field marks allowed reliable distinction of the 2 species in winter. During the winter, it is usually seen singly; it most often forages in shallow, protected waters.

Description
30–35″ (76–89 cm). The breeding plumage of this species is very similar to that of the Common Loon, although the white spots of the necklace and on the back are fewer and larger. The very large, pale, uptilted yellow bill makes this species distinctive. Birds in nonbreeding plumage are also similar to the Common Loon, but the adult Yellow-billed Loon's massive uptilted bill is yellowish, with a darkish line only on the basal part of the ridge. Though the crown is dark, like that of the Common Loon, the sides of the head and neck are whiter, the body coloration is brown rather than blackish, and the general effect is of a lighter-colored bird. A dark smudge or line is almost always present on the side of the head over the ear opening. The Yellow-billed Loon's back is more strongly barred with white than is the Common's. Winter adults often look larger than Common Loons; Yellow-billeds appear to have a "double-crested" crown more often than Common Loons do. Young Yellow-billeds have a bill more like the Common's, but with a warm, yellow cast.

Voice
Similar to calls of Common Loon, but louder and harsher; generally less vocal.

Similar Species
See Common Loon. Red-throated much smaller, paler, and grayer.

Range
Breeds along Arctic coastal areas north of tree line; in North America from northern Alaska nearly to Hudson Bay in Canadian Arctic, south to latitude of Great Slave Lake. Winters primarily along Pacific Coast from southeastern Alaska to Baja California; numbers vary annually. Also in Eurasia.   *Terence Wahl*

Winter plumage
1. *Pale bill with dark ridge on upper mandible.*
2. *Dark crown and nape shading into whitish underparts.*

Large size.

Winter plumage
1. *Yellowish, uptilted bill.*
2. *Brownish upperparts.*
3. *Dark mark or smudge behind eye.*

Breeding plumage
1. *Yellow, uptilted bill.*
2. *Black head.*
3. *Back checkered with small white spots.*
4. *White necklace.*

Grebes

(Family Podicipedidae)
Grebes are small to medium-size diving birds with elongated but
often somewhat rounded bodies. They are superficially similar
to the loons, but the neck-to-body ratio is greater owing to the
relatively longer neck. Like loons, grebes have a difficult time
taking off from the water and often dive when alarmed. Their flight
is weak but direct, with very rapid beats of the small, narrow wings.
Most grebes in breeding plumage have conspicuous head markings;
in nonbreeding plumage, most are dark above and light below.
Grebes have no visible tail, and the folded wings are generally not
discernible. These birds dive from the water's surface with a quick
forward leap; sometimes they submerge gradually. Grebes
characteristically preen with the body rolled over in the water,
exposing a great deal of the undersurface. Juvenile grebes (except
Westerns) are boldly streaked. All very young birds are carried on
the adults' backs. (World: 20 species. North America: 6 species.)
Scott B. Terrill

Least Grebe

Tachybaptus dominicus
Marshy or tree-lined ponds in southern Texas harbor the tiny Least
Grebe. It seldom flies and often hides in aquatic vegetation.

Description
10″ (25.5 cm). This bird has a short, blunt-tipped bill and yellow or
orange eyes. It is dark brownish-gray with a large white wing patch
and whitish belly. In breeding plumage, the head and neck are slate-
gray, the crown and throat black; in winter, the head is gray-brown,
the throat pale. Juveniles have some head stripes.

Voice
In alarm, sharp *peek*. Rattling trill, other calls in breeding season.

Similar Species
See Pied-billed and Eared grebes.

Range
Resident in southern Texas; rare in Southwest and upper Texas
coast. Central and South America, West Indies.   *Kenn Kaufman*

Pied-billed Grebe

Podilymbus podiceps
The most widespread and familiar member of its family in North
America, the Pied-billed Grebe inhabits large lakes and small ponds
—wherever there is marsh vegetation—but seldom appears on salt
water. Like other grebes, it is very much at home in the water and
awkward on land, rarely coming ashore. It dives easily to pursue
prey, and sometimes swims partly submerged, with only its head
exposed. It is seldom seen in flight; in taking off, it must patter
along the water's surface to gain momentum. During most of the
year it is not at all shy, but in breeding season it becomes more
secretive, hiding in the marsh, and at this season its odd calls may
be heard more often than the bird is seen.

Description
12–15″ (30.5–38 cm). The Pied-bill is a compact, short-bodied grebe
with a conspicuously short, thick bill. The adult is mostly dull brown
with fluffy white undertail coverts, a blackish-brown crown, and a
narrow white eye-ring. In breeding plumage the throat is black, and

Least Grebe
Pied-billed Grebe
Horned Grebe
Red-necked Grebe
Eared Grebe
Western Grebe

Breeding plumage
1. *Short bill.*
2. *Black crown.*
3. *Black throat.*
4. *Yellow eye.*
5. *Dark brownish-gray body.*

Small size.
Texas only.

Breeding plumage
1. *Short, whitish bill with black ring.*
2. *Dull brown color.*
3. *White undertail coverts.*

Compact, stocky body.

there is a black ring around the whitish bill; in winter the throat is
pale, and the bill is unmarked. The juvenile is variously striped,
especially about the head, but the stocky grebe shape and short,
thick bill identify it.

Voice
Calls frequently in breeding season. One long call begins with
lengthy series of odd, whinnying sounds, eventually slows down to
repeated, cuckoolike *cow-cow-cow* (or *cow-oo*) notes. Various other
mellow, clucking sounds.

Similar Species
Other grebes have proportionately thinner bills. Least Grebe
smaller, darker brown, with thinner bill, yellow or orange eyes.

Range
Breeds throughout most of North America from central Canada
south; winters on open water north to British Columbia, Great
Lakes region, and New England. Also throughout West Indies,
Central and South America.   *Kenn Kaufman*

Horned Grebe

Podiceps auritus
The Horned Grebe is less gregarious than the Western and Eared
grebes, especially during the breeding season. Like all other
grebes, it is highly adapted to water and dives with a quick,
graceful, closed-wing movement. The Horned Grebe can be confused
with the Red-necked and Eared grebes, but in both breeding and
winter plumages the neck and facial color as well as the facial
pattern are different. During the breeding season birds are found on
interior marshes, ponds, quiet lakes, and slow-moving rivers.
Horned Grebes winter on coastal salt water and nearby lakes.

Description
12–15″ (30.5–38 cm). In breeding plumage, the Horned Grebe has a
dark back contrasting with a rufous neck, breast, and flanks. The
dark-colored head region has conspicuous golden ear tufts, mainly
above the eyeline. The birds have a proportionally short, straight
bill and red eyes. The belly is white. Winter-plumage birds lack the
ear tufts and rufous neck, and have a dark head and back that
contrast with the white cheek, throat, and breast. In both plumages,
the birds show a distinct white speculum in flight.

Voice
Generally silent throughout much of year, but gives variety of trills,
harsh croaks, and high squeaks on breeding grounds.

Similar Species
Red-necked Grebe in breeding plumage has whitish throat and
cheek. Winter-plumage Red-necked larger, with less extensive
white facial area, heavier and longer gray neck, and dull yellow bill.
Eared Grebes have black neck and crown, with ear tufts extending
well below eyeline in breeding plumage; gray neck and cheek in
winter; upturned bill.

Range
Breeds from Alaska and northwestern Canada south to northern
Washington and east to Wisconsin. Winters on Atlantic Coast from
Nova Scotia to Texas, and on Pacific Coast from southeastern
Alaska to California. Known as "Slavonian Grebe" in Old World.
John T. Ratti

Winter plumage
1. *Short, pale bill.*
2. *Dull brown color.*
3. *White undertail coverts.*

   Compact, stocky body.

Winter plumage
1. *Dark crown and nape.*
2. *White cheek, throat, and breast.*
3. *Slender, straight bill.*

Breeding plumage
1. *Rufous neck.*
2. *Black head.*
3. *Golden ear tufts that do not extend below eyeline.*

Red-necked Grebe

Podiceps grisegena
Red-necked Grebes breed on shallow, marshy northern ponds and
lakes, where their floating nests can sometimes be seen among the
reeds. The species is most commonly observed in winter, when it
frequents open coastline, protected bays, and, occasionally, inland
lakes. These birds spend much of the day sleeping, but when feeding
are distinguished by the long, gray neck and long bill with a yellow
base. By late March or April, Red-necked Grebes molt into breeding
plumage. They sometimes form sizable flocks.

Description
17–22″ (43–56 cm). Breeding adults are distinctive with their
grayish-white cheeks, rust-red neck, and long, pointed bill. The
crown, nape, and back are dark. The bill appears straight in the field
but may be narrowly decurved; it has a yellow base and a blackish
tip and culmen. Red-necked Grebes can be recognized by their
short-bodied, long-necked, and long-billed profile. In winter
plumage, the neck is gray, but the pale area on the cheek remains
conspicuous; in some immatures, this cheek patch may be much
reduced. At close range the base of the bill is obviously yellow. The
gray crown appears flat-topped and angles sharply as it slopes down
the nape. In flight, Red-necked Grebes are superficially similar to
loons, but they are unique in showing 2 white patches on each wing;
both the white secondaries and white leading edge of the inner wing
contrast sharply with the dark upperparts.

Voice
On breeding grounds, varied wails, squeaks, and nasal brays.
Generally silent in winter.

Similar Species
See Eared, Horned, and Western grebes.

Range
Breeds from western Alaska across central Canada to Ontario, south
to Washington, Montana, northern South Dakota, and Minnesota.
Formerly farther east. Winters on both coasts, from Alaska
(including Aleutian Islands) to northern California, rarely farther
south, and from Newfoundland (infrequently) south to Long Island,
rarely to Florida. Occasional on inland lakes. Also in Eurasia.
Peter D. Vickery

Eared Grebe

Podiceps nigricollis
The small, slender Eared Grebe is found on marshy lakes and ponds
in summer and on coastal lakes, open bays, and the ocean in winter.
Eared Grebes are similar to Horned Grebes, but have a distinct
crest and a blackish neck and breast. The Eared Grebe is very
gregarious; large breeding colonies and winter flocks are common.
This species engages in elaborate courtship displays on the water,
and the birds are extremely vocal at nesting colonies.

Description
12–14″ (30.5–35.5 cm). In breeding plumage, the Eared Grebe is
quite striking, with a blackish head, throat, neck, breast, and back,
and rufous flanks. The head has an obvious blackish crest,
contrasting with the golden ear tufts that extend well below the
eyeline. The bill is slender, sharp, and slightly upturned. Winter-
plumage birds are dull grayish with a dark head and back; many
birds show a distinct white spot on the side of the head behind the
ear. In both plumages, the white speculum is visible in flight.

Immature
1. *Long, gray neck.*
2. *Long, straight bill.*
3. *Very little white on cheek.*

Breeding plumage
1. *Rufous neck*
2. *Whitish cheek.*
3. *Long, yellowish bill.*
4. *Two white patches on wing.*

Breeding plumage
1. *Black neck and head.*
2. *Golden ear tufts extending below eyeline.*
3. *Black crest.*

Nests in colonies.

Voice
A rhythmic, froglike *pu-weep* on breeding grounds.

Similar Species
Horned Grebes in winter plumage have white cheek, neck, and breast, and flatter crown; rufous neck and breast in breeding plumage. Winter-plumage Red-necked Grebes larger, with heavier head, longer neck, and larger, dull yellow bill.

Range
Breeds from British Columbia and Manitoba south to California and Texas. Winters on Pacific Coast from southern British Columbia to Guatemala, and inland from California, Nevada, Utah, New Mexico, and Texas south to Guatemala. Fairly frequent accidental on East Coast. Also in Old World.   John T. Ratti

Western Grebe

Aechmophorus occidentalis
These graceful divers of marsh, lake, and coastal waters form loosely spaced flocks of a few to several hundred birds throughout the year. Rarely seen in flight, Western Grebes are known for their elaborate aquatic courtship displays. Two color morphs were originally described in 1858 as separate species, the dark form being called the Western Grebe (*Podiceps occidentalis*) and the light form "Clark's" Grebe (*P. clarkii*). The birds were later assumed to represent distinct color types, and only 1 species is now recognized. However, recent research has shown that the 2 forms appear to function biologically as separate species. Although they are still considered 1 species, reclassification as separate species is possible.

Description
20–24″ (51–61 cm). The Western Grebe has a long, swanlike neck, bright red eyes, and a long, sharp bill. The top of the head, back of the neck, and the back are dark grayish-black, sharply defined against the white throat, foreneck, and breast. The facial pattern is the best characteristic for separating Western and "Clark's" Grebes. In Western Grebes, the eyes are completely surrounded by black crown feathers, and the lores vary from gray to black; in the "Clark's," the eyes are completely surrounded by white feathers. Rare intermediates have the black-and-white facial margin bisecting the eye horizontally. The Western generally has a uniformly dark back and flanks; "Clark's" usually has paler gray flanks and back speckled with white feathers. The Western's bill is dull greenish-yellow; "Clark's" has a brighter orange-yellow bill.

Voice
Western Grebe has 2-note call, *creet-creet;* "Clark's" call has 1 note, *creet.* Calls often carry great distances.

Similar Species
Winter-plumage Red-necked Grebe has shorter neck and bill, dull gray neck. Winter-plumage loons larger, with shorter necks.

Range
From British Columbia to central Mexico on West Coast, and from California and Washington inland to Dakotas; also in large portions of Manitoba, Alberta, and Saskatchewan. Rare on East Coast.
John T. Ratti

Winter plumage
1. *Dark crown and sides of head.*
2. *Whitish patch behind ear.*
3. *Dull gray body.*

   Often in flocks.

"Clark's" Grebe
1. *Long, slender, black-and-white neck.*
2. *White cheek extending above eye.*
3. *Orange-yellow bill.*

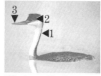

Western Grebe
1. *Long, slender, black-and-white neck.*
2. *Black crown extending to eye.*
3. *Dull greenish-yellow bill.*

Albatrosses

(Family Diomedeidae)
Albatrosses are huge seabirds with extremely long, proportionately
narrow, pointed wings; they have short, thick necks and large
heads, and most have short, blunt tails. They normally soar and
glide on their stiff, straight wings, somewhat like a Gannet (and can
cause confusion). However, in very strong winds the outer half of
the wing may be bent back at the wrist, as it is in gulls. On the
water, albatrosses sit tilted forward, with the bill pointed downward
and the body sloping up toward the rear; gulls, gannets, and boobies
sit with the bill and body horizontal. Six albatross species have the
common characteristics of a white body, a blackish area around or
over the eyes, and blackish back, wings, and tail; these birds are
traditionally known as "mollymawks." While the dark "brow" varies
among species, giving them different facial expressions, bill color
and underwing pattern are the most critical features among the
mollymawks. The mollymawks that occur regularly in our range are
the Laysan and the Yellow-nosed albatrosses. (World: 13 species.
North America: 7 species.)   *Stuart Keith*

Short-tailed Albatross

Diomedea albatrus
This very large, heavy-bodied, stout-billed albatross is intermediate
in size between the Wandering and the Laysan. Although the wings
are long, they are proportionately somewhat shorter than those of
other albatrosses. The Short-tailed progresses from a brown juvenal
plumage through a series of intermediate stages to a mainly white
adult plumage. While the brown juveniles and fully adult birds are
distinctive, subadults can be confusing. Formerly abundant in the
northwest Pacific, the Short-tailed was considered extinct by the
late 1940s. By 1954, a few birds had returned to nest on Torishima,
an island south of Japan; there are now estimated to be about 200
birds. Though strictly protected by the Japanese government, the
Short-tailed is one of the rarest and most endangered birds.

Description
37″ (94 cm); wingspan 84–90″ (213.5–228.5 cm). Adults have a white
body, including the back, and a broad black band at the tip of the
tail. The head and neck are washed with yellow-buff; the bill is pale
pink. The basal half of the upperwing is white, except for a dark
patch on the trailing edge; the outer half is dark with white primary
shafts; the underwing is white with narrow dark margins.
Juveniles are entirely dark brown at first, with a pink bill and pink
feet. Subadults have a "black-throated" stage, with a white face,
breast, and belly separated by a dark band across the throat. As the
throat becomes white, a blackish area remains from the top of the
head to the hindneck, continuing as a wedge down the side of the
neck and creating a black-hooded look. This hood is retained while

Immature

the back becomes contrastingly paler and mottled with white. The
forehead, face, and sides of the neck acquire a yellow tinge while the
dark hood is still present. White patches appear on the upperside of
the wing fairly early, eventually joining to form a continuous white
area; the uppertail coverts become white before the back does.

Similar Species
See Laysan and Black-footed albatrosses; also Wandering Albatross*.

Range
North American sightings in recent years mainly from Alaska; 1
from British Columbia, 1 from Oregon, and 3 from California. Nests
on Torishima, off Japan.   *Stuart Keith*

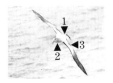

Adult
1. *White body.*
2. *Yellowish wash on head.*
3. *White basal half of upperwing.*

Large size.

Immature
1. *Entirely brown body and wings.*
2. *Pink bill.*
3. *Pink feet.*

Black-footed Albatross

Immature

Diomedea nigripes
The mostly dark Black-footed Albatross was once considered the only albatross one had any chance of seeing in North American waters. However, the great increase in pelagic trips by birders and by those studying marine life in offshore waters has resulted in numerous sightings of other species. As a result, people are now prepared for almost anything to turn up.

Description
27–29″ (68.5–73.5 cm); wingspan 76–84″ (193–213.5 cm). The Black-footed Albatross is mainly blackish-gray; at all ages it has some white at the base of the bill, a white mark under and behind the eye, and white primary shafts. The bill is dark brown, the legs and feet are black or grayish. The Black-footed becomes increasingly pale with age: white spreads from the base of the bill onto the crown, face, and throat; the belly becomes paler, and the vent, undertail coverts, and rump become white. Some very old or aberrant birds may have much white on the head, neck, tail, and underparts, leaving a brown breastband; the bill may become partly pinkish or yellowish and the feet may turn a dusky yellow.

Similar Species
Dark shearwaters much smaller. Juvenile Short-tailed Albatross larger, stockier, with pink bill and feet and no white in plumage. Old Black-footeds may resemble subadult Short-tailed, but Short-tailed has black hood and throat, white patches on upperwings, and dark undertail coverts and underside of tail.

Range
Breeds in Hawaiian Islands and on Torishima, off Japan (formerly also on other islands in North Pacific). Ranges widely in North Pacific north of about 10°N, reaching coasts of Alaska, Baja California, and Asia. Some present off our coasts all year, but most common in summer and fall.   *Stuart Keith*

Laysan Albatross

Diomedea immutabilis
The Laysan Albatross is the only mollymawk that occurs regularly off the west coast of North America (although the Shy* is accidental). The Laysan is one of the few albatrosses that have no separate juvenal or subadult plumages, thus making life easier for the birder; *immutabilis* means "unchangeable." This species is common in the northeast Pacific, especially off the Aleutians in summer, and off the mainland from British Columbia to southern California in winter. Except in the Aleutians, it usually remains several hundred miles offshore. Unlike the Black-footed Albatross, the Laysan does not show much interest in ships.

Description
31–32″ (79–81 cm); wingspan 80″ (203 cm). The Laysan is mainly white, with the back, tail, and upperwings gray-black. The underwing pattern, with dark patches on a white lining, is unique among albatrosses. There is a dark smudge in front of the eye and a minimal brow behind the eye. Some birds have a light gray wash on

On water
1. *Blackish-gray plumage.*
2. *White face.*
3. *Dark brown bill.*

In flight
1. *Blackish-gray plumage.*
2. *White primary shafts.*

In flight, from above
1. *White head and body.*
2. *Gray-black back, wings, and tail.*

Seldom follows ships.

the face below the eye, contrasting with the white crown and
producing a slightly capped effect; some have a creamy wash on the
head and neck (but not the yellow-buff of the Short-tailed
Albatross). The juvenile is like the adult. The Laysan's bill is either
gray with a dark tip or yellow with a gray tip. The sequence of
change in bill color from gray to yellow or green in maturing Shy
and Black-browed albatrosses suggests that gray-billed Laysans are
juveniles or subadults, and yellow-billed birds are adults.

Similar Species
Short-tailed Albatross larger, heavier, with massive pink bill. Adult
has yellow wash on head, white back, basal half of upperwing white;
subadult with mottled brown back also has dark hood on back of
head and neck, and white patches on upperwing. See Shy
Albatross*.

Range
Breeds on Hawaiian Islands; formerly also other islands in North
Pacific. Ranges widely in North Pacific, reaching Japan, Sea of
Okhotsk, Bering Sea, Gulf of Alaska, and western North America
south to northern Baja California.   *Stuart Keith*

Yellow-nosed Albatross

Diomedea chlororhynchos
Only 2 albatrosses have occurred in the North Atlantic with any
frequency—the Yellow-nosed and the Black-browed. The Yellow-
nosed has so far only been seen in the western part of the ocean,
whereas the Black-browed until recently had only appeared on the
eastern side. Like other mollymawks, the Yellow-nosed Albatross
bears a superficial resemblance to the larger dark-backed gulls, such
as the Great Black-backed and Western. But apart from having a
different shape, flying gulls may be distinguished at a distance by
white leading and trailing edges to the wings, which are lacking in
all mollymawks, and by their white tails. The white tail coverts of
mollymawks often extend over much of the tail in a shallow V, so
the birds appear to have a broad, dark band at the end of the tail.
Against a dark sea, the dark tail may not be apparent and the birds
may seem to have a very short white tail.

Description
29–34″ (73.5–86.5 cm); wingspan 76–83″ (193–211 cm). The Yellow-
nosed is a rather slim, elegant albatross with some delicate pale
gray on the head and neck that is visible only at close range. The
back, tail, and upperwings are blackish, and the rest of the body is
white. The underwing is white with a very narrow, dark trailing
edge and a somewhat broader dark leading edge. The rather slender
bill is black with a yellow culmen and pink tip. The juvenile has a
black bill and no gray on the head. With age, the ridge and tip of the
bill gradually become paler.

Similar Species
See Black-browed Albatross*.

Range
Breeds in southern Atlantic and Indian oceans, ranging west to
southern tip of South America and east to New Zealand. Eighteen
records for eastern North America (as of 1981), from Quebec to
Florida and Texas.   *Stuart Keith*

In flight, from below
White body.
Dark patches on white underwings.

Adult in flight
White wing linings with narrow, dark borders.
Slender bill.

Adult on water
Black upperparts.
Black bill with yellow ridge.

Often follows ships.

Fulmars, Gadfly Petrels, and Shearwaters

(Family Procellariidae)
These seabirds have nostrils enclosed in a tube or tubes on top of a
hooked bill; sexes and age classes are similar in appearance. Effects
of feather wear and molt may greatly alter the light-dark plumage
patterns of some species, as well as the basic blackish or brownish
coloration; under some light conditions, these birds may simply look
"dark." Four species of the North Atlantic—the Manx, Black-
vented, Audubon's, and Little shearwaters—are traditionally
known as "black-and-white" shearwaters. Flight is rapid, consisting
of several quick flaps and a glide down wave troughs, in up-and-
down wheeling arcs that increase in height with wind speed. In most
species, takeoff requires a pattering run across the surface. Almost
all species are gregarious. Some shearwaters plunge from the air or
dive from the surface for food. Nearly all are attracted to fishing
vessels. Most species occur well offshore in pelagic waters,
especially during migration; large numbers usually concentrate over
continental shelves, out of sight of land. (World: 66 species. North
America: 20 species.)   *Terence Wahl*

Northern Fulmar

Fulmarus glacialis
A medium-size "tubenose," the Fulmar appears to fly with rather
flat, stiff wings, lacking the flexed- or bowed-winged appearance of
shearwaters or the angled-winged look of gulls. Fulmars occur
primarily over offshore waters out of sight of land except near
nesting colonies, dispersing widely over cool pelagic waters when
not breeding. In peak years, nonbreeding birds may occur close to
shore or in harbors. These highly gregarious scavengers may occur
in huge flocks near fish-factory ships or spread out and fly low when
searching for food. Fulmars seldom dive for food.

Description
18–20″ (45.5–51 cm). Northern Fulmars are stocky and bull-necked
with a bulging forehead. The yellowish bill is relatively heavy and
short, with a prominent nostril tube. Both in flight and on the water,
the bird holds the bill pointed downward at an angle of about 45°. A
majority of Fulmars occurring in the North Atlantic are white with
gray mantles and wings; they may at first appear similar to gulls.
Birds occurring in the North Pacific are more varied, ranging from
virtually pure white to very dark gray; most seen south of the
northern Bering Sea are grayish and, in molt, quite mottled.

Voice
Quarrelsome-sounding cackling during squabbles over food, heard
away from nest sites.

Similar Species
Gulls have longer necks, slimmer bills without nostril tubes; leap
from water into more agile flight. Shearwaters of similar size
typically more slender, with thinner bills held more nearly
horizontal; wings narrower, more tapered, more flexed in flight.

Range
North Pacific population breeds from Alaska Peninsula and Aleutian
Islands north into Bering Sea and winters south to southern
California, with nonbreeders summering irregularly off west coast of
North America. Western Atlantic population breeds primarily in
Canadian Arctic, Greenland, and Iceland and winters south to
northeastern states and to edge of Gulf Stream off central East
Coast states. Range may be expanding. Also in Eurasia.
Terence Wahl

Northern Fulmar
Cape Petrel
Black-capped Petrel
Cahow
Mottled Petrel
Murphy's Petrel
Cook's Petrel
Stejneger's Petrel
Streaked Shearwater
Cory's Shearwater
Pink-footed Shearwater
Flesh-footed Shearwater
Greater Shearwater
Buller's Shearwater
Sooty Shearwater
Short-tailed Shearwater
Manx Shearwater
Black-vented Shearwater
Little Shearwater
Audubon's Shearwater

Dark phase
1. *Short, thick,
   yellowish bill,
   angled downward.*
2. *Dark gray plumage.*

   *Stocky, bull-necked
   build.
   Stiff-winged flight.*

Light phase
1. *White head and
   body.*
2. *Gray mantle.*
3. *Yellow bill angled
   downward.*

Black-capped Petrel

Pterodroma hasitata
This elusive, graceful gadfly petrel of the western North Atlantic
flies with characteristic *Pterodroma* arcing, alternating with flaps
and long glides on tilted wings.

Description
14–18″ (35.5–45.5 cm). This long-winged, long-tailed petrel generally
has a broad white collar and rump, contrasting with dark
upperparts. The underparts are white, with dark smudges at the
sides of the breast. The white underwing has black margins and tip,
with a diagonal black bar across the coverts.

Similar Species
See Greater Shearwater, Cahow*.

Range
Known to breed only in mountains of Hispaniola; migrates to
western edge of Gulf Stream.   *Ron Naveen*

Mottled Petrel

Pterodroma inexpectata
This is the gadfly petrel most likely to occur in the cool northeastern
Pacific almost exclusively over mid-ocean waters. In flight, it arcs up
much higher and zooms down faster than a shearwater.

Description
14″ (35.5 cm). This petrel is gray above, with dark bars on the
upperwing forming a flattened M. The bill is heavy, short, and dark,
the whitish forehead scaled-looking, and there is a dark mark around
the eye. A heavy black bar on the under secondary coverts and the
dark gray breast and belly are diagnostic.

Similar Species
See Cook's* and Stejneger's Petrels*.

Range
Nonbreeding season: North Pacific, Gulf of Alaska, and Bering Sea;
rare in coastal waters south to California in late winter and spring.
Breeds near New Zealand.   *Terence Wahl*

Cory's Shearwater

Calonectris diomedea
A regular visitor from late spring through late fall in the western
North Atlantic, Cory's Shearwater can sometimes be found in large
numbers with other shearwaters on its migration north. It has the
characteristic shearwater flap-and-glide flight pattern, but with
slower and floppier wingbeats. The large, yellowish bill, sometimes
with a dark tip, is distinctive.

Description
20–21″ (51–53.5 cm). Cory's is a very large, long-winged, pale-billed
shearwater, grayish-brown above and white below. It generally
favors warmer waters than do other shearwaters of the western
North Atlantic. The brownish-gray crown blurs into the paler chin
and white underparts. The large yellowish bill, sometimes with a
dark tip, is diagnostic among shearwaters. The upperparts and
wings generally appear uniformly gray-brown, although the primary
and secondary coverts may be darker. There are usually varying
amounts of white in the uppertail coverts, producing a more or less

In flight
1. Dark upperparts.
2. White collar.
3. White rump.
4. Long tail.

Rapid flight with flapping and gliding.

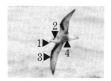

In flight
1. Short, heavy bill.
2. Dark mark around eye.
3. Heavy black bar on under secondary coverts.
4. Dark gray breast and belly.

In flight
1. Large, yellow bill.
2. Whitish underparts.

Large size.

distinct white rump band. The underwing is white with dusky brown
borders, especially on the trailing edges. The belly, underparts, and
undertail coverts are white. Cory's is bulkier and slightly longer-
winged than the Greater Shearwater, and much larger than the
black-and-white Manx and Audubon's shearwaters. In flight,
Cory's flaps deeply, with a relatively slow wingbeat; it sometimes
glides and soars more than other shearwaters do. The wings are
often bent at the wrist, giving Cory's a floppy-winged appearance.

Similar Species
Greater Shearwater has faster, stiffer wingbeats, although differing
wind conditions may make comparisons difficult. Greater has scaly-
looking upperparts, more distinct dark cap, more white on nape,
dark belly smudge (usually), more splotching on underwing, and
darker bill.

Range
Breeds in east-central Atlantic and Mediterranean. Migrant from
late spring through late fall to western North Atlantic; occasionally
to Maine and maritime Canada.   *Ron Naveen*

Pink-footed Shearwater

Puffinus creatopus
This large shearwater is commonly found over the outer continental
shelf off the west coast of North America. Birds often occur in loose
flocks of up to 50 or more birds; the species associates with other
shearwaters, especially near fishing vessels, and 1 or 2 are
occasionally seen from shore among feeding flocks of Sooty
Shearwaters. Distinctly larger than the Sooty, the Pink-foot has
noticeably slower wingbeats and soars more readily. While Sooties
dive frequently for food, Pink-foots are seldom seen to dive at chum.

Description
19″ (48.5 cm). The Pink-footed Shearwater is gray-brown above,
with the primaries darker than the inner wing and back. The
underwings are whitish, with variable amounts of irregular blackish
edging. The underparts are whitish, shading into the darker upper
surface and lacking the brilliant, pure white color of other "white-
bellied" shearwaters. The large, flesh-colored, dark-tipped bill and
pink feet are visible at close range.

Similar Species
Black-vented Shearwater smaller, with sharper contrast between
dark upperparts and white underparts; wingbeats very much faster.
Buller's Shearwater much "cleaner" in pattern. Streaked
Shearwater* larger, lighter brown above, pure white below; whitish
head has dark streaks visible at close range; light band across
uppertail coverts may be visible.

Range
Fairly common in summer over continental shelf from southeast
Alaska to California; occasional in winter off California. Presumably
migrates offshore along North and South America; may veer well
out to sea off Central America. Breeds on islands off southern Chile.
Terence Wahl

In flight, from side
1. *No distinct cap.*
2. *Uniform mantle with no scaling.*
3. *Bend at wrist*

Slow, floppy wingbeats.

In flight, from above
1. *Blackish-brown upperparts.*
2. *Pale bill with dark tip.*

Slow wingbeats. Soars occasionally.

In flight, from below
1. *Pale bill with dark tip.*
2. *Whitish underparts.*
3. *Pale feet.*

Flesh-footed Shearwater

Puffinus carneipes

The large, all-dark Flesh-footed Shearwater is an uncommon to rare visitor over the continental shelf off the west coast of North America. It is most often found among flocks of other birds at fishing vessels. In its behavior, slow wingbeats, and occasional soaring flight, the Flesh-footed is very similar to the Pink-footed Shearwater, to which it is closely related. Although it is seldom observed to dive off the West Coast, it reportedly does so readily in the Southern Hemisphere. While locating a single Flesh-footed in a flock of several thousand milling, diving Sooty Shearwaters may be difficult, a good look at this large, slower-flapping bird leaves little doubt as to its identity.

Description
19–20″ (48.5–51 cm). This large shearwater has a prominent, pale pink, dark-tipped bill contrasting sharply with the uniformly blackish-brown body and wings; the feet are flesh-colored. In good light, the undersides of the primaries and secondaries appear a shade lighter than the wing linings.

Similar Species
See Sooty and Short-tailed shearwaters, which have noticeably faster wingbeats. Dark-phase Northern Fulmar smaller, stubbier, paler, with different flight and posture.

Range
Occurs off West Coast from British Columbia to southern California, with records for Alaska. Nests near Australia, with part of population wintering in North Pacific.   *Terence Wahl*

Greater Shearwater

Puffinus gravis

The large Greater Shearwater flies with fast, stiff wingbeats. It has a capped appearance, and is larger than the Sooty, Manx, or Audubon's shearwaters, and not as bulky as Cory's. The dark belly smudge is diagnostic, but usually difficult to see. The light feather edgings on the upperparts give the Greater a scaly-backed appearance. During migration, it is often found in huge rafts, sometimes with other shearwaters. It glides, but for briefer periods than Cory's, the other large shearwater in the North Atlantic.

Description
19″ (48.5 cm). At close range, the Greater Shearwater generally shows a distinct dark gray-brown cap; the sides of the neck are broadly white; the white sometimes meets to form a white collar. The bill is long and slim. Most birds show white at the base of the tail; however, this patch may be indistinct or totally lacking. The upperparts are variably toned in browns and blacks, yielding a scaled or mottled appearance; the flight feathers are black. The

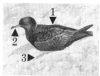

On ground
1. *Uniform dark plumage.*
2. *Pale bill.*
3. *Pale feet.*

In flight
1. *Uniformly dark plumage.*
2. *Pale bill.*

   Large size.
   Slow wingbeats.

In flight
1. *Distinct, dark cap.*
2. *Dark upperparts with scaling.*

   Fast, stiff wingbeats.

underwing is generally white, with dark margins and variable splotching from the axillars to the bend in the wing. The Greater's dark belly smudge, usually present but difficult to see, is diagnostic. The undertail coverts are dark.

Similar Species
Cory's upperparts more uniformly gray-brown, do not appear scaly. Cory's lacks dark belly smudge, has larger, yellowish bill (sometimes dark-tipped). Cory's flight usually slower, with less stiff, deeper wingbeats, but this distinction requires some experience. Sooty Shearwater slimmer, appears all dark. Black-capped Petrel has more dashing flight, with more soaring and swooping; generally has more pronounced white on nape and rump; lacks scaly appearance on upperparts and upperwing; bill shorter, stouter; lacks dark belly smudge.

Range
Breeds in far southern Atlantic, migrating north in austral winter to North Atlantic; extreme dates March through December.
Ron Naveen

Buller's Shearwater

Puffinus bulleri
This strikingly patterned, medium-size to large shearwater may appear in flocks of several hundred in the northeastern Pacific, though numbers vary from year to year. This species is more likely to occur in "pure" flocks than other shearwaters of the West Coast except for the Sooty. Buller's has not been observed to scavenge at fishing vessels, even when it occurs in the same locality, nor does it appear to dive for prey. Its flight is quite languid, buoyant, and wheeling, with slower wingbeats than the flight of other shearwaters; the birds often make tight, slow, near-vertical turns. These characteristics, combined with Buller's distinctive plumage pattern and habit of flocking, often make even distant birds stand out, and allow easier identification than is possible with other species.

Description
16½″ (42 cm). The pale gray upperparts, with sharply contrasting dark cap and dark M mark over the upperwing surface, together with the very clean, pure white underparts and wing linings, and slow, easy flight, make identification easy. Compared with other West Coast shearwaters, Buller's is broad-winged and wedge-tailed. The bill is long, thin, and dark; the tail is dark gray, and the uppertail coverts are pale gray.

Similar Species
Smaller Mottled Petrel also has dark M mark on upperwing but less cleanly patterned above; has dark gray patch on breast and belly and heavy black bar across under secondary coverts; in flight, arcs up much higher and zooms down faster, often tilting past vertical at top of arc. See Pink-footed Shearwater.

Range
Disperses to North Pacific during nonbreeding season: occurs off West Coast from British Columbia to California in fall; recorded from Gulf of Alaska. Breeds in New Zealand area.   *Terence Wahl*

In flight, from below
1. *White underparts with dark smudge on belly.*
2. *Distinct, dark cap.*

In flight, from below
1. *Pure white underparts and wing linings.*

   Slow wingbeats. Languid, buoyant flight.

In flight, from above
1. *Dark cap.*
2. *Light gray upperparts, with dark M on wings.*

   Often in tight flocks.

Sooty Shearwater

Puffinus griseus

The Sooty is the most abundant "tubenose," and the shearwater most commonly seen from shore in many parts of western North America. It occurs from the shore to the edge of the continental shelf in flocks of up to hundreds of thousands and is found over vast areas of the open ocean in small numbers. While not uncommon off the east coast of North America, it is much less abundant there. Other, less common species may be found among flocks of Sooties; this species serves as the yardstick for comparing field marks and behavior among shearwaters. Sooty Shearwaters have learned to forage at working fishing vessels. Huge, milling flocks plunging from the air on fish schools at sea or in the shoreline surf are impressive spectacles. Unlike most other tubenoses, Sooties dive readily and use their wings to swim underwater. Their flight is arcing, with several quick flaps and a glide, up and down in wave troughs and over crests, varying in height with wind speed.

Description

16–18″ (40.5–45.5 cm). The Sooty Shearwater is a medium-size, blackish-brown species with a long, thin, dark bill and dark feet. A silvery or whitish area on the wing linings is conspicuous in good light but may not be visible under some conditions; this feature also varies with molt. In good light, the plumage is a nearly uniform sooty brown, but often appears uneven or blotchy, with somewhat darker primaries and tail. The wings are long, narrow, and tapering, often appearing bowed or crescent-shaped in flight silhouette.

Voice

Gives nasal, bleating call at sea when competing for food around vessels.

Similar Species

See Northern Fulmar and Flesh-footed and Short-tailed shearwaters. Manx smaller, with white underparts.

Range

Spends nonbreeding season in temperate parts of North Atlantic and North Pacific oceans; occasional in Bering Sea. Recorded from Gulf of Mexico. Breeds in Southern Hemisphere. *Terence Wahl*

Short-tailed Shearwater

Puffinus tenuirostris

Abundant in cold North Pacific and Bering Sea waters, the Short-tailed Shearwater is very similar in appearance and behavior to the Sooty Shearwater; under most conditions, distinguishing between the 2 species can be difficult. The Short-tail is less regular in occurrence along the west coast of North America; its vast populations are largely unnoticed by North American observers except in western Alaska and the Bering Sea.

Description

14″ (35.5 cm). The Short-tail is a medium-size, dark brown or blackish shearwater. It is very similar to the more familiar Sooty Shearwater, but is slightly smaller, appears slimmer in build, and has a smaller head and a shorter bill. It often looks somewhat darker and more uniformly colored than the Sooty, with a rather velvety appearance. The head may show a vague dark cap, and there is often a rather sharply defined whitish patch on the throat. The forehead looks rounded, while the Sooty has a sloping forehead line

In flight
1. *Uniformly dark plumage.*
2. *Pale wing linings.*
3. *Dark bill.*

Arcing flight.

On water
1. *Uniformly dark plumage.*
2. *Dark bill.*

Often in large flocks.

In flight
1. *Short, dark bill.*
2. *Dark brown plumage.*
3. *Gray wing linings.*
4. *Dark feet.*

with a distinct "break" at the crown. The wing linings are usually a
rather even gray, narrowly outlined with a darker tone. In good
light, the wing linings appear obviously lighter than the upperparts,
but lack the whitish area typical of the Sooty Shearwater. The color
of the wing linings of the 2 species is variable, overlaps, and is by no
means definitive under all conditions. The Short-tail has a shorter
tail than the Sooty; it also appears to have a slightly faster wingbeat
and maneuvers more skillfully in flight. However, these are all
relative features, and under many conditions, differentiation
between the 2 species may not be possible.

Similar Species
See Sooty Shearwater. Flesh-footed larger, more uniformly dark,
with larger pinkish bill, broader wings; soars more frequently.

Range
Migrates to North Pacific for nonbreeding season; many enter the
Bering Sea in northern summer; seasonally abundant in Gulf of
Alaska. Irregularly uncommon to rare off West Coast from British
Columbia to California. Breeds near southern Australia.
Terence Wahl

Manx Shearwater

Puffinus puffinus
The long-winged, short-tailed Manx is the largest of the black-and-
white shearwaters in the western North Atlantic.

Description
12–15″ (30.5–38 cm). The Manx flies in bursts of stiff wingbeats
alternating with periods of gliding and banking. It is uniformly
blackish above, very white below, with sharp contrast between the
dark and white. The dark upperparts may extend slightly toward
the breast. The undertail coverts are white, and the feet often
project beyond the tail. The underwing is white, often narrowly
margined in black; the flanks may show some mottling.

Similar Species
See Audubon's, Sooty, Greater, Cory's, and Little* shearwaters.

Range
Usually breeds in northeastern Atlantic. Migrant to western North
Atlantic, may breed.   *Ron Naveen*

Black-vented Shearwater

Puffinus opisthomelas
One of the black-and-white shearwaters of the eastern Pacific, the
Black-vented Shearwater is now considered a separate species from
the Manx Shearwater of the North Atlantic. It is more brown-
backed and has dusky brownish rather than white undertail coverts.
It is often seen close to shore. The key to identifying the black-and-
white shearwaters is to focus on wingbeat, the comparative length
of wing and tail, and the color of the undertail coverts, which can
generally be seen when the shearwater glides and tilts. At times,
the mantle color can be helpful.

Description
12–15″ (30.5–38 cm). The Black-vented Shearwater appears
brownish-black above, white below, and has dusky brownish
undertail coverts. The axillars and flanks show some duskiness as
well. The brownish head color extends to well below the eye and
merges indistinctly with the dusky chin, throat, and neck. The
demarcation between the dark upperparts and the lighter

On water
1. *Dark plumage.*
2. *Rounded forehead.*
3. *Short, dark bill.*
4. *Pale throat patch.*

In flight
1. *Black cap and upperparts.*
2. *White underparts.*
3. *White undertail coverts.*

Slower wingbeat, longer wings, and shorter tail than Audubon's.

On water
1. *Brownish upperparts.*
2. *Dusky sides and breast.*
3. *No sharp distinction between back and underparts.*

underparts is not sharp. The sides of the breast are dusky, and this duskiness may extend across the breast. The leading edge of the underwing is whitish, while the trailing edge has a brownish border.

Similar Species
Manx Shearwater has white undertail coverts. Pink-footed Shearwater much larger, with heavier flight, darker wing linings, and grayish back.

Range
Fairly common late-fall and winter visitor to southern California waters; may be found in small numbers during spring and summer. Breeds in Revillagigedo Islands, Mexico.   *Ron Naveen*

Audubon's Shearwater

Puffinus lherminieri
The short-winged, long-tailed Audubon's is a small, active bird that flies with rapid, fluttery wingbeats and short glides, often using its tail as a rudder. It is prone to quicker turns and changes of direction than the Manx.

Description
12″ (30.5 cm). Audubon's Shearwater is blackish-brown above and light below. In flight, the flesh-colored legs may be visible against the dark brown undertail coverts but do not extend beyond the tail. There are often dark smudges on the sides of the breast.

Similar Species
Manx has slower wingbeats, glides and banks more often; has shorter tail and white undertail coverts; in good light appears darker above. See Little Shearwater*.

Range
Breeds in Bermuda and Caribbean. Regular to Gulf Stream from Carolinas to Florida. Casual to Gulf of Mexico and to Gulf of Maine.   *Ron Naveen*

In flight
1. *Light underparts.*
2. *Dark undertail coverts.*

Flight consists of much flapping and little gliding.

In flight
1. *Dark upperparts.*
2. *Light underparts.*
3. *Short wings.*
4. *Long tail.*

Rapid, fluttery wingbeats with short glides.

Storm-Petrels

(Family Hydrobatidae)
Storm-Petrels are the smallest petrels; identifying them requires
much experience and a careful comparison of their flight, feeding
habits, and relative size. Among all-dark, white-rumped species,
Wilson's flies directly, almost continuously flapping its rounded
wings, with only brief glides; it feeds by foot-pattering on the water.
In Leach's and the Band-rumped, the wings are more pointed and
bent; Leach's flies erratically, with deep, slow wingbeats and some
gliding, the Band-rumped more directly, with shallower, faster
wingbeats and shearwaterlike gliding. The rump patch of Wilson's is
square and large; that of Leach's is small, off-white, and triangular;
the Band-rumped's is whiter than Leach's and more rectangular.
Among all-dark, dark-rumped species, the Black is the largest, and
has deep wingbeats. The Ashy is smaller and has shallow wingbeats.
The Least is the smallest, and flies with quick, deep wingbeats.
(World: 20 species. North America: 10 species.)　*Ron Naveen*

Wilson's Storm-Petrel

Tail

Oceanites oceanicus
Wilson's Storm-Petrel flies swallowlike on continuously beating
wings, and glides occasionally. When feeding, it often "walks" over
the water with wings raised in a V.

Description
7″ (18 cm). Wilson's is blackish above and below, with a large,
square, contrasting white rump patch that extends to the undertail
coverts. The long legs and yellow webbed feet project beyond the
square or slightly rounded tail, but are difficult to see.

Similar Species
See Leach's and Band-rumped storm-petrels and discussion under
storm-petrel family. See also British Storm-Petrel*.

Range
Migrates in large numbers to North Atlantic during austral winter
(April through November). Regular in fall on Monterey Bay,
California. Breeds in Antarctic region.　*Ron Naveen*

White-faced Storm-Petrel

Pelagodroma marina
A fast, erratic flier, the White-faced darts from side to side and
proceeds with very shallow wingbeats and frequent glides. As it
feeds, the bird pushes off the surface, hopping over the waves.

Description
8″ (20.5 cm). The White-faced is dark gray above and pale below; it
has a distinct dark cap and a white face and chin that highlight a
dark line running through the eye to the ear coverts. The dark tail
and flight feathers accentuate the gray rump. The sides of the breast
are smudged with gray, and the white underwings have a broad,
dusky trailing margin. The White-faced has long legs and large,
yellow-webbed feet that extend beyond the square tail. It is about
the size of a Leach's but its paleness may make it look larger.

Range
Breeds in east-central Atlantic; a rare vagrant to western North
Atlantic waters, late summer and early fall.　*Ron Naveen*

In flight
1. *White rump extends to undertail coverts.*
2. *Rounded wings.*
3. *Square or slightly rounded tail.*

Swallowlike flight. Patters feet on water's surface.

In flight
1. *White face with dark eyeline and dark cap.*
2. *Dark sides of breast.*
3. *White wing linings and dark flight feathers.*

Erratic flight.

Fork-tailed Storm-Petrel

Oceanodroma furcata
The only pale storm-petrel of the North Pacific Ocean, this species prefers colder water, and is not likely to be confused with other storm-petrels. The Fork-tailed flies with deep, steady wingbeats.

Description
8″ (20.5 cm). The Fork-tailed Storm-Petrel is pale overall; medium gray above and lighter gray below, with a distinctive dark ear patch in sharp contrast with the rest of its face. The Fork-tailed is distinctly marked with dark wing linings and axillars that contrast sharply with the rest of the wing and the lighter underparts. This slate-black area is concentrated near the leading edge of the underwing and extends from the axillars to the bend of the wing.

Range
Breeds off coasts of southern Alaska, Washington, Oregon, and northern California. Casual winter and spring visitor off southern California; in northern California, occasionally seen in summer and early fall, rare in winter.   *Ron Naveen*

Leach's Storm-Petrel

Tail

Oceanodroma leucorhoa
On long, pointed, often bent wings, Leach's flies nighthawklike with deep wingbeats and much bounding and veering.

Description
8″ (20.5 cm). Leach's is dark brown above and below. The legs and feet do not extend beyond the forked tail. Most birds have a small, triangular, dusky white rump patch, bisected by dark feathers; some in the eastern Pacific have dark rumps.

Similar Species
See Wilson's and Band-rumped storm-petrels and discussion under storm-petrel family.

Range
Breeds in eastern Pacific from southern Alaska to Baja California; fairly common far offshore in summer (some winter records); in western North Atlantic from Newfoundland to Massachusetts from April to November; much scarcer to North Carolina.   *Ron Naveen*

Ashy Storm-Petrel

Oceanodroma homochroa
The Ashy Storm-Petrel is easily found in the huge storm-petrel flocks that gather each fall in California's Monterey Bay. It is chunky-looking and flies with very shallow wingbeats.

Description
8″ (20.5 cm). The dark-rumped Ashy has a tan or gray cast, a long, notched tail, and rounded wings that appear uniform in width. The wings are barely raised above the horizontal as it flies, and the wingbeats are not as deep as those of the Black, Leach's, or Least.

Similar Species
Other dark-rumped storm-petrels may be distinguished by comparative size and flight characteristics.

Range
Breeds in Marin County, California, California islands (Farallons, Santa Barbara), and Baja California (Coronadoes). Regular in southern California.   *Ron Naveen*

In flight
1. *Pale overall color.*
2. *Dark ear patch.*

*Deep, steady
wingbeats.
Dark wing linings
contrast with paler
underparts and
flight feathers.*

In flight
1. *White rump with
dark center.*
2. *Long, pointed wings
with distinct bend at
wrist.*

*Deep wingbeats.
Some Pacific birds
have dark rumps.*

In flight
1. *Dark rump and
long, deeply notched
tail.*

*Chunky build.
Shallow wingbeats,
with wings barely
raised above
horizontal.*

Band-rumped Storm-Petrel

Oceanodroma castro
This bird appears to be solitary and highly pelagic away from its
breeding grounds, and may occupy warmer, deeper waters than
other storm-petrels. It flies with shallower wingbeats than Leach's,
glides shearwaterlike, and often follows a horizontal, zigzag course.

Tail

Description
9" (23 cm). This species is dark brown above and below, with a
slightly forked tail and a narrow, rectangular white rump patch that
gives the bird a long-tailed look. The legs do not extend beyond the
tail. This bird often feeds with its wings held horizontally.

Similar Species
See Wilson's and Leach's storm-petrels.

Range
Breeds in eastern Atlantic and east-central Pacific. Occasional
midsummer to fall in western North Atlantic; casual to Gulf of
Mexico, May to October.   *Ron Naveen*

Black Storm-Petrel

Oceanodroma melania
This all-dark, dark-rumped storm-petrel can be distinguished by its
large size, long, pointed wings, and deep, steady wingbeats.

Description
9–10" (23–25.5 cm). This large, dark brown, long-legged, and dark-
rumped bird raises and lowers its pointed wings 60° above and below
the horizontal. At times it may fly with shallower wingbeats and
unpredictable glides.

Similar Species
Ashy smaller, flies with very shallow wingbeats. Least much
smaller; has short tail, more rapid wingbeats. See Leach's.

Range
Breeds on islands off California coast, Pacific coast of Baja
California, and in northern Gulf of California. Common summer to
early winter visitor to offshore southern and central California
waters, especially Monterey Bay in fall.   *Ron Naveen*

Least Storm-Petrel

Oceanodroma microsoma
Birders in southern California face the problem of distinguishing as
many as 4 all-dark and dark-rumped storm-petrels. The Least is the
smallest of the 4; size is a key field mark for this species. Its small
size and rapid wingbeats are often more readily perceived than its
short, wedge-shaped tail and very short wings.

Description
5–6" (12.5–15 cm). The Least Storm-Petrel is very small, all-dark
and dark-rumped, with very short wings and a very short, wedge-
shaped tail. It flies a rather direct course on rapid, deep wingbeats.

Similar Species
See Ashy, Black, and Leach's storm-petrels.

Range
Breeds in San Benitos Islands off Pacific Baja California, and
northern Gulf of California. Irregular visitor to offshore southern
California waters from August to October.   *Ron Naveen*

In flight
1. *Narrow rump patch extending to undertail coverts.*
2. *Rounded, short wings.*

Horizontal, zigzag flight.

In flight
1. *Long, pointed wings.*
2. *Dark rump.*

Large size.
Deep, graceful wingbeats.

In flight
1. *Short tail.*
2. *Short wings.*
3. *Dark rump.*

Small size.
Rapid, deep wingbeats.

Tropicbirds

(Family Phaethontidae)
Tropicbirds are basically all-white seabirds. Adults have distinctive long tail streamers, and are easily recognized as tropicbirds. Specific identification of juveniles and of adults without streamers, however, requires close examination of the back and upper surface of the wings. Wingbeat rhythm and bill color are also helpful, but should not be relied upon exclusively for identification. Tropicbirds fly with rapid, continuous wingbeats, interspersed with infrequent glides. These birds wander extensively in search of food. They are capable of much twisting and turning in flight, and they are adept plunge-divers. They swim on the water's surface with cocked tails. (World: 3 species. North America: 3 species.)   *Ron Naveen*

White-tailed Tropicbird

Phaethon lepturus
The White-tailed Tropicbird is the smallest member of its family. The adult has 2 broad, black patches stretching across the tertials and upper secondary coverts on the back and upperwing; these patches, which can sometimes be seen from below, are diagnostic. The White-tailed is the tropicbird most likely to be seen from the Dry Tortugas in Florida.

Description
15–16″ (38–40.5 cm) without tail streamers; 28–32″ (71–81.5 cm) with tail streamers. The White-tailed has relatively narrow wings and flies with a faster wingbeat rhythm than the Red-billed Tropicbird. Adults have bright white upperparts and underparts; the characteristic long, white tail streamers and broad black bands across the tertials and upper secondary coverts may be visible from below. The adult shows some dark before and behind the eye, but generally does not have a broad, dark line behind the eye and around the nape that is often visible in the Red-billed. The adult's bill is orange or orange-red. The juvenile lacks the long tail streamers and has widely spaced, dark barring on the back; otherwise, the upperparts are white. The bill is yellow at first and changes gradually to the adult's orange or orange-red color.

Immature

Similar Species
Adult Red-billed Tropicbird lacks broad, black bands across tertials and secondary coverts; wings broader at base; wingbeat rhythm slower; adult has larger, red bill. Adult and juvenile Red-billed have finely barred back, appearing gray or dusky at a distance; broadly spaced barring of immature White-tailed visible at greater distance.

Range
Western North Atlantic race breeds from Bermuda to Caribbean; another race breeds in tropical Pacific. Irregular offshore from Maryland to Florida (June to September); casual year round to Gulf of Mexico. Summer record from California.   *Ron Naveen*

White-tailed Tropicbird
Red-billed Tropicbird
Red-tailed Tropicbird

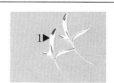

Adults in flight
1. *Narrower wings than Red-billed Tropicbird.*

Adult in flight
1. *Mainly white plumage.*
2. *Long tail streamers.*
3. *Broad, dark bands on secondary coverts and tertials.*

   Fast wingbeats.

Red-billed Tropicbird

Phaethon aethereus
The Red-billed is the largest tropicbird. It is a rare visitor to
western and eastern North American waters. Birders should use
caution in all tropicbird identifications: key field marks are found on
the upperwing and back, but the birds are usually seen from below.

Description
18–20″ (45.5–51 cm) without tail streamers; 36–42″ (91.5–106.5 cm)
with tail streamers. The Red-billed Tropicbird has broad-based
wings and flies with slower wingbeats than the White-tailed
Tropicbird. The adult's back is finely barred, lacking the White-
tailed's distinctive black bands across the tertials and secondary
coverts. The bill is large and red. There is often a strong black
eyeline extending from in front of the eye to, and around, the nape,
although this feature is variable. Juveniles lack the tail streamers,
have a yellow bill, and have a finely barred back like the adults.
At a distance, the barring of both the adults and juveniles appears
gray and indistinct.

Similar Species
Adult White-tailed smaller, lacks fine barring on back, and has
broad black bands across tertials and secondary coverts. White-
tailed has narrower wings and faster wingbeat; bill smaller, head
generally lacks strong, black eyeline. Juvenile White-tailed has
broader, more distinct barring on back; does not appear gray at a
distance.

Range
Very rare visitor to North Carolina waters; also rare summer and
early fall visitor to offshore southern California waters. Casual off
northern California and in winter. Native to tropics of western
Atlantic and eastern Pacific oceans.   *Ron Naveen*

Adult in flight

1. *Mainly white plumage.*
2. *Long tail streamers.*
3. *Fine bars on back, with no broad bands.*

Slow wingbeats.

Immature

1. *Yellow bill.*
2. *Barred back.*
3. *Tail lacks streamers.*

Boobies and Gannets

(Family Sulidae)
Five of the world's 9 species of sulids are found in our area. The
Northern Gannet is the Northern Hemisphere representative of the
world gannet complex, with other forms found in South Africa and
Australasia. Sulids are goose-size seabirds and, as a family, are
easily recognized by their large size, large, pointed bills and long
bodies tapered at both ends. They fly with strong, purposeful
wingbeats on stiff wings and often plunge-dive after subsurface
prey. Identification of adults is relatively easy, but first-year birds
are not as readily distinguishable, and require careful consideration
of the characteristic first-year—and in the Gannet's case, second-
and third-year—plumage that each species acquires. (World: 9
species. North America: 5 species.)   *Ron Naveen*

Masked Booby

Sula dactylatra
This is the large, white booby of tropical waters; its name derives
from its dark facial pattern. The Masked is the largest of the
boobies, and may be confused with the Northern Gannet, which it
resembles in size and adult and juvenal plumages.

Description
26–34″ (66–86.5 cm). From above, adults show a masked face, dark
wingtips and secondaries, a dark tail, and 2 small dark patches on
the back above the tail. Otherwise, adults are gleaming
white above and below. The chin is unfeathered. First-year birds
show a combination of a dark head and mantle separated by a white
collar (which, however, is variable and may be quite indistinct). On
the underparts, there is an inverted U- or V-shaped line dividing the
dark throat and upper breast from the paler lower breast and belly.
Adult plumage is gained in about 2 to 3 years.

Similar Species
Adult Northern Gannet lacks dark secondaries and dark tail. First-
year Gannet entirely dark; may show combination of light head
and dark mantle, in contrast to first-year Masked's dark head and
back separated by more or less distinct collar. From a distance,
however, first-year Gannet and Masked Booby must be carefully
distinguished, especially off Florida coast and in Gulf of Mexico.
First-year Red-footed smaller, appearing all-dark and often with
discernible breastband. First-year Brown Booby appears all-dark
with suggestion of adult's breast demarcation line. Adult white-
morph Red-footed Booby smaller, with light inner secondaries and
sometimes light tail; no dark patches.

Range
Regular visitor to Gulf of Mexico throughout year; often found in
Dry Tortugas. One winter record from southern California. Also in
tropical oceans worldwide.   *Ron Naveen*

Adult in flight
1. *Head and body white.*
2. *Dark flight feathers in wings and tail.*

First-year bird
1. *Head and back dark.*
2. *White collar.*

Blue-footed Booby

Sula nebouxii
The Blue-footed Booby is an irregular visitor from late summer to
early winter in the Salton Sea of southeastern California. Blue-foots
feed close to shore on their breeding grounds and are not as pelagic
as other members of the genus. There are many disputed records
from the Gulf of Mexico, where Blue-foots may easily be confused
with first-year Masked Boobies and first- and second-year Northern
Gannets.

Description
30–33" (76–84 cm). The adult Blue-foot is distinguished by its
streaked head and by the white patches on the nape and rump.
Often there is a third white patch on the tail. The adult otherwise
appears dark on the upperwing surface, with a slightly lighter and
barred appearance to the back and wing linings. The head is
streaked, and the throat, breast, belly, and undertail coverts are
white. From below, the tips and trailing edges of the wings are
dark. The wing linings are gray-brown; the inner lesser coverts are
paler, and the axillars are white. Often a small brown patch is
noticeable on the thigh. The feet and legs are bright blue. The
female's pupils often appear larger than the male's. First-year birds
are similar, but have more streaking on the throat and upper breast.
There is much variation, but they often show a sharp horizontal
demarcation line between the dark upper breast and throat and the
white lower breast and belly.

Similar Species
First-year Masked Boobies lack Blue-foot's white rump patch and
third patch that often shows on Blue-foot's tail. First-year Masked
has inverted U or V separating upper and lower breast, usually not
sharp horizontal line of first-year Blue-foot. Also see Brown and
Red-footed boobies and Northern Gannet.

Range
Very irregular late-summer visitor to Salton Sea and nearby
portions of southern California; sometimes lingers into early winter.
Blue-foots found in Salton Sea usually immatures and subadults.
Accidental in Gulf of Mexico. Also along Pacific coast of Central
America and northern South America.   *Ron Naveen*

Brown Booby

Sula leucogaster
This distinctive booby, with its brown upperparts and breast,
gleaming white belly, and white underwings broadly bordered with
dusky brown, is an inhabitant of tropical waters in the Atlantic,
Indian, and Pacific oceans, mainly between the Tropic of Cancer and
the Tropic of Capricorn. The Brown Booby is a regular visitor to the
Gulf of Mexico and to the Dry Tortugas off the southern tip of
Florida. It occurs much less frequently in the western North
Atlantic, where it is found off the coast from Florida north to the
Carolinas. It is occasionally seen in the vicinity of the Salton Sea in
southeastern California, and has been recorded on the Pacific Ocean
off the coast of southern California. The Brown Booby often feeds in
inshore waters, and unlike the Northern Gannet and most other
boobies, it readily perches on buoys, rocks, and in trees.

Description
26–29" (66–73.5 cm). The adult Brown Booby is easily distinguished
by its uniformly dark brown head, back, upperwings, and tail; broad

Adult in flight
1. *Pale, streaked head.*
2. *White patch on nape.*
3. *White patch on rump.*

First-year bird
1. *Dark head and breast.*
2. *Sharp demarcation between breast and belly.*

Shows white patches on nape and rump.

First-year bird
1. *Entirely dark plumage.*

dark margins on the leading and trailing edges of the white
underwing; the dark throat and breast; and a sharply defined
horizontal border between the very dark upper breast and the pure
white belly. The bill is yellow, and the legs and feet vary in color
from yellow to greenish-yellow. When viewed at close range, the
birds show a dark patch at the base of the bill just in front of the
eyes; this patch is generally more extensive in females than in
males. Birds in their first year appear wholly dark, with the belly
and underwings between the dark margins gradually becoming paler
as the birds mature. The horizontal demarcation line between the
dark breast and pale belly is present in first-year birds, but is
discernible only at close range. The full adult plumage is attained
after about 2 or 3 years.

Similar Species
Adult Brown Booby unmistakable. First-year Northern Gannet
larger than first-year Brown Booby; until head and underparts of
Northern Gannet become paler with age, may be difficult to
distinguish at a distance. First-year Blue-footed Booby smaller, with
white patches on nape and rump contrasting with dark back. First-
year Masked Booby has white patch on nape between dark head and
dark mantle, and inverted U- or V-shaped (not straight and
horizontal) line dividing dark upper breast from paler lower breast
and belly. First-year Red-footed Booby smaller, with narrower
wings and faster wingbeat; usually has indistinct band of dark
feathering on breast.

Range
Regular summer visitor to Gulf of Mexico and Dry Tortugas off tip
of Florida. Casual during rest of year in Gulf of Mexico. Rare
visitors may occur in western North Atlantic waters, especially off
Florida and occasionally northward. Casual in late summer in Salton
Sea area of California and Colorado River valley; very rare off coast
of southern California. Also in tropical Atlantic, Pacific, and Indian
oceans.   *Ron Naveen*

Red-footed Booby

Sula sula
The smallest of the boobies, the Red-footed is very common in
pantropical waters, but only an infrequent visitor to our area. There
are a number of color morphs, at least 3 of which may potentially be
found in North America.

Description
26–29″ (66–73.5 cm). The small size, narrow wings, and relatively
faster wingbeat of the Red-footed Booby may be helpful in
distinguishing this species from other sulids. The adult's red feet
and pale pink-and-blue facial skin are diagnostic; first-year birds
have drab gray feet. The white morph is gleaming white above and
below, with dark wingtips and outer secondaries; the innermost
secondaries are white. The tail is usually white, although some
white morphs from the Galapagos have dark tails. An all-dark brown
morph is found in the Galapagos; in the Caribbean, Galapagos, and
western Pacific there is a dark morph with a white tail. Some central
Pacific birds have dark bodies with white heads and tails. First-year

Immature

Adult in flight
1. *Upperparts dark brown.*
2. *Dark breast and white belly separated by sharp line.*
3. *Broad, dark margin to white wing lining.*

First-year bird perched
1. *Entirely dark plumage.*
2. *Yellow feet.*

Brown morph
1. *Brownish plumage.*
2. *Red feet.*
3. *Pale pink and blue facial skin.*

   In flight has fast wingbeat, narrow wings.

birds of all color morphs are brown above and slightly paler below, with the back and underparts variably lightening with age. There may be a band of darker brown feathering on the breast. Adult plumage is reached in 2 to 3 years.

Similar Species
First-year Northern Gannet much larger, all-dark with heavier flight; second- and third-year birds have light head, dark back, and white underparts; adult larger than white-morph Red-footed and has white inner and outer secondaries. First-year Masked Booby larger, usually has white nape patch and inverted U-shaped line separating dark upper breast and white lower breast and belly; adult has dark inner and outer secondaries and dark tail. Blue-footed has 2–3 white patches above. First-year Brown Booby larger; appears all-dark at distance, but at close range, dim breast line and broad underwing margins can be seen.

Range
Rare visitor to Dry Tortugas; accidental in Gulf of Mexico. Two fall records from Farallon Islands off San Francisco. Tropical oceans worldwide.   *Ron Naveen*

Northern Gannet

Sula bassanus

Although the adult Northern Gannet is distinctive, identification of younger Gannets requires some knowledge of the species' 4-year plumage sequence. Extreme care must be taken in spring and early summer in Florida and the Gulf of Mexico, where first- and second-year birds can be mistaken for first-year Masked or Brown boobies.

Description
35–40″ (89–101.5 cm). The Northern Gannet takes 4 years or more to reach adult plumage. The adult is quite distinctive: it has gleaming white upperparts, underparts, head, and tail, and obvious black upperwing tips from the wrist outwards. The underwing tips are not as dark and there is some white in the wing linings near the wrist. The bill is long, stout, and slate-gray; the feathered chin makes the bill appear pointed at both ends. Early in the first year, the young Gannet is generally all-dark. The head and underparts usually are the first areas to lighten, and do so earlier than the mantle and upperwing surface; a dark-backed, white-headed juvenile sulid may usually be safely identified as a Northern Gannet. In second-year birds, the mantle and rump begin to lighten, with many variations. There may be obvious white patches on the leading edge of the upperwing surface; or the white of the back and rump may surround a dark patch. Generally, the tail remains dark. Near the end of the second year, there is generally dark color only on the wingtips, secondaries, scapulars, rump, and tail. The secondaries and tail become white during the third year, and perhaps into the fourth.

Similar Species
See Masked Booby. Adult white-morph Red-footed much smaller, with dark outer secondaries, red feet, and pink and pale blue facial skin. First-year Brown Booby smaller, and shows semblance of breast demarcation line. First-year Blue-footed much smaller, often with dark breastband.

Range
Abundant breeder in Gaspé Peninsula of Quebec and Newfoundland, migrating south in September and October along eastern seaboard and into Gulf of Mexico. First-year birds tend to move farther south than older birds. Also in northeastern Atlantic.   *Ron Naveen*

White morph
1. *Plumage mainly white.*
2. *Dark wing tips and outer secondaries.*
3. *Red feet.*
4. *Pale pink and blue facial skin.*

   Small size.

Adult in flight
1. *Mainly white plumage.*
2. *Black wing tips and outermost secondaries.*
3. *Slate-gray bill.*

   Large size.
   Often plunge-dives.

Juvenile in flight
1. *Entirely dark head and upperparts.*

   Large size.
   Becomes paler on head and underparts as it grows older.

Pelicans

(Family Pelecanidae)
The Pelicans are very large water birds with heavy, broad bodies,
long necks, large, thick heads, and huge bills. The bill shape is
characterized not only by its size but also by its flat, wide upper
mandible that has a conspicuous hook at the tip. There is a large
distensible gular pouch on the lower mandible. Pelicans typically
stand in a very horizontal posture; they have short, stout legs and
webbed feet. When floating on the water, pelicans ride high, with
the long, large wings fitting loosely over the back. Airborne, they
are quite graceful, with a strong flight, deep wingbeats, and much
soaring. Pelicans usually fly in flocks in loose lines, often in a
gooselike V formation. (World: 8 species. North America: 2 species.)
Scott B. Terrill

American White Pelican

Pelecanus erythrorhynchos
The huge American White Pelican is one of North America's largest
birds, with a wingspread as wide as 9½ feet—rivaling that of the
California Condor. Floating buoyantly on the water's surface, the
White Pelican submerges its head and neck to scoop up fish in its
wide, flat bill; unlike the Brown Pelican, it never plunge-dives from
the air for food. Gregarious at all seasons, the White Pelican may
even fish cooperatively in shallow water, with several of the birds
lining up and herding the fish before them. Flocks fly in lines or V
formation and sometimes soar high in the air, wheeling in unison on
motionless flat wings. In flight, the head is folded back onto the
shoulders, heron-style.

Description
54–70″ (137–178 cm). The plumage of the adult is white except for
black primaries, primary coverts, and outer secondaries; the bill is
yellow. In the breeding season, the bill becomes brighter and
develops a raised "plate" or "fin" halfway along the upper mandible.
At this season, there is also a pale yellow patch on the upper chest
and a short, pale yellow crest on the back of the head; the latter is
replaced by dark gray before breeding is over. Immatures are
duskier than adults and have gray bills, but are still clearly
recognizable.

Similar Species
Wood Storks also soar in flocks and have similar wing pattern, but
have black inner secondaries, tail, and head; long legs always trail
beyond tail. Otherwise, American White Pelican should be
unmistakable; note that from distance very worn adult Brown
Pelicans can look surprisingly pale, with dark flight feathers.

Range
Breeds in widely scattered colonies on lakes in interior of western
Canada and northwestern United States, east to Minnesota and
south to northern California and Colorado; also locally on Texas
coast; formerly southern California. Winters in southern California
and along Gulf Coast to Florida; also in coastal Mexico. Migrant
through much of West and Midwest; casual strays reach
northeastern states.   *Kenn Kaufman*

American White Pelican
Brown Pelican

Adult in flight
1. *Long, flat bill.*
2. *Mainly white plumage.*
3. *Black wing tips.*

Huge size.
Often soars.

On water
1. *Long, flat bill.*
2. *White plumage.*
3. *Wings often held high above back.*

Huge size.
Often in flocks.

Brown Pelican

Pelecanus occidentalis
The Brown Pelican, a large bird of the coastal regions, has a very
large bill, a prominent, unfeathered throat pouch, and a wingspread
of up to 7½ feet. Commonly found along beaches, bays, and tidal
estuaries, and only rarely on fresh water, it feeds exclusively on
fish, diving head-first from heights of 20 to 50 feet to capture its
prey. Individual birds may become rather tolerant of humans and
seek handouts at marinas and piers and around fishing boats. In
flight, the neck is folded back heron-style. The flight is characterized
by strong strokes alternating with glides; small groups of birds often
make various formations. The Brown Pelican frequently flies
skimming just above the surface of the water, but unlike the
American White Pelican it seldom soars.

Description
42–54″ (106.5–137 cm). The adult in nonbreeding plumage has a
white head and neck; in breeding season the hindneck and nape are
cinnamon-brown. The body and wings are gray-brown or silvery
brown; the primaries and secondaries are dark gray-brown. The
large bill is gray, and the throat pouch is black. The sexes are alike.
In the immature Brown Pelican, the head, upper neck, wings, and
back are brown, and the base of the neck and the underparts are
white. Some worn adults can appear quite pale.

Similar Species
White Pelican white in all plumages with black primaries and some
black secondaries.

Range
Breeds locally from southern California and North Carolina south to
Florida, West Indies, Venezuela, and Chile. Regularly occurs on
Pacific Coast north to Washington and rarely to British Columbia;
on Atlantic Coast occasionally to New England and Nova Scotia.
Regular post-breeding visitor to lower Colorado River and Salton
Sea, California.   *Paul W. Sykes, Jr.*

Pelicans

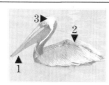

Breeding adult
1. *Long, flat bill.*
2. *Gray-brown body.*
3. *White head.*

Large size.
Often dives for fish.

Immature
1. *Head and neck*
   brown, not white.

Cormorants

(Family Phalacrocoracidae)
Cormorants are medium-size to large darkish water birds with
elongated bodies and relatively long, rather stout necks. The head
looks like a slightly wider extension of the neck,and the bill is long
and noticeably hooked at the tip. The tail is relatively long, wide,
and wedge-shaped. The legs are set far back on the body, and the
bird's stance is very upright. Like anhingas, cormorants when
perched often spread the wings to dry their feathers. In North
America, adult cormorants frequently show a metallic sheen to their
blackish plumage and have crests, filoplumes, or white flank patches
during breeding season. The immatures of most species are
noticeably paler on the underparts. At close range, the brightly
colored bare skin in the facial and gular region can be seen.
Generally, cormorants are gregarious. In flight, the wingbeats are
slower than those of loons and have a characteristic "rolling" aspect.
Swimming cormorants often hold the head and bill at an upward tilt.
They dive with a forward leap. (World: 33 species. North America: 6
species.)   *Scott B. Terrill*

Great Cormorant

Phalacrocorax carbo
This species is the largest of the North American cormorants.
Confined to maritime areas in eastern Canada during the summer, it
is also the only cormorant likely to be encountered in winter from
New England north. From February through early summer, adults
can readily be distinguished by their conspicuous white flank
patches; this is the only eastern cormorant so marked. Both sitting
and in flight, the Great Cormorant appears to have a heavy, angular
head and a longer bill than the Double-crested Cormorant. When not
swimming, it is most often observed perched in small groups on   *First-year bird*
offshore rocks, navigation towers, or buoys. The Great Cormorant,
like other cormorants, often assumes a spread-eagle posture at rest.
In flight, its large size and heavy wingbeats make it appear quite
gooselike. The Great Cormorant is rare in our range in summer.

Description
34–40″ (86.5–101.5 cm). Adults in breeding plumage are essentially
black throughout, but the chin and sides of the face are white. From
early spring through early summer, white feathers appear on the
back of the crown, nape, and sides of the upper neck, in addition to
the conspicuous white flank patches. The throat pouch is yellow. In
winter, the white feathers on the chin and sides of the face have
brownish tips that wear off by early spring. Immatures, while
highly variable, are typically blackish-brown above with a pale
throat, light brownish neck and chest, and a gleaming white belly.
The throat pouch is pale yellow.

Similar Species
Double-crested Cormorant only species with overlapping range;
smaller and slimmer, with slenderer head and bill profile, orange-
yellow throat pouch, and no white flank patches. Immature Double-
crested variable, but usually has paler neck and chest and brown
belly—reverse of immature Great Cormorant.

Range
Breeds locally along coast from Newfoundland and Quebec south to
Nova Scotia and New Brunswick. Winters regularly from breeding
areas south to New Jersey, in small numbers to coastal Virginia;
casually to Georgia. Numbers are increasing. Also in Old
World.   *Wayne R. Petersen*

Great Cormorant
Double-crested Cormorant
Olivaceous Cormorant
Brandt's Cormorant
Pelagic Cormorant
Red-faced Cormorant

Immature
1. *Thick neck.*
2. *Dusky neck and chest.*
3. *Whitish belly.*

Large size.

Adult
1. *Heavy head and bill.*
2. *Throat pouch yellow.*

Large size.

Double-crested Cormorant

Phalacrocorax auritus
A large, gangly cormorant widespread in North America, the
Double-crested is the only one likely to be found inland north of the
Mexico borderlands. Its breeding locations in many regions change
from year to year as interior wetlands are "improved." The Double-
crested is highly adaptive and uses a variety of habitats, both
marine and terrestrial. In the nonbreeding season, Double-cresteds
usually appear singly or in small family groups. In general, they fly
at a higher altitude than other cormorants. In flight they may be
distinguished by their long tails, crooked necks, and long heads.

Description
26–32″ (66–81.5 cm). This large, long-tailed cormorant flies with a
distinctive crook in the neck, its long, large head riding above the
body centerline. Adults are black with iridescent green and purple
above. The large, unfeathered throat pouch is yellow-orange, and
the bill is black. Juveniles are pale, flat brown above; they have
varying amounts of whitish below, on the foreneck, breast, sides,
and, in some individuals, on the belly and flanks. The unfeathered
throat pouch and the lower mandible are yellow; the base of the
upper mandible is sometimes yellow as well. All ages have black
feet. The iris is brown in immatures, blue-green in spring adults.

First-year bird

Similar Species
See Great, Olivaceous, and Red-faced cormorants. Brandt's
Cormorant has shorter tail, flies with neck straight or very slightly
kinked. Juvenile and nonbreeding Brandt's may have extensive tan
feathers bordering throat pouch, but not bright yellow unfeathered
throat pouch of Double-crested. Pelagic Cormorant small with much
thinner neck, head, and bill; flies with neck straight out.

Range
Breeds from Aleutians to Gulf of California; in southern Idaho and
northern Utah; from Saskatchewan, eastern Montana, and Western
Nebraska to northern Great Lakes; in lower Mississippi Valley; from
Newfoundland to Long Island; and from Chesapeake Bay south
through Florida and along Gulf Coast to eastern Texas. Winters
along entire West Coast; on East Coast from Long Island south; in
Mississippi and Rio Grande river systems; and along Gulf Coast
south to Central America.   *Richard W. Stallcup*

Olivaceous Cormorant

Phalacrocorax olivaceus
One of the most widespread waterbirds in the American tropics, the
Olivaceous Cormorant reaches our area mainly in coastal Texas and
Louisiana. In appearance and general habits it resembles a small,
long-tailed version of the Double-crested Cormorant; it frequents
both salt water and fresh water and often perches in trees.

Description
24–28″ (61–71 cm). The adult is black, usually with a dull or
brownish tinge; the throat pouch and base of the lower mandible are
a dull buff-yellow. The eyes are green. In breeding plumage there is
a narrow white border behind the throat pouch, and the plumage is
generally a glossier black. Immatures are dull grayish-brown, a bit
paler below, the throat and breast fading to buff or even whitish.

Similar Species
In North America overlaps only with Double-crested Cormorant,
and must be carefully distinguished from that species. White border
to throat pouch of breeding Olivaceous is diagnostic, but some

In flight
1. *Distinct crook in neck.*
2. *Long tail.*

   Often flies high above water.

Adult
1. *Orange-yellow throat pouch.*
2. *Glossy black upperparts.*

   Large size.

Breeding plumage
1. *Slender bill.*
2. *Dull yellow or buff throat pouch comes to point below eye.*
3. *White border to throat pouch.*
4. *Slender neck.*
5. *Long tail.*

Double-cresteds, especially in several western populations, have noticeable white plumes elsewhere on head in breeding season. In Double-crested, throat pouch and adjacent areas often bright orange, but can be dull yellow; in Olivaceous, these areas never brighter than buff-yellow. Rear border of pouch below bill tapering to more of a point below and behind eye in Olivaceous, more smoothly rounded in Double-crested; not always easy to discern. Proportionately longer tail of Olivaceous detected most easily in flight by comparing extension of tail behind wings to extension of head and neck in front of wings: in Olivaceous, these 2 are about equal; in Double-crested, head-neck length is nearly twice tail length. With experience, Olivaceous may be identified by slimmer neck, smaller head, and thinner bill. At close range note tips of scapulars bluntly pointed in Olivaceous, rounded in Double-crested.

Range
Permanent resident in coastal regions and up some large rivers in Texas and Louisiana, and locally in southern New Mexico. Wanders regularly to southern Arizona and southern Oklahoma, casually to adjacent states. Also in American tropics.   *Kenn Kaufman*

Brandt's Cormorant

Phalacrocorax penicillatus
Brandt's is a rather large, robust cormorant of the Pacific Coast of North America, the Gulf of California, and neighboring offshore islands. During the breeding season, it nests in colonies on flat or gently sloping surfaces of islands. It remains generally gregarious during the entire year and can often be seen in large flocks flying low over ocean swells. Brandt's Cormorant is a shallow diver and is usually found feeding in the water beyond the intertidal zone. The birds are frequently seen in large numbers at feeding frenzies, diving with a forward leap to take small fish from just beneath the surface of the water.

Description
28–31″ (71–78.5 cm). This rather large, short-tailed cormorant flies with the neck held straight, but often with a slight bend at the base so that the head is lower than the centerline of the body. The head is large, distinctly thicker than the neck, and shows no crest. The bill is long and stout. Adults are dark brownish-black, the feathers showing comparatively little iridescence. Adults in breeding plumage have a striking, sky-blue, bare throat pouch bordered by yellowish throat feathers, and bristly white plumes that form wispy eyebrows. The juvenal plumage of this species is basically flat, dark brown, but not as dark as the corresponding plumage of the Pelagic Cormorant; there is a V of tan to buff on the upper breast that often extends down toward the center of the lower breast and belly. The bill, legs, and feet are black at all ages and seasons. The iris is dark in immature birds and bright blue in spring adults.

Similar Species
Pelagic Cormorant smaller, longer-tailed, more slender, with thinner neck and bill; head not distinctly thicker than neck; in flight neck held out straight, without slight bend at base, so that centerline of neck and body parallel to water; adult Pelagic shows much more iridescence; in breeding plumage has large, white flank patches, at close range shows small, red throat pouch; juvenile Pelagic darker, more uniform. Double-crested Cormorant longer-tailed, flies with distinct crook in neck, with head held above centerline of body; at close range shows bright yellow, unfeathered throat pouch with no blue; juvenile Double-crested has varying amounts of whitish on underparts.

Immature
1. Slender bill and small head.
2. Dull yellow or buff throat pouch comes to point below eye.
3. Slender neck.
4. Long tail.

Immature
1. Large head.
2. Thick neck.
3. Tan or buff breast.
4. Short tail.

Adult
1. Large head.
2. Thick neck.
3. Brownish-black plumage with little iridescence.

Range

Along Pacific Coast of North America from south coastal and
southeastern Alaska (where rare but has bred), south in increasing
numbers to central California, then south in diminishing numbers to
the southern tip of Baja California, and occurring north in Gulf of
California on peninsular side, more seldom on Sonoran side (at least
3 breeding colonies in Gulf of California). Accidental near Fresno,
California, and at Lake Patagonia, southern Arizona.
Richard W. Stallcup

Pelagic Cormorant

Phalacrocorax pelagicus
This small, slender cormorant of the North Pacific Ocean is almost
exclusively a bird of surf-battered, rocky shorelines. Although it
regularly enters large sounds and bays, and may forage for short
distances up some major rivers, the Pelagic Cormorant makes its
home on the windswept outer coast. It nests on steep sea cliffs that
are inaccessible to predators, often in close proximity to others of its
kind. When feeding, Pelagics dive for fish in shallow water, often in
the intertidal zone, but they are also capable of very deep dives.
They are usually solitary foragers, seldom taking part in feeding
frenzies like those of Brandt's Cormorant. In flight they can be
distinguished as far away as they can be seen by their characteristic
silhouette: a long-tailed cormorant with its neck held out straight,
without a bend or crook, and with the head scarcely thicker than the
neck.

Description

20–23″ (51–58.5 cm). The Pelagic is a small, long-tailed cormorant
that flies with the neck held straight out, showing no bend or crook.
The head is slight, barely thicker than the neck, and the bill is
distinctly slender. In flight, the centerline of both the body and the
neck is parallel to the surface of the water. Adults are dark, showing
much oily-green iridescence on the feathers of the back and wings,
and with varying amounts of purple on the neck. From early spring
through summer, the small, red throat pouch, the large, oval white
patches on the flanks, and the "double-crested" appearance (with a
crest on the forecrown and another on the hindcrown) will readily
distinguish this species. The juvenile is darker and more uniformly
colored than any other North American cormorant, being entirely
blackish-brown with only occasional medium-brown feathers on the
sides of the neck and breast. Birds in their second summer are black
and show some iridescence; they lack the white flank patches and
red throat pouch of the adult in breeding plumage. At all ages, the
bill appears largely dark.

Similar Species

Red-faced Cormorant (Alaska only) larger, with thicker, pale bill.
Brandt's Cormorant larger, shorter-tailed, more robust, with head
distinctly thicker than neck; Brandt's flies with neck straight out but
often bent, with head below centerline of body. Double-crested

Adult in flight
1. *Thick neck held out straight, without kink.*
2. *Head thick and held low.*
3. *Short tail.*

Adult in flight
1. *Thin neck held out straight, without kink.*
2. *Snakelike, slender head.*
3. *Small bill.*
4. *White flank patch in breeding season.*

Head of breeding adult
1. *Small, dark bill.*
2. *Red throat pouch.*
3. *Purple iridescence on neck.*

Cormorant larger, with larger head, stockier neck; flies with distinct crook in neck and head held above centerline of body.

Range
Pacific Coast from northern Alaska (summer only, rare), including Aleutians and virtually all major offshore islands, south to central Baja California. Breeds as far north as Kotzebue Sound and St. Lawrence Island in Bering Sea. Accidental away from marine environments. Also on northeast coast of Asia.
Richard W. Stallcup

Red-faced Cormorant

Phalacrocorax urile
The Red-faced Cormorant is confined to the Bering Sea and the adjacent coasts and islands of the North Pacific Ocean. It is larger than the Pelagic Cormorant, a similar species that is also found in Alaska waters.

Description
31–35″ (78.5–89 cm). The medium-size Red-faced Cormorant displays large white flank patches from winter to midsummer. The lower mandible and the base of the upper mandible are pale buff, the tip and rest of the upper mandible are dark. The throat pouch is bright blue, edged with orange-red. The bare facial skin, including the forehead, is bright scarlet or bright red-orange. Immatures show much white on the neck and breast.

Similar Species
Pelagic Cormorant smaller, with thinner, more serpentine neck, dark red facial skin that does not extend to forehead, and with thinner, blackish bill; thicker, paler bill will distinguish Red-faced from Pelagic in all plumages in flight. Brilliant scarlet or orange-red facial skin of Red-faced can be seen a great distance, whereas Pelagic, with black bill and dark red facial skin, looks completely dark-headed at any distance. Juveniles of these 2 species can be distinguished by size and by thickness and color of bill. See Double-crested Cormorant, Brandt's Cormorant.

Range
Bering Sea and adjacent waters of northern North Pacific Ocean. In North America, resident in Alaska from Pribilof and Aleutian islands east along Alaska Peninsula to Kodiak Island archipelago and islands of Prince William Sound.   *Daniel D. Gibson*

Immature
1. Very dark, uniform plumage.
2. Small, dark bill.
3. Long tail.

   Small size.

Immature
1. Deep, pale bill.

   Larger than Pelagic Cormorant.

Breeding adult
1. Pale blue bill.
2. Red-orange facial skin.
3. White flank patch.

Anhingas

(Family Anhingidae)
Anhingas are large, primarily freshwater birds with an extremely
long, slender neck. The neck takes on a peculiar curve caused by a
hinge mechanism in the vertebrae; the resulting posture is unique to
anhingas. The body is large and elongated, exaggerated by a long,
graduated tail. The head is small, but the bill is very long, narrow,
and sharply pointed. Anhingas swim deeply, often completely
submerged except for the neck and head. They can often be
observed perched on snags or limbs, standing upright on short
sturdy legs with their broad wings open to dry. Anhingas are
excellent fliers and often soar for some time on long, wide wings and
fanlike tails. The wingbeats are deep and powerful. (World: 4
species. North America: 1 species.)   *Scott B. Terrill*

Anhinga

Anhinga anhinga
The fish-eating Anhinga is rather cormorantlike, with a long tail, a
long, slender neck, and a straight, pointed bill with which it spears
its prey. It dives from the surface like a cormorant, capturing fish as
it swims. It is common in freshwater swamps, marshes, ponds,
lakes, and along rivers, but is also found on salt water, particularly
in Florida. Anhingas frequently swim with the body submerged and
only the head and neck visible, giving them a serpentlike appearance
that explains the nickname "Snakebird." They often perch with their
wings partly extended to dry. Flight consists of flaps and glides with
the tail spread fanlike and the neck extended. The Anhinga
sometimes soars to great heights.

Description
32–36″ (81.5–91.5 cm). The black male has conspicuous white plumes
on the upper surface of the wings and back, and a yellow bill. The
female is similar, but has a buff-colored head, neck, and upper
breast. Immatures are similar to the female, but are more brownish.

Similar Species
Cormorants have hooked tip of bill and much shorter neck and tail;
lack white dorsal plumes.

Range
Breeds from west-central and eastern Mexico, southern and eastern
Texas, southeastern Oklahoma, southern and eastern Arkansas,
western Tennessee, central Alabama, southern Georgia, and eastern
North Carolina south to southern Brazil and Ecuador. Winters along
Gulf Coast north to South Carolina. Occasionally disperses north of
breeding range.   *Paul W. Sykes, Jr.*

Anhinga

Adult male
1. *Long, slender neck.*
2. *Slender, pointed bill.*
3. *Long tail.*
4. *Plumage black, with white plumes on upperparts.*
5. *Often soars to great heights with tail fanned.*

Adult female
1. *Head, neck, and breast buff-colored.*

Frequently swims with only head and neck above surface.

Frigatebirds

(Family Fregatidae)
Frigatebirds are very large, long, highly aerial birds with very long
pointed wings and long, deeply forked tails. The birds are large but
very light, with a very high ratio of wing surface area to body
weight; this makes them exceptionally dynamic soarers. They are
often seen in large numbers soaring along coastal areas, where they
frequently ride thermals to great altitudes. Both on land and on
water, frigatebirds are quite awkward. They usually perch in trees,
the large wings forming immense shoulders that protrude far
forward. The thick neck is rather long, and the head is relatively
small and rounded. The bill is long and noticeably hooked at the tip.
Adult male frigatebirds are almost entirely black, while females and
immatures show varying amounts of white, especially on the
underparts. Frigatebirds often chase and steal food from other
birds. They also forage in flight, taking food from the surface of the
water, or even from land, without alighting. (World: 5 species.
North America: 2 species.) · *Scott B. Terrill*

Magnificent Frigatebird

Fregata magnificens
Champion gliders of the avian world, Magnificent Frigatebirds fly
with deep, deliberate wingbeats and long glides. They often soar for
long periods and rise to great heights. Frigatebirds are strictly
marine, generally staying close to shore; they secure their food in
flight by snatching it from the water's surface or by robbing gulls
and terns. They do not generally alight on the water.

Immature

Description
37–45″ (94–114.5 cm). The Magnificent Frigatebird has long,
narrow, pointed wings with a prominent angle at the wrist, and a
wingspread of up to 8 feet. The tail is long, narrow, deeply forked,
and often folded in a point; the slender bill is hooked at the tip. The
male is black, with a red throat pouch that is inflated during
breeding and in the vicinity of nesting colonies. The female is black
with a white breast, and immatures are black with a white head,
neck, and breast. The shape of these large seabirds is diagnostic.

Similar Species
See Lesser Frigatebird.*

Range
Breeds locally from lower Florida Keys (Marquesas group),
Bahamas, and Bermuda south through West Indies to islands off
Venezuela and southern Brazil, both coasts of Central America
south to Galapagos Islands and Ecuador. Regular north of breeding
range throughout the year on Atlantic and Gulf coasts of Florida,
and sparingly north in summer on Atlantic Coast to Cape Hatteras,
and to northern Gulf of Mexico and coastal southern California and
Salton Sea. Storms may drive individuals inland or north of usual
range. *Paul W. Sykes, Jr.*

Magnificent Frigatebird
Lesser Frigatebird

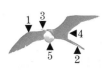

Adult male
1. *Long, narrow wings, with crook at wrist.*
2. *Long, deeply forked tail.*
3. *Long bill hooked at tip.*
4. *Black plumage.*
5. *Red, inflatable throat pouch.*

Adult female
1. *Black, with white breast and no red throat pouch.*

Flies with much gliding and soaring.

Herons

(Family Ardeidae)
Although herons vary in size from fairly small to very large, all have
elongated bodies with long, often slender necks. The bills in most
species are long and taper evenly to a sharp point. These slender-
legged birds may forage while standing or may perch motionless
and slowly await prey, which they take with a rapid thrusting
extension of the neck. In flight, the wingbeats are regular and
strong; unlike storks, ibises, and cranes, herons fly with the neck
folded onto the back. The long legs protrude beyond the short,
squared, or slightly rounded tail. Many species have ornamental
plumes on the head and upperparts; these plumes are highly
developed in the breeding season. (World: 62 species. North
America: 14 species.)   *Scott B. Terrill*

American Bittern

Botaurus lentiginosus
In summer, the American Bittern is usually found in fresh or
brackish marshes, especially among cattails and rushes. In
migration and during winter, it occupies a slightly wider range of
habitats. Normally solitary and secretive, it is most often seen flying
low over marshes, or skulking at the water's edge. This bird often
freezes with its bill pointed up in the air; in this posture, it is nearly
invisible against a backdrop of marsh.

Description
23–27″ (58.5–68.5 cm). The American Bittern is a brownish,
streaked, medium-size bird, with lighter brown and more streaked
underparts. A black neck stripe and the dark brown primaries and
secondaries contrast strongly with the lighter brown of the body and
the rest of the wing. At close range, its plumage reveals a subtle,
complex, understated beauty; in high breeding plumage, it has
small, seldom seen, bright green areas on its back. The legs are dull
green, the bill a dark buff. The sexes are similar. Immatures are
lighter brown and lack the black neck stripe.

Voice
Usually silent. On breeding territory, a loud, resonant *pump-per-
lunk* or *plum-puddin*, usually repeated 3–5 times. When flushed,
sometimes utters a low, repeated *kok-kok-kok*.

Similar Species
Immature night-herons darker, lack contrast between dark wing
tips and rest of upperparts, have no black neck patch; flight of night-
heron slower, usually higher, and not as steady. Green-backed
Heron smaller, with bright yellow legs; lacks black neck stripe.
Other herons readily perch in trees; bitterns rarely do so.

Range
Breeds from southeastern Alaska, central British Columbia, and
southern Mackenzie east to southern Quebec and Newfoundland;
south locally to southern California, New Mexico, Texas, and
Florida. Rare breeder south of northern California, Utah, Plains
States, Ohio River valley, and Virginia. Winters from southern
British Columbia, Utah, New Mexico, central parts of Gulf States,
and southern New England south to southern California, Gulf of
Mexico, and along Atlantic Coast.   *Henry T. Armistead*

American Bittern
Least Bittern
Great Blue Heron
Great Egret
Chinese Egret
Little Egret
Snowy Egret
Little Blue Heron
Tricolored Heron
Reddish Egret
Cattle Egret
Green-backed Heron
Black-crowned Night-Heron
Yellow-crowned Night-Heron

In flight
1. *Brown head and body.*
2. *Dark primaries and secondaries.*

Standing adult
1. *Brown, streaked plumage.*
2. *Black neck stripe.*

Often freezes with neck and bill pointed upward.

Least Bittern

Ixobrychus exilis
This very small heron is most often seen making short flights low over marshes. Even more furtive and secretive than the American Bittern, it seldom flies, preferring to walk rail-like or to clamber through reeds, cattails, and marsh grasses. The body is about the size of a snipe's or meadowlark's, although the long legs and bill make it seem bigger. This species freezes in the same manner as the American Bittern. It prefers freshwater marshes, but occasionally breeds in brackish areas, especially in the South.

Description
11–14″ (28–35.5 cm). The Least Bittern is an extremely small heron with large, conspicuous, pale buff wing patches, and rich, dark chestnut on the rest of the wings and sides of neck. The head and back are black in males, chestnut in females and immatures. The legs are dull greenish, and the bill is pale. An extremely rare color phase, "Cory's Least Bittern," formerly more common, has a similar pattern, but with rich chestnut replacing the buff on the wings.

Voice
Soft, low *coo-coo-coo*, very similar to call of Black-billed Cuckoo. Usually 3–5 *coos* repeated at fairly frequent intervals during breeding season, especially at dawn, sometimes at night. Call is often only clue to its presence. Other harsher notes when flushed.

Similar Species
Unmistakable. Green-backed Heron much larger, with wings completely dark. Rails lack buff wing patches.

Range
Breeds locally from southeastern Oregon, southern Manitoba, Michigan, Ontario, and southern New Brunswick south to southern California, Arizona, Rio Grande valley, Gulf States, and southern Florida. Winters from northern California, Arizona, coastal Texas, and Florida south into Mexico; rarely farther north. Also in Central and South America.   *Henry T. Armistead*

Great Blue Heron

Ardea herodias
Standing about 4 feet tall with a wingspan of 7 feet, the Great Blue is our largest heron and the most widespread of its family in North America. It flies with slow, labored wingbeats, and is found in all wetland environments. It usually hunts by standing motionless in shallow water and waiting for prey to come within striking distance. An all-white color morph, the "Great White" Heron, was considered a separate species until 1973.

Description
50–54″ (127–137 cm). The adult has a white head with the sides of the crown and nape black, and short plumes projecting to the rear. The neck is light gray, with a whitish ventral stripe; the bill is large and yellowish; the body is blue-gray, and the legs are dark. The immature is similar to the adult, but paler, with a black crown and no head plumes. The "Great White Heron" is wholly white, with greenish-yellow legs and feet. An intermediate form, called "Würdemann's Heron," is dark with white head.

Displaying adult
1. *Large, buff wing patches.*

Adult male
1. *Buff neck and underparts.*

Small size.
Secretive habits.

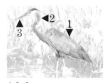

Adult
1. *Blue-gray body.*
2. *Long neck.*
3. *Yellow or pale bill.*

Large size.

Voice
Hoarse croak; usually silent.

Similar Species
Other dark herons smaller, lack black-and-white head and yellow
bill. Great Egret smaller, with less massive bill and black legs and
feet. Sandhill Crane has entire plumage rather uniform gray or
gray-brown, and has black bill; flies with neck fully extended.

Range
Breeds throughout southern Canada south to Mexico, southern
Florida, and Cuba, except in high mountains. Post-breeding
dispersal north into southern Alaska, central Canada, and into
nonbreeding areas in United States. Winters from coastal British
Columbia, central United States, and southern New England south
to northern South America. White morph breeds in Florida Bay,
Cuba, and coastal Yucatán; some post-breeding dispersal north
through peninsular Florida, occasionally beyond. "Würdemann's"
found primarily in Florida Bay and Keys.   *Paul W. Sykes, Jr.*

Great Egret

Casmerodius albus
The Great Egret has a worldwide distribution. In North America, it
is among the most common and widespread of the herons, typically
found in freshwater and saltwater marshes and lagoons, lakes, and
ponds. It is usually seen stalking its prey slowly in shallow water.
Next to the Great Blue Heron, it is our largest heron.

Description
37–41" (94–104 cm). The Great Egret is white in all plumages, with
a yellow bill and black legs and feet. In breeding plumage, it has
long, lacy plumes on the back.

Similar Species
Great White Heron larger, with massive yellow bill and yellowish
legs. White phase of Reddish Egret smaller, with flesh-colored,
black-tipped bill, bluish legs. Immature Little Blue Heron smaller,
with bluish, dark-tipped bill and greenish legs. Snowy Egret
smaller, more slender, with slender black bill, black legs, and yellow
feet. Immature Cattle Egret may have yellow bill and black feet,
but much smaller, with yellow legs.

Range
Breeds from southern Oregon and California south through western
Mexico to southern South America, and from west-central Texas,
southeastern Minnesota, Illinois, Ohio, southern Ontario, and Long
Island south through West Indies and South America. Post-breeding
dispersal north into Washington, Michigan, southern Ontario and
Quebec, and Maritime Provinces, occasionally beyond. Winters from
northern California across southern United States, and south along
coast from New Jersey through South America. Also in Old World.
Paul W. Sykes, Jr.

"Great White" Heron
, *White plumage.*
, *Yellow bill.*
, *Yellow legs.*

Florida only.

Nonbreeding plumage
, *White plumage.*
, *Long neck.*
, *Yellow bill.*
, *Black legs and feet.*

Large size.

Breeding plumage
. *Long, lacy plumes on back.*

Snowy Egret

Egretta thula
The Snowy Egret is a small, slender heron that can be found in most wetland habitats. It is more active when feeding than most other white herons, rushing about and shuffling its feet in shallow water to frighten its prey out of hiding.

Description
22–26″ (56–66 cm). The Snowy Egret is white in all plumages. The bill is black and slender, less deep at the base than the bills of other white herons; the lores are yellow and unfeathered. During the breeding season it has prominent plumes on the head, back, and breast. The legs are black, and the feet are bright yellow. Leg and foot color in immatures is not as distinct as in adults, but the pattern is usually evident. For a period, the immature has a yellow stripe up the rear of the leg.

Similar Species
White-phase Reddish Egret larger, stockier, with flesh-colored, black-tipped bill. Immature Little Blue Heron has larger body, with bluish, dark-tipped bill, dark lores, and greenish legs. Great and Cattle egrets have yellow bills. See Little Egret*. Snowy has more slender head, neck, and body than all these herons.

Range
Breeds locally on coast and in Central Valley of California and Nevada east to eastern Colorado, southern Oklahoma, lower Mississippi Valley, and Long Island; south through Florida, West Indies, Central and South America. Post-breeding dispersal north to Oregon, Nebraska, Great Lakes, and Atlantic Canada. Winters in much of California, along southern Colorado River, Gulf Coast; also south along Atlantic Coast from Virginia to Florida, and south through South America.   *Paul W. Sykes, Jr.*

Little Blue Heron

Egretta caerulea
The medium-size Little Blue Heron is found in wetland habitats of eastern North America, including coastal areas, freshwater lagoons, and swamps. Like many members of its family, this bird stalks its prey quietly in shallow water. The plumage of the immature is quite different from that of the adult.

Description
25–29″ (63.5–73.5 cm). The adult is slate-blue with a maroon or purple head and neck. The bill is bluish with a black tip; the legs are bluish-green. Immatures are white with blue-gray lores. Birds changing from immature to adult plumage are pied blue and white.

Similar Species
Reddish Egret larger, with thicker, shaggy neck, flesh-colored, black-tipped bill, bluish legs; neck and head of dark-phase Reddish Egret rusty, not purplish. Snowy Egret has slender black bill, yellow lores, black legs; feeds much more actively. Louisiana Heron dark, with contrasting white belly.

Breeding adult
1. *White plumage.*
2. *Slender black bill.*
3. *Black legs.*
4. *Yellow feet.*

   Active, sprinting feeding behavior.

Immature
1. *Yellow stripe on back of leg.*
2. *Yellow feet.*

Immature
1. *White plumage.*
2. *Pale bill with dark tip.*
3. *Bluish-green legs.*

Range
Breeds from Texas, Oklahoma, southern Illinois, and southern
New England south to Gulf Coast, Florida, and West Indies; also
throughout much of South America. Post-breeding dispersal north in
interior to North and South Dakota, Michigan, southern Ontario,
and southern Quebec, and to Nova Scotia on Atlantic Coast. Winters
from New Jersey south to Gulf Coast and Florida.
Paul W. Sykes, Jr.

Tricolored Heron

Egretta tricolor
The slender Tricolored Heron is most common in salt marshes and
coastal lagoons, but is also found in freshwater marshes near the
coast. It is an active feeder, running about to capture small fish, but
may also stalk its prey slowly, often wading into deep water.

Description
24–28″ (61–71 cm). An unmistakable dark, slate-blue heron with a
white belly and rump. There are maroon feathers at the base of the
dark neck (and at the base of the back plumes during breeding
season). The distal portion of the plumes is buff to cinnamon. A
white stripe extends from the base of the bill to the breast.

Range
Breeds along coast from New Jersey south to northern South
America. Post-breeding dispersal north to Oklahoma, Arkansas, and
coastal New England. Most individuals in northern part of breeding
range move south in colder months. Rare but regular visitor to
southern California.   *Paul W. Sykes, Jr.*

Reddish Egret

Egretta rufescens
The Reddish Egret is primarily a bird of saltwater flats and lagoons
and is rarely found far from the coast. This uncommon, stout,
medium-size heron has both white and dark color phases; the dark
phase predominates in Florida and Texas. This species is a very
active feeder in shallow water, employing a special technique known
as "canopy feeding." By foraging with the wings extended over the
water, the bird creates pools of shadow, through which it can more
easily spot its prey. The Reddish Egret is the only North American
heron that uses this feeding method.

Description
27–32″ (68.5–81.5 cm). The dark-phase Reddish Egret has a gray
body with a rust-colored head and neck; the white phase is totally
white. Some birds are intermediate—dark with a scattering of white
feathers. In the adult, the bill is flesh-colored and dark at the tip,
the legs are blue, and the plumes on the head and thick neck give
the bird a shaggy appearance.

Adult
1. *Slate-blue back and wings.*
2. *Maroon-purple head and neck.*
3. *Bluish bill with dark tip.*

Adult
1. *Dark gray-blue neck and upperparts.*
2. *White belly.*

Adult, dark phase
1. *Gray body.*
2. *Rust-colored head and neck.*
3. *Shaggy plumes on neck.*
4. *Pinkish bill with dark tip.*

Similar Species
Little Blue Heron more slender; has bluish bill with dark tip and
bluish-green legs. Great, Snowy, and Cattle egrets may resemble
white-phase Reddish Egret. Great Egret larger, with black legs and
feet; all-yellow bill lacks black tip. Snowy Egret smaller, more
slender, with black bill. Cattle Egret smaller, with shorter neck,
orange-red bill, pinkish legs.

Range
Breeds locally on coast of Texas; in southern Florida from Tampa
south to Florida Bay and in Florida Keys, Bahamas, West Indies,
both coasts of Mexico, and Central America. Wanders north along
both coasts of Florida, and across northern Gulf of Mexico; rarely
north to North Carolina.   *Paul W. Sykes, Jr.*

Cattle Egret

Bubulcus ibis
The least shy, least aquatic, and most silent of our herons is the
Cattle Egret. This small, stocky, short-necked white heron is highly
gregarious. It frequents a great variety of habitats: pastures,
freshwater and salt marshes, fallow and plowed fields, orchards,
citrus groves, road shoulders and median strips, vacant lots, lawns,
and other open grassy areas. It often associates with large hoofed
mammals, particularly cattle, capturing insects and other small prey
disturbed by these animals' movements. A recent immigrant from
the Old World, this species is believed to have reached the Western
Hemisphere on its own from Africa. First recorded in northern
South America in the late 1880s, it had arrived in Florida in the
early 1940s and was found breeding there in 1953 at Lake
Okeechobee. The population increased rapidly, and has continued to
spread through North America. The Cattle Egret is now the most
abundant and widespread heron in Florida.

Description
19–21″ (48.5–53.5 cm). The breeding adult is white, with buff on the
crown, back, and breast, and with an orange-red bill and coral-pink
legs. Nonbreeding adults and immatures are pure white with yellow
bills and yellow or greenish legs (although immatures can sometimes
have black legs). The bill is short and stout, with feathers along a
short distance of the undersurface of the lower mandible. The legs
are also short. Birds foraging in citrus groves in Florida often
become stained from pesticides and herbicides and may exhibit odd
coloring on the plumage.

Similar Species
Great Egret much larger, with long black legs. All other white
herons larger, with longer necks and different colored bills.

Range
Breeds in southern California, Utah, Colorado, New Mexico, Texas,
Michigan, Ontario, and southern Maine, south to Florida, West
Indies, and Central and South America. Post-breeding dispersal and
wandering birds occur north to southern British Columbia, south-
central Canada, and Maritime Provinces. Widespread in Old World.
Paul W. Sykes, Jr.

Adult, white phase
1. *White plumage.*
2. *Pinkish bill with dark tip.*
3. *Bluish legs.*

Breeding adult
1. *Short, stout, yellow bill.*
2. *Buff crown.*
3. *Buff breast.*

   Small size. Often forages in association with livestock.

Nonbreeding adult
1. *Short, stout, yellow bill.*
2. *Plumage entirely white.*
3. *Pale legs.*

Green-backed Heron

Butorides striatus
A dark, crow-size heron, the Green-backed Heron is widespread and occupies a variety of habitats: wet woodlands, streams, lake shores, swamps, marshes, and coastal wetlands. It is equally at home in freshwater or saltwater areas, and often occurs singly. The Green-backed is the only small, dark heron present in much of the northern part of its range. When disturbed, it will stretch its neck, erect its crest, and flick its tail downward. A common species with a rapid flight, the Green-backed Heron may nest by itself, in mixed colonies of other heron species, or in small, pure colonies of its own.

Description
15–22″ (38–56 cm). The small, dark adults have a rich chestnut head and sides, with a black crown, blue-gray back and wings, and a white streak down the throat and underparts. The bill is dark; the bright yellow legs are conspicuous. Immatures are similar but duller and browner, with heavily streaked underparts and vague, buff-colored edging on the wing coverts.

Voice
A loud, emphatic *skouwp*, especially when flushed, often repeated. Also a measured *guk, guk, guk, guk*. When flying overhead or at night, gives less emphatic version of *skouwp* call, *keeyou*. Slower, quieter, almost slurred *kee-you-wuh* when at rest or concealed, especially in deep woods.

Similar Species
Little Blue Heron larger, lacks bright yellow legs. American Bittern larger, longer-winged, browner; has prominent black neck stripes. Least Bittern much smaller, with buff wing patches.

Range
Breeds from southern British Columbia and Washington south to southern California, Arizona, and New Mexico, and from North Dakota, Ontario, and southern New Brunswick south to Gulf Coast and southern Florida. Winters from central California south and east along southern parts of border states, coastal sections of Gulf States, Florida; on Atlantic coast north to North Carolina, rarely farther north. Also in Central and South America and Old World.
Henry T. Armistead

Black-crowned Night-Heron

Nycticorax nycticorax
The Black-crowned Night-Heron is common throughout most of its range in North America. It is small, stocky, short-billed, short-necked, and short-legged. As its name implies, it is most active at night, roosting during the day. When perched or standing, it has a hunched posture. This species occupies many different wetland habitats, including marshes, wooded swamps, and forests along rivers and streams. Flying with deep strokes on arched wings, it holds its neck curled so that the head and the back form a straight line.

Description
23–26″ (58.5–66 cm). The adult Black-crowned Night-Heron has a black cap and back, pale gray wings, whitish underparts, and a red eye. The immature is dull gray-brown with numerous light spots on the upperparts and streaks on the underparts. The legs are yellow in adults, duller in immatures; in flight the toes extend beyond the tail.

Adult
1. *Blue-gray back and wings.*
2. *Chestnut head and neck.*
3. *Orange-yellow legs.*

Small size.
Loud skouwp call.

Immature
1. *Streaked underparts.*
2. *Indistinctly barred upperparts.*

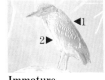

Immature
1. *Dull gray-brown upperparts with light spots.*
2. *Streaked underparts.*

Voice
A loud, flat *kwawk*, heard at dusk and at night or when bird is
flushed from roost.

Similar Species
Immature Yellow-crowned Night-Heron is slate-brown with fine,
light spots on upperparts; in flight, entire foot projects well beyond
tail (this characteristic alone can distinguish the 2 species).
American Bittern lacks pale spots on upperparts; has blackish
primaries and secondaries, different shape and flight.

Range
Breeds throughout much of United States and south-central and
southeastern Canada (north to New Brunswick). Wanders a great
deal. Post-breeding dispersal covers most of United States not
within its breeding range (except northern Rocky Mountain region)
and north into southern Canada. Winters in southwestern and
southeastern United States, and along Atlantic Coast as far north as
southern New England. Also in American tropics and Old World.
Paul W. Sykes, Jr.

Yellow-crowned Night-Heron

Nycticorax violaceus
The Yellow-crowned Night-Heron is similar in size, shape, and
posture to the Black-crowned, but is less common and somewhat
more active during the day. In flight, it looks more like a miniature
Great Blue Heron than like a Black-crowned. It is found in a wide
range of saltwater and freshwater habitats.

Description
22–28″ (56–71 cm). The adult is pale gray with a black head, a
yellowish forehead, and white crown and cheek patch. The immature
is slate-brown with fine, light spots on the upperparts and streaks
on the underparts. The legs are yellow and somewhat longer than
those of the Black-crowned Night-Heron. In flight, the entire foot
extends beyond the tail.

Voice
A loud *kwawk*, slightly higher pitched than call of Black-crowned.

Similar Species
Black-crowned Night-Heron has bill less deep at base; immature
browner, less finely spotted on upperparts; in flight, adult and
immature have wings less strongly 2-toned; only toes (not entire
foot) project beyond tail.

Range
Breeds in south-central United States north to Minnesota, along
Gulf Coast from Texas to Florida, north along Atlantic Coast to
southern New England, south into South America. Post-breeding
dispersal north to eastern Colorado, Iowa, southern Ontario, and
Atlantic Canada. Winters on Gulf Coast, Florida, and along Atlantic
Coast to southeastern North Carolina.   *Paul W. Sykes, Jr.*

Adult
1. *Black cap.*
2. *Black back.*
3. *Gray wings.*
4. *Whitish underparts.*

   Loud kwawk *call.*

Adult
1. *Gray body.*
2. *Black head with white crown and cheek patch.*
3. *Stout bill.*

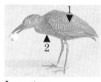

Immature
1. *Slate-brown upperparts with fine spots.*
2. *Streaked underparts.*

Ibises and Spoonbills

(Family Threskiornithidae)
This family comprises a group of medium-size to large wading birds
with elongate bodies, long necks, and long legs. These birds have
either long, thin, decurved, and bluntly pointed bills or spatulate-
tipped bills. The flight is usually direct on fast, strong wingbeats,
with little soaring. Unlike herons, ibises and spoonbills fly with the
neck extended. These birds are gregarious and are often seen flying
in lines or other tight flock formations. (World: 33 species. North
America: 5 species.)   *Scott B. Terrill*

White Ibis

Eudocimus albus
The White Ibis is a small, locally common wader with a large,
slender, down-curved bill. It flies with rapid wingbeats, holding the
neck extended as it alternates between flapping and gliding. The
White Ibis is a highly gregarious species and congregates in flocks
that fly in long lines or V formations. These birds feed in all types of
wetlands, as well as grassy or plowed fields. White Ibises inhabit
lagoons, swamp forests, and mud flats along much of the Atlantic
and Gulf coasts.

Description
22–28″ (56–71 cm). The adult White Ibis is white with black-tipped
primaries; the black areas are generally hidden except when the bird
is in flight. The bare facial skin and the bill are red; the bill is
strongly decurved. The legs are red during the breeding season,
slate-colored at other times. The immature has a mottled brown
head and neck, brown upper body, white rump and belly, brown to
pinkish bill, and brown legs.

Similar Species
Adult White Ibis unmistakable. Immature Glossy Ibis wholly
brown, lacking white on rump and belly present in White Ibis.
Limpkin brown with white spots and streaks.

Range
Breeds and winters along Atlantic Coast from North Carolina to
Florida and along northern Gulf Coast; also from Mexico to northern
South America. Post-breeding dispersal north of breeding range.
Paul W. Sykes, Jr.

White Ibis
Scarlet Ibis
Glossy Ibis
White-faced Ibis
Roseate Spoonbill

Adult
1. *Red, decurved bill.*
2. *White plumage.*
3. *Black wing tips.*
4. *Flies with neck and legs extended.*

Often in flocks.

Immature
1. *Decurved bill.*
2. *Brown body and wings.*
3. *White belly.*

Glossy Ibis

Plegadis falcinellus
The Glossy Ibis is a dark wading bird with a long, down-curved bill. At home in marshes and estuaries, this bird appears heronlike when wading, with an upright posture unlike that of curlews, to which it is sometimes compared. The Glossy Ibis flies with rapid, ducklike wingbeats, holding its neck and legs extended and slightly drooped. Plumage color changes seasonally, as does the color of the bare facial skin. This species has recently expanded its range in North America, and may now be found in the same areas as the very similar White-faced Ibis.

Description
19–26″ (48.5–66 cm). Adults in spring and summer plumage are rich chestnut with a metallic purple gloss on the head, neck, underparts, and shoulders. The lower back, wings, and tail are somewhat more greenish or brassy. The facial skin is gray with a white border above and below but not extending around the back of the eye. At the height of the breeding season, this skin becomes a dark cobalt-blue with pale blue borders, and the usually gray bill acquires a pinkish tinge. The iris is always brown; the legs are gray-brown. In winter, most of the chestnut is lost, the body feathering becomes a dark metallic green, and the head and neck are finely streaked with dark brown and white. At this season, the facial skin is plain dull gray, but many individuals retain a trace of the pale blue border, particularly on the upper portion of the face. Juvenile birds look like winter adults with no trace of chestnut feathers; the adults often retain a few of these feathers in winter.

Similar Species
White-faced Ibis very similar, but in breeding plumage has prominent border of white feathers around face; maroon facial skin, bill, and legs; iris is red. Winter adults distinguishable only by iris color; juveniles indistinguishable. Curlews much smaller, paler.

Range
Breeds from coastal Maine south along Atlantic Coast, across southern peninsular Florida and west along Gulf Coast to Texas. Also in West Indies and Old World.   *H. Douglas Pratt*

White-faced Ibis

Plegadis chihi
The White-faced Ibis is the western counterpart of the Glossy Ibis and in North America is much more abundant and widespread than the latter. The 2 are identical in behavior and general appearance, but during spring and summer the White-faced has a prominent band of white feathers encircling the eye and the bare facial skin. At other times, the 2 are difficult, if not impossible, to distinguish. They occur together regularly only in southern Louisiana, but wanderers of both species can be seen outside this region.

Description
19–26″ (48.5–66 cm). Plumages of the White-faced Ibis are identical to those of the Glossy, except for the white facial border of the breeding adult. The facial skin is rich maroon during the breeding season, but fades to dull gray in winter. It never shows even a trace of the Glossy's pale blue facial border. The bill, legs, and feet are gray, but become strongly tinged with maroon when breeding. The iris is brown in first-year birds, dark red in adults.

Winter adult
1. *Long, decurved bill.*
2. *Dark plumage.*
3. *Streaked head and neck.*
4. *Brown eye.*

Breeding adult
1. *Long, decurved bill.*
2. *Dark plumage.*
3. *Pale border on facial skin.*
4. *Brown eye.*

   Often in flocks.

Breeding adult
1. *Long, decurved bill.*
2. *Dark plumage.*
3. *White feathers bordering maroon facial skin.*
4. *Red eye.*

Similar Species
See Glossy Ibis. Red iris distinguishes adult White-faced, but
juvenile Glossy and White-faced indistinguishable.

Range
Breeds from Oregon east sporadically to Minnesota, south to
California, Utah, and Nebraska, and in coastal regions of Texas and
Louisiana, south to central Mexico. Post-breeding wanderers occur
between these areas, as well as northward. Withdraws from
northern states in winter.   *H. Douglas Pratt*

Roseate Spoonbill

Ajaia ajaja
The Roseate Spoonbill is a medium-size, bright pink wader with a
spatulate bill. It is rare and local in shallow freshwater and
saltwater wetlands and is most often found near the coast, where it
builds stick nests in dense bushes and low trees. The Spoonbill feeds
by moving its bill sideways in long arcs through the water,
consuming shrimps, small fish, and whatever other nutrients the
water offers. Holding the neck extended, the Roseate Spoonbill flies
with a series of slow wingbeats often followed by glides. Although
spoonbills bear a superficial resemblance to flamingos, a good look
should enable one to tell these 2 species apart.

Description
30–34″ (76–86.5 cm). Unmistakable. The adult has a naked, greenish
head; the neck, upper breast, and upper back are white. The
upperwing coverts and legs are red, and the remainder of the body
plumage is bright pink; the tail is bright orange. The immature has a
feathered head and is largely white; the pink color of the adult is
acquired gradually.

Similar Species
Flamingos are also large pink wading birds, but have a shorter,
sharply hooked bill with black tip, and longer neck.

4

Range
Breeds and winters locally along coast of Texas, southwestern
Louisiana, and southern Florida south through Greater Antilles to
southern South America. Post-breeding dispersal along coast of
Texas and Louisiana, north through peninsular Florida.
Paul W. Sykes, Jr.

Winter adult
1. *Long, decurved bill.*
2. *Dark plumage.*
3. *Streaked head and neck.*
4. *Red eye.*

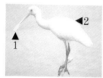

Immature
1. *Long, flat, spoonlike bill.*
2. *Pale pinkish plumage.*

Adult
1. *Long, flat, spoonlike bill.*
2. *Pink wings with red coverts.*
3. *White neck and upper breast.*
4. *Flies with neck and legs extended.*

   Often in flocks.

Storks

(Family Ciconiidae)
These are large, long-legged wading birds with sturdy bodies, long necks, and rather stout, somewhat rounded heads. The bills are long and deep, and in most species taper to a blunt point. The amount of feathering on the head varies among species; some birds have heads partially bare, while others lack feathering entirely. Members of this family have long, wide wings and are dynamic soarers; the deep wingbeats alternate with intermittent gliding. These birds fly with neck extended, unlike herons, and unlike pelicans have their long legs trailing far beyond the tail. (World: 17 species. North America: 2 species.)   *Scott B. Terrill*

Wood Stork

Mycteria americana
The Wood Stork is a large, mostly white, long-legged wading bird found in the vicinity of freshwater and coastal swamps and marshes. Storks are highly gregarious, usually occurring in small to quite large flocks, although there are occasional strays outside of the normal range. Storks feed on small fish, which they capture by probing with their long bills in shallow water, as they wade through still pools, drying marshes, or along the margins of lakes and streams. They nest in colonies in cypresses, mangroves, or other woody swamp vegetation. Flocks of Wood Storks spend much of each day soaring high above wetland regions and roost either in tall trees or on banks along waterways. Wood Storks fly with the long neck and legs fully extended.

Description
35–45″ (89–114.5 cm). The Wood Stork is entirely white except for the glossy black primaries, secondaries, and tail. The wings are long and rounded, and the tail is quite short. The adult has a blackish bill and a blackish, scaly-looking, unfeathered head and neck that give rise to the local nicknames "Flinthead" and "Ironhead." The immature has a pale yellow bill and a dull grayish-brown feathered head and neck.

Similar Species
White Ibis much smaller, with thinner, decurved bill, and black only on tips of outer primaries. High-soaring White Pelican has similar wing pattern, but has white tail and very short legs; lacks long neck. See Whooping Crane.

Range
In United States, storks nest in Florida and southern Georgia, very rarely in other coastal swamps between Texas and South Carolina. Post-breeding dispersal from Mexican and Florida colonies carries flocks north during summer and early fall to southern Salton Sea in California, lower Colorado River, and from Texas east to South Carolina along coastal plain and lower Mississippi Valley. Rare wanderers in summer may appear much farther north, especially along major waterways or coastlines. Widespread in Central and South America.   *John C. Ogden*

Jabiru
Wood Stork

In flight
1. *White body.*
2. *Black flight feathers.*
3. *Dark head and neck.*

   *Often soars in
   wheeling flocks.*

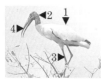

Standing adult
1. *White plumage.*
2. *Dark, naked head
   and neck.*
3. *Long legs.*
4. *Stout, decurved bill.*

Flamingos

(Family Phoenicopteridae)
Members of this family are well known for their striking plumages,
long, elegant shapes, and bizarre bills. Although the body is rather
rounded, the very long, slender neck and long, thin legs give
flamingos a very stretched appearance, especially as they fly rapidly
on strong wingbeats. The bill is unique, curving abruptly downward
in the middle. This odd shape further dominates the profile of these
birds because the head is very small and rounded. (World: 5 species.
North America: 1 species.)   *Scott B. Terrill*

Greater Flamingo

Phoenicopterus ruber
The Greater Flamingo, a rare vagrant to Florida, is a slim, pink
wading bird with an extremely long neck and legs. Rarely seen in
fresh water, it prefers highly saline environments, where it forages
with its bill and sometimes its head submerged. In flight, the neck is
extended and slightly drooped; the very long neck and legs give this
bird a most distinctive appearance. Escaped birds from collections
may turn up in various parts of the continent.

Description
50″ (127 cm). The adult Greater Flamingo is rose-pink with black
primaries and secondaries; the bill is thick, sharply bent, and white
with a black tip. The immature is paler pink with a grayish head and
neck.

Similar Species
Roseate Spoonbill also large and pink, but has long, spatulate bill,
shorter neck.

Range
In New World, breeds in West Indies, coastal Yucatán in Mexico,
and Galapagos Islands; not known to breed in wild in Florida.
Occurs regularly in very small numbers in Florida Bay and
occasionally on Florida Keys. At least a few are probably wild
individuals, but most are birds that have escaped from captivity.
Greater Flamingos now found north of southern tip of Florida are
probably all birds that have escaped. Also in Old World.
Paul W. Sykes, Jr.

Greater Flamingo

In flight
1. *Very long, thin neck.*
2. *Long, thin legs.*
3. *Pink body with black wing tips.*

   Often flies in long lines.

Standing adult
1. *Rose-pink plumage.*
2. *Long, curved neck.*
3. *Heavy, bent bill with black tip.*

Swans, Geese, and Ducks

(Family Anatidae)
Swans, geese, and ducks represent a diverse group of waterbirds.
All except the mergansers have broad, flattened bills that are
rounded at the end and have a hard nail on the tip of the upper
mandible. Birds in this family also have 4 toes: the front 3 are
webbed, and the hind toe is free. Most of these birds have short or
medium-length legs, which are set relatively far apart, and stout
bodies. (World: 148 species. North America: 57 species.)

Whistling-Ducks
These ducks have long necks, flat-crowned heads with abruptly
rising foreheads, and long, robust bodies. They stand very upright;
in flight, the neck is extended, and the legs trail well beyond the
tail. These ducks make whistling sounds, most frequently in flight.

Swans .
The swans include the largest waterfowl. These familiar birds have
very long, slender necks that are topped with small, rounded heads;
the bills are gooselike, and the bodies are large and long. Adults of
North American species are white; immatures are brownish-tinted.

Geese
Geese are longer-necked than ducks and have bills that are
noticeably deep at the base. Most species are larger than ducks; in
all species, the sexes are similar. Geese walk easily; many spend a
large part of their time feeding on land or in shallow areas.

Wood Ducks
Wood ducks have small bills with a conspicuous decurved nail at the
tip and long, tapered tails. These birds perch in trees and nest in
cavities; they prefer quiet, shaded ponds and streams.

Dabbling Ducks
These ducks do not normally dive for food. Instead, they thrust the
head, neck, and breast underwater, and tilt the tail straight up.
They also feed from the surface and onshore. Most have a bright
iridescent wing patch called a speculum. Most species are sexually
dimorphic; females have wing patterns like the males'.

Bay Ducks
These diving birds often inhabit deeper water than dabbling ducks.
Males of most North American species have pale body plumage with
dark rumps, breasts, and heads that show either iridescent or
reddish colors. Bay ducks do not have a speculum, but in flight the
wings often look variably 2-toned. Females are brownish but retain
the characteristic shape of each species; head and bill shape are
especially useful features.

Sea Ducks
These excellent divers inhabit coastal areas or lakes and ponds with
deep fresh water. Adult males are for the most part boldly
patterned, often with black and white. Some have wing patches;
these are usually white or white with some black, not iridescent.
The generally drab, darkish females can usually can be identified by
shape and profile; they often share the wing pattern of the male.

Stiff-tail Ducks
These agile divers are primarily found in fresh and brackish water.
All have wide, short bodies with stout necks supporting rather large
heads. The bills are long, wide at the top, variably swollen at the
base, and slightly upturned toward the tip. The rather long, stiff,
sharply tapered tail is often held straight up. The large feet, placed
far to the rear of the body, make these ducks clumsy on land. Stiff-
tails often ride very low in the water.   *Scott B. Terrill*

Fulvous Whistling-Duck
Black-bellied Whistling-Duck
Tundra Swan
Whooper Swan
Trumpeter Swan
Mute Swan
Bean Goose
Pink-footed Goose
Greater White-fronted Goose
Snow Goose
Ross' Goose
Emperor Goose
Brant
Barnacle Goose
Canada Goose
Wood Duck
Green-winged Teal
Baikal Teal
Falcated Teal
American Black Duck
Mottled Duck
Mallard
Spot-billed Duck
White-cheeked Pintail
Northern Pintail
Garganey
Blue-winged Teal
Cinnamon Teal
Northern Shoveler
Gadwall
Eurasian Wigeon
American Wigeon
Common Pochard
Canvasback
Redhead
Ring-necked Duck
Tufted Duck
Greater Scaup
Lesser Scaup
Common Eider
King Eider
Spectacled Eider
Steller's Eider
Harlequin Duck
Oldsquaw
Black Scoter
Surf Scoter
White-winged Scoter
Common Goldeneye
Barrow's Goldeneye
Bufflehead
Smew
Hooded Merganser
Common Merganser
Red-breasted Merganser
Ruddy Duck
Masked Duck

Fulvous Whistling-Duck

Dendrocygna bicolor
The Fulvous Whistling-Duck is a bird of broad, open marshlands; in
North America today it is most likely to be found in flooded
agricultural land and rice fields. This bird often feeds at night; pairs
and small flocks tend to fly around in the morning and evening,
calling frequently. In flight, this species has a distinctive silhouette:
the wings appear broad and rounded, the feet extend beyond the tip
of the tail, and both the head and feet droop below the level of the
body. Although it was formerly known as the "Fulvous Tree-Duck,"
this species seldom perches in trees.

Description
18–21″ (45.5–53.5 cm). The adult is a rich buff-yellow on the head,
neck, and underparts, with a darker brown strip running down the
center of the crown and hindneck, and some whitish streaking on the
neck. A strip of white feathers along the flanks sets off the buff
underparts from the dark brown back. The bill is dark gray; the legs
are bluish-gray. In flight, the undersides of the wings are
conspicuously blackish, the upperwings are dark without obvious
pattern, and a narrow white crescent is visible on the rump. The
immature resembles the adult but is slightly duller and shows
less contrast.

Voice
Hoarse but penetrating whistle, *ka-wheeah* or *ki-wheeeh*, often
given in flight.

Similar Species
See immature Black-bellied Whistling-Duck.

Range
Fairly common summer resident (less common in winter) in
southern California (Imperial Valley), and in coastal Texas and
Louisiana; in recent decades also resident in southern Florida.
Wanders sporadically, and singles or small flocks may turn up
practically anywhere in North America. Also widespread in tropical
America, Africa, and southern Asia.   *Kenn Kaufman*

Black-bellied Whistling-Duck

Dendrocygna autumnalis
Favoring less open country than the Fulvous Whistling-Duck, this
strikingly patterned species is usually found at tree-lined ponds.
Unlike the Fulvous Whistling-Duck, the Black-bellied regularly
perches in trees, often roosting on low branches above the water,
and sometimes—especially when alarmed—perching quite high. It
has the distinctive whistling-duck shape and flight silhouette, but is
larger than the Fulvous and appears heavier in the air.

Description
20–22″ (51–56 cm). The Black-bellied Whistling-Duck is a large,
long-necked, strong-legged, and broad-winged bird. Adults are rich
chestnut on the crown, nape, back, lower neck, and chest; they are
gray on the face and throat, and black on the lower breast and belly.
White coloring on the upperwing is usually visible at rest, and
flashes boldly in flight: the white occupies most of the wing coverts
and the bases of the primaries, leaving a broad black trailing edge
and a narrower brown leading edge to the wing. The wing linings

In flight
1. *White flank stripe.*
2. *White patch on rump.*

On water
1. *Bright buff neck and breast.*
2. *Dark wings.*
3. *White flank stripe.*
4. *White rump.*

Gooselike shape.

Standing adult
1. *Long neck.*
2. *Long legs.*
3. *Chestnut and black plumage.*
4. *Red bill*

Upright posture. Often perches in trees.

are blackish, as are the rump and tail. The bill is waxy pinkish-red, with some blue-gray at the tip; the legs and feet are usually pinkish. The immature's pattern foreshadows that of the adult, but in muted tones of grayish-brown, and lacks any chestnut, deep black, or sharp contrast. The immature's bill, legs, and feet are dark gray.

Voice
Melodious whistles; most frequent pattern *pit-che wee che, che che chee;* emphasis on high third syllable, last 3 notes descending.

Similar Species
Adults unmistakable. Fulvous Whistling-Duck similar to dark-billed immature, but much brighter; lacks white wing patch.

Range
Breeds locally (and sometimes winters) in south-central Arizona; common in summer, uncommon in winter in southern Texas. Escaped birds have bred in wild in southern Florida. Casual vagrants reach southern California and probably New Mexico and Louisiana; those seen elsewhere most likely escaped birds.
Kenn Kaufman

Tundra Swan

Cygnus columbianus
The Tundra Swan is the most widespread swan in North America. It is commonly encountered in winter and during migration along the Atlantic and Pacific coasts and on sizeable reservoirs and lakes in the interior of the continent. These large, pure white birds undertake long, sustained migrations to and from the Arctic regions of North America and northeastern Siberia, where they nest near ponds and sloughs on the open tundra. The total North American population, which has been censused on the wintering grounds, now numbers more than 100,000 birds. In areas where both the Tundra and Trumpeter swans are likely to occur, distinguishing between the 2 species can be quite difficult without close study of the birds on the ground or in the water, especially when the birds are not calling.

Description
47–58″ (119.5–147.5 cm). This medium-size swan is entirely white, with a black bill and black legs and feet. Occasionally the feathers on the head and neck may acquire a rust-colored stain from iron in the tundra ponds where the birds feed. There is usually a small, oblong yellow spot at the base of the bill just in front of the eye, but this spot may be absent or difficult to see. The crown and forehead show a rounded profile. When the Tundra Swan is standing or swimming, it holds the head and neck erect. At close range, note the thin black base of the bill that ends in a sharp angle immediately in front of the eye, so that the eye seems to be isolated on the white face. Juveniles in fall plumage are pale dusky grayish, with dusky pink, dark-tipped bills. Immatures acquire the white adult plumage and mostly dark bill by the spring following the year in which they were hatched. An East Asian subspecies, "Bewick's" Swan (*C. c. bewickii*), is a rare vagrant to the northwest Pacific Coast; it is similar to the North American race but the bill shows more yellow, extending in a small band across the base of the upper mandible.

Voice
In migration, series of mellow, high-pitched notes: *hoo-ho-hoo,* reminiscent of Snow Goose.

Similar Species
Trumpeter Swan larger, lacks any yellow on bill; angle at base of bill wider, encompassing eye; profile of crown and forehead long and

In flight
1. Red bill.
2. Large, white wing patch.

Immature
1. Dusky-gray tinge to plumage.
2. Pinkish, black-tipped bill.

Adult
1. White plumage.
2. Neck held straight up.
3. Black bill with small yellow spot in front of eye.

Often in flocks. Loud, mellow flight call.

flat, not rounded; call low-pitched and trumpetlike. Whooper Swan
(Alaska only) larger, with conspicuous, broad yellow patch
extending in wedge from base of bill to beyond nostril. Mute Swan
has different head and bill profile; neck generally curved, not
straight; orange bill has black knob at base; voice much weaker.
Snow and Ross' geese smaller, with black primaries and short
pink bill.

Range
Breeds from northeastern Siberia and Arctic and western coastal
Alaska to Alaska Peninsula, across Arctic Canada to Baffin and
Nottingham islands. Winters mainly along coast from southern
Alaska through British Columbia to Pacific states and northern Baja
California (casual); also in southern Great Basin to northern New
Mexico; and in mid-Atlantic states, rarely to Gulf Coast. "Bewick's"
Swan vagrant to Washington, Oregon, and California.
Theodore G. Tobish Jr.

Whooper Swan

Cygnus cygnus
Whooper Swans breed chiefly north of the Arctic Circle across most
of Eurasia; they occur mainly as winter visitors to North America in
Alaska's Aleutian Islands. In the Old World, the Whooper is the
most common swan, wintering in very large numbers in rather small
areas, as the Tundra Swan does in North America. Large flocks of
the East Asian population winter in the northern islands of Japan.
Its habitat preference is similar to that of other northern swans; the
species nests on shallow inland or tundra lakes and marshes. Named
for its unique call, the Whooper Swan seems to be more vocal than
other North American swans. The validity of most sightings outside
Alaska is subject to doubt, owing to the possibility that the birds
escaped from waterfowl collections.

Description
56–70″ (142–178 cm). The Whooper Swan is similar in size, shape,
and head and bill profile to the Trumpeter Swan, but the bill has a
conspicuous, broad yellow patch that extends in a wedge shape from
the base of the bill to beyond the nostril, covering at least half the
bill length. The bird often holds its head forward in a curved or
kinked posture, as does the Trumpeter Swan. Like other swans,
immature Whoopers are dusky with a pinkish, black-tipped bill.
Spring immatures retain the dusky plumage mainly on the head and
neck, but the bill obtains partial orange-yellow patches at the base.

Voice
Principal flight call a double, low-pitched *whoop-whoop*. When
alarmed, often utters a single bugled note.

Similar Species
Adult Trumpeter and Tundra lack large yellow patch at base of bill.
Immature Trumpeter in spring has solid dark bill. Rare "Bewick's"
Swan smaller, has half as much yellow on bill; call different.

Range
In North America, small numbers regularly winter in central and
western Aleutian Islands and rarely in Pribilof Islands; latest spring
record there is 8 May. Single records from northwest Alaska, and in
fall from south coast of Alaska. One old record from Maine. Breeds
primarily across northern Eurasia; formerly bred in Greenland.
Theodore G. Tobish Jr.

"Bewick's" Swan
1. *Large, yellow patch at base of bill.*

Adult
1. *White plumage.*
2. *Yellow patch on bill extends in wedge to beyond nostril.*
3. *Flat forehead profile.*

*Large size.
Bugling call.*

Immature
1. *Dusky tinge to plumage.*
2. *Heavy, pinkish bill with dark tip.*

Large size.

Trumpeter Swan

Cygnus buccinator
Once severely reduced in numbers, the Trumpeter Swan has made
a comeback aided by conservation and local reintroductions. This
species is conspicuously larger than the Tundra Swan. Its deep,
booming, sonorous call distinguishes the Trumpeter from all other
North American swans. The North American population is split into
resident and migratory groups. Trumpeters can be seen year-round
in Wyoming and Montana in Yellowstone National Park and Red
Rock National Wildlife Refuge.

Description
58½–72″ (149.5–183 cm). The adult is entirely white, like the Tundra
Swan. The long bill lacks any yellow at the base; the forehead and
the bill profile are long and flat, reminiscent of a Canvasback. When
seen at close range, the salmon-pink mandible edges on the closed
bill are usually visible. When not alert, the Trumpeter holds its
proportionally longer neck in a slightly curved, drooping position,
with a subtle kink at the base. The area at the base of the bill
includes a wider angle of black than the same area in the Tundra
Swan, encompassing the eye instead of isolating it. Fall immatures
are dusky, but the dusky pink bill has a black base and tip; the gray-
brown immature plumage is retained into spring.

Voice
Series of loud, low-pitched, trumpetlike notes on 1 pitch: *koo-hoh*.

Similar Species
Tundra Swan smaller, with yellow spot at base of bill, more rounded
head, and shorter bill profile; different call. Mute Swan larger;
"sails" on water; calls weaker. See Whooper Swan.

Range
Two distinct breeding populations in northwestern North America.
One migratory group breeds from interior and south coastal Alaska
into parts of northern British Columbia, locally in Alberta and
southwest Saskatchewan; winters from southern Alaska to coastal
Washington, rarely to Oregon and California. Another population is
mainly resident, scattered across areas of northern Great Basin,
including parts of Idaho, Montana, and Wyoming. Introduced birds
reside in refuges in eastern Washington and eastern Oregon.
Theodore G. Tobish Jr.

Mute Swan

Cygnus olor
Introduced to North America in the mid-19th century, the Mute
Swan is often seen in park and aviary ponds, reservoirs, rivers, and
coastal bays. Although semi-domesticated and often hand-fed, it is
aggressive and can be dangerous at the nest. It is not particularly
gregarious, but may congregate in open bays or along coastlines. It
can be confused with the Tundra and the Trumpeter swans.

Description
50–60″ (127–152.5 cm). About half of the Mute Swan's length is
made up of its extremely long neck. This large bird weighs from 18
to 33 pounds—sometimes more—and has a wingspan of 60 inches or
longer. The adult is white with a pink bill that becomes orange-red
in breeding season; the knobbed bill is black at the base and
around the eye. The female is smaller than the male, with a smaller
bill knob. The iris is hazel; the legs and feet are black, paler in the
"Polish" variety. Immatures are dirty gray-brown in the first year;
in the second year they grow whiter, and show some brown flecking

Immature
1. *Grayish tinge to plumage.*
2. *Pinkish, black-tipped bill.*
3. *Rounded forehead.*

Adult
1. *White plumage.*
2. *Bill black, with no yellow spot at base.*

Large size.
Deep, trumpeting call.

Adult
1. *White plumage.*
2. *Gracefully curved neck.*
3. *Pinkish or orange bill with black knob at base.*

Usually tame.
"Sails" on water.
Common near towns.

on the wings; the bill is blue-gray, and lacks a knob. The swimming posture is diagnostic: the heavy neck is gracefully curved, and the head is down-turned; the wings are often raised and fluffed in a "sailing" position, and the tail is elevated. Except for the angle where the bill and knob join the head, this swan is flat-headed (a good field mark). It flies low, with slow, deep, powerful wingbeats and head and neck outstretched.

Voice
Variety of low snorts, grunts, and hisses. Most distinctive is swooshing, *vaou, vaou* of wings, audible for half a mile.

Similar Species
See Tundra and Trumpeter swans.

Range
East Coast from Massachusetts to New Jersey, especially eastern Long Island, with enclave in Grand Traverse Bay, Lake Michigan. May be introduced almost anywhere. Populations probably include both wild and domesticated birds. Most populations nonmigratory. Native to mid-latitude Eurasia.   *Robert Arbib*

Bean Goose

Anser fabalis
This Eurasian goose regularly reaches North America in the spring, migrating to the Bering Sea area of western Alaska. Represented by several subspecies, it ranges widely across northern Eurasia, breeding in quite diverse habitats including northern tundra, interior taiga, and alpine meadows. As a member of the genus *Anser*, it most closely resembles the White-fronted Goose. In the western Aleutian Islands, the Bean Goose is the only regular migrant goose. Its low-pitched flight call is unique and distinguishes it from all other geese.

Description
29–36" (73.5–91.5 cm). The Bean Goose is a large, long-necked goose very similar to the White-fronted Goose. The head and neck are a uniform dark gray-brown, darker than the rest of the body. In flight, the primaries, secondaries, and wing coverts are dark gray. The large, long black bill has an irregular orange band across the middle. Immatures are uniformly dusky gray-brown and have mostly solid dark bills. All ages have unmarked pale grayish underparts.

Voice
Low, lazy, single or double *ong-angk*, usually on 1 pitch.

Similar Species
White-fronted Goose smaller, paler, especially on head and neck, with white on face, smaller pink bill, and dark flight feathers contrasting with wing coverts; also has different call. Immatures distinguished by size and shape of bill color and call.

Range
Regular rare spring migrant in central and western Aleutian Islands. A few scattered spring records from farther north in Bering Sea. Native to Eurasia.   *Theodore G. Tobish Jr.*

Immature
1. Gray-brown plumage.
2. Gracefully curved neck.

On water
1. Brownish plumage.
2. Dark head and neck.
3. Dark bill with orange band across middle.

Low-pitched, lazy, honking call.

Standing
1. Dark head and neck.

Large size.

Greater White-fronted Goose

Anser albifrons
This is a dark, medium-size goose common in central and western North America. It breeds in the Arctic, favoring higher inland tundra. In migration and winter it frequents open country, feeding in fields or shallow water, usually resting near the water's edge toward midday. During migration, the flocks often fly quite high in lines or V-formation, sometimes dropping down very steeply to a favorable habitat. White-fronts occur with other geese, tending to maintain their own flocks and family groups rather than to mix randomly.

Description
26–34″ (66–86.5 cm). The adult is mostly gray-brown, variably barred with black on the lower breast and belly. The rump and undertail coverts are white. A white patch (the "front") surrounds the base of the bill, which is generally pink. The legs and feet are orange. Immatures lack the white "front" and the black bars on the belly; they appear uniformly dark brown, with a paler belly, white rump and undertail coverts, pink bill, and orange feet. The Greenland race, *A. a. flavirostris*, a casual stray to the Atlantic Coast, has an orange bill, and its plumage tends to be quite dark.

Voice
High-pitched, melodious laughing or barking sound, usually of 2–4 syllables.

Similar Species
Immature blue-phase Snow Goose resembles immature White-front, but has dark bill and feet; paler blue-gray upperwing coverts noticeable in flight. In Alaska, Bean Goose larger; darker, especially on head and neck; lacks white on face; has larger black bill with orange band; lacks dark flecking on belly. Some similar dark geese kept in captivity; escaped birds may be mistaken for White-fronts.

Range
In North America, breeds in Alaska and Arctic Canada; winters mainly from southern British Columbia south through California, in coastal Texas and Louisiana, and in Mexico. Wanders to East Coast; so do some Greenland birds, but latter normally winter in British Isles. Widespread in Eurasia.   *Kenn Kaufman*

Snow Goose

Chen caerulescens
There are 2 races of the Snow Goose, the "Lesser" and the "Greater." The "Lesser" Snow Goose (*C. c. caerulescens*) has 2 color phases—a dark phase (the so-called "Blue" Goose) and a white phase (the Snow Goose). The "Greater" Snow Goose (*C. c. atlantica*) is believed to have only a white phase. Snow Geese migrate in large flocks and fly in a peculiar undulating fashion, forming wavy lines rather than the well-defined V of Canada Geese. The white-phase "Lesser" Snow Goose is a common migrant to mid-America and the Pacific flyway, while the dark phase is rarely found west of the eastern Great Plains. The "Greater" Snow Goose is restricted to the Atlantic flyway as far south as South Carolina. Both races feed extensively on rootstocks and the shoots of bulrushes and marsh grasses, but have recently adapted to feeding on waste grain and pasture grasses.

Description
Lesser: 27–31″ (68.5–78.5 cm); Greater 28–33″ (71–84 cm). Adults of

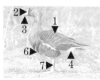

Adult
1. *Brown plumage.*
2. *White face.*
3. *Pink bill.*
4. *White undertail coverts.*
5. *White V on uppertail coverts.*
6. *Barring on belly.*
7. *Orange feet.*

Immature
1. *Uniformly brown plumage.*
2. *No white on face.*
3. *Pink bill.*
4. *Orange feet.*

Immature Snow Goose
1. *Sooty-gray upperparts.*
2. *White underparts.*

Snow Goose

"Blue" Goose

the "Greater" and the white-phase "Lesser" Snow Geese are entirely white except for black wing tips and carmine bill, legs, and feet. Immatures are a sooty gray on the top of the head, back of the neck, back, and wing coverts, but mostly whitish below, with black wing tips. Adult "Blue" Geese have slate-gray bodies, with white heads and upper necks, whitish tail coverts, and varying amounts of white on their bellies. Their wings are a pearl-gray with black primaries, and, like their white counterparts, they have carmine bills, legs, and feet; the bill has black "lips." The drab immature "Blue Goose" is almost entirely brownish-gray, lighter below, with gray wing coverts, a white chin spot, and a dark purplish-gray bill and feet.

Voice
Generally most vocal of waterfowl; call shrill, scratchy *uh-uk*, somewhat similar to yelp of fox terrier.

Similar Species
Ross' Goose smaller, with shorter neck, stubbier bill, faster wingbeats, and more highly pitched call. Emperor Goose has dark tail coverts, scaly appearance; lacks black "lips" on mandible; does not overlap in range with blue-phase Snow Goose. Immature White-fronted Goose has pink bill, orange feet.

Range
"Lesser" breeds from Wrangel Island, Siberia, to Baffin Island, south along western and southwestern coasts of Hudson Bay to James Bay. Winters from Puget Sound through California in West; in Nebraska, southeastern Iowa, Kansas, Missouri, Illinois, and Oklahoma in Midwest; south through New Mexico, Texas, Louisiana, and panhandle of Florida, and into Mexico. Largest winter concentrations in Central Valley, California, and coastal Louisiana and Texas. "Greater" breeds on several Arctic islands, northwestern Greenland, and in extreme northeastern Canada; wintering grounds range from northeastern United States to mid-Atlantic Coast.   *Frank C. Bellrose*

Ross' Goose

Chen rossii
A diminutive white goose with black wing tips, Ross' Goose inhabits the Far West—particularly California—from fall to spring. A rare species a few decades ago, it has become surprisingly abundant in recent years. Although it associates with the similar but larger "Lesser" Snow Goose, Ross' often maintains the integrity of its flocks. Recently, hybrids with "Lesser" Snow Geese have been reported, as well as a blue phase that is similar to the "Blue" Goose of the Snow Goose.

Ross'

Description
21–26″ (53.5–66 cm). The adult Ross' Goose is white except for black wing tips, and a carmine bill, feet, and legs. This species' small body, short, stubby bill, short neck, rapid wingbeat, and high-pitched call all constitute distinguishing characteristics. The sexes are alike. Some adults may show warty protuberances between the nostrils and the base of the bill. Immatures are very pale gray and lighter in tone than immature Snow Geese.

Snow

"Blue" Goose
1. *Dark gray body.*
2. *White head and neck.*

Adult Snow Goose
1. *White plumage.*
2. *Pink bill with black "lips."*
3. *Black wing tips.*

Usually in flocks. Shrill, yelping call.

Adult
1. *Short, stubby pink bill.*
2. *Short neck.*
3. *White plumage.*
4. *Black wing tips.*

Small size. Higher-pitched call than Snow Goose.

Voice
High-pitched call similar to bark of small dog; higher and less
melodious than call of Snow Goose.

Similar Species
"Lesser" Snow Goose larger, more abundant; has longer bill and
neck and lower-pitched call.

Range
Breeds in limited locations in high Arctic, mostly adjacent to Queen
Maud Gulf of Northwest Territories, but also at Southampton Island
and delta of McConnell River, Hudson Bay. Winters almost
exclusively in Central Valley and at Salton Sea, California; also in
small numbers along Rio Grande, New Mexico, and on Texas coast.
In migration, large numbers stop along south border of Alberta and
Saskatchewan; at Freezeout Lake, Montana; and in Klamath Basin
and Sacramento Valley, California.   *Frank C. Bellrose*

Emperor Goose

Chen canagica
Most of the world's Emperor Geese live in western Alaska. Strictly
maritime, they breed on tundra near pools or just above the high-
tide line.

Description
26–30" (66–76 cm). This smallish, stocky, short-necked goose has a
stubby pink bill and orange legs. The medium blue-gray body
feathers and wing coverts, fringed with black and white, appear
scaly. The delicately rounded head and hindneck are pure white;
chin, throat, and foreneck are black. The underparts are uniformly
dark and scaly; the tail is white. Immatures appear dusky gray.

Voice
Common flight call aloud, musical, *cla-ha, cla-ha.*

Range
Breeds on Bering Sea coast in Alaska; winters from Bristol Bay and
Alaska Peninsula to Commander and Aleutian islands, east
to Kodiak Island; rarely farther south.   *Theodore G. Tobish Jr.*

Brant

Branta bernicla
In winter, the small Brant is ubiquitous along the coastal bays and
eelgrass communities of both coasts; in spring and fall, it undertakes
a long migration to and from its breeding grounds in the High
Arctic. The Pacific race (the "Black" Brant) is dark-bellied, while the
Atlantic population is pale-bellied; at one time these were considered
separate species. A very dark goose, the Brant is on the average
only a few inches longer than the Mallard. Flocks in the air can
usually be distinguished from other geese by their constantly
shifting, erratic formations; they fly in small groups rather than long
lines or Vs. Nonbreeding birds usually undertake most of the
northward spring migration and can be distinguished by their worn
plumage and the pale feather edges retained from the previous fall.

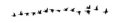

Description
22–26" (56–66 cm). The Brant is a small, stocky, dark-backed goose
with a black head, neck, and breast. A small, whitish patch is
present on both sides of the neck below the throat; in the "Black"

Immature
1. *Short, stubby bill.*
2. *Short neck.*
3. *Very pale gray plumage.*

Adult
1. *White head and hindneck.*
2. *Scaly blue-gray upperparts.*
3. *Black throat and foreneck.*
4. *White tail and undertail coverts.*

Loud, musical call.

"Black" Brant
1. *Dark belly.*
2. *Short, black neck.*
3. *White collar.*
4. *White undertail coverts.*

Small size.
Low, growling call.

Brant the white forms a thin collar. The underparts are variously marked with black, especially in the "Black" Brant. The extreme lower belly, undertail coverts, and lower flanks are white, contrasting with the dark upperparts and breast, and, in the "Black" Brant, with the dark belly (although some "Black" Brants have pale bellies). This contrast is most evident in flight, or at close range on the water. The short, stubby bill and the legs are blackish.

Voice
Less vocal than other geese; utters low, soft, growling sound.

Similar Species
Canada Goose larger, longer-necked, with large white facial patches, pale breast, and larger bill. Barnacle Goose has wholly white face, pure white underparts, scalloped upperparts.

Range
Breeds in high latitudes of Arctic from Arctic coast of Alaska and Yukon-Kuskokwim deltas to Baffin Island and across northern coastal Mackenzie. Migrates and winters primarily along Pacific and Atlantic coasts; in West to Gulf of California; in East occasionally south to north-central Florida.   *Theodore G. Tobish Jr.*

Barnacle Goose

Branta leucopsis
This very rare Old World vagrant sometimes occurs with migrating or wintering Canada Geese. Most in our range are escaped birds.

Description
25–28″ (63.5–71 cm). Adult has barred black and gray mantle, dark primaries, and black crown, nape, and neck. Face, belly, and flanks white; narrow black line extends from eye to black bill. Breast, legs, and feet black. Juvenile similar but duller.

Voice
A barking, terrierlike *gnuh*, sometimes rapidly repeated.

Similar Species
See Brant and Canada Goose.

Range
Rare vagrant, primarily in Northeast; scattered reports west to Mackenzie and Great Plains. Breeds in Greenland and northern Eurasia. Common in captivity.   *Joseph A. Grzybowski*

Canada Goose

Branta canadensis
For most people in North America, the word "goose" instantly conjures up a vision of the widespread and numerous Canada Goose; this bird, with its distinct V-shaped flock formation and clear, musical honking call, is familiar to many, throughout the continent. The extensive geographic range of this abundant species, together with its fidelity to specific breeding localities, has led to a number of racial variations. Although many expert ornithologists do not believe that all races of the Canada Goose have yet been identified, 11 subspecies are currently recognized, representing a tremendous range of morphological variation. These races pose varying degrees of identification difficulties; at times biologists have resorted to using the terms "large," "medium," and "small" in distinguishing birds whose winter populations mix. Canada Geese are basically grazers by nature, but have recently adapted to feeding on cereal grains and cultivated green forage; this adjustment has in part been responsible for an enormous increase in the species' numbers over the last few decades.

Atlantic race
1. *Light belly.*
2. *Short, black neck with small white patch.*
3. *White undertail coverts.*

Small, stocky build.

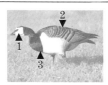

Adult
1. *Large white face patch.*
2. *Gray-and-black barring on back.*
3. *Black breast contrasting with white belly and flanks.*

Small size.

"Giant" Canada Goose
1. *Black head and neck.*
2. *White cheek patch.*
3. *White undertail coverts.*

Very large size.

Description
Small races: 22–27″ (56–68.5 cm); medium and large races: 32–48″
(81.5–122 cm). All sex and age classes of all races of Canada Geese
have the following characteristics in common: black bill, legs, and
feet; black head and neck with a white cheek patch that usually
covers the throat; gray-brown to dark brown back and wings; and a
dull gray to dark brown breast and sides—in most races, these are a
lighter shade than the back. Other common characteristics are the
white belly, flanks, and undertail coverts, and a black rump and tail
separated by a white V bar formed by the white uppertail coverts.
Some races are very large, such as the "Giant" Canada Goose (*B. c.
maxima*); others, like "Richardson's" Canada Goose (*B. c.
hutchinsii*) and the "Cackling" Canada Goose (*B. c. minima*), are
very small.

1

Voice
Call ranges from resonant *uh-whonk* of larger races to yelping, high-
pitched *unc* of smaller ones. In general, larger races utter longer,
less frequent, more sonorous calls.

Similar Species
Brant almost entirely confined to seacoasts; black head lacks white
cheek patch, and dark upper body almost black. Barnacle Goose has
wholly white face, black breast, white belly and flanks.

Range
Small races breed mostly north of 60° latitude from northern Alaska
through Northwest Territories to Baffin Island, south to Aleutian
Islands, and northern Alberta and Saskatchewan. Large and
medium races breed largely south of 60° latitude from southeastern
Alaska, British Columbia, Alberta, Saskatchewan, Manitoba,
Ontario, Quebec, and Newfoundland south to northeastern
California, Nevada, Utah, Colorado, Kansas, Missouri, Illinois,
Tennessee, and Ohio. All races winter across much of United States
and into northeastern Mexico. Although mixing of races commonly
occurs on wintering grounds, certain races are more prevalent in
different areas.   *Frank C. Bellrose*

Wood Duck

Aix sponsa
The colorful Wood Duck is the most abundant breeding duck in the
eastern United States. It nests in tree cavities and nest boxes,
sometimes in cities and towns adjacent to rivers and lakes. From
spring to late summer, Wood Ducks are usually found in pairs or
small flocks, but during the fall and winter they frequently form
large flocks, especially at favored feeding and roosting areas. These
birds inhabit the placid waters of streams, ponds, swamps, wooded
sloughs, and lakes. When swimming, they ride higher on the water
than other ducks, nodding their heads in a manner similar to coots,
and often with the tail held at a 45° angle from the horizontal.

Description
15–21″ (38–53.5 cm). Adults of both sexes have crested heads, white
bellies, and long tails. The white trailing edge of the secondaries is
apparent against the dark back and upper surface of the wings. The
male's crest is iridescent green with 2 white streaks, one extending
back from the bill, the other from the eye. The white throat has 2

Medium-size race
1. *Flies in wedge-shaped formation.*

Smaller in size and shorter-necked than "Giant" Canada Goose.

"Cackling" Canada Goose
1. *Very short neck.*
2. *Stubby bill.*

Very small size.

Breeding male
1. *Striped crest.*
2. *Bold, white face pattern.*
3. *Red bill.*
4. *Red eye.*
5. *Buff flanks.*
6. *Long tail.*

prongs extending upward; the burgundy chest is stippled with white and separated from the bronze side feathers by a "finger" of black and white. A red eye and a partially red bill complete this colorful array. The female has a gray head and crest, an elliptical white eye patch, and a grayish-brown chest and sides with whitish spots.

Voice
Male: ascending *ter-we-ee*, heard at flock feeding and roost sites; female: squealing *wee-e-e-ek* or *woo-e-e-e-ek* alarm call.

Similar Species
American Wigeon has large white speculum; lacks crest. Hooded Merganser has slender bill, white patches on wings, faster wingbeat, and more direct flight, often low over water.

Range
Breeds from southern British Columbia and western Montana south to southern California and from north shore of Lake Superior east to Nova Scotia and south to Florida and Texas. Winters throughout breeding range in Far West, particularly in central California; east of Great Plains, largely from Virginia and Missouri south to coastal Texas and tip of Florida.   *Frank C. Bellrose*

Green-winged Teal

Anas crecca
The smallest of puddle ducks, the Green-winged Teal flies in moderate to large flocks that twist, turn, and dive in tight unison. The swift wingbeat and proportionately long, narrow wings of this bird yield an impression of very rapid flight. This abundant species prefers to feed on mud flats, shallow marshes, lake borders, and occasionally shallow, flooded grain. During fall migration, the sexes sometimes segregate into separate flocks.

Description
12–16″ (30.5–40.5 cm). The whitish belly, dark upperwings, and iridescent green speculum distinguish this species from the Blue-winged Teal. In breeding plumage, males exhibit a striking, slightly crested rust-colored head, with an iridescent green face patch sweeping back from the eye. Males of the American race (*A. c. carolinensis*) have a vertical, sometimes crescent-shaped white stripe separating the breast and sides; the Aleutian race (*A. c. nimia*) and the Eurasian race (*A. c. crecca*) have a bold horizontal white line between the gray flanks and back and a cream-colored line above the green face patch. Females of all races are a drab gray-brown with a dark eyeline and a buff triangular patch on the dark undertail coverts. In eclipse plumage, drakes are difficult to distinguish from females and immatures.

Male, Eurasian race

Voice
Male: clear whistle, once or in series; female: airy, diffuse quack.

Similar Species
Blue-winged Teal has conspicuous blue wing patch and dark belly; breeding-plumage males exhibit gray-blue head with contrasting white facial crescent.

Range
American race breeds from Arctic Alaska, Saskatchewan, Manitoba, Ontario, Quebec, Newfoundland, and Maritime Provinces south to northern California, Colorado, Minnesota, Wisconsin, and northern New England. Winters across North America from southern Canada to southern United States, Mexico, and northern South America. Much more abundant west of Missouri River in United States. Aleutian race confined to Aleutian islands. Eurasian race rare visitor to Atlantic and Pacific coasts.   *Frank C. Bellrose*

Female
1. *Dark upperparts.*
2. *White eye patch.*
3. *Pale belly.*
4. *Long tail.*

Squealing alarm call.

Female
1. *Green speculum.*
2. *Whitish belly.*
3. *Dark upper wings without light patches.*

Small size.

Breeding male, American race
1. *Rust-colored head with green face patch.*
2. *Vertical white stripe on side.*

Eurasian race has horizontal white stripe on side.

Falcated Teal

Anas falcata
This East Asian dabbling duck was named for the male's
conspicuously elongated ("falcate") inner flight feathers. Its large
size and propensity for salt water give it an unteal-like character.
The Falcated Teal is an irregular migrant in the Aleutian and
Pribilof islands of Alaska, but since it is commonly kept in waterfowl
collections, the origin of birds seen south of Alaska is questionable.
In flight, the drake superficially resembles a male Mallard; on the
water, however, its unique plumage pattern allows quick
recognition. The female is surprisingly similar to a female Eurasian
Wigeon; less so to a female Gadwall.

Description
19″ (48.5 cm). About the size of a Gadwall, the male Falcated Teal is
unmistakable. It has a silver-gray back and sides, with a black and
gray scalloped breast and black undertail coverts flanked with a buff
patch. The chestnut and iridescent green head is crested on the
nape; a white throat and white spot low on the forehead further
distinguish the male. The distinctive, sickle-shaped inner flight
feathers drape over the sides, overlapping the base of the tail. The
female has a plain gray-brown head and a cool brown barred and
mottled body. The belly of the female is dark brown, and the bill is
solid dark gray. The whitish outer tail feathers are distinctive on the
female; sometimes there is a semblance of a crest on the nape. Both
sexes have blackish legs and a dark greenish, iridescent speculum
bordered fore and aft with white.

Voice
Male: a low-pitched, teal-like whistle; female: a Gadwall-like quack.

Similar Species
Female Eurasian Wigeon differs subtly from female Falcated Teal;
has pinkish, unscaled sides and white belly; smaller, rounder head;
smaller, delicate, bluish bill, tipped with black. Female Gadwall has
white speculum, orange on sides of bill, and yellowish feet.

Range
Rare but regular in spring and casual in fall in central and western
Aleutian Islands; casual in Pribilof Islands. Records from British
Columbia and California probably of escaped birds. Breeds and
winters in northeastern Asia and Japan.   *Theodore G. Tobish Jr.*

American Black Duck

Anas rubripes
Rarely found west of the Midwest, the Black Duck becomes
increasingly abundant eastward, reaching peak numbers on the
Atlantic Coast north of the Carolinas. So strong is its resemblance
to the female Mallard that it is often called the "Black Mallard."
Where both species are common, pairs or small flocks of Black
Ducks mingle among multitudes of Mallards. On the East Coast,
however, Black Ducks frequent marshes and estuaries, where they
are not likely to mix with the Mallard.

Description
20–25″ (51–63.5 cm). The Black Duck is mainly sooty-brown with
little contrast; the head and neck are somewhat lighter than the
body, the wings have a purplish speculum bordered with black. The
feet and legs are carmine (brighter in the male); the bill is bright
yellow in the adult male, mottled black in the female, and olive-
green in the immature. In flight, the white wing linings create a
vivid contrast against the very dark body.

Breeding male
1. *Large, drooping, iridescent crest.*
2. *White throat.*
3. *Silvery-gray back and sides.*

   Large size.

Female
1. *Suggestion of crest.*
2. *Barred flanks.*
3. *Dark gray bill.*

   Large size.

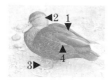

Standing bird
1. *Sooty-brown body.*
2. *Pale head and neck.*
3. *Carmine legs and feet.*
4. *Purple speculum.*

Voice
Quack almost identical to Mallard's.

Similar Species
Male Mallard has green head, brown chest, white belly and tail
feathers; female Mallard lighter brown with white-bordered
speculum. Sexes also alike in Mottled, Florida, and Mexican ducks
but lighter than Black Duck; restricted in range to extreme southern
United States, where Black Duck seldom occurs.

Range
Breeds in northern Alberta, northwestern Manitoba, western
Minnesota, and Wisconsin; majority of breeding population in
northeastern United States and Canada; reaches Hudson Bay and
Ungava Peninsula in north; south along Atlantic Coast to Cape
Hatteras, North Carolina. Winters largely in eastern United States
south of Great Lakes and St. Lawrence River to northern Gulf
Coast; most abundant along Atlantic Coast from New Brunswick to
Georgia.   *Frank C. Bellrose*

Mottled Duck

Anas fulvigula
The Mottled Duck is a large, common, surface-feeding duck found in
Florida and along the Gulf Coast. A pale version of the American
Black Duck, it is found mainly in freshwater marshes, ponds,
pastures, and fields, but also on coastal waters and salt marshes.

Description
21–24″ (53.5–61 cm). This duck is mostly pale brown to tawny. It
has an unstreaked buff throat, a yellow bill, and silvery wing linings.
The pale sides of the head and neck are a useful field mark. The
white bar on the trailing edge of the speculum may be obscured or
lacking in some individuals, especially in Florida.

Similar Species
See American Black Duck and female Mallard.

Range
Entire Gulf Coast and most of Florida; into northeastern Mexico.
Florida population nonmigratory.   *Paul W. Sykes, Jr.*

Mallard

Anas platyrhynchos
The Northern Hemisphere's most abundant and cosmopolitan duck,
the familiar and adaptable Mallard has been domesticated for
centuries. It is especially abundant in the interior of North America,
where, during the fall and winter, it feeds extensively on waste
grain in harvested fields. These hardy birds winter as far north as
open water and food permit; on favored lakes, marshes, and swamps
they are often seen congregating in flocks of many thousands and
forming huge "rafts."

Description
20–28″ (51–71 cm). The breeding male's green head and neck,
separated from a dark brown chest by a narrow white ring, are
highly diagnostic. At rest, the folded wings form a dark line
separating the gray sides and back. The black rump and tail coverts
contrast with the white outer tail feathers. The female is a rather
uniform mottled brown, lighter and less mottled on the head and
belly. In flight, the dark blue speculum, bordered in front and back

In flight
1. *Flashing, white wing linings.*
2. *Dark body.*
3. *Pale head.*

On water
1. *Medium-brown body and tail.*
2. *Pale head, with unmarked throat.*
3. *Yellow bill.*
4. *White bar on trailing edge of speculum.*

Female
1. *Uniformly mottled, brown body.*
2. *Dull orange and brown bill.*
3. *Whitish tail feathers.*
4. *Dark blue speculum with white borders fore and aft.*

by white, alternates with the flash of white wing linings, helping to distinguish both sexes from other ducks. The proportionately broad wings and short tail make the wings look as though they are placed farther back on the body than in other species. During the summer, the males assume an eclipse plumage and resemble the female. Both sexes of the "Mexican" Duck (*A. p. diazi*), a subspecies of the Mallard, are similar to the female Mallard but darker; they are lighter than the Black Duck.

Voice
The most vociferous of ducks, uttering a very wide variety of familiar quacks.

Similar Species
American Black Duck and Mottled Duck have sexes colored alike, both similar to female Mallard but darker, especially Black Duck. Mottled Duck confined to states along Gulf Coast (Louisiana, Alabama, and Texas) and Florida; Black Duck largely east of Great Plains.

Range
Breeds from Alaska into Midwest and Northeast; south in West almost to Mexico and in East to mid-Atlantic states. Winters almost entirely in United States as far north as Washington, Montana, North Dakota, Wisconsin, and New York. Most abundant in Arkansas; Louisiana; Texas Panhandle; Platte river of Nebraska and Colorado; Snake River, Idaho; and Columbia Basin, Washington. Also in Eurasia. "Mexican" Duck restricted to several localities in southeastern Arizona, along Rio Grande in New Mexico, in southwestern corner of state, and in western Texas.
Frank C. Bellrose

Northern Pintail

Anas acuta
A trim, slender bird, the Northern Pintail is the most streamlined of waterfowl. It cleaves the air in graceful flight on long, narrow wings. Males in breeding plumage have especially long tails that constitute almost one-fourth of their total length. Rivaling the Lesser Scaup in number, the Pintail is the second or third most abundant North American duck; it is most numerous west of the Mississippi River in winter, particularly in California and along the Gulf Coast of Louisiana and Texas. Pintails frequent shallow lakes and marshes, feeding in deeper water than other dabblers.

Description
20–30″ (51–76 cm). The male Pintail in breeding plumage has a chocolate-brown head with a white streak extending upward from its white neck, breast, and belly. The gray back and sides are separated by an elliptical black patch. The black upper- and undertail coverts contrast with the white flank and belly; the tail feathers are gray, except for the long black central pair. Females

Breeding male
1. *Green head.*
2. *Chestnut breast.*
3. *Blue speculum.*

"Mexican" Duck
1. *Brown plumage; paler than Black Duck, paler than female Mallard.*
2. *Speculum with white borders.*

Breeding male
1. *Brown head.*
2. *Slender neck with white stripe.*
3. *Gray body.*
4. *Thin black central tail feathers.*

are a mottled dark brown above, with a lighter brown head and breast and a shorter tail. Juveniles and eclipse males resemble females. The bill is blue-gray, and the legs and feet are gray in both sexes. In flight, the green speculum of the male and the brown speculum of the female, both with white on the trailing edge, are good field marks.

Voice
Male: a short, piping, whistling note; female: a harsh quack.

Similar Species
Mallards chunkier with blue speculum, slower wingbeat. Gadwall has grayish-white speculum. Blue-winged Teal smaller, with blue shoulder patch.

Range
Breeds from northern Alaska across northern Canada to Labrador, south to southern California, across to northeastern Nebraska, northern Illinois and Iowa, Lakes Ontario and Erie, St. Lawrence River, and Maine. Winters along Pacific Coast from British Columbia to Mexico and Colombia; across southern United States to Atlantic Coast from Long Island to Georgia.   *Frank C. Bellrose*

Garganey

Anas querquedula
A long-distance migrant from the Old World with elongated, sickle-shaped scapulars, the Garganey is a rare vagrant to both coasts of North America. Drake Garganeys are quite distinctively plumaged, but the female plumage shows little difference from the female Blue-winged or Cinnamon teal. This common dabbler of Eurasia is regularly recorded during migration in the Aleutian Islands.

Description
14–16″ (35.5–40.5 cm). The Garganey is roughly the size of a Blue-winged Teal, but its bill is wider and longer, more like the bill of a Cinnamon Teal. The drake has a dark purple head with a prominent white eyebrow curving back onto the upper nape. The breast is black to the water line, accentuating the silvery sides and flanks. The lower back and the uppertail and undertail coverts are mottled brown and buff. The long, dark-centered, white-edged scapulars overlap the sides. The female's plumage is similar to that of female North American teals, but with caution the female Garganey can be distinguished by its facial markings: a bold eyebrow line, set off by a long dark eyeline, and usually a pale, circular spot on the cheeks at the base of the bill. Both sexes have chalky grayish lesser and median wing coverts and a greenish speculum with white borders (brighter in the male). The bill and legs are dull gray.

Voice
Male: low, cackling single notes; female: a loud, teal-like quack.

Similar Species
Female Blue-winged Teal usually has less contrasting light-and-dark facial pattern with less obvious eyebrow; yellow legs, and darker bill. Female Green-winged Teal has shorter bill, lacks facial pattern and grayish wing coverts. Female Cinnamon and Blue-winged teals have deeper, more clear-blue forewing.

Range
Regular spring and fall migrant in central and western Aleutian Islands; casual there in summer. Casual migrant on both coasts and accidental elsewhere on continent. Breeds widely across Eurasia, from Iceland to northeast Asia; winters to north-central Africa.
Theodore G. Tobish Jr.

Female
1. *Slender neck.*
2. *Long tail.*
3. *Bluish bill.*
4. *Mottled brown body.*

Female
1. *Contrasting pattern of light and dark lines on face; distinct eyebrow.*

Male
1. *Dark head with white eyebrow.*
2. *Long, pointed scapulars.*

Blue-winged Teal

Anas discors
The widespread Blue-winged Teal commonly nests in grassy areas
near potholes, sloughs, and shallow marshes. In general, it is the
first duck to migrate south in the fall and the latest spring migrant
northward. Groups of these ducks prefer to feed on aquatic plants in
shallow marsh vegetation or on mud flats. The Blue-winged Teal is a
swift duck that twists and turns as it flies in small, compact flocks.
The Green-winged Teal is similar in flight, but is more prone to
aerial acrobatics and generally occurs in larger flocks.

Description
14–16½″ (35.5–42 cm). In flight, the small size and chalky blue wing
patch distinguish the Blue-winged Teal from most other ducks.
Under some light conditions, the blue wing patch may appear white.
While at rest or on the water, the wing patch is usually hidden, and
the features readily spotted at a distance are the white facial
crescent and the white flank patch just before the tail of the
breeding-plumage male. Breeding males exhibit a bluish-gray head
and neck, and a tan breast and sides with brown spots. Females are
rather uniformly gray-brown, with a dark line through the eye and a
buff or whitish patch on the lores. Both sexes have a green speculum
and brownish underparts. During the fall, all plumages appear
similar. Adult males gain breeding features by mid-November or
December, but immature males do not begin to show distinguishing
characteristics until late winter.

Voice
Male: a peeping whistle or *keck-keck-keck;* female: a faint quack.

Similar Species
See Green-winged and Cinnamon teals. Female Northern Shoveler
can usually be distinguished even in flight by large, spoon-shaped
bill.

Range
Breeds from intermountain region of British Columbia to
Newfoundland south to northern California, Colorado, New York,
and to some degree down central Atlantic seaboard. Occasional to
locally common breeder throughout United States under favorable
water conditions. Winters from Texas to Carolinas, south through
Mexico to Central and South America.   *Frank C. Bellrose*

Cinnamon Teal

Anas cyanoptera
A denizen of western marshes, the small Cinnamon Teal is most
abundant in the wetlands flanking Utah's Great Salt Lake. Here and
in other wetlands of arid regions, the Cinnamon Teal virtually
replaces the Blue-winged Teal. Usually the Cinnamon Teal occurs in
smaller flocks than either the Blue-winged or Green-winged teal.

Description
14½–17″ (37–43 cm). The male in breeding plumage has an almost
completely cinnamon-red head and body. The wings are similar to
those of the Blue-winged Teal, but are a more chalky blue that
appears whitish in reflected sunlight. In contrast to the bright
plumage of the male, females are a mottled brown, more even on the
back and more streaked below. Females, juveniles, and males in
eclipse plumage are similar and can be distinguished from their
Blue-winged Teal counterparts only under the most favorable
conditions. The bill is dark, fairly long, and somewhat spatulate at
the tip. The cheek and neck of the female are tawny; the forehead

Breeding male
1. *Bluish-gray head with white crescent on face.*
2. *White flank patch.*
3. *Blue-gray wing coverts visible in flight.*

Small size.

Female
1. *Gray-brown plumage.*
2. *Bill shorter and slenderer than Cinnamon Teal's.*
3. *Pale spot on lores and distinct dark line through eye.*

Small size.

Female
1. *Reddish-brown plumage.*
2. *Bill longer and broader than Blue-winged's.*
3. *Indistinct facial pattern.*

Small size.

slopes gradually to the top of the slightly flattened head. The male's eye is red in all plumages.

Voice
Male: a low, whistled peep; female: a harsh *karrr, karr, karr*.

Similar Species
Blue-winged Teal has shorter, less spatulate bill; breeding male has more waxy blue tone to wing; cheek and neck of female less tawny, with steeper forehead; eclipse male less reddish, lacks orange eye. Shoveler has large, spatulate bill. Ruddy Duck has white face patch and blue bill.

Range
Breeds from southern British Columbia (Caribou-Chilcotin Parklands) to just north of Mexico City; and from marshes adjacent to Pacific Coast east into western Dakotas, Nebraska, Kansas, Oklahoma, and Texas. Winters from Sacramento Valley of California south through Central America, primarily in Mexico north of Yucatan. Occurs rarely farther east in migration, usually in flocks of Blue-winged Teal.   *Frank C. Bellrose*

Northern Shoveler

Anas clypeata
A fairly common duck of North American lakes and marshes, the Northern Shoveler is most abundant west of the Mississippi River. This species migrates south early and returns north rather late, generally flying in small flocks of 5 to 10 individuals. In flight, the unusually long, downward-angled bill and the somewhat humped appearance of the back give the Shoveler a distinctive blocky look. Shovelers prefer to feed in shallow water; they are often seen swimming slowly with the neck extended and the bill skimming the surface or partially submerged.

Description
18–20″ (45.5–51 cm). The single most diagnostic characteristic of the shoveler is the large, spatulate bill, which is longer than the head. Drakes in breeding plumage are colorful, with a dark green head and neck, a white breast, rust-red sides and belly, white rear flanks, and a black tail with white outer tail feathers. This pattern of alternating light and dark colors is useful in identifying birds both in flight and at rest. Females are a drab mottled brown with light wing linings. Both sexes have a green speculum and blue-gray upperwing coverts. Eclipse drakes and immatures are similar to females. Immatures and most adults do not gain full breeding plumage until midwinter.

Voice
Male: a low raspy chuckle, seldom heard except in spring; female: a feeble quack.

Similar Species
Blue-winged Teal smaller, with smaller bill. Mallard drake has smaller bill, lacks alternating light-dark color pattern; female Mallard has smaller bill, dark blue speculum.

Range
Breeds from Alaska south and east to Saskatchewan and Manitoba, south to northern California, Colorado, Nebraska, Wisconsin, and to limited degree in marshes of Great Lakes region; also local, at least occasionally, in Northeast to western Nova Scotia. Winters from Oregon across southern half of United States to Arkansas and Maryland, south to Texas, Mexico, and Florida; mostly in California and coastal Louisiana.   *Frank C. Bellrose*

Male
1. *Cinnamon-red head and underparts.*
2. *Blue-gray wing coverts visible in flight.*

Small size.

Breeding male
1. *Broad, spatulate bill.*
2. *Green head.*
3. *White breast.*
4. *Rust-red flanks.*

Female
1. *Broad, spatulate bill.*
2. *Brown plumage.*
3. *Blue-gray wing coverts visible in flight.*

Gadwall

Anas strepera

The nondescript Gadwall is one of the most difficult ducks to identify in the field. Gadwalls are usually encountered in small to medium-size flocks; they appear more streamlined in flight than the Mallard, but less so than the Pintail. Gadwalls are more prone to dive than other dabbling ducks. The Gadwall's numbers have increased substantially recently, principally in central North America; the range has also extended eastward considerably.

Description

18–22½″ (45.5–57 cm). This is the only dabbling duck with white in the speculum; this distinctive flight characteristic is seldom visible at rest, when it is concealed by the gray flank feathers. The male is mottled gray-brown with black uppertail and undertail coverts and a sandy brown head. On the water, the contrast of the undertail coverts and body is distinctive; at close range the rusty scapulars on the folded wing are also noticeable. The female is a fairly uniform mottled brown. At close range, the narrow gray bill, edged with orange, distinguishes the female from the female Mallard. In flight overhead, both sexes display a white belly and wing linings sharply outlined by dark feathers.

Voice

Male: *kack-kack* and whistle; female: a soft, Mallardlike quack.

Similar Species

American Wigeon has white patch on upperwing coverts. Female Mallard has blue speculum and wider, orange bill. American Black Duck larger, darker; lacks white belly and speculum. Female Northern Pintail has longer neck and bluish bill. Green-winged Teal smaller, with green speculum. In Alaska, see Falcated Teal.

Range

Breeds from central Alaska, Alberta, Manitoba, and Minnesota to southern California, Utah, Colorado, and Texas Panhandle; most nest in Dakotas and Prairie Provinces; uncommon in Northeast. Winters across southern half of United States from California to Chesapeake Bay, south to Texas, Louisiana, and Florida, and on to Mexico and Guatemala. Also in Old World.   *Frank C. Bellrose*

Eurasian Wigeon

Anas penelope

Although it is not known to breed in North America, the Eurasian Wigeon is a regular visitor here, especially along the Atlantic and Pacific coasts. It is most often observed as a lone bird in a flock of American Wigeons, or rarely with Mallards or Northern Pintails. In much of its behavior, the Eurasian Wigeon is similar to the American Wigeon.

Description

16½–20½″ (42–52 cm). The gray back and sides and the russet-red head with a cream-colored crown stripe distinguish Eurasian drakes in breeding plumage from American Wigeons. Positive identification of females and immatures is difficult in the field. Adult female Eurasian Wigeons have 2 color phases: red-phase females have russet-red heads, necks, chests, backs, sides, and flanks, with a much redder tinge than American Wigeon females; gray-phase birds are almost identical to female American Wigeons, but tend to have darker heads. In both color phases, the axillars are finely speckled

Female
1. *Narrow gray bill, edged with orange.*
2. *Forehead steeper than female Mallard's.*
3. *Dark tail feathers.*
4. *Small white wing patch visible in flight.*

Breeding male
1. *Gray body.*
2. *Sandy-brown head.*
3. *Black undertail coverts.*
4. *Small white wing patch visible in flight.*

Breeding male
1. *Russet head with cream-colored forehead and crown.*
2. *Gray back and sides.*
3. *Large white wing patch visible in flight.*

with dark gray; this speckling is absent in the American Wigeon.
The bill is pale blue with a dark tip.

Voice
Male: a shrill, 2-note whistle; female: a low quacking note.

Similar Species
Male American Wigeon has brownish head, white crown, and green
band sweeping back from eye; female has pure white wing linings.

Range
Regular visitor along Atlantic and Pacific coasts during fall and
winter; in interior during spring. Common transient in Aleutian
Islands. Breeds in Eurasia.   *Frank C. Bellrose*

American Wigeon

Anas americana
A common duck of ponds and marshes, the American Wigeon is
often observed in the company of diving ducks. More than any other
dabbler, the Wigeon may be considered an "aquatic grazer,"
preferring to feed on the vegetative portions of aquatic plants. This
medium-size duck flies rapidly in compact flocks; its flight behavior is
more erratic than that of all other dabblers except that of the teals.
The American Wigeon is an early fall migrant, heading south on the
heels of the Blue-winged Teal and Pintail.

Description
18–23″ (45.5–58.5 cm). American Wigeons have medium-size bodies,
rather round heads, narrow wings, short bills, and wedge-shaped
tails. Both sexes have an elliptical white belly outlined with brown;
the white wing linings are obvious in overhead flight and somewhat
similar to those of the Gadwall and Wood Duck. The breeding
drake's most distinctive flight feature is a rectangular white patch
on the upperwing coverts, but this is scarcely visible when the
wings are folded. At rest, the brownish head with white to cream or
buff crown and the green band sweeping back from the eye, the
pinkish brown breast and sides, and the white rear flank feathers
bordered by black undertail coverts are all diagnostic of breeding-
plumage males. The female has a grayish head that contrasts with
the pale gray-brown sides and chest. Eclipse drakes resemble
females. Both sexes have a pale blue bill tipped with black that is
apparent at short range and distinctive among dabblers.

Voice
Male: 3 clear whistling notes, middle note higher-pitched; female: an
infrequent low quacking note.

Similar Species
See Eurasian Wigeon and Gadwall. Female Mallard larger than
female Wigeon, has longer orange bill and blue speculum.

Range
Breeds from Alaska tundra to James Bay and south to Oregon,
Utah, Wyoming, and Dakotas. Winters from British Columbia to
New England and south through California, Texas, Louisiana, and
Florida to Central America and West Indies.   *Frank C. Bellrose*

Female
1. *Reddish tinge on head and flanks.*
2. *Pale blue bill with dark tip.*
3. *Large white wing patch visible in flight.*

Female
1. *Grayish head.*
2. *Pale blue bill with dark tip.*
3. *Large white wing patch visible in flight.*

Breeding male
1. *White crown.*
2. *Green band on side of head.*
3. *Large white wing patch visible in flight.*

   Whistling flight call.

Common Pochard

Aythya ferina
The Common Pochard of Eurasia bears a close resemblance to its
North American counterparts, the Canvasback and Redhead. Once
considered accidental in North America, Common Pochards are
now found annually as spring migrants in the central and western
Aleutian and Pribilof islands of Alaska. The size of a Redhead but
like the Canvasback in shape and coloration, this species is easy to
identify in spring by the bold pale blue band across its bill. Pochards
breed inland on fresh water, mainly on steppes and plains; they
generally winter on large interior lakes and coastal bays.

Description
18″ (45.5 cm). The adult male has a deep chestnut head and neck, a
black breast to the water line, and a black rump and undertail
coverts. The back, flanks, and upperwing feathers are pale silvery
gray, paler than those of the Redhead. Both sexes have dark gray
bills with a pale blue band encircling the bill just behind the nail; this
band is slightly reduced in females. The female plumage recalls a
Canvasback, but shows a pale gray shade to the back and a thin
buff-colored line from the eye to the border of the ear coverts. Both
sexes have the sloping, more pointed head and bill shape of the
Canvasback, but in smaller dimensions. The iris is reddish or
orange-red; both sexes have a dull gray wing stripe in flight.

Voice
Male: a soft, nasal wheeze; female: a harsh *karr*.

Similar Species
Male Redhead darker on back and sides, with steeper head and bill
profile, gray-blue bill with black tip, and yellow iris. Female
Canvasback larger, with more extremely sloping head profile;
longer, solid-colored bill. Female scaups have white wing stripes,
white feathering at base of bill, and yellow iris. Female Tufted Duck
has darker body; different head and bill profile.

Range
In North America, occurs as regular spring migrant and summer
visitor to central and western Aleutian and Pribilof islands.
Accidental on Alaska mainland in spring. Breeds across Northern
Eurasia.   *Theodore G. Tobish Jr.*

Canvasback

Aythya valisineria
Canvasbacks prefer large inland lakes and coastal freshwater bays—
areas abounding with aquatic plants. In fall and winter, they form
large groups at a few traditional spots; in spring migration they
disperse more and favor smaller bodies of water. Canvasbacks have
a rapid wingbeat and fly faster than most other ducks. Small flocks
in flight form a wedge-shaped pattern, their oscillating wings
providing a flickering of white; this feature is a good field mark.

Description
19–22″ (48.5–56 cm). At rest, adult males show a chestnut-red head
and neck, a black bill, and a red eye. They have a black breast, and a
white back, sides, and belly; the extensive white back is more
evident than in other species. The tail and uppertail and undertail
coverts are black. Females and juveniles have brown heads and
necks; in the fall, the backs are a lighter brown, becoming
increasingly dappled with gray as the season progresses. The head
shape is distinctive, with a long, sloping black bill.

Female
1. *Dark gray bill with pale blue band.*
2. *Thin buff line behind eye.*
3. *Sloping forehead.*
4. *Gray tinge on back.*

Male
1. *Chestnut head and neck.*
2. *Dark gray bill with pale blue band.*
3. *Sloping forehead.*
4. *Silvery-gray upperparts.*

Male
1. *Chestnut head and neck.*
2. *Broadly sloping forehead and long black bill.*
3. *Whitish back, sides, and inner wing.*

Voice
Largely silent except during spring courtship. Male: cooing call;
female: quacks and low, guttural purring call.

Similar Species
Redhead male has gray back, rounded head, different bill shape and
color. Male Greater and Lesser scaup have grayer backs, black
heads, and dark wings in flight with white band at trailing edge.

Range
Breeds from Alaska to Nebraska, and in certain intermountain
marshes of Washington, Oregon, northern California, Nevada,
Montana, and Wyoming. Winters along Pacific Coast from British
Columbia to Jalisco, Mexico, particularly in San Francisco Bay; in
interior, in highlands of Central Mexico, Gulf Coast from Veracruz,
Mexico, to Florida; limited numbers reach as far north as lower
Great Lakes; almost half of population winters in Atlantic flyway
from Vermont (rare) to central Florida; largest number on
Chesapeake Bay.   *Frank C. Bellrose*

Redhead

Aythya americana
Redheads are the most common members of the genus *Aythya* that
nest in intermountain wetlands of western North America. In
migration, they usually occur individually, in pairs, or in small
flocks, but on favored wintering grounds they may gather in rafts of
thousands. Redheads usually fly fairly low over the water in tight,
wedge-shaped flocks; they have rapid wingbeats and engage in little
dodging or flaring. They feed on aquatic plants more extensively
than other divers, and tend to frequent shallow lakes and marshes.

Description
18–22″ (45.5–56 cm). Drakes in breeding plumage have a roundish,
bright red head, black lower neck and chest, gray back, white belly,
black tail, and black tail coverts. Females and immatures are a
rather uniform tawny brown with white bellies. At close range, the
long blue-gray bill tipped with black is noticeable in both sexes. The
dark-and-light color pattern of the male is visible at a good distance
on the water; the gray back is darker than that of scaup and much
darker than the whitish back of Canvasbacks. Female Redheads are
paler brown than the scaup and Ring-necked in similar plumages.

Voice
Male: courtship call a catlike *me-ow*, frequent in late winter and
spring; female's call infrequent, usually inaudible.

Similar Species
Canvasback larger with wedge-shaped head; male has whitish back,
female has gray back. Male scaup have dark iridescent head and
lighter gray back; female darker brown; lack pale streak behind eye.
Male Ring-necked has dark, puffy head and black back; female
darker brown.

Range
Breeds from northeastern British Columbia to western Ontario,
south to northern California (rarely to southern California and
Arizona), Utah, Colorado, Nebraska, and Iowa. Greatest breeding
concentrations in marshes of Great Salt Lake and parklands of
southern Canada. Winters largely in southern United States and
along Atlantic seaboard; majority winter along Gulf Coast from
Yucatan Peninsula to Apalachee Bay, Florida.
Frank C. Bellrose

Female
1. *Sandy-brown head and neck.*
2. *Broadly sloping forehead and long, black bill.*
3. *Grayish back.*

Male
1. *Chestnut head and neck.*
2. *Blue bill with black tip.*
3. *Black breast.*
4. *Gray back.*
5. *Pale gray secondaries.*

Female
1. *Tawny-brown head and body.*
2. *Steep forehead.*
3. *Blue bill with black tip.*

Ring-necked Duck

Aythya collaris
A small, dark, gregarious bird, the Ring-necked Duck might
appropriately be known as the "Ring-billed" Duck because of the
conspicuous white band that rings its dark bill; the chestnut collar
for which the species is named is at best a poor field mark. Ring-
necks breed on small freshwater marshes, ponds, and bogs and
frequent more forested areas than other diving ducks. In migration
and winter, they may form sizable flocks on large lakes and tidal
estuaries. Although Ring-necks are diving ducks, they often "up-
end" in shallow water. Their flight is very rapid and agile.

Description
14–18″ (35.5–45.5 cm). The male is very dark above, appearing black
at a distance, though at closer range a glossy purple or greenish
sheen on the head is visible. At a distance, the best field mark is a
prominent white vertical wedge that separates the black chest from
the gray flanks. In profile, the head appears peaked near the back of
the crown. The white band across the otherwise dark gray, black-
tipped bill is also diagnostic; a discrete, thin line of white feathers
separates the bill from the head. Females have a similar but less
exaggerated profile. They are dark gray-brown with a conspicuous
eye-ring and down-curved eyeline separating the darker crown from
a somewhat paler cheek; the bill has a white ring. There is pale
feathering at the base of the bill. In flight, both sexes have pale gray
secondaries and slightly brown primaries.

Voice
Male: a low-pitched whistle; female: a scauplike, purring growl.

Similar Species
See Tufted Duck, Redhead, and Greater and Lesser scaup.

Range
Limited to New World. Breeds from Alaska, Northwest Territories
across central Canada to Maritime Provinces, south to Washington,
Minnesota, northern New York, southern Maine; rarely south to
California, Arizona, northern Indiana, and Massachusetts. Absent
from Rocky Mountains. Winters from Washington, southern Illinois,
and New England south to Caribbean, Central America. Rare
wanderer to Europe.   *Peter D. Vickery*

Tufted Duck

Aythya fuligula
This rare visitor to North America occurs chiefly on Alaska's outer
islands, where it has now become quite regular. In recent years,
Tufted Ducks have also been found wintering regularly in very small
numbers along the Pacific Coast south to California. Closely related
to scaup, Tufted Ducks are notably small birds that prefer lakes,
tidal estuaries, and city ponds. They are often found in association
with mixed flocks of freshwater ducks, usually Ring-necked Ducks,
scaup, and Canvasbacks.

Description
16–18″ (40.5–45.5 cm). Adult males have a rounded, black head with
a purple gloss. The thin black crest can be very difficult to see, but
when visible it is diagnostic; the plume is frequently shorter on
immature males. The starkly black back contrasts sharply with the
pure white flanks, although first-winter males and males molting
into breeding plumage sometimes have duskier, brownish flanks.
The notably broad, gray-blue bill has a large, conspicuous black tip,

Female

1. *Dark gray-brown plumage.*
2. *Pale eye-ring and line behind eye.*
3. *High, steep forehead and peaked crown.*
4. *Dark gray bill with white ring and black tip.*

Male

1. *Dark gray bill with white ring and black tip.*
2. *Peaked crown.*
3. *White, vertical mark on sides of breast.*
4. *Black back.*
5. *Black wings with gray wing stripe.*

Male showing no crest

1. *Rounded, black head.*
2. *Gray bill with dark tip.*
3. *Black wings with white stripe.*
4. *White flanks.*

much wider than on scaup; in rare cases there is an inconspicuous
white band posterior to the black nail. The eye is yellow in both
sexes, though not as bright in the female. Female Tufted Ducks
require close observation for certain identification; they generally
have darker backs than female scaup, with dark brown to blackish
upperparts that contrast with the paler brown flanks and sides,
which may be mottled with yellowish or dull white feathers.
Occasionally there is some pale feathering at the base of the female's
bill, which is usually less extensive and less sharply defined than in
female scaup, but is sometimes more prominent. The female's short
head plume, if observable, is diagnostic. Some female Tufted Ducks
have obviously white undertail coverts, but these may be difficult to
observe. Males in eclipse plumage resemble females, though males
are generally grayer and lighter on the flanks. In flight, both sexes
show a broad white wing stripe that becomes grayer on the outer
primaries.

Similar Species
Female Ring-necked Duck has peaked head shape, dark eyes, and
white eye-ring and eyeline. Female and juvenile Greater Scaup very
similar to Tufted Duck, but generally paler above; white wing stripe
shorter, less bold; female has white feathering at base of bill;
juvenile has no feathering and much less contrast between back and
flanks. Juvenile Lesser Scaup has head slightly more peaked and
shorter wing stripe in flight. Both scaup have narrower black tip to
bill and lack white undertail coverts.

Range
Regular in small numbers in Alaska, especially on outer islands; not
known to breed there. Very rare but regular in winter along Pacific
Coast south to southern California. Records on Atlantic Coast have
suspicious affinity to major urban areas, which suggests that most, if
not all, East Coast records are of escaped or released aviary birds; 1
unimpeachable Atlantic Coast record from St. John's,
Newfoundland, in January 1982. Abundant in Europe and Asia.
Peter D. Vickery

Greater Scaup

Aythya marila
In late fall and winter, large rafts of Greater Scaup, commonly
called "Bluebills," can be seen diving for mollusks in open bays and
harbors and on large unfrozen lakes. Flocks numbering in the
thousands may also occur on the open ocean well beyond the
breakers. Greater Scaup generally prefer more open marine
environments; their close relatives, the Lesser Scaup, are more
likely to be found wintering on less saline, brackish bays. As is well
known, the 2 scaup species are very similar and require experience
and favorable conditions for reliable identification.

Description
15–20″ (38–51 cm). The male Greater Scaup has a blackish head, a
black chest, and a brownish-black tail and rump. Its gray mantle is
usually paler than the Lesser's; it has a white abdomen and white
flanks that are usually unmarked. The bill is pale blue with a black
tip; the eyes are bright yellow, and there is typically a greenish
sheen to the head. The most useful and consistent field mark for

Female
1. *Rounded head, sometimes with crest.*
2. *Dark back contrasting with paler flanks.*
3. *Gray bill with dark tip.*

Male with crest
1. *Wispy crest on back of black head.*
2. *Black back.*
3. *White flanks.*

Female
1. *Rounded brown head with large white patch at base of bill.*
2. *Pale blue bill.*
3. *Dark brown back.*
4. *Gray-brown flanks.*

identifying these birds on the water is the distinctive shape of the head: the Greater Scaup has a rounded or slightly flat-topped profile, while that of the Lesser is more pointed toward the rear of the crown. Females have dark brown upperparts, gray-brown breasts and flanks, and white abdomens. In winter, females have well-defined and often extensive patches of prominent white feathers at the base of the bill that usually meet on the forehead. This white feathering is absent or much reduced in juvenile scaup. Summer females often lose these feather patches, and a white crescent develops on the ear coverts; many West Coast birds may retain this crescent year-round. The female's eye is a dull dark yellow. As with the male, the head shape of the female is distinctive. In flight, Greater Scaup of both sexes have a white wing stripe extending through the speculum and most of the primaries.

Voice
Courting male: soft coos, whistles, and purring notes; female: harsh, growling *kerr*. Usually silent in winter, although flocks occasionally break into chorus of odd *scaup* calls.

Similar Species
Ring-necked Duck has different head shape, darker mantle, obviously ringed bill, and white blaze on sides. Female Ring-necked has white eye-ring, eyeline and different head profile. Male Tufted Duck black-backed, plumed. Female Redhead lacks distinct white patches about bill; has pale streak behind eye, pale chin, and dark eye. See Lesser Scaup.

Range
In North America, breeds on tundra and forested ponds from Alaska through central Canada to Hudson Bay, sparingly east to Magdalen Islands. Winters on Pacific Coast from Aleutian Islands south to northern California, infrequently farther south. On Atlantic, from Canadian Maritimes south to Florida (a few) and along Gulf Coast. Sometimes winters inland on large lakes and rivers. Also breeds in Far North in both New and Old worlds.   *Peter D. Vickery*

Lesser Scaup

Aythya affinis
Unlike the Greater Scaup, the Lesser is strictly a New World species. It is believed to be either an offshoot of its larger circumpolar relative, or perhaps a descendant from a common ancestor. The 2 species do not occupy the same breeding habitat, however; nor do they share a common wintering range, although there is some overlap. Lesser Scaup are very much birds of the Canadian prairies, where they commonly breed on small ponds, marshes, and sloughs. They are late nesters; their young do not hatch until early July, and they are among the last waterfowl to migrate south. In winter, Lesser Scaup are abundant on protected harbors and in brackish bays.

Description
15–18″ (38–45.5 cm). Like the Greater Scaup, the male Lesser Scaup has a blackish head, black chest, and brownish-black tail and rump. Its gray mantle is usually somewhat darker than the Greater's, and it has more obvious vermiculations on its white flanks. The abdomen

Birds in flight

1. *Long white wing stripe.*

Usually in flocks. Often in large rafts in winter.

Breeding male

1. *Rounded head.*
2. *Black chest.*
3. *Black rump.*
4. *Gray back.*
5. *Pale blue bill with dark tip.*

Breeding male

1. *Pale blue bill with black tip.*
2. *Peaked head.*
3. *Black chest.*
4. *Black rump.*
5. *Pale gray back.*
6. *Short white wing stripe.*

is white; the bill is pale blue with a black tip, and the eyes are bright
yellow. The Lesser Scaup more often has a purplish sheen to the
head, rather than the greenish lights of the Greater; however, this
characteristic is variable and of limited value in the field. The head
of the Lesser is pointed toward the rear of the crown, in a manner
that suggests the exaggerated profile of the Ring-necked Duck.
The female has dark brown upperparts, a gray-brown breast and
flanks, and a white abdomen. In winter, the female develops white
facial patches at the base of the bill; these often meet at the
forehead, but they are not usually as prominent as in the Greater
Scaup. Juveniles lack or have diminished white feathering at the
base of the bill. In summer, the female's facial patches sometimes
disappear, and a white crescent may develop on the ear coverts. The
female's eye is a dull dark yellow. In flight, both sexes show a white
wing stripe on the speculum, and dull dark gray primaries.

Voice
Courting males: a soft *whee-ooo.* Can utter loud whistles, deep
scolding notes, and loud *scaup* calls when alarmed. Generally silent
in winter.

Similar Species
Male Greater Scaup larger, has usually unmarked white flanks; head
rounded or flat-topped, not pointed; bill wider, with longer nail; may
have more greenish gloss to head. Female has more extensive white
feathering at base of bill; may appear slightly rust-brown. Both
sexes of Greater have white wing stripe through speculum and most
of primaries. Ring-necked Duck has more exaggerated profile,
darker mantle, white ring on bill, and white blaze on flank; female
Ring-necked has white eye-ring and eyeline, and different profile.
Female Redhead lacks white patches about bill; has pale streak
behind eye, pale chin, and dark eye.

Range
Breeds from central Alaska east through Canada to Hudson Bay,
and south locally to Colorado, Nebraska, the Dakotas, and western
Minnesota; rarely farther east. Winters along Pacific Coast from
British Columbia south through California and Central America; on
Atlantic Coast from southern New England to Florida, Gulf Coast,
West Indies, and South America.   *Peter D. Vickery*

Common Eider

Somateria mollissima
This large, heavy sea duck is common in winter along much of the
northern Atlantic Coast and in coastal Alaska. In fall, very large
flocks gather in favorite feeding areas, where one can sometimes see
several thousand birds diving for mussels or simply rafting together.
Long lines of these heavy eiders can frequently be observed flying
low over the ocean; the flight is slow and steady, occasionally
interspersed with short glides. Common Eiders typically hold their
bills pointing down toward the water; King Eiders generally keep
their bills parallel to the water.

Description
23–27" (58.5–68.5 cm). Adult males are easily recognized by their
white upperparts, black flanks, and black crown extending below the
eye. The rear of the crown is divided by a thin, white median stripe.
The nape and ear coverts are a pale lime-green color. The breast
sometimes has a rose-pink blush. A white flank spot just before the
tail interrupts the black flank. The bill is yellow-green in most races;

Eclipse male
1. *Pale blue bill with black tip.*
2. *Dark head with trace of white at base of bill.*
3. *Mottled breast.*
4. *Dark back.*

Female
1. *Pale blue bill with dark tip.*
2. *Peaked brown head with small white patch at base of bill.*
3. *Dark brown back.*
4. *Gray-brown flanks.*

Female
1. *Rich brown plumage.*
2. *Barred flanks.*
3. *Long, sloping forehead.*

   Large size.
   Heavy build.

the bare frontal shield that extends up the forehead is pointed in the
northern race (*S. m. borealis*) and rounded in the abundant eastern
race (*S. m. dresseri*). The Pacific race (*S. m. v-nigra*), sometimes
considered a separate species, has a bright orange bill with a black
V on the chin. Female Common Eiders are typically rich brown; the
flanks are barred with linear (rather than crescent-shaped) streaks,
and the crown is darker; however, color can vary considerably, and
some females appear pale gray, sandy gray, or nearly black. In all
variations, the distinctive head shape with the long, sloping bill is
diagnostic. The immature male develops a white breast in its first
winter, and may superficially resemble a King Eider. Males in
eclipse plumage are generally dark-bodied except for the white wing
patches.

dresseri

v-nigra

borealis

Voice
Male: a long, hollow moan, a soft pigeon-like coo, and *kor-kor-kor*
notes; female: harsh croaks, groans, and quacks.

Similar Species
Female and immature King Eiders have steeper forehead, shorter
bill, and usually hold bill parallel to water; females have crescent-
shaped marks on flanks. American Black Duck has different bill
shape, white wing linings, lacks barring on flanks. In Alaska, see
Spectacled Eider.

Range
In North America, nests near salt water from western Alaska across
Canada, Maritimes, and Newfoundland south through Maine;
recently to northern Massachusetts. Pacific populations winter from
Aleutian Islands south, rarely to British Columbia. Atlantic birds
winter from Labrador and Newfoundland along New England coast
to Long Island; rarely farther south. Also in Eurasia.
Peter D. Vickery

King Eider

Somateria spectabilis
It is perhaps unfortunate for so many birders that the King Eider's
distribution is restricted to the Far North. In North America, these
birds have a breeding range limited to northern Alaska and Canada,
and a wintering range that reaches only a little farther south.
However, these birds can be great wanderers, and small numbers
occur regularly along the Atlantic Coast and on the Great Lakes.
King Eiders are more likely to occur farther south than Common
Eiders, especially along the Pacific Coast. Finding a King Eider on a
frozen winter day provides one of the keenest pleasures for winter
birdwatchers.

Description
21–24″ (53.5–61 cm). Adult males are splendid, unmistakable birds
with black backs, soft blue-gray crowns, green cheeks, and a
distinctive orange bill shield. The modified scapulars or "sails" on
the back are a noteworthy field mark, and a prominent white flank
patch is obvious at considerable distances. The somewhat concave

— Common

King

Immature male

1. *Long, sloping forehead.*
2. *White breast.*
3. *Dark brown body.*

Usually found with adults.

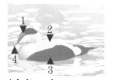

Adult male

1. *Long, sloping forehead and black crown.*
2. *White back.*
3. *Black flanks.*
4. *Usually holds bill pointed toward water.*

Large size.

Adult male

1. *Orange bill shield.*
2. *Black back.*
3. *White wing patch.*
4. *Usually holds bill parallel to surface of water.*

bill process, slightly humped forehead, and rounded crown give this species a unique profile that is apparent from some distance; head shape is the bird's most readily identifiable feature. Immature males in fall are dull brown to black and generally have a conspicuous yellow-orange to flesh-colored bill. Identification of female King Eiders requires close attention and favorable conditions; when mixed with a flock of Common Eiders, female Kings appear shorter, usually with a richer, rusty-brown body, and frequently with a tawny or gray head, especially about the chin and throat. First-winter females tend to be a richer orange-brown; older birds are more sandy-colored. At close range and under excellent conditions, it is possible to observe the dark, subterminal, crescent-shaped marks on the female King's flank feathers, which are quite different from the straighter barring of the female Common Eider.

Voice
Male: a low, dovelike, cooing call; female: hoarse croaks.

Similar Species
Adult male unmistakable. Immature male usually has orange bill; useful for identification of Atlantic Coast birds, but may not separate species from immature male Common Eiders of Pacific race. Slightly concave profile of bill, "bumped" front, and rounded crown are most useful diagnostic characteristics. Head of both sexes generally held higher than Common Eider's. Female Common Eider has linear streaks on flanks. Black Duck lacks flank marks and has different head shape. See female Steller's Eider.

Range
In North America, breeds in northern Alaska and arctic Canada south along Hudson Bay. Winters on Bering Sea and Aleutian Islands, casually south to Washington and California; uncommon on Atlantic Coast from Labrador to Long Island, and rarely south to Florida. Sometimes found inland on Great Lakes and elsewhere; most likely eider to be found on fresh water. Also in Eurasia.
Peter D. Vickery

Spectacled Eider

Somateria fischeri
A large marine duck, the Spectacled is the rarest of the eiders. Named for its peculiar facial feathering, which resembles large spectacles about the eyes, this eider breeds on the coastal plains of the Bering Sea and the Arctic Ocean, usually nesting in tall grass near standing water. This is one of the last species of North American breeding birds whose winter range is an uncertainty.

Description
21–22" (53.5–56 cm). The drake is distinctively marked; it is black from well up on the breast to the undertail, white above, and has an apple-green head. Conspicuous, white, circular spectacles outlined with a thin black line surround the eyes. The facial feathering covers the base of the orange bill to the nostrils. In flight, the drake is black below and white above. The female is mostly barred with dark brown and tawny-buff, and has a pale, unmarked buff throat and fairly well-defined spectacles. The female's bill is small and dark gray, covered to the nostril with feathers. The head profile is similar

Immature male
1. *Dull brown or blackish plumage.*
2. *Bright yellow-orange bill.*

Female
1. *Forehead profile steeper than Common Eider's.*
2. *Crescent-shaped marks on flanks.*

Female
1. *Sloping forehead with feathers extending over base of bill.*
2. *Pale spectacles.*
3. *Tawny plumage.*

to that of the Common Eider, but the head is smaller and thinner and the bill appears shorter. First-year males in winter and spring have frosted heads, white spectacles, and a suggestion of the adult male's head patterning, but without the male's green coloring. The body of first-year males is whitish-buff above and dark brown below.

Voice
Rarely heard; utters a faint *hoo-hoo.*

Similar Species
Male Common Eider larger, with white breast and paler face and nape. Female Common and King eiders less tawny, lack spectacles, and show more of bill below feathering. First-year male Common and King show head and bill patterns suggesting adults'.

Range
Breeds from northeastern Siberia to Beaufort Sea and eastern Arctic Coast of Alaska, south to Yukon-Kuskokwim deltas of western Alaska, where largest breeding populations occur. Winter range largely unknown, but probably at sea along southern edge of Bering Sea pack ice.   *Theodore G. Tobish Jr.*

Steller's Eider

Polysticta stelleri
Called the "Little Eider" by Siberian explorers of the Bering Sea, Steller's is the smallest of the eiders—about the size of a Greater Scaup. It occurs in a limited range only slightly more extensive than that of the Spectacled Eider. When swimming, Steller's Eider often holds its tail erect and angled upward. Like other eiders, it has an elongated profile. These birds molt offshore in large rafts.

Description
18–19″ (45.5–48.5 cm). The adult male is mostly whitish on the head and back and on the sides as far as the water line. A chestnut tinge on the feathers of the chest and flanks blends into dark chestnut underparts as far as the undertail. The throat and back are black, and a small black spot can usually be seen on the side of the breast. At close range, 2 greenish patches are visible on the forehead and nape. Females are a very dark, rich brown, mottled but appearing uniform at a distance. The female's squarish head profile, large, unfeathered bill, and whitish area about the eyes are all distinctive. Both sexes have a purple speculum with white borders. First-year males are rarely encountered, but show an intermediate plumage between that of the male and the female, pale above but lacking any bright coloring.

Voice
Low, growling series of calls near nesting areas; usually silent rest of year.

Similar Species
Male Steller's Eider unmistakable. All other female eiders are larger, have clearly barred, paler plumage, feathering extending down on the bill, and more rounded heads; lack purple speculum. Female scoters blackish.

Range
Breeds locally on eastern Arctic Coast of Alaska and south to St. Lawrence Island and Yukon-Kuskokwim deltas; also in Arctic Siberia. Winters along southwest coast of Alaska to Aleutian Islands and Kodiak Island, base of Alaska Peninsula, and western Prince William Sound. Casual in northern coastal British Columbia. *Theodore G. Tobish Jr.*

Adult male
1. *Green head with white spectacles.*
2. *Black underparts extend farther forward than Common Eider's.*
3. *White back.*

Adult male
1. *White head.*
2. *Unfeathered bill.*
3. *Chestnut breast and underparts.*
4. *Black back.*

Small size.

Female
1. *Rich brown, mottled body, appearing uniform at distance.*
2. *Small head and blunt bill.*

Usually on salt water.
Dives frequently.

Harlequin Duck

Histrionicus histrionicus
The Harlequin Duck, with its boldly patterned face and body, is one
of the loveliest of North American waterfowl. Sometimes called
"Lords and Ladies," these small ducks winter along the outer ledges
of rugged coasts, enduring even the heaviest surf with grace and
ease. More numerous on the Pacific Coast, small flocks can be found
from Alaska to California frequenting rocky shores, jetties, log
booms, and exposed surf beaches. Harlequin Ducks are notably less
common along the Atlantic Coast; rarely they winter inland on large
lakes. They nest along fast-moving streams and rivers; like Dippers,
they are able to swim and walk underwater, foraging for caddisfly
larvae and other invertebrates. Their flight is fast and agile, with
many twists and turns; they usually fly low over the water.

Description
14–19″ (35.5–48.5 cm). Harlequin Ducks are small, short-billed,
dapper birds that ride the surf easily. At a distance, both sexes look
very dark on the water. Males are gray-blue with darker, slate-blue
heads. They have a conspicuous white, crescent-shaped patch at the
base of the bill that is connected to a chestnut stripe along the side
of the crown. There is a white ear patch and a white blaze along the
side of the neck. The chestnut flanks have a vertical white stripe
near the bend of the wing; an incomplete white collar circles the
base of the neck. The scapulars and inner secondaries are white. The
female is dark gray-brown with 3, or occasionally 2, white spots on
the head. A white patch bordering the chin sometimes overlaps onto
a second patch in front of the eye; a third, immaculate white spot is
prominent on the ear. Fall immatures resemble females; young
males assume adult plumage, except for their plain wings, as the
first winter progresses. In flight, Harlequins appear small and
notably long-tailed; they lack any obvious white on the wing.

Voice
A mouselike squeak, giving rise to colloquial name "Sea Mouse."
Male: a low whistle with 2 longer notes and descending trill; female:
sharp, whistled call of 1–4 notes.

Similar Species
Female Bufflehead plumper, with single, elongated white mark
behind eye, and white wing patch visible in flight. Female and
immature Surf Scoters larger, with very different profile; facial
spots larger, less circular, less sharply defined. Female Oldsquaw
has more white on face.

Range
Breeds on turbulent streams and rivers from Alaska inland along
mountain streams to Alberta, rarely south to Colorado. In eastern
Canada from Baffin Island, Labrador, Newfoundland (rare) to Gaspé
Peninsula. Winters abundantly in Aleutian Islands, regularly to
northern California, sparsely farther south; on Atlantic Coast from
Labrador south uncommonly to New England and Long Island;
rarely south to Virginia and Maryland. Casual to Florida; rare on
inland lakes. Also breeds in Iceland and eastern Siberia.
Peter D. Vickery

Breeding male
Slate-blue head with white crescent at base of bill and white spots on sides of head. Gray-blue body. Chestnut flanks. White stripes on back visible in flight.

Molting male
Dark gray head with white crescent at base of bill. Trace of white breastband. White pattern in wings.

Female
Dark gray-brown head with two or three white spots. Dark gray-brown body.

Found on swift streams or in surf near rocks. Small size.

Oldsquaw

Clangula hyemalis
The Oldsquaw, aptly called the "Long-tailed Duck" in Britain, breeds on Arctic tundra, but is most frequently observed along both coasts during the winter. In early spring, males become increasingly vocal, emitting an odd, musical call. As courting activity intensifies, flocks spring into flight, dashing about madly before abruptly splashing back down into the water. Unlike most ducks, Oldsquaws have distinct breeding and winter plumages.

Description
16–21″ (40.5–53.5 cm). Only male Oldsquaws have the characteristic long central tail feathers. Males in breeding plumage are largely dark brown with prominent white cheeks, flanks, and undertail coverts. Breeding females are largely gray-brown with a less sharply defined facial pattern and a pale, off-white area on the side of the neck. There is considerable plumage variation during molt. Males in winter plumage are pale with a white neck, crown, and rump; the buff-gray facial patch extends over the bill and becomes dark brown on the upper neck. The flanks, scapulars, and upper back are pale gray; the chest, lower back, and long tail feathers are dark brown. The short black bill has a pinkish-orange transverse stripe. Winter females are browner above with pale flanks and a distinct facial pattern. Both sexes have plain, dark wings in flight.

Breeding male

Voice
During courtship, *poorh-poordle-ooh*, easily recognized even when bird is out of sight.

Similar Species
Male Oldsquaw unmistakable. Female Harlequin Duck smaller and darker than female Oldsquaw, with 3 (occasionally 2) facial spots.

Range
Breeds on coastal tundra ponds from Alaska and northern Canada to Hudson Bay and Labrador. Winters on Pacific from Alaska to Washington and Oregon, uncommonly farther south; on Atlantic Coast from Labrador to South Carolina; less frequently to Gulf Coast. Occasionally winters on deep open lakes, especially Great Lakes. Very rare transient in interior western states. Also in Eurasia.   *Peter D. Vickery*

Black Scoter

Melanitta nigra
Known as the "Butterbill" because of the large orange knob at the base of its bill, the Black Scoter is the smallest and least abundant of the 3 scoters. In the East, it is the first scoter to migrate south in the fall and the last to fly north in spring, often lingering well into May. Interestingly, nonbreeding first-year birds summer south of the breeding range in larger numbers than the other 2 more numerous scoters. Black Scoters gather at traditional, somewhat local feeding areas, where they are quite numerous; they may be infrequent elsewhere.

Female

Description
17–21″ (43–53.5 cm). The Black Scoter carries its distinctive, round head high, holding the bill parallel to the water. Adult males are black and have an orange knob, or process, on the bill. Females and juveniles are dark brown; they have obviously paler cheeks that contrast sharply with the blackish crown and nape. Young males become black and develop a yellowish bill process during their first

Immature male

Winter female
1. *White head with dark patches.*
2. *Short bill.*
3. *All-dark upperparts.*

Winter male
1. *White head with dark patches.*
2. *Bold black-and-white back pattern.*
3. *Long, thin black tail feathers.*
4. *Wings dark in flight.*

Female
1. *Dark bill and head with pale cheeks.*
2. *Dark body.*

   Silvery wing linings visible in flight.

winter. In flight, the undersurface of the Black Scoter's flight
feathers is silvery and contrasts with the darker wing linings.

Voice
More vocal than other scoters. Male: a melodious whistle, also
plaintive *coar-loo*, similar to curlew's call; female: a hoarse croak.

Similar Species
See White-winged Scoter. Winter Ruddy Duck, sometimes confused
with female Black Scoter, has pale flanks, brighter cheek patch;
female Ruddy has dark stripe across cheek, generally occupies
freshwater habitat.

Range
Circumpolar; in North America breeds irregularly from western
Alaska to Newfoundland. Winters from Aleutian Islands to southern
California, and from Newfoundland to South Carolina; a few to
Florida. Rare on Gulf Coast and large lakes inland.
Peter D. Vickery

Surf Scoter

Melanitta perspicillata
As the name suggests, Surf Scoters—or "Skunk-heads" as they are
frequently called—are often found diving for shellfish in the rolling
breakers along our coastal beaches. Both Surf and White-winged
scoters share a similar diving technique in which the inner wing is
extended and contracted in a modified underwater "flight." Unlike
the other 2 scoters, Surfs are limited to the New World, although
vagrants have occurred in Europe.

Description
17–21″ (43–53.5 cm). Surf Scoters are large-headed birds that
typically hold their bills at an angle to the water. The species
characteristically alights on the water, holding the wings extended
up over the back. Adult males are black with a prominent white
nape patch, a smaller white patch on the forehead, and a large, very
bright, multicolored bill that extends onto the side of the face. Adult
females are dark brown and usually show 2 distinct whitish facial
patches and a dull whitish nape patch; the latter is often difficult to
see. Females have large, swollen bills and a flat profile that suggests
a Common Eider. Juveniles have 2 white face spots, pale breasts,
and lack the white nape. In their first winter, immature birds begin
to display sexual dimorphism: young males become blacker,
acquiring some bill color; they develop the white nape, but not the
frontal patch.

Immature male

Voice
Generally silent; during mating season utters low whistles and
guttural croaks.

Similar Species
See White-winged Scoter.

Range
Breeds near freshwater ponds from western Alaska to Labrador.
Winters on Pacific from Aleutian Islands to southern California and
northern Mexico, on Atlantic from southern Newfoundland to
Florida and occasionally Gulf Coast. Small numbers winter on Great
Lakes.   *Peter D. Vickery*

Adult male
1. *Orange bill process.*
2. *Rounded head.*
3. *Solid black plumage.*
4. *No white in wings.*

Silvery wing linings visible in flight.

Adult male
1. *White patches on black head.*
2. *Brightly colored bill.*
3. *Solid black plumage.*
4. *No white in wings.*

Female
1. *Large bill.*
2. *Pale spots on sides of dark head.*
3. *Dark brown body.*

Shows no white in wings.

White-winged Scoter

Melanitta fusca
These scoters are common in winter along both coasts. In migration,
long lines of these heavy birds fly low over the water, their white
speculums distinctive. Called the "Velvet" Scoter in Europe.

Description
19–24″ (48.5–61 cm). The largest of the scoters, the White-winged is
a short-necked, heavy-headed bird. Adult males are black with a
small white crescent rising up from below and behind the eye. The
reddish-orange bill has a white ridge and a pronounced black knob
on the upper mandible; it is generally held pointed downward. Black
feathering on the bill extends almost to the nostril, making the bill
less obvious than in the Surf Scoter. Females are dark brown with
obvious white secondaries; they usually have 2 obscure white facial
patches, 1 on the ear and the other before the eye. The bill is dark
and the head profile is somewhat concave. Both sexes show a white
speculum in flight. In the fall, juveniles are dark brown with a pale
abdomen, a white speculum, and conspicuous white facial spots. In
winter, immatures begin to show sexual dimorphism, and the facial
patches become obscure. Young males acquire some color on the bill.

Voice
A low bell-like whistle; also a hoarse or guttural, rattling croak.

Similar Species
Male Surfs have obvious white front and nape patches and more
prominent bill. Male Black Scoters smaller, have bright orange bill
process and lack any white on head. Black Scoters carry bills
parallel to water. Female Surfs generally, but not always, have
more prominent white facial patches than female White-wings; adult
female Surfs have dull whitish nape patch, not easily seen. Surf's
head profile flatter, less concave; bill swollen at base, extending
farther onto face. In flight, White-winged shows white speculum.

Range
Breeds from Alaska to western Ontario, possibly farther east, south
to northern Washington and northern North Dakota. Winters on
Pacific from Aleutian Islands to Baja, California; on Atlantic from
southern Newfoundland to South Carolina; infrequently on Great
Lakes, rarely on Gulf Coast. Also in Eurasia.   *Peter D. Vickery*

Common Goldeneye

Bucephala clangula
Migrating late in the fall and early in the spring, the Common
Goldeneye is often identified by the whistling of its rapidly beating
wings—this sound gives rise to the bird's common nickname, the
"Whistler." Common Goldeneyes winter as far north as open water
and animal food supply permit. They are most common on coastal
bays and the Great Lakes; elsewhere they frequent large lakes,
impoundments, and rivers. They fly fast in small, compact flocks,
their chunky bodies distinguishing them from mergansers.

Description
16–20″ (40.5–51 cm). Common Goldeneyes are large, compact ducks.
The adult male is a study in black and white; its most noticeable
feature is a knobby, blackish-green head with a white circular patch
between the eye and bill. The black back appears to merge with the
head, but when the head is raised, a white neck becomes evident.
The belly and sides are white. Both sexes have black wings with a
large white patch that extends almost across the base. The female

Immature female
1. *Long bill.*
2. *Pale spots on sides of dark head.*
3. *Dark brown body.*

Shows white speculum on wing.

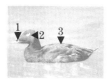

Adult male
1. *Reddish-orange bill with black knob at base.*
2. *Small white mark behind eye.*
3. *Black body.*
4. *White speculum on wing.*

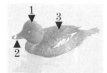

Female
1. *Brown head.*
2. *Dark bill with small yellowish patch.*
3. *Grayish back and sides.*

has a brown head, a grayish back and sides, and a white breast and belly. Juveniles and males in eclipse plumage resemble females.

Voice
During courtship, male utters loud whistling call; otherwise silent.

Similar Species
Male Barrow's Goldeneye has purplish, longer head, smaller white wing patch, crescent-shaped white facial spot, more black on sides; female darker overall, with chocolate-brown, elongated head; has darker breastband, less white in folded wing. Juveniles nearly identical. Barrow's shows smaller, stubbier bill in all plumages, Bufflehead smaller; male has large white patch on puffy, rounded head; female has elongated white facial mark. Mergansers more elongate with slender bills.

Range
Breeds largely in coniferous forest country of Alaska, Canada, and northern United States. Winters in small numbers throughout continental United States, mostly in northern half; less numerous farther south in West. Also in Old World.   *Frank C. Bellrose*

Barrow's Goldeneye

Bucephala islandica
Barrow's Goldeneye may be seen infrequently in winter on the Pacific Coast from Alaska to San Francisco Bay, and on the Atlantic Coast from the Gulf of St. Lawrence to Long Island. It is accidental elsewhere at that season. Like the Common Goldeneye, Barrow's can be identified by the whistling of its wings in flight.

Description
16–20″ (40.5–51 cm). Like the male Common Goldeneye, the male Barrow's has contrasting black-and-white plumage. The adult male Barrow's has a white crescent-shaped cheek patch on the purplish head that is somewhat elongated by the long nape feathers. There is a white patch on each wing, smaller than in the Common as a result of more black covert feathers near the leading edge. Female and juvenile Barrow's have a dark brown head with a puffy hindcrown, white chest, breast, and belly; the bill is yellow to pinkish-orange, subject to seasonal change.

Voice
Mewing and grunting notes given during courtship; otherwise silent.

Similar Species
Male Common Goldeneye has greenish head, larger white wing patch; female has paler brown, more elliptical head and less yellow in bill. Juveniles almost indistinguishable.

Range
Two populations: larger, in West, breeds in mountains from Alaska south to Oregon and southern Wyoming. Winters mainly along Pacific Coast south to San Francisco Bay area; small numbers winter on mountain streams in Northwest. Small eastern population breeds on northeast coast of Labrador. Fairly large numbers winter in certain spots in New Brunswick and Prince Edward Island; small numbers observed in winter off New England coast and inland; rarely south to Long Island. A few records on Great Lakes; regular in small numbers on Colorado River in Nevada and Arizona (winter); elsewhere casual or accidental.   *Frank C. Bellrose*

Adult male
1. Glossy green head with round white spot at base of bill.
2. White sides.
3. Black back.

Wings whistle in flight.

Adult male
1. Glossy purple head with crescent-shaped white spot at base of bill.
2. Less white on sides than in Common Goldeneye.
3. White wing patch smaller than Common Goldeneye's.

Female
1. Brown head.
2. More yellow or orange on bill than on Common Goldeneye's.
3. Darker body than Common Goldeneye's.

Bufflehead

Bucephala albeola

The sprightly little Bufflehead, known to many as the "Butterball," is the smallest of North American waterfowl. It nests along forested lakes, in holes excavated by flickers and other large woodpeckers. Buffleheads are most frequently encountered in winter, as small flocks sport about protected bays, harbors, and ice-free lakes. They are generally quite tame, and have a spirited disposition. Their flight is very fast with rapid wingbeats.

Description
13–15½" (33–39.5 cm). The large-headed, small-bodied profile of this species is distinctive. Adult males are easily recognized by their iridescent dark heads with a broad, triangular white patch extending across the nape and rear of the crown. The neck and underparts are white; the back and rump are black. Males in flight have a prominent white wing patch occupying most of the inner wing. The female has a dark gray-brown head and neck, with an oval white cheek patch extending backward from just below and behind the eye. The female's upperparts are dark brown; the underparts are largely gray, except for a white chest and belly. In flight, the white wing patch is restricted to the secondaries.

Voice
Male: a squeaky whistle and low guttural note; female: a hoarse croak or quack.

Similar Species
Male unmistakable. Female Harlequin Duck has 3 more or less round white face patches. Male Hooded Merganser has somewhat similar face pattern, but longer bill and brownish flanks. See Common Goldeneye.

Range
In West, breeds from southern Alaska through forested regions of Canada, east to Ontario and western Quebec, south rarely to northern California, northern Wyoming, and northern North Dakota. Winters on Pacific from Aleutian Islands to coast of Mexico; on Atlantic from southern Newfoundland (rare) to Florida and Gulf Coast. Regular in winter on fresh water as far north as Great Lakes.   *Peter D. Vickery*

Smew

Mergellus albellus

The Smew is a rare vagrant to our area from Siberia and possibly northern Europe. In recent years, small numbers of this small, beautiful merganser have been found annually, especially in fall and winter, off the western and central Aleutian Islands of Alaska. While the Smew is accidental elsewhere, several winter records for British Columbia, Washington, and most recently California may suggest a developing pattern along the Pacific Coast. Farther east, the Smew is extremely rare, but has been seen in Ontario, Quebec, New York, and Rhode Island. Like the Hooded Merganser and Common Goldeneye, the Smew nests in tree cavities along streams and ponds; in winter it prefers fresh water or brackish inlets.

Description
14–16" (35.5–40.5 cm). Smews are very small ducks with a shorter, somewhat stouter bill and a comparatively larger, puffier head than other mergansers. Males in breeding plumage appear very white; the bleached-looking head is accented with a black spot at the base

Female
1. *Dark head with long white cheek patch.*
2. *Dark upperparts.*
3. *White speculum.*

Small size.

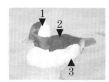

Adult male
1. *Dark head with large white patch above and behind eye.*
2. *Black back.*
3. *White sides.*
4. *White speculum.*

Small size.

Adult male
1. *White head with black eye patch.*
2. *White crest with black stripe.*
3. *Two thin black bars on white side.*

Plumage mainly white.
Small size.

of the bill that encompasses the eye. The inconspicuous white crest, not always raised, is framed below with a black V-shaped blaze that meets at the nape. The black back and slightly vermiculated flanks, the 2 vertical black bars on the sides of the breast, and the horizontal black line (bordering a grayer one), all give the male a striking effect. Females have a dark gray body, a bright cinnamon-brown head, and a distinctly white lower cheek and neck; the female's breast and flanks are usually paler than the upperparts. Eclipse males resemble females, and have the same white cheeks, but have blacker upperparts and more prominent white upperwing coverts. Males in flight are black and white, with black wings interrupted by an extensively white bar across the inner wing. Females in flight are gray-bodied, brown-headed, and white-cheeked; they also have conspicuous white median secondary coverts.

Range
In North America, recorded in Alaska, British Columbia, Washington, California, Quebec, Ontario, New York, and Rhode Island. Rare spring transient in western Aleutians. Breeds and winters in Eurasia.   *Peter D. Vickery*

Hooded Merganser

Lophodytes cucullatus
Unlike the other mergansers, the handsome Hooded Merganser occurs exclusively in North America. Hooded Mergansers prefer to nest in tree cavities along secluded woodland ponds and streams.

Description
16–19″ (40.5–48.5 cm). This duck's small thin bill and crested head give it a distinct profile. Males in breeding plumage have a glossy black head with a neat, rounded crest and a prominent white head patch starting behind the eye. The crest is bordered in black on the rear edge; the white patch can expand or flatten dramatically. The male has a black bill and yellow eyes. The blackish-brown back contrasts with the rusty, faintly vermiculated flanks, which are separated from the white breast by 2 vertical black bars. The long tertials are white-striped and conspicuous. Females are dark with a grayish-brown head and a prominent rust-orange crest. The back is dull black; the flanks are brownish-gray, and the chin and throat are paler. The bill is orange near the base. Eclipse-plumage males resemble females but have heavier mottling about the head and neck. Juveniles have a diminished crest; immature males develop the white head patch during their first winter. In flight, these ducks look long-tailed; males are boldly black and white with a flashy wing pattern; females have restricted white secondary tips.

Voice
Courting male: strange, froglike *croooo;* also rolling, croaking note.

Similar Species
Female Wood Duck has bold, elongated eye-ring; iridescent blue inner wing in flight. See Bufflehead.

Range
Breeds from southern Alaska to Nova Scotia, south to Oregon and Idaho, east to Maine and Massachusetts. Infrequent and local breeder in Mississippi Valley and southeastern United States, excluding Florida; does not breed in Great Plains. Winters on fresh water from British Columbia and New England south to California, Texas, Florida, and northern Mexico. Scarce in Arizona, New Mexico, and Plains States.   *Peter D. Vickery*

Female
1. *Cinnamon-brown head with white cheek.*
2. *Gray upperparts.*

Small size.

Female
1. *Thin bill.*
2. *Orange-rust tinge to crest.*
3. *Dull black back.*
4. *Small white speculum.*

Slender build.

Adult male
1. *Thin bill.*
2. *White crest with thin black border.*
3. *Rusty flanks.*
4. *Black back.*

Slender build.

Common Merganser

Mergus merganser
These large, sleek ducks are usually found on streams, rivers, and
lakes. They are slow to take off as they patter across the water, but
their flight is strong, fast, and direct. Common Mergansers nest in
tree cavities and are among the earliest spring migrants.

Description
22–27″ (56–68.5 cm). All mergansers are easily identified by their
slim-billed, long, sleek profiles; Common Mergansers are the
largest. Adult males have a smooth, blackish head that appears
iridescent green at close range; the eye is dark. The long, straight
scarlet bill, with a serrated upper mandible, is usually held parallel
to the water and appears heavier and thicker at the base than that
of the Red-breasted. The nostril, visible at close range, is set nearly
halfway down the bill. The dark upperparts contrast sharply with
the extensively white, sometimes salmon-pink flanks and breast.
Females are gray, with a slightly crested, warm brown head, brown
neck, and a red bill. The brown upper neck and the white lower neck
and breast are sharply divided; the white chin is sharply defined
against the warm brown head. Males in flight flash an extensively
white inner wing; females have a white speculum.

Voice
Usually silent; sometimes low *qua-auk*, guttural calls, or hisses.

Similar Species
Male Red-breasted darker, with crest; has dark-speckled pink
breast and bright red eyes; in flight, appears dark-chested, with 2
dark bars separating white inner wing. Female Red-breast lacks
sharply defined white chin; may appear double-crested; in flight, has
smaller speculum with dark bar. Bill of both sexes slenderer,
thinner at base; nostril closer to base.

Range
Breeds from southern Alaska through central Canadian forests to
Newfoundland, south to northern California, Arizona, and New
Mexico, east to Wisconsin, Michigan, Connecticut; occasionally
farther south. Winters from Alaska to Newfoundland, south to
southern California, northern Mexico, and Florida. Also in Europe
and Asia.   *Peter D. Vickery*

Red-breasted Merganser

Mergus serrator
Unlike the larger Common Merganser, the Red-breast is completely
at home on salt water; in migration, it also occurs regularly on fresh
water. This species usually nests on the ground. Both mergansers
are called "Sawbills" for the serrated edge of the upper mandible.

Description
19–26″ (48.5–66 cm). Smaller and much darker than the male
Common Merganser, the male Red-breasted has a glossy, crested
(sometimes double-crested) greenish-black head, bright red eyes,
and a thin red bill that appears uniformly slim throughout its length.
The upperparts are dark; the flanks are pale gray with black
vermiculations. The salmon-pink breast has heavy black streaking
and may appear black at a distance. The conspicuous white collar,
incomplete on the back of the neck, is perhaps the species' most
prominent field mark when identifying individuals far offshore. The
female has a gray body and a bright, cinnamon-brown head which
often appears more obviously crested than the female Common

Adult male
1. *Thin red bill.*
2. *Glossy green head with dark eye and scanty crest.*
3. *White breast and sides.*
4. *Much white on back and wings.*

   Long, slender build.

Female
1. *Thin red bill.*
2. *Brown head with ragged crest.*
3. *Sharp border between brown head and white breast.*
4. *White speculum.*

   Long, slender build.

Adult male
1. *Thin red bill.*
2. *Glossy green head with crest and red eye.*
3. *Streaked pinkish breast.*
4. *Gray flanks.*
5. *Black back*

   Long, slender build.

Merganser's; the white breast merges gradually into the brown neck, and the pale chin fades smoothly into the dark cheek. In both sexes, the nostril is set close to the base of the slim bill. In flight, these birds have a long, slender profile. Males are dark-breasted; the white inner wing is divided by 2 noticeable black bars. Females show a restricted white speculum interrupted by a dark bar.

Voice
Generally silent; occasionally hoarse croaks. Courting males make catlike *yeow-yeow* calls.

Similar Species
See Common Merganser.

Range
Breeds from Alaska across northern Canada to Newfoundland, south to northern British Columbia, northern midwestern states to Maine; occasionally to coastal New Jersey. Winters from Aleutians to southern California and northern Mexico; from Newfoundland to Florida and Gulf Coast; also on Great Lakes. Widespread in Europe and Asia.   *Peter D. Vickery*

Ruddy Duck

Oxyura jamaicensis
The Ruddy Duck is the most common and widespread of North America's 2 species of "stiff-tails." These are small, chunky diving ducks with large, flat bills, short necks, and relatively long, stiff tails that are often held at an angle above the surface of the water. Except when they are courting, Ruddy Ducks seem sluggish or lethargic. Although their flight is rapid, with fast, whirring wingbeats, they fly rather infrequently, and have to patter over the surface of the water for some distance before becoming airborne. They nest on marshy lakes and ponds. Nonbreeding birds at all seasons gather in flocks on larger bodies of water. They tend not to mix freely with other species of ducks, although they sometimes associate with American Coots.

Description
15–16″ (38–40 cm). The Ruddy Duck's shape—stocky, short-necked, large-headed and with a long, stiff tail—is distinctive throughout the year. The adult male in breeding plumage (March to July) is bright ruddy brown, with pure white cheeks, a black cap and nape, and a bright powder-blue bill. The center of the lower breast, the belly, and the undertail coverts are white. In fall and winter, the ruddy brown of the adult male is replaced by gray, the cap and nape become duller, and the bill is gray. Females and immature Ruddy Ducks resemble winter males, except that the cheek is a duller off-white, crossed below the eye by a horizontal dark line that can be vague in some birds and lacking in young males by midwinter.

Voice
Silent most of year; utters a few low nasal sounds during breeding season.

Similar Species
Masked Duck (rare and local in Texas and Florida) similar in shape but smaller; shows white patch in secondaries in flight; breeding-plumage male has black mask on face and forecrown, heavy spotting on sides; females, nonbreeding males and immatures have blackish crown, buff eyebrow, dark eyeline, and dark horizontal stripe across cheek below eye. Female Black Scoter resembles winter-plumage male Ruddy Duck, but larger, darker-bodied, with proportionately smaller bill.

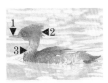

Female
1. *Thin red bill.*
2. *Brown head with ragged crest.*
3. *No sharp border between brown head and breast.*

Long, slender build.

Winter male
1. *Dark cap and white cheeks.*
2. *Grayish body.*
3. *Long tail.*

Small size. Chunky build and short neck.

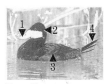

Breeding male
1. *Blue bill.*
2. *Black cap and white cheek.*
3. *Rufous body.*
4. *Long tail.*

Chunky build.

Range

Widespread breeder in western North America from northern
British Columbia and southern Northwest Territories east to
Manitoba and western Ontario, south to northern Mexico; scattered
nesting northwest to Alaska and east to New England; sporadic on
Long Island, New York, and in northern New Jersey. Winters
mainly along coast well south into Mexico and north to British
Columbia, Kansas, and New England: a few to Great Lakes;
northern limit of winter range varies depending on availability of
open water. Also resident in West Indies and South America.
Kenn Kaufman

Masked Duck

Oxyura dominica
Rare and irregular in its occurrences along our southern borders,
the Masked Duck—our second "stiff-tail"—is a species that we
know very little about. It frequents dense marshes, where it may
remain out of sight much of the time. On occasion, however, it is
found at the edge of open water, apparently undisturbed by the
presence of observers. It seems to be most active at dawn and dusk;
it takes flight more easily and perhaps more often than the Ruddy
Duck.

Description

12–14″ (30.5–35.5 cm). The Masked Duck resembles the Ruddy
Duck in shape but is smaller, with a smaller bill. Unlike the Ruddy,
it has a white patch on the secondaries; this feature is often
concealed when the bird is at rest. The adult male in breeding
plumage is mostly a rich ruddy brown. A black "mask" covers the
fore part of the face and crown, and there is heavy black spotting on
the sides and flanks; the bill is pale blue. The male in "winter
plumage" (which it wears about half the year, not necessarily in our
winter months) is medium brown, darker above, and heavily spotted
or scaled with blackish markings. It has a strong head pattern with
a blackish crown and buff eyebrow; the face has 2 horizontal streaks,
1 the blackish eyeline and the other a dark, horizontal stripe that
crosses the pale cheeks. The bill is gray. Females and immatures
resemble the winter-plumage male.

Similar Species

See Ruddy Duck.

Range

In United States, occurs irregularly in southern and eastern Texas
and has bred there; small numbers appear most winters in Florida.
Wanderers recorded in several states north to Wisconsin and
Massachusetts. Widespread in American tropics, including West
Indies.   *Kenn Kaufman*

Female
1. *Large bill.*
2. *Pale cheek crossed by dark line.*
3. *Long tail.*

Chunky build.

Female
1. *Blackish eyeline and dark line on cheek.*
2. *Brown body with blackish bars or spots.*

Small size.
Chunky build.
Very secretive.

Adult male
1. *Blue bill.*
2. *Black face patch.*
3. *Ruddy-brown plumage.*

Small size.
Chunky build.
Very secretive.

New World Vultures

(Family Cathartidae)
New world vultures are large, dark birds with long, broad wings and very obviously naked heads. Members of this group are exceptionally adept at soaring, with most species often soaring vast distances. Vultures are often seen in large numbers in the air, at a carcass, or at communal roosts. No family member is capable of true vocalizations. (World: 7 species. North America: 3 species.)
Scott B. Terrill

Black Vulture

Coragyps atratus
A large black raptor, stubby in all respects, the Black Vulture is a bird of the open skies. Its range is generally more southern than that of the Turkey Vulture, and it is less common in most areas where the 2 birds occur together. Much less skillful at soaring than the Turkey Vulture, the Black Vulture is more apt to soar in tight circular patterns, holding its wings more horizontally rather than in a shallow V. The Black Vulture often makes 4 to 5 quick wingbeats —as rapid as a crow's—between sails. This trait, together with its stubby build, makes it identifiable in the air at great distances.

Description
23–27″ (58.5–68.5 cm). The Black Vulture is black with a gray head and pale legs and feet. White patches at the base of the primaries are conspicuous in flight. This species appears less pin-headed than the Turkey Vulture; its wings are comparatively short, as is its squarish tail, which projects just slightly past the wings. All of these characteristics make for a much chunkier, stubbier, heavier appearance than the Turkey Vulture's.

Voice
Essentially silent; rarely utters hisses, grunts, or croaks.

Similar Species
See Turkey Vulture. Eagles soar on flat wings.

Range
Breeds from southern Arizona (but not California or New Mexico), most of Texas and Arkansas, lower Ohio River valley, southeastern Pennsylvania, and rarely southern New Jersey south to Mexico, Gulf of Mexico, and southern Florida. Range extending slightly northward; retreats from northern range limits in winter. Also in West Indies, Central and South America.   *Henry T. Armistead*

Black Vulture
Turkey Vulture
California Condor

In flight
1. *Short, broad wings with white at base of primaries.*
2. *Short, squarish tail.*

Flies with several rapid wingbeats between sails.

Perched
1. *Black plumage.*
2. *Naked gray head.*
3. *Pale legs and feet.*

Large size.

Turkey Vulture

Cathartes aura
The most common "buzzard" throughout most of its range, this
species is a large, long, blackish raptor almost the same size as an
eagle. Its lighter secondaries and primaries contrast strongly with
the bird's otherwise blackish appearance—so much so that these
wing feathers may appear whitish when seen from below in bright
light. It is usually seen soaring in search of carrion or perching on
utility poles and dead trees with wings spread. Turkey Vultures
may also be observed roosting in tall woods, or at road kills along
highways. They soar in loose groups or singly; like other large
raptors, they are much harder to find on windless or rainy days.
These birds have a tilting, tentative manner of soaring, and a slow,
deep, laborious flapping in calm air; they hold their wings in a
shallow V.

Description
26–32″ (66–81.5 cm). The Turkey Vulture is a large, blackish,
soaring raptor with a 6-foot wingspread, a naked, small-looking red
head, and a rather long tail. The adult's red head appears dark at
even fairly close range; immatures have a gray head. The light gray
secondaries and primaries contrast strongly with the bird's
otherwise blackish-brown plumage. The legs are dull orange. The
wing profile in flight is a very distinctive characteristic: the wings
are held in a shallow V, called a dihedral, with the outer primaries
separated. This bird often seems off balance when soaring; it tilts
and shifts as if suddenly bereft of supporting winds. Turkey Vulture
nestlings are white.

Voice
Usually silent; a grunt or hiss when disturbed.

Similar Species
Black Vulture chunkier, with stubby tail, shorter wings, and white
patches at base of primaries; flies with flatter wings, faster and more
shallow wingbeats. Black Vultures soar in tighter circles and when
in groups generally fly closer together than Turkey Vultures.
Immature Turkey Vulture has gray head like Black Vulture, but
flight posture different. Bald and Golden eagles hold wings
horizontally, not in V. Osprey has kink in wings when soaring. In
Southwest, see Zone-tailed Hawk.

Range
Breeds from southern British Columbia, Prairie Provinces, southern
Ontario, and northern New England south to Mexico, Gulf of
Mexico, and southern Florida. Uncommon in northern part of range,
but increasing and expanding there. Winters from central
California, southern Arizona, southern New Mexico, Texas,
southern Ohio River valley, and New Jersey south. Also breeds and
winters in West Indies and Central and South America.
Henry T. Armistead

In flight
1. *Long, narrow, blackish wings.*
2. *Pale flight feathers.*
3. *Long, narrow tail.*

Holds wings in shallow V.
Tilts while soaring.

Immature perched
1. *Black plumage.*
2. *Small, dark head.*

Adult
1. *Black plumage.*
2. *Naked red head.*

Slenderer in build than Black Vulture.

California Condor

Gymnogyps californianus
The largest land bird in North America, the California Condor is
mostly blackish in color, with a wingspan of up to 9 feet—twice the
size of the Turkey Vulture's wingspan. Condors are most often seen
soaring around mountain and ridge tops, or coasting high over
intervening valleys in the rugged chaparral- and pine-covered
mountains in a limited region of central and southern California.
Condors nest in caves or on rocky cliff ledges, and very rarely in
large, hollow trees. They roost on cliffs or in tall conifers in
mountainous regions, and spend much time preening and sunning
themselves; they take to the air only after the sun has been up for
several hours. This species feeds on carrion, often in the grass-
covered foothills adjacent to the high mountains. Formerly more
widespread in western North America, the California Condor has
markedly declined in numbers during the last century, and is now in
danger of extinction. Birds take 5 to 7 years to reach breeding age,
and in the wild, females lay only a single egg every other year. The
young condor is cared for by its parents for nearly a year and a half
after hatching. These birds are very sensitive to human disturbance,
and will abandon a roosting site or nesting place if frightened away
by intruders. The few remaining breeding areas are closed to the
public year-round; the best way to see a condor is to stand atop a
nearby mountain and wait for one of these rare birds to appear in
the sky.

Description
45–55″ (114.5–149.5 cm). The California Condor is unmistakable
when seen clearly. The adult is black with an unfeathered red and
orange head. It has a pale, narrow wing stripe above the
secondaries on the upper side of the wing, and a large, triangular
white patch on the wing linings. The immature is gray-headed until
the third or fourth year, with varying amounts of gray mottling on
the white wing linings; the upper wing stripe is often less
pronounced or absent. In level flight, condors sail in a very steady,
direct fashion, as if plowing through the air; the wings are held at a
slight angle above the horizontal. California Condors display a
characteristic wing movement during soaring flight in which the tips
are rapidly flexed downward and backward and then returned to the
original position in a single continuous movement.

Similar Species
Golden Eagle and Turkey Vulture smaller, with pale areas on
different parts of underwings. Golden Eagle has proportionately
larger head and slimmer body. Turkey Vulture has decidedly more
buoyant, tilting flight. Both have proportionately longer, slimmer
tails.

Range
Confined to California, in foothills and higher mountains of coastal
and inland ranges adjacent to southern portions of San Joaquin
Valley.   *John C. Ogden*

Immature in flight
1. *Broad wings with spread primaries.*
2. *Short tail.*
3. *Dark wing linings.*
4. *Dark head.*

Huge size. Soars with wings held horizontally.

Adult in flight
1. *Broad wings with spread primaries and white wing linings.*
2. *Short tail.*
3. *Reddish head.*

Huge size.

Adult perched
1. *Black plumage.*
2. *Whitish bar on upper wing.*
3. *Naked red and orange head.*

Huge size.

Hawks and Eagles

(Family Accipitridae)
Members of this large, diverse group of diurnal birds of prey range
widely in size, but all are excellent flyers. Raptors have powerful
bills with a strongly curved, sharply tipped upper mandible.
Members of this family generally have strong legs with long,
powerful talons for capturing prey. At the base of the bill there is a
rounded, membranous growth, known as the cere. In most groups,
the sexes are alike. The Osprey has long-toed, sharp-taloned feet
with shiny spicules on the pads. Kites have long, relatively narrow,
pointed wings and long tails; they are bouyant, swift, and agile in
flight. Harriers are elongate, long-winged, and long-tailed; they
often soar for long periods of time. Eagles are large with broad,
very long wings, large heads, and very large bills. Most species soar
extensively and flap only occasionally. Accipiters have short, very
rounded wings and long tails. They fly with rapid wingbeats and
varying amounts of gliding. Buteos have stout bodies and broad,
rounded wings; the tails are short and broad. (World: 218 species.
North America: 27 species.)   *Scott B. Terrill*

Osprey

Pandion haliaetus
The Osprey is a fairly large raptor, intermediate in size between
buteos and eagles. It feeds almost exclusively on live fish, and is
typically associated with water. However, when suitable nest sites
are unavailable near water, it may nest considerable distances
inland. Ospreys hunt from perches overlooking the water and while
hovering and gliding at moderate altitudes; when capturing fish,
they often submerge completely. Their large stick nests are
typically built in dead trees, but Ospreys are easily attracted to
artificial platforms and commonly nest on a variety of manmade
structures, including telephone poles, windmills, old duck blinds,
and channel markers.

Description
22–25″ (56–63.5 cm). The Osprey is brown to brownish-black above
and white below; it has brownish-black marks at the wrist, and buff
to brown speckling on the breast. The head is white with a dark
crown and a wide, dark brown eye stripe. Juveniles are similar to
adults, but have broad, buff edging on the back and more extensive
streaking below. In flight, Ospreys can be distinguished by the
white underparts and the pronounced crook in the long, narrow
wings, as well as by the blackish marks at the wrist.

Voice
Quite vocal, especially during nesting season. When alarmed, a
series of loud cries in succession: *kip kip kip kiweek kiweek*. During
courtship and about the nest, a variety of soft whistling and chirping
calls.

Similar Species
Subadult Bald Eagle similar in some plumages, but larger,
splotchier; lacks definite crook in wings in flight.

Range
Breeds from northwestern Alaska and north-central Canada south
to Baja California, Sonoran coast, and Gulf States. Winters from
southern United States south as far as Chile and Argentina.
Nonbreeding subadults (second-year birds) remain on wintering
grounds through northern summer.   *David L. Evans*

In flight
1. *Long wings with crook at wrist.*
2. *Black mark at wrist on wing linings.*

Adult perched
1. *White head with dark crown and eye stripe.*
2. *Dark brown upperparts.*

Usually found near water.

Hook-billed Kite

Chondrohierax uncinatus
"Kite" is a loosely applied term; the 5 North American kites all
belong to different genera and have different feeding habits, shapes,
and flight styles. Reaching our range only in southern Texas, the
Hook-billed feeds largely on land and tree snails, and thus has little
need for fancy aerial maneuvers. In flight, it proceeds with several
rapid, loose-jointed flaps, followed by a disproportionately slow,
unsteady glide.

Description
15–17″ (38–43 cm). In flight, the Hook-billed's silhouette is
distinctive: the long, oval wings are very rounded at the tips and
narrow at the bases; the tail is long and fanlike. Black-and-white
barring in the primaries is very conspicuous from below; the
underside of the tail has 2 wide whitish bands and a narrow white
tip separated by 2 wide black bands. The large, long-hooked bill is
often obvious. The cere and facial skin are green, and the eyes of
adults are whitish. The typical adult male is slate-gray on the back
and wings, blue-gray on the head, and finely barred with gray on the
underparts. The typical adult female is sooty brown on the back,
brownish-gray on the head, with a rufous collar crossing the nape
and rufous bands on the underparts. The immature has dark eyes
and a blackish cap and back separated by a white collar; the
underparts are mostly whitish, with some indistinct barring on the
sides. A black phase occurs farther south and could turn up in
Texas; it is entirely black except for some white barring in the outer
primaries and 1 broad white band across the center of the tail.

Voice
Musical whistle; harsh chatter when disturbed.

Similar Species
Gray Hawk has smaller bill, dark eyes, different flight silhouette;
lacks bold barring on outer primaries. Cooper's, Sharp-shinned,
Red-shouldered, and Broad-winged hawks also have reddish barring
on underparts but different flight silhouettes.

Range
Local permanent resident in extreme southern Texas, along Rio
Grande between Falcon Dam and Santa Ana National Wildlife
Refuge. Widespread in American tropics.   *Kenn Kaufman*

American Swallow-tailed Kite

Elanoides forficatus
This distinctive, graceful raptor has long pointed wings, a deeply
forked swallowlike tail, and striking color pattern. It is locally
common in forests near water; in migration it forms large flocks.

Description
20–25″ (51–63.5 cm). Unmistakable. The adult has a white head,
neck, underparts, and wing linings; the back, wings, and deeply
forked tail are black. Immatures have the pattern and color of the
adult, but are duller, with fine streaks on the head and breast.

Voice
A high-pitched alarm call: *eee-eee-eee*, *pee-pee-pee*, or *kee-kee-kee*;
a high-pitched hissing whistle; also several other calls.

Range
Breeds locally from Louisiana along Gulf Coast to Florida, and north
to coastal South Carolina; occasionally to Great Lakes and New
England. Winters south of our range.   *Paul W. Sykes, Jr.*

Adult male
1. *Large, long-hooked bill.*
2. *Blue-gray head.*
3. *Slate-gray back.*
4. *Fine gray bars on underparts.*

Adult female
1. *Large, long-hooked bill.*
2. *Sooty brown back.*
3. *Rufous collar.*
4. *Rufous bands on underparts.*
5. *Long, fan-shaped tail with 2 wide, pale bands.*

In flight
1. *Deeply forked black tail.*
2. *White wing linings.*
3. *White head and underparts.*

Graceful and swallowlike in flight.

Black-shouldered Kite

Elanus caeruleus
The Black-shouldered Kite is often found watching for rodent prey
from an exposed perch, usually in open country with scattered
groves of trees. It also hunts by flying at low to moderate heights
over fields, frequently pausing to hover on rapidly beating wings.
Slightly gull-like in appearance, this bird flies with languid, floppy
wingbeats, gliding with wings held above the horizontal and usually
angled slightly at the wrist. Once reduced in numbers almost to the
point of extinction in the United States, the Black-shouldered Kite
has made a major comeback.

Description
15–17″ (38–43 cm). The Black-shouldered Kite has long, pointed
wings, a long, square-tipped or slightly notched tail, a rounded
head, and a small bill. The adult has a white head and underparts,
pale gray back, and medium gray upperwings, with black lesser and
median coverts. The tail is white with pale gray central feathers,
but appears white from below. The underside of the wing is whitish,
with some gray showing through the flight feathers, and usually a
dark patch or smudge at the wrist. The eyes are red, the legs and
feet yellow. The immature is generally pale but has a rusty brown
chest, brown streaking on the head, heavy brown scaling on the
back, much blackish on the upperside of the wings, and a dark band
near the tip of the tail.

Voice
A rich, descending whistle, *teew*, sometimes repeated.

Similar Species
Mississippi Kite smaller, much darker in all plumages, with different
flight style. See adult male Northern Harrier.

Range
Widespread permanent resident in lowlands of California (except
desert regions) and southern Texas; winter resident and scarce
breeder in Oregon. Strays to adjacent states (apparently with
increasing frequency), also to Florida, Mississippi, and elsewhere.
Widespread in American tropics and warmer regions of Old World.
Kenn Kaufman

Snail Kite

Rostrhamus sociabilis
The Snail Kite is a wide-ranging species of the New World tropics
that barely reaches the United States. It is an uncommon bird in our
area, although it is abundant in other parts of its range. It is found
in freshwater marshes, where it hunts for the apple snail (*Pomacea
paludosa*), which under normal conditions is the bird's sole food. The
thin, sharply curved and pointed bill is well adapted for extracting
the mollusk from its shell. The flight is slow and buoyant; when
hunting on the wing, the Snail Kite executes tight, graceful turns on
broad, rounded wings that droop slightly at the tips. These highly
gregarious and somewhat nomadic birds are greatly affected by
drought or drainage of marshes.

Description
16–18″ (40.5–45.5 cm). The Snail Kite's tail in all plumages shows a
broad white patch at the base that is visible from above and below,
with a black subterminal band, and a narrow white to buff terminal
band; the basal white patch is visible at a considerable distance.

Immature
1. *Rust-brown streaks on white breast.*
2. *Whitish tail with dark band near tip.*

Adult
1. *Whitish head and body.*
2. *Black shoulder.*
3. *White tail.*
4. *Long, pointed wings.*
5. *Square-tipped tail.*

Slender build.

Female
1. *Strongly hooked, long, thin bill.*
2. *Brown upperparts.*
3. *Streaked breast.*

White at base of tail in flight. Broad, rounded wings.

When the bird is perched, the tips of the wings extend about half an inch beyond the tail. The adult male is slate-black, with black primaries and secondaries; the feet and base of the bill are orange or red. The adult female and immatures are brown above; they have a light eyebrow, white to buff underparts with heavy, brown streaks, and orange or yellow feet. Immatures generally cannot be distinguished from adult females in the field.

Voice
Alarm call a *kak-kak-kak-kak*, uttered in series. Other calls include *kor-ee-ee-a kor-ee-ee-a* and a bleating sound.

Similar Species
Female and immature Northern Harriers more slender; have longer, narrower, pointed wings; white patch on rump, not on tail; flight is more direct, with wings held in shallow V.

Range
Resident locally in southern Florida. Also in Cuba, and from eastern Mexico south to southern South America.   *Paul W. Sykes, Jr.*

Mississippi Kite

Ictinia mississippiensis
The Mississippi Kite flies like a giant Purple Martin; it glides and circles on flat wings, with only minor adjustments of wing and tail position for control, but it can put on sudden bursts of speed. This migrant insect-feeder tends to nest in loose colonies. Despite its name, it is most abundant on the southern Great Plains, where it nests in groups of tall trees next to open country.

Description
14″ (35.5 cm). This bird's shape is a good field mark: perched birds have very long wing tips, small, rounded heads, and small bills. In flight, the wing usually shows little or no angle at the wrist. The wing tips come to a blunt point, and the wings never appear very broad; the tail looks square-tipped or slightly notched, except when fully spread. The mostly gray adult is palest on the head, black on the tail, and has no strong pattern except on the upper wing, where the whitish secondaries contrast with the dark gray upperwing coverts and blackish primaries. From below, the wings are a smooth, smoky gray, darker at the tips and toward the trailing edges. The feet are dusky yellow; the eyes are red. The immature is blackish-brown above, streaked with brown below; its black tail has several pale bars visible from below. One-year-old birds resemble adults, but retain bars on the tail (and often some on the wing linings), and lack the whitish patch on the secondaries.

Voice
A thin whistle, usually 2-syllabled.

Similar Species
Soaring Peregrine Falcon has similar flight silhouette but falcons lack all-black tail and whitish patch on upper side of secondaries. Female and immature Merlin and Peregrine Falcon have patterned faces and barring on underside of primaries and secondaries.

Range
Common summer resident of southern Great Plains from Kansas to Texas; uncommon to fairly common in Southeast; locally as far north as Illinois and Carolinas and west to Colorado and Arizona. Has recently increased in numbers and expanded breeding range; strays have appeared in many areas. Winters in South America.
Kenn Kaufman

Adult male
1. *Strongly hooked red or orange bill.*
2. *Slate-black plumage.*
3. *Red or orange feet.*
4. *White patch at base of tail.*
5. *Broad, rounded wings.*

Adult
1. *Pale head.*
2. *Dark gray body and wings.*
3. *Black, square-tipped tail.*
4. *Long, pointed wings.*

   Graceful flight.

Immature
1. *Blackish-brown upperparts.*
2. *Streaks on underparts.*
3. *No strong facial pattern.*
4. *Bars in tail.*

Bald Eagle

Haliaeetus leucocephalus

Adult

Immature

Subadult

The Bald Eagle is a fish-eating bird of impressive size with long, broad wings and a large, strong bill. During the breeding season, it is closely associated with large bodies of water, which provide an abundant source of food. This species' large stick nests are typically built in supercanopy trees, but in the Aleutians, northern coastal regions, and other areas where suitable trees are scarce, the nests are placed on ridges, cliffs, and sea stacks. Bald Eagles usually hunt from perches adjacent to the water, but are also known to pursue their prey in flight. During the winter, major concentrations of these birds occur near dams, wildlife refuges, and other areas with ice-free water. In recent decades the Bald Eagle population has been badly reduced by pesticides, but the species is now making a moderate comeback.

Description
30–43″ (76–109 cm). Adults are light to chocolate-brown, with a white head and tail. Juvenal and subadult plumages are highly variable, ranging from brownish-black to light mottled tan, with white spotting and marbling on the wing linings and flight feathers. In general, the body becomes lighter with successive molts until the third or fourth year, when the typical adult plumage is attained.

Voice
Series of harsh, squeaky, metallic chitters and screams, sometimes interspersed with guttural, grunting sounds.

Similar Species
Juvenile Golden Eagles have well-defined areas of white on tail and wings; lack white or silver in wing linings; have smaller bill.

Range
Formerly bred throughout North America north of Mexico; centers of abundance remain in Alaska and Canada south of tree line, Washington, Oregon, northern Idaho, Great Lakes States, Maine, Chesapeake Bay, California, Arizona, and Florida. Southeastern populations move north in summer as far as Nova Scotia and New Brunswick. Bulk of northern population winters from southern Canada south along major river systems, Great Plains, and intermountain regions.   *David L. Evans*

Northern Harrier

Circus cyaneus

This species is the only North American representative of the harriers, a group of hawks more diversified in the Old World. It hunts primarily on the wing, quartering fields and marshes, covering up to 100 miles a day. Formerly called the Marsh Hawk, the Northern Harrier is a bird of marshlands, grasslands, and prairies; it preys on a variety of animals, which it regularly detects solely by means of its keen hearing. When hunting, this species is one of the most acrobatic and agile of North American raptors. During the breeding season, the male performs an elaborate courtship flight that consists of a series of U-shaped maneuvers, with a stall and wingover when the bird reaches the top of each "U." The Northern Harrier is commonly observed at concentration points of raptor migration, quite often in soaring flight. It nests on the ground in dense cover, or occasionally in deeper, more bulky nests built in shallow water. During the winter, the Northern Harrier sometimes roosts communally, occasionally in groups of as many as 80 or 90 birds.

Adult
1. *White head with large yellow bill.*
2. *White tail.*
3. *Dark brown body.*

Immature
1. *Dark brown body.*
2. *Heavy black bill.*
3. *Subadults show pale mottling on body and wings.*

Huge size.

Immature male
1. *Rich brown upperparts.*
2. *Rust-brown breast and belly.*

Shows white rump in flight.

Description
16–24″ (40.5–61 cm). This species is a slender-bodied hawk with a
long tail and wings, long slender yellow legs, distinct facial disks,
and a conspicuous white rump patch. In flight, the wings are
typically held in a shallow V. Adult males are pale gray on the head,
back, and wings; the tail is also gray, and crossed with 6 to 8 pale
gray-brown bands. The neck, throat, and upper breast are gray or
gray-brown, becoming paler gray to whitish on the lower breast and
belly. There is cinnamon or brown spotting on the legs and flanks;
the wing linings and undertail are white, the ends of the outer
primaries are black. The eyes are yellow. Adult females are
brownish on the head, back, and wings; the brownish tail is crossed
with 6 to 8 darker bands. The neck, throat, and breast are light
brown to cream-colored and streaked with darker brown. The belly
and wing linings are buff to cream-colored with cinnamon to
brownish streaks and spots; the ends of the outer primaries are
black. Eyes are brown, becoming mostly yellow by the third year.
Immatures are similar to adult females but richer brown above and
are smooth rust brown on the breast and belly in the fall. Immature
males have grayish eyes; females' eyes are dark brown.

Voice
Nest-alarm call a rapid, nasal, chattering *ke ke ke ke ke*.

Similar Species
Red-tailed and Rough-legged hawks larger, have broader wings and
proportionately shorter tails.

Range
Breeds from northern Alaska and Canada south to northern Baja
California, Mexico, and southern United States. Absent from
Southeast in summer. Winters from southern Canada to northern
South America; occasionally observed in Caribbean.
David L. Evans

Sharp-shinned Hawk

Accipiter striatus
Distinguishing among the 3 accipiter species—the Sharp-shinned
Hawk, Cooper's Hawk, and the Northern Goshawk—is one of the
most difficult problems in identification of North American raptors,
especially where the immatures are concerned. The accipiters are
sexually dimorphic with little or no overlap in size between the
sexes; this disparity is only slightly less than that among the
different species. Nonetheless, size and flight style remain among
the most reliable means of identification. The Sharp-shinned Hawk
is a shy, secretive woodland hawk that preys on small to medium-
size birds. During the breeding season it is found in coniferous and
mixed conifer-aspen-birch forests in the northern United States and
Canada, as well as in mountainous areas; it is less commonly seen in
other types of woodland in the United States. Large concentrations
of migrating birds occur in fall and spring along mountain ridges,
lake shores, and coasts; these formations provide updrafts and serve
as leading lines or barriers to migration. In migration and during
winter, these hawks occur in almost any type of habitat with trees

In flight
1. *White rump.*
2. *Narrow wings held in shallow V.*
3. *Long, narrow tail.*

Usually seen quartering over open country.

Adult male
1. *Pale gray head and upperparts.*
2. *Long, narrow tail.*

Slender build.

Immature
1. *Brownish upperparts.*
2. *Cream-colored underparts with streaks on breast, barring on flanks.*
3. *Long, narrow tail.*

or shrubs. They take their prey in sudden, swift attacks from
inconspicuous perches, or during fast, stealthy flights through the
woods.

Description
Male: 10–11½″ (25.5–29 cm); female: 12–13½″ (30.5–34.5 cm). A
small accipiter, the Sharp-shinned Hawk is characterized by long
narrow legs, short rounded wings, and a long tail crossed with 4
straight dark bands. Adults are dark blue-gray above; the
underparts are white, barred with rufous or cinnamon. The eyes are
yellow-orange to deep red, becoming redder with age. Immatures
are brownish above, often spotted with white on the mantle. The
underparts are cream-colored, with teardrop-shaped cinnamon or
brown streaks on the breast, diamonds or arrowheads on the
abdomen, and barring on the flanks. The eyes are pale yellow. In
flight, the head rarely extends beyond the wing line.

Voice
Nest defense call a high, shrill *kik kik kik kik*.

Similar Species
Of the 3 accipiters, Sharp-shinned Hawks most buoyant fliers, flap
wings fastest. Cooper's Hawk intermediate in this respect;
Goshawks, with highest wing loading, flap most slowly and appear
heaviest in flight. Accipiters exhibit number of subtle differences
among species; although these are variable and show some overlap,
they can often provide confirmation of identification under good
viewing conditions. See Cooper's Hawk and Northern Goshawk.

Range
Breeds from tree line in Alaska and Canada south to southern
United States; scarce in Southeast. Winters from British Columbia
and northern United States south to Panama, Gulf Coast, and
Bahamas.   *David L. Evans*

Cooper's Hawk

Accipiter cooperii
This accipiter is a secretive woodland hawk that preys on medium-
size birds and mammals, and, in the West, small reptiles. It occurs
in various types of mixed and deciduous forests and open woodlands
during breeding season. Cooper's can be commonly observed at
concentration points of raptor migration; in the East, it is less
common than the Sharp-shinned Hawk, but the 2 are roughly equal
in number in the Rockies and the West. Cooper's occurs in a wide
variety of habitats during migration and winter. It hunts in typical
accipitrine style, using available cover for concealment, or springing
from inconspicuous perches.

Description
Male: 15–17½″ (38–44.5 cm); female: 17–19½″ (43–49.5 cm). A
medium-size accipiter, Cooper's Hawk is characterized by short,
rounded wings, and a very long rounded tail; the tail is crossed by 4
dark straight bands and has a wide white terminal band. Adults are
dark blue-gray above, and white, barred with rufous or cinnamon

Immature

1. *Whitish spots on upperparts.*
2. *Long tail notched or squared at tip.*

Adult

1. *Dark blue-gray upperparts.*
2. *White underparts barred with rufous.*
3. *Tail notched or square at tip.*
4. *Rounded wings.*

Small size.

Adult

1. *Dark blue-gray upperparts.*
2. *Fine rufous bars on underparts.*
3. *Tail rounded at tip.*
4. *Rounded wings.*

Large size.

below. The eyes are yellow-orange to deep red, becoming redder with age. Immatures are brownish above, often spotted with white on the mantle, and white to cream-colored below, with cinnamon or brown streaks on the breast, abdomen, and flanks. The undertail coverts are usually unmarked. The eyes are pale yellow.

Voice
Nest-defense call a harsh, raspy *cac cac cac cac.*

Similar Species
Sharp-shinned Hawk has proportionately longer wings, appears shorter, with smaller head; in flight, head appears even with, or behind, leading edge of wings. Male Sharp-shin's tail more notched or square; female's slightly more rounded but not as obviously so as Cooper's. Immature Sharp-shin and immature Northern Goshawk more heavily streaked below; appear darker at a distance.

Range
Breeds in southern Canada and entire United States south to northwestern Mexico. Winters in central and southern United States, south to Costa Rica.   *David L. Evans*

Northern Goshawk

Accipiter gentilis
The Goshawk is the largest North American accipiter, inhabiting areas in the forested regions of Canada and the extreme northern United States, extending south into the Rocky Mountains and northern Appalachians. It hunts in typical accipitrine fashion, preying on birds and mammals as large as grouse, pheasants, ducks, and snowshoe hares. It is normally nonmigratory, remaining on the breeding range throughout the winter months; however, during the cyclical population lows of snowshoe hares and Ruffed Grouse that occur every 9 to 11 years, large numbers of Goshawks, most of them adults, move south in search of food. These irruptions may extend as far as the southern United States. During years when no irruption occurs, considerable numbers of juveniles—mostly males—are observed at northern concentration points of raptor migration. These movements which rarely bring the birds south of their usual breeding range, appear to be the result of a normal dispersal mechanism rather than a response to a reduction in the food supply.

Description
Male: 21–23½″ (53.5–59.5 cm); female 23–25½″ (58.5–65 cm). In its overall proportions, eye-color sequence, and plumage of the immature, the Goshawk is very similar to Cooper's and Sharp-shinned hawks. Adults are pale to dark blue-gray on the back, with a blackish cheek and crown, set off sharply by white eyebrows. The breast is whitish, with gray to gray-black barring; this is quite heavy in females, but appears finely vermiculated in older adult males. Younger adults, especially females, have wide, black shaft-streaking on the breast, which tends to obscure the barring. The tail is broad, moderately rounded, and crossed with 5 to 6 dark bands; these are much reduced in some older adults. The white terminal band on the tail is narrower than in Cooper's. The legs and feet are stockier than those of Cooper's or the Sharp-shinned, reflecting a greater dependence on mammalian prey. Immature Goshawks have a cream- to buff-colored eyebrow; this feature not particularly conspicuous in immature males. The undertail coverts are streaked or spotted.

Voice
Nest-defense call a loud, high-pitched (not raspy) *cac cac cac cac.*

Immature
1. *Brownish*
   upperparts.
2. *Whitish underparts*
   with fine streaks.
3. *Rounded tail.*
4. *Short, stocky legs.*

Large size.

Adult
1. *Blue-gray*
   upperparts.
2. *Whitish underparts*
   with gray barring.
3. *Bold white eyebrow.*
4. *Long tail.*

Large size.

In flight
1. *Rounded wings.*
2. *Long, banded tail.*
3. *Pale underparts.*

Large size.

Similar Species
Cooper's Hawk has proportionately longer, more rounded tail;
terminal band wider, dark barring of tail more even; undertail
coverts lack spotting or streaking; adult lacks white eyebrow. See
Sharp-shinned Hawk.

Range
Breeds in forested areas from tree line in Alaska and Canada south
through Cascades, Sierra Nevada, and in Rocky Mountains to
northwestern Mexico; east to Black Hills of South Dakota, northern
Great Lakes States, and northern Appalachian Mountains. Usually
winters on breeding range; may extend as far south as Gulf States
during periodic invasions related to food shortage.
David L. Evans

Common Black-Hawk

Buteogallus anthracinus
This local southwestern hawk is most often encountered along
perennial streams with extensive, mature riparian forests, upon
which it is entirely dependent. In flight, the adults are easily
identified by their primarily blackish plumage, wide wings, and
broad black tail crossed in the middle by a wide white band and
tipped with a narrow white line. Although it usually forages from
low perches over running water, the Common Black-Hawk is
frequently observed soaring on level wings high above its riverine
habitats.

Description
20–23″ (51–58.5 cm). The Common Black-Hawk is a stout, dark
raptor with very broad wings (caused by long secondaries) and a
short, broad tail. The entire plumage of the adult is blackish, except
for a broad white median band and a narrow white terminal band on
the tail. There is a small whitish area toward the base of the
primaries, but this area is not always visible. The cere and legs are
yellow; the lores are grayish to yellowish. The immature Common
Black-Hawk has dark brown to blackish-brown upperparts, with a
buff eyeline, a buff nape streaked or blotched with blackish, and a
dark malar stripe. The underparts are buff and are marked with
long, irregular black streaks. The tail is buff and is crossed by about
6 narrow blackish bands.

Voice
Characteristic vocalization a series of shrill, high-pitched, whistled
screams: *whee-wheee-we-we-we-we* or *fle-fle-flee-fle-fle-fle-fle*, with
longest syllable generally higher and louder than rest; most often
heard when flushed from nesting area.

Similar Species
Perched adult Zone-tailed Hawk has tail crossed by several black
and white bands of relatively even width, not single wide white
band; light bands on upper surface of tail appear gray rather than
white; in flight, wings held in dihedral, obviously 2-toned with dark
linings and lighter flight feathers; wings and tail longer and
narrower. Adult Harris' Hawk appears dark at distance, but
chestnut on wings and legs usually visible; white band on long,
narrow tail at base, includes undertail and uppertail coverts. Zone-

Immature
1. *Pale eyebrow.*
2. *Brownish upperparts.*
3. *Whitish underparts with bold streaking.*
4. *Long tail with jagged bands.*

   Large size.

Immature
1. *Dark upperparts.*
2. *Buff eyebrow.*
3. *Buff underparts heavily streaked and blotched.*
4. *Black tail with several light bands.*

Adult perched
1. *Blackish plumage.*
2. *Yellow cere.*
3. *Yellow legs.*

   Stout build.

tailed and Harris' hawks also have narrow white tips to tail, visible
from both sides.

Range
Primarily neotropical. In United States, breeds from northwestern
Arizona and extreme southern Utah south and east to southwestern
New Mexico and, rarely, western Texas (Davis Mountains).
Occasional in Rio Grande valley. Most common in central Arizona
and extreme west-central New Mexico. Winters primarily from
northern Mexico south. Also in Central and South America.
Scott B. Terrill

Harris' Hawk

Parabuteo unicinctus
This beautiful bird primarily inhabits arid desert scrub and, to a
lesser extent, river woodlands of the Southwest. A fairly common
bird in its range, it is generally associated with thorn-scrub habitats,
such as mesquite, palo verde, and large cacti. Harris' Hawks
frequently perch conspicuously on telephone poles, large cacti, and
snags; when flushed, they often fly low and alight not far from their
original perch. Occasionally Harris' Hawks are seen soaring very
high, usually at midday. These long-legged, long-tailed birds often
perch with the body held less upright and more horizontally than
many other hawks. Harris' will breed year-round, often with more
than 2 birds helping to raise the young. Consequently, Harris'
Hawks are often seen in small groups.

Description
18–23″ (45.5–58.5 cm). The adults are black or brownish-black with
the shoulders, wing linings, and thighs a rich chestnut. The upper-
and undertail coverts and the base and tip of the tail are white. The
cere and legs are yellowish. Immatures have dark brownish
upperparts, with rusty and brown-blotched shoulders. The
underparts are buff, heavily streaked with blackish-brown; the base
of the upper surface of the tail and the rump are whitish. The rest of
the tail looks like that of the adult, but the dark area consists of
narrow, dark barring, and the light areas tend toward buff.

Adult

Voice
Most common call a harsh, loud hiss, initiated with a hard *k* sound,
then tapering off; usually heard only near breeding site.

Similar Species
See Common Black-Hawk and Zone-tailed Hawk. Immature Red-
shouldered Hawk (not generally found in same habitat) streaked
above as well as below, and generally lighter in overall appearance,
with fewer bars on tail.

Range
Resident from central Arizona and southern (primarily
southeastern) New Mexico through southern Texas into Mexico and
Central and South America.   *Scott B. Terrill*

Adult in flight
1. *Broad, short wings.*
2. *Short, broad tail with single white band.*

Immature
1. *Rusty, brown-blotched shoulders.*
2. *Heavy streaks on buff underparts.*
3. *Chestnut thighs.*

Shows whitish tail base and rump in flight.

Adult
1. *Dark upperparts with chestnut shoulders.*
2. *Dark breast.*
3. *Chestnut thighs.*
4. *White rump and base of tail.*
5. *White tail tip.*

Gray Hawk

Buteo nitidus
This rather rare hawk is found primarily in riparian willow, cottonwood, and sycamore groves in the San Pedro and Santa Cruz river drainages of Arizona, where its habitat is threatened.

Description
15–18″ (38–45.5 cm). Adults are pale gray above, white below with heavy gray barring, and several black and white bars on the tail. The cere and legs are bright yellow; the eye is dark brown. The gray wing linings contrast with the mostly white flight feathers; narrow, dark barring becomes more distinct toward the trailing edge, and each flight feather is black-tipped. The rump and undertail coverts are white; the head is slightly crested. Immatures are streaked with buff, rust, and dark brown on the crown, nape, and above; they have a prominent, dark whisker mark, and buff eyebrows. The underparts are off-white, with rows of long, irregular dark brown blotches; the tail has dark and light gray bars. The eyes are dark.

Voice
Loud, clear, whistle: *who-fleearr*, second syllable higher, tapers off rather mournfully. Also *flu-fleeaa* or descending *fleerrr*.

Similar Species
Immature Gray and Broad-winged hawks distinguishable only with care. Generally, Gray Hawk shows finely barred thighs; immature Broad-winged usually (but not always) has bolder dark markings on thighs and usually has paler, finer markings on underparts. Most immature Gray Hawks have rust-colored or dark rufous streaking and blotching on upperparts; immature Broad-winged lacks rusty tone. Gray Hawk also usually has bolder malar stripes. Immature Broad-winged has brown crown finely streaked with white; Gray's crown irregularly streaked with buff or rust. Broad-winged has yellowish eye; Gray Hawk's is brownish.

Range
Southeastern Arizona represents northwestern extreme of breeding range; a few winter records. Very rare in New Mexico and primarily in winter, lower Rio Grande valley; Davis Mountains, Texas, in spring. Existence very precarious in United States. Widespread in New World tropics and subtropics.   *Scott B. Terrill*

Red-shouldered Hawk

Buteo lineatus
This hawk inhabits moist deciduous woodlands, seeming to prefer mature forests. It obtains most of its varied prey by still-hunting from perches. It is migratory only in the northern parts of its range, tending to migrate much later than other hawks of comparable size.

Description
17–24″ (43–61 cm). The Red-shouldered Hawk is a slim, narrow-winged, long-tailed buteo. The adult is blackish-brown to brown above, with extensive black-and-white checkering, especially on the wings, and rufous streaking and edging, particularly on the shoulders. The uppertail coverts are white-tipped, and the tail is blackish with 4 to 7 narrow white bands. The breast, belly, and wing linings are rufous with black shaft streaks; there is a white crescent-shaped patch, or "window," at the base of the outer primaries. The trailing edges of the wings are scalloped; in flight, the tips of the wings are drooped. Immatures are brownish above and show little or no rufous. They are cream- or buff-colored below, heavily

Adult
1. *Gray head and upperparts.*
2. *Gray barring on underparts.*
3. *Yellow cere.*
4. *White rump.*
5. *Black and white bars on tail.*

Immature
1. *Buff-brown upperparts and crown with dark streaks.*
2. *Pale underparts with irregular blotches.*
3. *Buff eyebrow and dark whisker.*

Immature
1. *Brownish, mottled upperparts.*
2. *Cream or buff underparts with dark streaks and blotches.*
3. *Pale "windows" in wings.*

streaked and blotched with dark brown; the wing linings are dark.
The tail is brownish-gray with 7 dark bands.

Voice
During courtship, loud, screaming *kee yar*, dropping in pitch and
typically uttered 2–4 times. Largely silent at other times.

Similar Species
Broad-winged Hawk plumper, with shorter wings; has cream-
colored to white wing linings, lacks white crescent-shaped patch at
base of primaries. Immature Broad-winged tends to be paler below,
with finer streaks. See Northern Goshawk and Red-tailed Hawk.

Range
Breeds east of Great Plains from southern Canada south to Gulf
Coast, and south along Gulf to central Mexico. Isolated population
breeds in California, with occasional records from southwestern
Oregon and northern Baja California; very rare to casual in interior
Southwest. Winters throughout breeding range south of Canada,
although sparsely in extreme northern United States.
David L. Evans

Broad-winged Hawk

Buteo platypterus
The Broad-winged Hawk is a small, stocky buteo that primarily
inhabits large tracts of mixed deciduous forests in central and
eastern North America. A tame bird, it is often observed sitting
along roadsides and clearings as it hunts for a wide variety of prey.
The Broad-wing's migration is less protracted than that of other
species; the bulk of the population passes through an area within
several days. When conditions are favorable, hundreds of birds form
huge flocks, or "kettles," that soar to the top of thermals and then
glide to another. In this way, they expend less energy during the
long flight to their South American wintering grounds.

Description
14–19″ (35.5–48.5 cm). Adults are dark brown or grayish-brown
above, with white-tipped uppertail coverts. The tail is dark, with a
very narrow pale terminal band, broad white median band, and a
narrower white band near the base. The breast and belly are
whitish, with reddish-brown or rufous barring, becoming finer and
more distinctive on the belly. The wing linings are whitish; the
trailing edge of the wings below is dark. The primaries are dark-
tipped and show no pronounced white patch at the base. Immatures
are brown or cinnamon-brown above, often showing some white
spotting on the back. The breast and belly are cream-colored, with
brownish streaks; the wing linings are pale buff to whitish, generally
unmarked. The tail is grayish and crossed with 5 or 6 narrow, dark
bands. There is an extremely rare melanistic phase.

Voice
Characteristic call a very high-pitched, long *pe-heeeeeeee*.

Similar Species
Narrow, dark, straight trailing edge of wing in adult Broad-winged
distinctive. Cooper's Hawk has proportionately much longer tail.
See Red-shouldered, Gray, and Red-tailed hawks.

Range
Breeds from central Alberta to Nova Scotia, south to eastern Texas
and Florida. Rare but regular in fall in coastal California. Very rare
transient in interior West; 2 records for British Columbia. Winters
in southern Florida; also southern Mexico south to Peru and Brazil;
a few winter almost annually in California.   *David L. Evans*

Adult
1. Brownish, streaked upperparts.
2. Rufous shoulder.
3. Rufous breast and barring on underparts.
4. Pale "windows" in wings.
5. Several light tail bands.

Adult
1. Uniform dark brown upperparts.
2. Rufous barring on underparts.
3. Two white bands in tail.

Immature
1. Brown upperparts with whitish spots or bars.
2. Cream-colored underparts with dark blotches.
3. Grayish tail with several dark bands.

Short-tailed Hawk

Buteo brachyurus
In our area, this chunky, broad-winged hawk occurs in Florida, where it is rare; it inhabits mixed woodland-savannah regions. This species soars with its wings held flat and with a pronounced upturn to the outer primaries. It dives for prey from great heights.

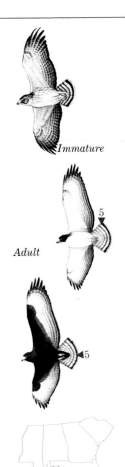

Immature

Adult

Description
15–17″ (38–43 cm). The most common color phase in Florida has primarily sooty black underparts; the undersides of the tail, the primaries, and the secondaries are pale gray (palest at the base of the primaries). There is thin, dark barring on the flight feathers, and 2 or 3 narrow dark tail bars, the outermost being the darkest. Light-phase birds are pure white on the underparts and usually show only a single, narrow subterminal tail bar. Apart from a narrow white chin and throat, the head of the light-phase adult is solid dark brown, creating a hooded appearance. Immatures are basically like the adult, but both phases have darker and more numerous tail bands. The light-phase has buff or pale ocher underparts, which are either unstreaked or have inconspicuous dark shaft streaks on the sides and flanks. The dark phase is mostly dark below, with some light mottling on the belly, chin, and wing linings. In all plumages the cere, legs, and feet are bright yellow.

Voice
Distress call a high-pitched squeal, *keeeea*, dropping slightly at end. Also a less intense, *keee* or *kleee*. Usually silent away from nest.

Similar Species
In Florida, adult Red-shouldered and Broad-winged hawks have different color and pattern of breast and belly, and much darker, more numerous tail bands. Immature Red-shouldered and Broad-winged show varying amounts of dark streaking on underparts, unlike unstreaked light-phase immature Short-tail. Both Red-shoulder and Broad-winged soar with flat wing tips. Behavior, size, and tail patterns should distinguish Short-tail.

Range
Peninsular Florida: in spring and summer, rarely seen north of counties bordering lower Suwannee River; in winter, apparently restricted to south Florida. Has occurred in Texas. Widespread in Central and South America.   *John C. Ogden*

Swainson's Hawk

Buteo swainsoni
Swainson's Hawk is a common inhabitant of the Great Plains and relatively arid areas of western North America. It builds rather flimsy nests in shrubs and trees along wetlands and drainages and in windbreaks in fields and around farmsteads. It is a lanky, small-footed buteo that preys on small mammals, birds, large insects, reptiles, and amphibians, hunting primarily from perches such as fence posts and low trees, or from vantage points on the ground; in winter, it is apparently much more insectivorous. During both winter and summer, Swainson's tends to be less sedentary than other buteos, moving about in response to locally high concentrations of prey. It often sails with its wings held in a shallow V. During migration to Argentina—its primary wintering grounds —it forms immense flocks that are particularly impressive as they funnel through Central America.

Description
19–22″ (48.5–56 cm). One of the best field marks for all plumages of

Light phase
1. *Dark upperparts.*
2. *White underparts.*
3. *Yellow cere.*
4. *Yellow legs and feet.*
5. *Several bands in tail.*

   Soars with tips of primaries upturned.

Dark phase
1. *Dark upperparts.*
2. *Dark underparts.*
3. *Yellow cere.*
4. *Yellow legs and feet.*
5. *Several bands in tail.*

   Only all-dark buteo in Florida.

Light-phase immature
1. *Dark brown upperparts with broad pale edges.*
2. *Buff underparts with variable spotting, often forming a bib.*
3. *Wing tips extend beyond tail.*

Swainson's is the long wings with distinctively pointed tips; when the bird is at rest, both the long, pointed wings and the long tail are apparent. Adults are dark brown above with fine pale brown to cinnamon feather edging. The tail is gray-brown with about 6 narrow dark bands and a wider dark subterminal band. Below, the white throat looks like a bib against the brownish breast, which has fine black shaft streaks. The belly, legs, and wing linings are cream-colored, lightly mottled and barred with brown or rufous, and contrasting with the very dark flight feathers. Dark-phase adults are sooty brown all over, except for the undertail coverts, which are buff-colored, often with dark barring. As in all melanistic buteos, the flight feathers are similar to those of the light phase; Swainson's Hawks exhibit a continuum of plumage variations between the dark and normal phases. Immatures and 1-year-olds are blackish-brown above with some pale streaking on the crown, and often with broader feather edgings. They are buff below, with highly variable spotting, which is sometimes very heavy on the breast, and forms the bib effect seen in adults. The dark-phase juvenile is similar to adults, but often darker.

Voice
Long, whistled *kieeer*, higher-pitched and more plaintive than Red-tailed Hawk's call.

Similar Species
All other melanistic buteos (Red-tail, Rough-leg, Ferruginous, and Broad-wing) lack buff undertail coverts and have white or light gray flight feathers. Red-tail has larger bill, different look to head.

Range
Breeds primarily in Great Plains and arid regions of western United States, extending less commonly to interior Alaska, northern Mexico, and western Minnesota, Illinois, Missouri, and south-central Texas. Winters mainly in Argentina, although winter range has become less concentrated owing to control of migratory locusts (major food source) there. Small group, primarily immatures, known to winter in southern Florida since about 1950; many erroneous wintering records from large parts of the continent.
David L. Evans

White-tailed Hawk

Buteo albicaudatus
The bulky White-tailed Hawk is an uncommon buteo of the Texas grasslands and coastal prairies. As is true of other hawks, the White-tailed's flight silhouette is an important field mark. The broad wings taper to bluntly pointed tips; the wings are held in a shallow V when the bird is soaring. The shortness of the tail is not always apparent when the bird is in flight, but when it perches, the wing tips extend beyond the end of the tail.

Description
23–24″ (58.5–61 cm); wingspan to 4½′. The adult is blue-gray above, with extensive rufous on the upperwing coverts and scapulars; the rump and tail are white, with a black tail band near the tip. The underparts are white with a variable amount of fine dark barring on the flanks and thighs. The white wing linings contrast strongly with the dark flight feathers. Immatures are variable but are always much darker, mostly blackish above and below, with part of the chest or belly pale. The tail is pale brown or whitish with many fine

Dark-phase adult
1. *Sooty brown plumage.*
2. *Light undertail coverts.*
3. *Head appears small.*
4. *Wings extend beyond tail.*

Light-phase adult
1. *Dark brown upperparts.*
2. *Brown breast.*
3. *Pale belly.*
4. *Pale wing linings.*
5. *Dark flight feathers.*
6. *Rather pointed wings for a buteo.*

Adult
1. *Gray upperparts.*
2. *Rufous upperwing coverts.*
3. *White underparts.*
4. *White tail with black band near tip.*

dark crossbands, creating a grayish effect; the wing linings, when seen from below, are darker than the flight feathers.

Voice
Clear, 2-syllabled *keeyah, keeyah;* sometimes high-pitched chatter.

Similar Species
Immature might be confused with other dark buteos having pale tails. Dark "Harlan's" form of Red-tailed most similar, but tail feathers mottled and streaked lengthwise with darker gray; soars with wings held more horizontally. Dark-phase Rough-legged slimmer, tail longer with dark band at tip, more contrast on underwing. Dark-phase Ferruginous longer-winged, longer-tailed, has more contrast on underwing, with secondaries usually very whitish; body more uniformly maroon-brown. Dark-phase Swainson's has darker, more strongly banded tail.

Range
Uncommon permanent resident on Texas coastal plain; local inland. Widespread in open country south to Argentina.   *Kenn Kaufman*

Zone-tailed Hawk

Buteo albonotatus
In flight, with its wings held in a shallow V, the Zone-tailed Hawk looks remarkably like a Turkey Vulture—with which it often associates. Zone-tailed Hawks are fairly common but local in canyons and wooded river bottoms of the Southwest.

Description
18–23″ (45.5–58.5 cm). The Zone-tailed Hawk has all-blackish plumage except for 3 to 4 light tail bands that appear gray from above and white from below; the cere and legs are yellow. In flight, both the wings and tail appear long and narrow; black wing linings and fine dark-and-light barring on the flight feathers (which appear solid gray at a distance) give the underwing a 2-toned look. The white bands on the tail are most noticeable in flight. Immatures are similar to adults but slightly paler, with white spotting on the underparts. The tail above is grayish, with narrow blackish bars on the upper surface; below, it is whitish with gray bars; the outermost bar is the widest.

Voice
A loud, descending scream, similar to Red-tailed's but less shrill.

Similar Species
Turkey Vulture has naked, reddish head; tail wider, lacks pale bands. Blackish dark-phase Swainson's Hawk resembles immature and often holds wings in slight dihedral, but has wider wings and tail, more typical buteo shape; upper surface of tail dark brownish, with blackish barring above, usually buff or rust markings on upperparts and wing linings. Dark-phase "Harlan's" form of Red-tailed Hawk similar to immature but conspicuously spotted with white on upperparts and wing linings, has broader wings and tail; does not carry wings at angle; tail generally not as evenly barred, being more or less whitish, with dark subterminal band. See Common Black-Hawk.

Range
Breeds from southern California (very rare), northwestern, central, and southeastern Arizona, southern New Mexico, and southwestern and central Texas south through Mexico into South America. Very rare north of Mexico in winter.   *Scott B. Terrill*

Immature
1. *Body dark and blotchy.*
2. *Pale tail.*
3. *Wing linings paler than flight feathers.*

Adult
1. *Blackish plumage.*
2. *Dark tail with white bands.*
3. *Yellow legs.*
4. *Yellow cere.*

Adult in flight
1. *Narrow tail with white tail bands.*
2. *Long, narrow wings.*

Flies like Turkey Vulture.

Red-tailed Hawk

Buteo jamaicensis
A common and familiar raptor throughout North America, the Red-tailed Hawk is highly variable in color. There are often 2 color phases, a "normal" or light phase and a melanistic phase, with some intergradation between them. Some subspecies can be distinguished in the field, although adjacent races interbreed, and confusing intermediates are impossible to identify to subspecies with certainty. The Red-tail is a large, stocky, broad-winged, and usually dark-headed buteo; because of the great variation in plumage coloration, these general characteristics are often helpful in distinguishing this species from other buteos. Immature birds tend to look somewhat more slender—longer-winged and longer-tailed—than adults. Red-tailed Hawks are found in a wide variety of habitats, ranging from open woodlands and fields to plains and deserts with scattered trees. In general, the breeding ranges of the major subspecies coincide with broad habitat zones. Eastern Red-tails are birds of open woodlands and fields; their breeding range extends to the Great Plains. The western race (*calurus*) and "Krider's" Red-tail are birds of more open country, while "Harlan's" Red-tail breeds in forested areas of southwestern mainland Alaska. Red-tails are commonly observed soaring, especially in spring and summer, or still-hunting from a perch overlooking an open area. Small rodents and rabbits form the bulk of the Red-tail's diet, but it also feeds on a variety of other mammals, as well as on birds, snakes, lizards, and large amphibians. Birds in the northern part of the species' range are migratory, but many will remain through the winter as long as sufficient food is available. While it is possible to see many Red-tails in a single day at a favored migration spot, the species is seldom seen in large flocks like those of Swainson's and Broad-winged hawks. Some nonmigratory pairs occupy territories during the winter, and at this season it is usual to find these birds fairly evenly spaced out over the countryside. There has been some uncertainty about the status of both "Krider's" and "Harlan's" Red-tails; they have been considered color phases, races, and separate species, and are now considered to be subspecies of the Red-tailed Hawk.

Description

19–25″ (48–63.5 cm). Typical adult eastern Red-tailed Hawks, and birds from southeastern Alaska, are brown to dark brown on the upperparts, often lighter brown on the head and nape, and mottled with white or rufous on the mantle. The uppertail coverts may be whitish suffused with rufous or, more commonly, rufous with brownish or darker rufous barring. The tail is reddish, usually brick-red, with a narrow black subterminal band and a narrow white tip. On the underparts these birds are cream-colored, with variable cinnamon to black streaking on the sides of the breast, a broad band of dark barring and streaking across the belly, and barring on the legs. The wing linings are whitish, with a brown or chestnut-brown patagial stripe and a dark, crescent-shaped wrist patch. The primaries and secondaries are crossed with 6 to 8 narrow dark bars. Immatures are similar to adults on the upperparts, but lack the rufous cast on the back and uppertail coverts. They are also similar below, but do not have the cinnamon cast, and are spotted and streaked rather than barred. The tail is grayish-brown or brown, with about 7 narrow dark bands. Melanistic birds are absent or extremely rare in the eastern population. Adults and immatures of the western race (*B. j. calurus*) tend to be dark-headed, more heavily marked on the underparts, and more rufous-colored than the eastern birds. The tails of adults have a variable number of

Immature

**Immature eastern
Red-tailed Hawk**
1. *Dark head and
   upperparts.*
2. *Whitish underparts
   with dark spots and
   streaks.*
3. *Grayish-brown tail
   with several narrow,
   dark bands.*

**Adult eastern
Red-tailed Hawk**
1. *Dark head and
   upperparts.*
2. *Brick-red tail.*
3. *Bars and streaks on
   belly.*
4. *Dark patagial stripe
   and wrist patch on
   underwing.*

**Dark-phase western
race (*calurus*)**
1. *Dark upperparts.*
2. *Dark underparts.*
3. *Banded tail with
   reddish cast.*

   Stocky build.

incomplete black bands in addition to the subterminal band, which is typically wider. The tails of immatures usually have a reddish cast. Melanistic individuals are common; they are dark brown below, with a rufous-brown breast; the flight feathers are similar to those of normal-phase birds. Some melanistic immatures may have whitish or buff streaking on the underparts. "Krider's" Red-tailed Hawk (*B. j. krideri*) is much paler than the eastern Red-tail, with more white on the head, back, and upper surface of the wing. The tail is whitish; it is sometimes tinged with pink near the tip in adults, and is normally banded in immatures. The band of barring and streaking across the belly is greatly reduced. The inner primaries are often paler than the adjacent secondaries and outer primaries. "Harlan's" Red-tailed Hawk (*B. j. harlani*) is a very distinctive form, once considered a separate species. It probably occurs only in the melanistic phase; supposed light-phase birds, showing characteristics of *harlani* (primarily in the tail) are probably hybrids with *calurus* or *alascensis*. Adults are black with white spotting above and below, in contrast to melanistic *calurus*, which is dark brown or rufous-brown without white spotting. The wing linings are dark, with heavy white spotting; the tail is grayish or white, occasionally tinged with cinnamon, and variably streaked and mottled with black. Immatures are similar to melanistic *calurus*, but are typically darker, with white spotting instead of streaking.

Voice
Nest-defense call a raspy, descending *tseer;* sometimes given at other times when bird is irritated or disturbed.

Similar Species
Swainson's Hawk lacks belly band, has dark bib in adult and some immatures; has pale wing linings and dark flight feathers. Ferruginous Hawk larger; adults immaculate below, with rusty brown legs, whitish tail; immatures nearly immaculate below, with basal half of tail white. Rough-legged Hawk has large, dark wrist patch; tail white at base. Red-shouldered Hawk smaller; below, has white crescent-shaped wing patch on outer primaries; adults have 4–7 white bands in tail. Broad-winged Hawk noticeably smaller, with no distinguishing marks on underwing; lacks belly band; adults have 2 white bands in tail. Melanistic Swainson's has buffy tail coverts, dark flight feathers below. Melanistic Ferruginous has tail and flight feathers similar to normal phase. Melanistic Rough-legged discernibly darker with wrist patch on underwing; tail dark, sometimes with 1–3 white tail bands. See also White-tailed Hawk.

Range
Breeds from southern Alaska, Yukon, southern Northwest Territories, southern Quebec, and Maritime Provinces south to Florida, West Indies, and Central America. Winters from southern Canada southward. "Krider's" Red-tail breeds in southern Prairie Provinces of Canada south to Colorado and Nebraska; winters south to central Mexico. "Harlan's" Red-tail breeds from tree line in Alaska, Yukon, and Northwest Territories south to interior northern British Columbia and northern Alberta; winters in southern Kansas, southwestern Missouri, western Arkansas, Oklahoma, and northern Texas; has occurred as a vagrant elsewhere.   *David L. Evans*

Intergrade between "Harlan's" and *B.j. calurus*

1. Tail tinged with rufous, with many narrow, wavy dark bands.

Adult "Harlan's"

1. Dark plumage with white spots.
2. Grayish tail with variable streaking or mottling.

Adult "Krider's"

1. More white on head and upperparts than in eastern Red-tail.
2. Pale inner primaries.
3. Whitish tail tinged with pink near tip.

Ferruginous Hawk

Buteo regalis
The largest of the North American buteos, the Ferruginous Hawk is
a long-winged, pale-headed bird that inhabits unbroken terrain in
the Great Plains and arid intermountain regions of western Canada
and the United States. This species utilizes a variety of nesting
sites, including ground nests on low hillsides, cut banks and buttes,
trees in open country and along drainage areas, power-line
structures, and haystacks. Its diet is restricted, consisting primarily
of rabbits, hares, and ground squirrels, although it will take other
prey. The Ferruginous Hawk may watch for prey from a perch or on
the ground, while soaring with wings above the horizontal, or in
low, rapid flight over open country. Unlike the Rough-legged Hawk,
the Ferruginous hovers only occasionally. Nesting birds sometimes
hunt cooperatively for larger prey.

Description
22–27″ (56–68.5 cm). Typical adults are brownish above and paler on
the head, with cinnamon or rufous feather edgings, especially on the
back and shoulders. They are whitish below, with a few dusky or
rufous bars on the flanks. In flight, the wings above show a white
patch on the outer primaries. The wing linings are white, with a
dark crescent at the wrist and a narrow chestnut patagial stripe.
The thighs are chestnut-brown with heavy black barring and are
feathered to the toes. The tail is whitish to silvery, often with
cinnamon or reddish near the tip. Immatures are dark brown above
with some white spotting on the mantle. The breast is cinnamon,
fading to whitish within a few months after the bird leaves the nest;
the belly and flanks are pale cinnamon to whitish, with scattered
dark spots and streaks. The immature's tail is white on the basal
half, brownish-gray with several indistinct dark bars on the distal
portion. The legs are white to pale cinnamon, never chestnut-brown,
and have scattered dark flecks. The dark, or melanistic, phase
makes up 2 to 5 percent of the population in most areas; dark-phase
birds are a rich, dark brown below as well as above; the flight
feathers are the same as in light-phase birds, although somewhat
duskier. There are no intergrades between the light and dark phases
as there are in the Rough-legged, Swainson's, and Red-tailed hawks.

*Dark-phase
immature*

Voice
Less vocal than other buteos; nest-defense call a sharp, descending,
high-pitched *kree-a-ah.*

Similar Species
Pale Red-tailed Hawk stockier, broader-winged, and lacks chestnut-
brown thighs. Light phase Rough-legged Hawk has dark belly, bold
black wrist mark, and lacks chestnut-brown thighs. See also
melanistic Red-tailed, Swainson's, and Rough-legged hawks.

Range
Breeds in semiarid western plains and cold desert from southern
Alberta, Saskatchewan, Manitoba, and North Dakota south to
northern Arizona, New Mexico, and Kansas. Winters over much of
breeding range south to Baja California, northern Mexico, and
Texas; casual farther east.   *David L. Evans*

Light-phase immature
. *Dark brown uppparts.*
. *Whitish tail with indistinct dusky bars toward tip.*

Light-phase immature
. *White underparts.*
. *Scattered dark spots on belly, flanks, and legs.*

Light-phase adult
. *Brownish uppparts with rufous edgings.*
. *White breast.*
. *Whitish tail with reddish near tip.*
. *Chestnut thighs.*
. *Chestnut patagial stripe and dark crescent on underwing.*

Rough-legged Hawk

Buteo lagopus
A northern buteo that breeds in the Arctic and subarctic, the
Rough-legged Hawk frequents open, unwooded terrain and nests on
rock ledges, hillsides, or short trees. It hunts small mammals from
perches or on the wing, often hovering or quartering the ground at
low altitudes. Breeding success fluctuates markedly; numbers seen
during the winter in southern Canada and the United States largely
reflect the phase of the lemming cycle farther north. During winter,
Rough-legs sometimes form communal roosts, with as many as 20
birds returning to a single tree at nightfall.

Light-phase
immature

Description
19–24″ (48.5–61 cm). The Rough-legged Hawk is a large buteo with
long wings that are usually held above the horizontal when soaring
or gliding. Plumages are quite variable, with many intergradations
between the light and dark phases. The light-phase adult is
brownish to grayish-brown above, with some rufous, and with white
to buff feather edgings. The head is pale; the uppertail coverts are
white, and barred with blackish-brown. The tail is usually white at
the base, sometimes with dark spotting or incomplete bars, and has
a broad, dark subterminal band and a white tip. Adult light-phase
males often have a larger, white basal area with 2 or 3 well-defined,
dark subterminal bands. The breast is typically cream-colored or
buff, with scattered brownish spots and streaks; in some light-phase
adults this spotting may be quite extensive. The belly is usually
uniformly dark brown to blackish, sometimes with white or buff
spotting; in some adults, however, especially males, the belly may
be whitish with dark spotting. In flight, the wing lining appears
whitish, with dark brown spotting and a blackish wing patch at the
wrist. Light-phase immatures have paler heads, more blackish on
the belly, and a single blackish subterminal tail band. Dark-phase
birds vary from dark brown to jet black above and below; the wing
linings often show a discernibly darker wrist patch. The tail varies
from a nearly uniform brown to dark brown or black, with several
white bands.

Dark-phase adult

Voice
Squeal or screech, ending on lower note, *kee-we-uk;* given during
nesting season when excited or alarmed.

Similar Species
Red-tailed Hawk broader-winged, stockier, with white rump patch
smaller than white base of Rough-legged's tail. Ferruginous Hawk
lacks black belly. See melanistic Red-tailed, Ferruginous, and
Swainson's hawks.

Light-phase
adult

Range
Breeds in Arctic and subarctic south to Aleutian Islands, Manitoba,
and Newfoundland. Winters from southern Canada south to
California, Arizona, New Mexico, Oklahoma, Tennessee, and
Virginia.   *David L. Evans*

**Dark-phase
immature**
1. *Dark plumage.*
2. *Contrasting dark
   wrist patch.*
3. *White base to tail.*

*Tail sometimes dark
with 1–3 white
bands.*

Adult male
1. *Tail white at base,
   with well-defined
   subterminal bands.*
2. *Belly spotted with
   white and buff.*

*Frequently hovers.
Holds wings in
shallow V.*

Light-phase adult
1. *Brownish above with
   light feather edgings.*
2. *Blackish belly.*
3. *White tail base.*
4. *Black wrist mark on
   underwing.*

Golden Eagle

Aquila chrysaetos
The Golden Eagle is most abundant in the mountainous and hilly
regions of the western part of North America, and scarce in the
East. During the winter it is sometimes found far from its breeding
areas, especially in the southern Great Plains and at various wildlife
refuges, where it may feed on crippled waterfowl. Most of its prey is
taken on the ground; it hunts from perches or, more frequently than
smaller raptors while soaring at great heights with its wings held
horizontally (rather than in a shallow V). This species' nest is
typically a large structure of sizable sticks and branches; it is placed
on a suitable cliff ledge or, in some areas, in trees. During courtship,
soaring and undulating flight displays are frequent. The Golden
Eagle's huge size, broad wings, and relatively small bill are
distinctive.

Description
30–40″ (76–101.5 cm). Adults are uniformly brown to dark brown,
sometimes paler on the back owing to faded or worn plumage. The
crown and nape feathers are edged with golden-buff or tan.
Immatures and subadults are similar to adults, but usually darker.
Their wings have a white, circular patch centered on the outer
secondaries and inner primaries, which is replaced as the dark adult
feathers molt in during the second or third year. The juvenile's tail
is white at the base with the terminal half to one-third dark brown;
over a period of 2 to 3 years, tail feathers are replaced by feathers
with less basal white, and finally by dark, banded adult feathers.
The white wing patch tends to disappear before the white basal area
on the tail. Thus a second-year bird might show a reduced wing
patch and a typical immature tail; a third- or fourth-year bird might
show no wing patch, while still retaining a reduced white area at the
base of the tail.

Voice
Typically silent; mewing cries and melodious yelping call, *weeo-hyo-
hyo-hyo*, during courtship.

Similar Species
Immature Bald Eagle has larger bill, broader wings; often shows
much white blotching on back and underparts. See Turkey Vulture,
Black Vulture.

Range
Breeds in mountainous and hilly country from northwestern Alaska
and Canada south to Mexico and east to Texas, Dakotas, and
southern Saskatchewan; sporadically to Labrador. A few pairs
remain in northern Appalachians. Winters from northern British
Columbia, Alberta, Manitoba, and eastern Canada; south into
Mexico. Very rare migrant at principal raptor-watching stations in
Northeast, wintering in very small numbers in mid-Atlantic states.
Not known to breed in Northwest. Also in Eurasia and North
Africa.   *David L. Evans*

Immature in flight
1. *Long, narrow wings with white at base of flight feathers.*
2. *Dark body.*
3. *Broad white band at base of tail.*

Large size.

Subadult in flight
1. *Long, narrow wings with little or no white at base of flight feathers.*
2. *Dark body.*
3. *Reduced white band at base of tail.*

Large size.

Adult
1. *Golden-buff crown and nape.*
2. *Solid dark brown plumage.*
3. *Entirely dark tail.*

Large size.

Falcons

(Family Falconidae)
These streamlined, swift birds of prey fly powerfully and display
great agility in flight. Most falcons fly with very strong wingbeats
alternating with extremely rapid, often sustained glides, but these
birds are especially well known for their spectacular diving abilities.
While foraging, most species will hover at least occasionally;
1 species, the American Kestrel, hovers almost constantly. Like
most raptors, the falcons have a strongly decurved, sharp upper
mandible that is used for tearing prey. Unlike accipiters, members
of the genus *Falco* have a conspicuous toothlike projection on the
cutting edge of the upper mandible near the tip; this is called a
"tomial tooth." Falcons can be identified in flight by their long,
pointed wings and long, relatively narrow tails that appear squared
or tapered toward the top when folded. Also characteristic of the
family is a bold whisker mark on the side of the head. As is true of
the Accipitridae, females are larger than males. (World: 62 species.
North America: 8 species.)   *Scott B. Terrill*

Crested Caracara

Polyborus plancus
This is an uncommon local scavenger of open arid and semiarid
scrublands and prairies; it spends considerable time on the ground.
Description
21–25″ (53–63.5 cm). Adult has white head with black crest, white
neck, and black lower back and upperwing. Breast and upper back
barred; tail long, white, finely barred, with broad black subterminal
band. In flight, black wing lining shows large white patches.
Immature similar but browner, with streaked breast. At all ages,
base of bill and face reddish, unfeathered; feet yellow.
Voice
Alarm call a grating *trak-trak-trak*.
Range
Southern Arizona and New Mexico (rare), southern and east-central
Texas, southwestern Louisiana, and central Florida; to northern
South America.   *Paul W. Sykes, Jr.*

American Kestrel

Falco sparverius
The smallest North American falcon, the American Kestrel is widely
distributed in habitats that include deserts, forest openings,
marshes and grasslands, agricultural and suburban areas, and even
big cities. It is frequently seen hunting from perches overlooking
open land. It also hunts on the wing, hovering frequently. It feeds
on small vertebrate animals throughout the year but often
concentrates on grasshoppers and other large invertebrates when
such prey is abundant. The Kestrel often pumps its tail up and down
when perched, especially after landing. It nests in tree cavities,
crevices in buildings, and holes in earth banks or cliffs.
Description
7½–8″ (19–20 cm). The American Kestrel is a small falcon with long,
pointed wings. Males have a rufous back with narrow black barring,
which is more pronounced on the lower back. The upperwing coverts
are bluish-gray, and the black primaries are spotted with white; the
tail is red, with a black subterminal band and a white tip. The crown

Crested Caracara
Eurasian Kestrel
American Kestrel
Merlin
Aplomado Falcon
Peregrine Falcon
Gyrfalcon
Prairie Falcon

Adult

1. White head and neck with black crest.
2. Dark upperparts.
3. Streaked or barred breast.
4. Long legs.
5. White tail with black band.
6. White wing patches.

Female

1. Rufous upperparts with black barring.
2. Two mustache marks on cheek.
3. Rufous, banded tail.

Often hovers.
Pumps tail after alighting.

is slate-blue, usually with a central rufous patch; the throat and
cheeks are whitish, with 2 vertical black stripes. The nape is buff or
apricot, with a broad dark streak, or "eyespot." Below, the Kestrel
is buff to cinnamon or rufous, with variable black spotting that
becomes heavier on the flanks and midsection. The female is rufous-
brown above, with black barring; the underparts are buff, blotched
and streaked with darker rufous and brown. The head is similar to
the male's, but somewhat duller, and has a rufous-brown crown.

Voice
A high-pitched *klee klee klee klee*, given rapidly in series of 3–6
when bird is excited or alarmed. During courtship, a variety of
whining cries and chitters.

Range
From near tree line in Alaska and Canada south into Mexico.
Breeding populations in Canada and northern United States migrate
south in winter as far as Central America and Panama.
David L. Evans

Merlin

Falco columbarius
This small, fast-moving falcon feeds almost entirely on small to
medium-size birds. In the open, the Merlin hunts with a series of
shallow stoops, continuing if unsuccessful; this bird seldom glides.
Merlins will take prey by stooping from great heights, though they
do so less frequently than the larger falcons; along coastlines, they
are often seen taking shorebirds. Merlins generally nest in or near
open areas, often near water. Like other falcons, they often use the
old stick nests of crows, ravens, magpies, or other raptors; they are
also known to nest in cavities and on the ground. Three races,
corresponding to major habitat types, exist in North America.

Description
10–12" (25.5–30.5 cm). Adult males are a slate blue-gray above, with
a dark gray crown finely streaked with black. The tail is dark and
has a whitish terminal band and 2 or 3 grayish bands. Below, males
are tan or buff with brown streaking. Adult females and immatures
are similar to adult males, but are dark brown above and have gray
to buff tail bands. Merlins have a less striking facial pattern than
Kestrels or Peregrines, and a poorly defined mustache. The
primaries above are black with uniform, well-defined white spots.
F. c. richardsoni is paler; adult males are light gray above; adult
females and immatures are tan to light brown. *F. c. suckleyi* is
much darker than *columbarius*, dark chocolate-brown above and
darker below in all plumages; the dark tail lacks pale crossbands.

Voice
When alarmed or irritated, harsh, rapid, high-pitched *ki ki ki ki ki*.

Similar Species
See American Kestrel, Peregrine Falcon, and Sharp-shinned Hawk.

Range
F. c. columbarius: Breeds in boreal forest regions of northern
North America. Winters from southern breeding range to northern
South America. *F. c. richardsoni:* Breeds in prairie-parkland
regions of central Canada and northern Great Plains. Winters from
southern breeding range to northern Mexico. *F. c. suckleyi:* Breeds
in humid Pacific coastal regions and offshore islands. Primarily
resident, but some birds range to west in winter. All races rare in
East except along coast.   *David L. Evans*

Male
1. *Bluish, pointed wings.*
2. *Red tail with dark band near tip.*
3. *Two mustache marks on cheek.*

Adult male
1. *Blue-gray upperparts.*
2. *Darker crown.*
3. *Pointed wings.*
4. *Dark tail with light gray bands.*
5. *Streaked underparts.*

Immature
1. *Dark brown upperparts.*
2. *Dark tail with gray or buff bands.*
3. *Face pattern less striking than American Kestrel's.*

Aplomado Falcon

Falco femoralis
This swift, graceful, medium-size falcon has all but disappeared from
the United States, where it formerly occupied arid southwestern
grasslands with scattered yucca, thorn scrub, and cacti. Most recent
reports from our range are erroneous or unsubstantiated. This
falcon appears very light and dexterous in flight, pursuing even
insects and small birds on the wing. It often perches on conspicuous
tree tops, or cacti. It appears very long-tailed, even for a falcon.

Description
15–18″ (38–45.5 cm). The Aplomado Falcon has contrasting and
conspicuous head markings consisting of a dark gray crown and a
white to off-white eyebrow that extends to the nape, forming a
collar; the postocular stripe, whisker, and posterior nape are dark
gray, contrasting boldly with an otherwise white background. The
breast is white to buff, with varying degrees of black streaking; this
stands out from the blackish sides and belly, which usually have
some thin white barring. The thighs, undertail coverts, and flanks
are a rich cinnamon; the upperparts are gray. The tail has
alternating dark and light gray bands, sometimes with brownish to
buff tones. In flight, the wing linings appear boldly checkered with
dark gray to gray-brown and white or buff. The cere and legs are
yellow. The immature resembles the adult, but is browner above,
with more uniform wing linings. The face pattern is the same; the
underparts are rich buff, with bold blackish streaks on the breast
and plain blackish sides. There is a cinnamon-breasted phase.

Voice
Series of *kaks* similar to calls of other falcons, but higher-pitched
than those of large falcons. Also a shrill *keek* or *eek*.

Similar Species
Prairie Falcon can have black axillars extend to belly, but paler,
stockier, shorter-tailed; lacks pronounced patterning. Peregrine
larger, stockier, without light eye stripe; underparts lack bold
contrast between belly and breast.

Range
Mexico south to Tierra del Fuego (including Trinidad). Formerly in
southern Arizona, New Mexico, and Texas. No recent records from
Arizona; very few from Texas and New Mexico.   *Scott B. Terrill*

Peregrine Falcon

Falco peregrinus
As the focal point of early inquiries into the effects of DDT and
other chemical contaminants on wildlife, the Peregrine Falcon has
become a symbol of the struggle against environmental pollution. It
vanished as a breeder in the eastern United States and suffered
severe declines throughout its range except in the Pacific
Northwest, where it is essentially nonmigratory. Declines in most
regions have reversed, and restocking efforts with captive-bred
birds have bolstered native populations, resulting in the
establishment of several breeding pairs both in the East and the
West. The Peregrine Falcon shows an impressive display of speed
and power when pursuing its prey, whether in direct pursuit or in
swift dives from above. It feeds primarily on medium-size birds,
including passerines, shorebirds, alcids, pigeons, and waterfowl. It
does not build its own nest but uses ledges, potholes, or small caves
on high cliffs, sea stacks, and Arctic cutbanks and river slopes.
Peregrines occasionally nest on various man-made structures,
sometimes within large cities; typically, however, they nest near

Immature
1. *Heavy streaks on breast.*
2. *Bold face pattern with white eyebrow.*
3. *Long tail.*

Adult
1. *Bold face pattern with white eyebrow.*
2. *Dark sides and belly.*
3. *Cinnamon thighs, undertail coverts, and flanks.*
4. *Long tail.*

Adult
1. *Black head and malar stripe.*
2. *Slate-gray upperparts.*
3. *Barred underparts.*
4. *Pointed wings.*

   Large size.

lakes, rivers, marshes, coasts, and other areas providing abundant prey. Northern populations are highly migratory, going as far as southern South America. During migration, they tend to follow the shorelines of the Great Lakes, coasts, and barrier beaches.

Description
15–20″ (38–51 cm). Adults are bluish to dark slate-gray above, with a black head and black malar stripes. Below, they are tinged with buff-cinnamon to dark rufous in some races, off-white in others; all races show dark spotting and barring. The Pacific Coast race (*F. p. pealei*) tends to be considerably darker; northern birds (*F. p. tundrius*) tend to be lighter. Juveniles are brown to bluish-brown above, with white to buff feather edging and dark malar stripes; below, they are buff or sandy with dark streaking. In northern birds, the juvenile's head may be quite pale, and often appears tan.

Voice
Rather noisy during breeding season, with a variety of wails and cries; when excited or alarmed, *hak hak hak hak*, given repeatedly.

Similar Species
Merlin much smaller, usually darker; lacks distinctive mustache. Prairie Falcon has dark wing linings and axillars. Gyrfalcon has longer wings, somewhat broader at base, and longer tail; undersides and back usually show less contrast. Other falcons lack Peregrine's very bold facial markings.

Range
Breeds north of tree line in Alaska and Canada as far north as Queen Elizabeth Islands; south to mid-Canada and Pacific Northwest, extending south to Mexico in Rocky Mountains. Some reestablished breeding pairs in northeastern and western United States. Pacific race breeds in Aleutian Islands south to Queen Charlotte Island; largely resident. Northern populations highly migratory, reaching Argentina and Chile. Also in Old World.
David L. Evans

Gyrfalcon

Falco rusticolus
The largest and most powerful of falcons, the Gyrfalcon is an essentially permanent resident in the Arctic. It usually breeds in remote areas and is rarely observed, but it can be relatively common in areas of abundant prey. Gyrfalcons breed on ledges or in potholes, and in small caves in cliffs or old raven or raptor nests. This species preys primarily on birds ranging in size from redpolls to large ducks and geese, with ptarmigan usually providing the bulk of its diet. Small mammals, including lemmings, voles, and arctic hares, are also taken. The Gyrfalcon is less inclined to take prey from a high stoop than the Peregrine; more often it directly pursues and captures its prey on or close to the ground. During winter, this bird remains on its breeding grounds if prey is available; juveniles and birds breeding in higher latitudes normally follow the ptarmigan migration as far as the southern tundra and tree line.

◄3

Description
20–25″ (51 to 63.5 cm). This falcon's broader, less pointed wings and

Immature
1. *Dark malar stripe.*
2. *Brown upperparts.*
3. *Buff, streaked underparts.*

Large size.

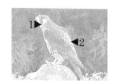

Immature
1. *Dark malar stripe.*
2. *Bluish-brown upperparts with buff feather edging.*

Gray phase
1. *Gray-brown upperparts.*
2. *Long tail.*
3. *Broad wings.*

Very large size.

longer tail give it an accipitrine appearance. There is considerable
variation in plumage; the upperparts range from white with dark
spotting, barring, and streaking and nearly immaculate underparts
to uniform black or dark brown with pale feather edging.
Intermediate gray or brownish-gray phases are most common.
Juveniles are typically more heavily streaked below than adults.

Voice
Similar to Peregrine's call but louder and harsher.

Similar Species
See Peregrine Falcon and Northern Goshawk.

Range
Breeds from high Arctic tundra south to southwestern Alaska and in
partly forested subarctic regions to Ungava Peninsula and northern
Labrador. Winters from middle of breeding range south to boreal
forest, occasionally as far as northern limits of United States; very
rarely farther south to northern California, Colorado, Missouri,
Pennsylvania, and New Jersey. Also in Eurasia.   *David L. Evans*

Prairie Falcon

Falco mexicanus
A large falcon of arid regions, the Prairie Falcon is a locally common
bird that breeds in the mountains, foothills, and riverine
escarpments of western North America. This species nests almost
exclusively on suitable ledges of cliffs and low escarpments or,
occasionally, in stick nests constructed on cliffs by ravens, hawks, or
eagles. It preys on a variety of mammals, birds, reptiles, and
insects, with proportions varying with local and seasonal abundance;
it hunts from perches or in a low, rapid, searching flight, usually
capturing prey on or near the ground. In drier regions, there is
sometimes a post-breeding migration to intermountain valleys and
the Great Plains.

Description
14–18″ (35.5–45.5 cm). A large falcon, the Prairie is more slender
than the Peregrine. Adults are brown to sandy brown above, with
indistinct buff feather edgings; below they are creamy white with
brown spotting or streaking on the breast and belly and barring on
the thighs. The axillars, part of the wing linings, and the upper
flanks are dark brown with indistinct white spotting. Juveniles are
similar to adults, darker brown above and darker buff below, with
heavier streaking.

Voice
Call similar to Peregrine's when alarmed or excited, sharp *kik kik
kik kik*. Variety of wails and whining cries during courtship.

Similar Species
Peregrine Falcon slightly larger, darker, with bolder facial
markings.

Range
Breeds from central British Columbia, Alberta, and western North
Dakota south to Baja California, New Mexico, and northern Texas.
Winters from northern part of breeding range east sparingly to
Mississippi River; casual east to Michigan, Illinois, South Carolina,
and possibly Georgia; south to central Mexico.   *David L. Evans*

White phase
1. *Plumage largely white.*

   Very large size.

In flight
1. *Dark wing linings.*

   Slimmer build than Peregrine Falcon's.

Perched
1. *Faint mustache.*
2. *Sandy-brown upperparts.*
3. *Lightly marked underparts.*

Guans, Curassows, and Chachalacas

(Family Cracidae)
This is a family of medium-size to large birds that frequent tropical forests and brushlands. All have long tails, long necks, rather chickenlike bills, and strong legs. Most species spend much time in trees, and many—especially the chachalacas—have loud and distinctive voices. (World: 44 species. North America: 1 species.)
Kenn Kaufman

Plain Chachalaca

Ortalis vetula
Dawn in the woods of southern Texas owes much of its tropical flavor to the chorus of the Plain Chachalaca. Perched in the tree tops, members of a flock call at the same time but not in unison, creating a discordant clatter. The efforts of one flock usually inspire neighboring flocks to join in, until the woods ring with the noise of their calls. When moving about in trees, the birds bound from branch to branch, with or without the assistance of their wings; going from one tree top to another or to the ground, they fly with several quick flaps followed by a flat-winged glide. Normally Chachalacas are shy and difficult to observe, but in some Texas parks and refuges they have become accustomed to humans and may be easily approached as they feed by the roadsides.

Description
20–24″ (51–61 cm). This chachalaca species is named for its plain, mostly gray-brown color—darker on the back, wings, and tail, slightly grayer on the head, becoming paler to buff-white on the lower underparts. The tail has a slight greenish gloss, and the outer feathers are tipped with dull white or buff. There is a small patch of bare reddish skin on the throat, but this is not always evident in the field.

Voice
Best-known call a loud, grating *cha-cha-lac*, repeated rhythmically for long periods in chorus; low-pitched and guttural from adult males, much higher-pitched from females and immatures. Usually pace is set by one old male, with higher voices filling spaces between his calls. Many other miscellaneous cackling and growling notes.

Range
Resident from lower Rio Grande, Texas, south to Costa Rica. Introduced on Sapelo and Blackbeard Islands, Georgia.
Kenn Kaufman

Plain Chachalaca

Adult
1. *Long tail with pale tip.*
2. *Chickenlike bill.*
3. *Strong legs.*
4. *Gray-brown color, darkest above.*

Gives raucous calls in flocks at dawn.

Adult
1. *Bare reddish patch on throat.*

Pheasants, Grouse, and Quails

(Family Phasianidae)
This is a large, diverse group of primarily terrestrial birds with
stocky or heavy bodies and thick, short legs; their large toes are
spread wide for walking and scratching. The bills are usually shorter
than the head and have deep bases and strongly curved culmens.
These birds often have bare skin or ornamental feathering around
the head or neck. The wings are short and broad. Most species fly
low to the ground, covering short distances on very rapid, weak
wingbeats. In North America, all species in the subfamily
Phasianinae have been introduced. They are represented by
medium-size to large terrestrial birds. The partridges have short
tails, the pheasants have very long tails; in flight, the tails of both
groups are fan-shaped. Partridges and francolins have very rotund
bodies and short stocky necks with relatively large, rounded heads.
Pheasants are more elongated with smaller heads on longer, thinner
necks. Most members of the subfamily have boldly patterned
plumage. Grouse and ptarmigans (subfamily Tetraoninae) are stocky
and medium-size to fairly large, with somewhat elongated bodies.
They differ from the Phasianinae in having partly or fully feathered
legs; ptarmigans have feathered toes and relatively short legs.
Members of this subfamily are also distinguished by the feathered
covering over their nostrils. The plumages are generally patterned
in brown, gray, black, or white. The males of most species have
small, short, colorful patches of skin over the eyes. Courting
behavior is varied; some species make booming sounds, while others
perform elaborate dances in traditional areas known as leks. Some
grouse have bare, distensible skin pouches that are inflated during
these displays. Turkeys (subfamily Meleagridinae) are large, long-
necked ground birds. The head is very small and naked, with
brightly colored blue and red skin patches. The legs are stocky but
long; the conspicuous tail appears wide and fan-shaped in flight. The
plumage is a mixture of rust, brown, black, and white, with many
metallic overtones. Odontophorinae are small, rotund ground birds
with short tails, stocky necks, and rounded heads. Most species have
a plume or crest on the head. In general, sexes have distinct
plumages. These highly gregarious birds are often associated with
brushy areas; all species have distinctive loud calls. (World: 212
species. North America: 21 species.)   *Scott B. Terrill*

Gray Partridge

Perdix perdix
This species calls during most of the year and is often heard but not
seen at dawn and dusk. It is most easily seen in fall and winter, in
coveys along roads and in open agricultural land.

Description
11–14″ (28–35.5 cm). Round, stocky; breast and upper back gray;
face and throat orange-brown; large dark spot on belly; reddish-
brown bars on flanks; rufous outer tail feathers show in flight.

Voice
A hoarse *keee-uk;* first note higher. A rapid cackle when flushed.

Similar Species
See Northern Bobwhite. Chukar has white face and throat with
black border, lacks dark belly spot; occurs in rocky, steep terrain.

Range
Washington and Oregon east to Minnesota and Wisconsin; portions
of Alberta, Saskatchewan, and Manitoba south to Utah and
Nebraska. Scattered populations in Northeast.   *John T. Ratti*

Gray Partridge
Black Francolin
Chukar
Ring-necked Pheasant
Spruce Grouse
Blue Grouse
Willow Ptarmigan
Rock Ptarmigan
White-tailed Ptarmigan
Ruffed Grouse
Sage Grouse
Greater Prairie-Chicken
Lesser Prairie-Chicken
Sharp-tailed Grouse
Wild Turkey
Montezuma Quail
Northern Bobwhite
Scaled Quail
Gambel's Quail
California Quail
Mountain Quail

Adult
1. *Gray breast and upper back.*
2. *Orange-brown face.*
3. *Dark patch on belly.*

Shows rufous outer tail feathers in flight.

Black Francolin

Francolinus francolinus
The Black Francolin, a chickenlike species native to southern Asia and the Middle East, has been introduced to many parts of the world as a game bird. In the continental United States it has become established only in a small area of southwestern Louisiana. Outside the breeding season, the birds are very shy and will run before a pursuer rather than flush, making them difficult quarry. Trying to observe a Black Francolin can be equally frustrating, except during the breeding season from April to June, when the colorful males choose high, exposed perches from which to utter their peculiar songs. In Louisiana, the Black Francolin is found most often along rice-field levees or in open pastureland with scattered shrubs.

Description
13–14″ (33–35.5 cm). Adult males are mostly black with a prominent white cheek patch, a chestnut collar, bold white spots on the lower neck, sides, and flanks, and fine white barring on the rump and center of the tail. The belly and undertail coverts are chestnut. The wing coverts and scapulars are pale sandy brown with dark brown centers; the flight feathers are barred with the same colors. Females and juveniles are sandy brown, barred and spotted with dark brown above and below, and with a chestnut patch on the hindneck. The legs and feet are orange-red in both sexes.

Voice
A loud, far-carrying *click*, *kick-kirrick*, *kick ki-dick*, more like insect's stridulation or electric buzzer sending Morse code than like bird song; unmistakable.

Similar Species
Northern Bobwhite much smaller, has dark legs.

Range
Introduced and established in southwestern Louisiana (Cameron and Calcasieu parishes); also in Hawaii and Guam. A few individuals still seen in southern Florida, although introductions there failed. Undocumented reports from southeastern Texas. Native to India and Middle East.   *H. Douglas Pratt*

Chukar

Alectoris chukar
This elusive game bird, introduced from Europe and Asia, inhabits open, rocky, sparsely vegetated dry mountain slopes and canyons.

Description
13″ (33 cm). Chukars have a grayish head, back, rump, and breast. The whitish throat and cheek is bordered by a black necklace. The white flanks have black vertical bars. The rufous outer tail feathers show in flight. The bill, eye-ring, legs, and feet are pinkish-red.

Voice
A loud, rapid *chuck-chuck-chuck*, often producing laughing effect.

Similar Species
See Northern Bobwhite, Gray Partridge.

Range
British Columbia, Alberta, Washington, and California to Montana and Colorado. Introduced locally in East.   *John T. Ratti*

Female
1. *Sandy-brown color.*
2. *Chestnut patch on hindneck.*
3. *Red-orange legs.*

Male
1. *Black head and breast.*
2. *White cheek patch.*
3. *Chestnut collar.*
4. *Red-orange legs.*

Adult
1. *Black necklace.*
2. *Vertical black bars on white flanks.*
3. *Rufous outer tail feathers.*

Ring-Necked Pheasant

Phasianus colchicus
The Ring-necked Pheasant, a native of Asia, is one of the most successful and well-known introduced birds in North America. Its spectacular multicolored plumage, long tail, and chickenlike appearance make this species difficult to mistake. The birds are swift runners and strong flyers, preferring agricultural land, especially areas with field border cover and interspersed patches of idle brush or woodlots. Nonetheless, they are highly adaptable to diverse habitat types; in the Midwest, cattail marshes provide an important winter habitat. In farm country, pheasants may be heard "crowing" from a distant field; when the ground is snow-covered, they are seen along roadsides, where they seek gravel needed to pulverize grain passing through the gizzard.

Description
Male: 30–36″ (76–91.5 cm); female: 20–26″ (51–66.5 cm). The male pheasant has an iridescent blue-green head and a greenish and slightly elongated crest with cream-colored edging. Brightly colored red skin forms a patch on the cheek and around the eye. Most birds have an incomplete white necklace that is most obvious on the sides of the neck. The body is richly colored with bronze, gold, and iridescent bluish-green feathers, showing prominent dark spots on the flanks and light spots on the back. The rump has elongated grayish-green to brown feathers; the tail is long and pointed. In flight, males show grayish-green shoulder and rump patches. The female is mottled brown and has a shorter tail.

Voice
Loud, rapid, raspy double squawk, *caw-cawk* or *ca-ca*, followed by muffled flurry of wingbeats. Most males cackle when taking flight.

Similar Species
Sharp-tailed Grouse similar to female but has shorter tail with white outer tail feathers.

Range
Populations established on most midlatitude agricultural lands from Alberta and Saskatchewan south to Washington, northern California, Utah, and Kansas, east to Virginia and New England. Scattered populations elsewhere. Native to Asia.   *John T. Ratti*

Spruce Grouse

Dendragapus canadensis
The trusting behavior of the Spruce Grouse, or "fool hen," is its most noteworthy trait. Humans may approach to within a few feet before the bird retreats. This small grouse, which is uncommon in most of the southern portions of its range, inhabits large tracts of conifers, especially where living branches reach to the ground and where there are numerous small forest openings. In much of its eastern range, this bird is particularly fond of bog edges. Although Spruce Grouse can live in forests of any short-needled conifers, they generally favor mixtures of jack pine or lodgepole pine and spruce throughout much of their range. The courtship display of males in spring features strutting, tail-spreading, and periodic short flights with exaggerated wingbeats. The male "Franklin's" Grouse, a form inhabiting the Rocky Mountain region, produces a double wing-clap at the end of its flight display.

Description
13–16″ (33–40.5 cm). The male Spruce Grouse has a black upper

Male
1. *Glossy green head with red face patch.*
2. *White necklace.*
3. *Long tail.*

Female
1. *Mottled brown plumage.*
2. *Pointed tail with no white markings.*

Female
1. *Dark barring on plumage.*
2. *Short, fan-shaped tail.*

Inhabits coniferous forest.

breast and throat, a black tail tipped with orange, white-tipped
undertail coverts, a finely barred gray and black rump, and a
crimson comb above each eye. The male "Franklin's" Grouse lacks
the orange tip of the tail but has white-tipped uppertail coverts. The
combs of males in normal posture vary in size, depending upon the
age of the bird and the intensity of agitation. The female is generally
brown with black barring. There is much individual variation in the
basic color, ranging from gray-brown to reddish-brown. All females
have a narrow buff band across the tip of the tail.

Voice
Male threat call, seldom uttered, a guttural *krrrrk, krrrrk, krrk,
krrk, krrk*, said to be lowest-pitched vocal sound of any North
American bird. Territorial females produce chickenlike *prrp prrrp
prrp prrp prrp prrp prp prp prp*, rising in volume in first few
syllables, then falling.

Similar Species
Ruffed Grouse occasionally as tame, but spotted rather than barred,
with dark band near tip of tail and contrasting ruff feathers on sides
of neck. Female Blue Grouse similar but larger, with black tail
(usually with grayish terminal band visible).

Range
Across North America in boreal forest from southern border of
tundra in Alaska south to northern and eastern Washington, eastern
Oregon, and in Rocky Mountains to Idaho, Montana, and western
Wyoming; from northern edge of Canadian prairies south to central
Ontario north of the farmlands, and through Minnesota, Wisconsin,
and northern Michigan east to Adirondack Mountains of New York,
northern Vermont and New Hampshire, Maine, and Nova Scotia.
William L. Robinson

Blue Grouse

Dendragapus obscurus
This is a common, unwary bird, and the largest grouse in forested
areas of western North America. Its identifying characteristics are
its large size, hooting, flutter-flight displays, tame nature, and habit
of flaring the tail feathers and erecting a white rosette of neck
feathers while displaying. Blue Grouse are unique in migrating down
to lower elevations to breed in spring and back to high altitudes in
winter. Like the Spruce Grouse, Blue Grouse are often called "fool
hens"; they are extremely tame and may be approached closely.
They prefer somewhat open forests, especially forest edges and
ridges with scattered trees and shrubs or mixed coniferous and
deciduous trees.

Description
Male: 17–19″ (43–48.5 cm); female 18½–22½″ (47–57 cm). Males are
gray to bluish-gray with slight brown or black mottling on the
feathers of the head, nape, back, and wings. The breast and belly
are gray and unmottled; the flanks have white markings. Females

Male "Franklin's" Grouse

1. *Red comb over eye.*
2. *Black throat and upper breast.*
3. *Uppertail coverts with white tips.*
4. *Black tail without buff tip.*

Male Spruce Grouse

1. *Red comb over eye.*
2. *Black throat and upper breast.*
3. *Uppertail coverts without white tips.*
4. *Black tail with buff tip.*

Female

1. *Breast without barring.*
2. *Black tail with gray terminal band.*

are brown with black barring or mottling on the head, scapulars, chest, and flanks. The breast and belly are gray and lack barring. In both males and females the tail is black and squared; in most birds there is a gray terminal band, although in some this band may be indistinct. During their display, males fan the tail, raise the yellow-orange to red combs over the eyes, and fan the white, black-tipped feathers of 2 rosettes, 1 on each side of the neck. The bare skin in the center of these rosettes is yellow in birds of most of the species' range, but red to purple in birds of the Rocky Mountains.

Voice
Males: 5–7 low hooting notes; females: clucking and cackling. Hooting of Rocky Mountain birds audible at about 50 yards, but calls of other races can be heard at greater distances, up to several hundred yards.

Similar Species
Male Spruce Grouse much smaller, with black breast patch conspicuously barred with white, black-and-white barred back feathers, and brown terminal band on tail. Female Spruce Grouse has white-and-black barred underparts, and orange terminal tail band. Ruffed Grouse has gray or brown tail with black subterminal band.

Range
Resident from southeastern Alaska and Yukon Territory east to Northwest Territories, and southward along coast to northern California; in mountains to central California, northeastern Nevada, northern Arizona, Colorado, and northern New Mexico. Extremely rare in mountains of southern California.   *Harold J. Harju*

Willow Ptarmigan

Lagopus lagopus
Largest of the 3 species of ptarmigan, the Willow Ptarmigan is a medium-size grouse with a chunky body, short legs, short tail, and rather stubby but powerful wings. It lives in arctic and alpine areas, at lower elevations than the Rock Ptarmigan, in places where water is plentiful and shrubs are tall; these birds sometimes move in winter to brushy areas within the forest. Remaining in family groups from May to August, Willow Ptarmigans gather in flocks and become nomadic in fall and winter. Unlike male Rock Ptarmigans, male Willows help to raise the brood. Loud calls often reveal the birds' presence in spring and autumn, but ptarmigans are usually quiet in midsummer and winter.

Description
14–16″ (35.5–40.5 cm). The Willow Ptarmigan has the 3-plumage annual cycle typical of ptarmigans. The primaries of all adult North American ptarmigans are white throughout the year. The tail feathers of both the Willow and Rock ptarmigans are dark brown or

Typical male
1. Squared, black tail with gray terminal band.
2. White rosette of feathers on side of neck, with bare yellow skin in center.

Rocky Mountain male, displaying
1. Red skin in center of white rosette.

Female in summer
1. Warm brown plumage with yellow barring on underparts.

black, tipped with white. Ptarmigans' toes are feathered to the base
in summer and to the tip in winter. Willow Ptarmigans have pure
white body plumage from late fall to spring. The male in breeding
plumage has a bright rust-brown head and neck and a white body.
Later the white is replaced by reddish-brown feathers on the back
and underparts. In midsummer a partial postbreeding molt brings
new brownish feathers to the body and neck of adults. Females in
summer plumage are warm brown with prominent yellow barring on
the breast, belly, and flanks. Chicks are downy for a few days, then
grow yellow-flecked brown body feathers and primaries. By late
summer juveniles have new white primaries, and white body
feathers appear by fall.

Voice
Breeding male a loud, staccato call, *go-back, go-back* or *tobacco,
tobacco, tobacco*, at end of display flight; other guttural calls. Easily
distinguished from snoring rattle of Rock Ptarmigan and high squeal
of White-tailed Ptarmigan. Females call chicks with purring and low
clucking sounds.

Similar Species
Rock Ptarmigan slightly smaller, with much smaller bill; has black
eye stripe in winter, brown, not rust-colored, in summer plumage.
White-tailed Ptarmigan smaller, with smaller bill and white tail
feathers.

Range
Alaska east to Ellesmere Island and Newfoundland, south to
mountains of British Columbia and Alberta; does not reach as far
north in central Canadian Arctic as Rock Ptarmigan. Winters south
to forested parts of central Canadian provinces. Also in Eurasia.
Robert B. Weeden

Rock Ptarmigan

Lagopus mutus
This species lives high in hilly tundra with low heath and willows.
Far northern populations may migrate hundreds of miles.

Description
12–14″ (30.3–35.5 cm). Winter plumage white, with black loral stripe
in males and a few females, and black tail; both sexes have red
comb, larger in males. Bill slim. Summer plumages brown, with
gray flecking (males) or yellow barring (females).

Voice
Males: long, far-carrying snore at end of display flight; females:
clucking and purring with young. Silent in winter and midsummer.

Similar Species
See Willow and White-tailed ptarmigans.

Range
Aleutians, Alaska, northern Canada. Winters south to edge of
boreal forest. Also in Eurasia, Greenland.   *Robert B. Weeden*

Breeding male
1. *Rust-brown head and neck.*
2. *White body.*

Winter plumage
1. *Pure white plumage without black eye stripe.*
2. *Large bill.*
3. *Black feathers in tail.*

Winter plumage
1. *Pure white plumage with black eye stripe.*
2. *Small bill.*
3. *Black feathers in tail.*

White-tailed Ptarmigan

Lagopus leucurus
The small White-tailed Ptarmigan lives above tree line most of the
year. While it occupies rocky tundra areas from May through
October, it frequents areas dominated by willow, birch, and alder
shrubs at or slightly below tree line during most of the winter.
Annual local migrations are common; in winter, females move
farther and occur in larger flocks than males.

Description
12–14″ (30.5–35.5 cm). Throughout the year, this small grouse has
white wings, a white tail, and feathered legs and toes. The bill is
intermediate in shape between those of the Willow and Rock
ptarmigans. In white winter plumage, the sexes are virtually
indistinguishable. Males begin to molt into breeding plumage before
females—usually from late April to early May. The male's breeding
plumage is typified by coarsely barred brown feathers with finer
bars of black and yellow on the back, scapular, and upper tail
regions; the long tail coverts conceal the white tail feathers, except
when the bird flicks its tail or takes flight. Head and neck feathers
are black-tipped, while feathers of the lower breast, belly, and
undertail coverts remain white. Breeding-plumage females are
coarsely barred black with finer bars of yellow on the back,
scapulars, and upper tail. The upper breast and belly are barred
yellow and black, with yellow predominating. The first postbreeding
molt of males starts in late June; that of females in mid- to late July.
The feathers on the back, scapulars, upper tail, and upper breast
replaced during this molt are identical in both sexes; they are finely
vermiculated and slightly speckled with brown and gray. After the
second postbreeding molt, the winter plumage appears. Both sexes
have pale orange to crimson eye stripes; these can be exposed when
the birds are breeding, brooding, or excited. Eye stripe color may
change seasonally. White-tailed Ptarmigan have heavily feathered
legs and toes. Newly hatched chicks are rich brown on the back to
gray and buff on the flanks. Juvenile flight feathers are gray, and
eventually replaced by white primaries, secondaries, and rectrices
starting at about 3 to 4 weeks of age. With the first postnatal molt,
the natal down is replaced by finely vermiculated feathers, speckled
gray and brown, with occasional coarsely barred black spots. The
second postnatal molt of juveniles results in white winter plumage
identical to that of adults. Plumage of the young of the year and of
all age classes in winter are similar in both males and females.

Voice
Males: a high pitched *ku-kriiee, kriiee* during breeding season; also a
kuk-kuk-kuk while stationary or running. Females: a low-pitched
cluck when alarmed or when with chicks.

Similar Species
Rock and Willow ptarmigans have white wings and black tails.
Females and winter birds quite similar but lack white tail. Male
Rock Ptarmigan remains white until after peak of breeding.
Breeding male Willow Ptarmigan has rusty head and neck. In late
summer, male Rock and White-tailed ptarmigans similar except for
tail color and bill size.

Range
Breeds above tree line in high mountains from south-central Alaska,
British Columbia, Yukon Territory, Northwest Territories, Alberta,
south to Washington, Montana, Wyoming, Colorado, and northern
New Mexico. Recently successfully introduced into Sierras in
northeastern California, Wallowa Mountains in Oregon, and Uinta
Mountains in Utah.   *Clait E. Braun*

Winter plumage
1. *Pure white plumage without black eye stripe.*
2. *No black in tail.*

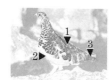

Breeding male
1. *Barred brown plumage on upperparts.*
2. *White lower breast and belly.*
3. *Long uppertail coverts conceal white tail.*

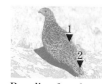

Breeding female
1. *Coarsely barred upperparts.*
2. *Long uppertail coverts conceal white tail.*

Ruffed Grouse

Bonasa umbellus
The Ruffed Grouse is the most widely distributed resident game
bird on the continent. It is most common in hardwood forests with
dense undergrowth, especially where aspens are present. The
Ruffed Grouse may be best known by the male's "drumming"
display, heard most often in the spring; while standing erect on a
log, rock, or other elevated site, the male snaps its wings forward,
producing a distinctive sound like that of a chain saw or tractor
starting up. In territorial or courtship display the male spreads its
tail, extends the neck ruff, and droops the wings in a manner
resembling a turkey. Females are most likely to use this display
when their broods are threatened. When the bird is alarmed, a crest
may be erected on the head. Although normally quite secretive, this
species' need to feed on tree buds makes it conspicuous in tree tops,
usually at dawn or dusk, during winter when snow covers the
ground. Ruffed Grouse prefer to walk, run, or freeze rather than to
fly; flight is usually a last resort to escape an enemy.

Description
15–19″ (38–48.5 cm). Both sexes have similar coloration, the body
being generally mottled and varying from gray to light brown.
Flank feathers are light gray or tan with prominent dark bars. The
tail may range from a chestnut-red to silver-gray. In warmer
climates all birds are red-tailed, while in colder climates the grayer-
tailed birds become more common. The tail, which varies in color
and pattern among individuals, has 5 to 11 transverse bars and a
black or chocolate-colored subterminal band. The prominent neck
ruff is always the same color as the tail band. This ruff is more
conspicuous on the male than the female, but is extended by both
sexes when displaying. Feathering on the legs may be sparse or
absent in warmer climates but quite dense in colder climates; in
winter, horny growths (pectin) develop on the toes to aid the birds
as they feed in trees.

Voice
Assorted, seldom-heard clucks, hisses, and other vocal sounds. A
loud *chuck* similar to call of red squirrel. Male "drums" with wings
frequently at night and in morning, especially during spring, but
may be heard at any time in any season; usually repeated at
4-minute intervals.

Similar Species
Sharp-tailed Grouse chunkier, generally lighter brown, with pointed
tail; lives in more open cover. Spruce Grouse generally darker, with
prominent rust-colored or yellowish band on tip of tail; seldom
occurs in hardwoods, but may occur with Ruffed Grouse in northern
coniferous forests. Adult Blue Grouse larger and darker; juvenile in
Rocky Mountains lacks subterminal tail band.

Range
Resident from central Alaska, Yukon, Mackenzie, Saskatchewan,
northern Ontario, southern Quebec, and southern Labrador south to
northern California, northern Utah, Wyoming, South Dakota,
Missouri, Kentucky, northeastern Alabama, and northern Georgia.
Introduced to Newfoundland and northeastern Nevada.
Gordon W. Gullion

Displaying male
1. *Fanned tail with black subterminal band.*
2. *Raised black neck ruffs.*

Brown form
1. *Brown plumage.*
2. *Chestnut-red tail.*
3. *Barred flanks.*

Gray form
1. *Gray plumage.*
2. *Silver-gray tail.*
3. *Barred flanks.*

Sage Grouse

Centrocercus urophasianus
The Sage Grouse is the largest species of grouse in North America, with males often weighing from 5 to 7 pounds. It occurs throughout the sagebrush-dominated rangelands of western North America. This species is entirely dependent upon forms of sagebrush, primarily big sagebrush, for food from October to May and for cover throughout the year. It is most abundant where sagebrush provides 15 to 50 percent of the ground cover. Mixed flocks make annual migrations of up to 48 miles and more throughout much of the year, though females are nonmigratory immediately prior to and during nesting. Sage Grouse gather for mating on leks, or traditional display grounds, during the period from late March to late May; during peak periods, several hundred birds may be present. While this grouse is frequently abundant in suitable habitats, its cryptic coloration and secretive nature make it difficult to locate outside of the breeding season.

Description
Male: 27–34″ (68.5–86.5 cm); female: 18–24″ (45.5–61 cm). For most of the year, both sexes are brown to gray-brown with pointed tails, black bellies, and white-tipped (in males) or streaked (in females) undertail coverts. Breeding males have large white air sacs on the breast, a black bib in the upper center of the air sacs, and long (100 + mm) filoplumes extending from the sides of the upper throat back over the white collar of the air sacs. Males appear twice as large as females and, apart from size, can be distinguished from females by the black basal area of the lower mandible and the white or grayish-white specialized feathers covering the air sacs on the upper breast. Both sexes have a dull yellow-green to yellow eye stripe that is visible in males during the breeding season. Chicks are cryptically colored pale gray to gray-brown. The juvenal plumage is pale gray-brown with white shaft streaks similar to, but lighter than, those of adult females. After the postjuvenal molt in late September or early October, juvenile males begin to acquire feathers of the breeding plumage. The legs and toes of Sage Grouse are feathered, and the toes appear light yellow to dull green.

Voice
During breeding display, males give a *plop-plop* or bubbling sound as air is released from air sacs. Females may give a cackle or *quak-quak* call during breeding period. Calls at other times of the year not audible at a distance.

Similar Species
All other North American grouse substantially smaller than male Sage Grouse. Blue Grouse males similar in size to female Sage Grouse, but slate- to blue-gray with square tail feathers, red-yellow eye stripes and white rosettes (not easily seen except in breeding season) around yellow to crimson air sacs. Female Blue Grouse smaller and browner with more black-barred feathers. Sharp-tailed Grouse much smaller; have shorter, square-tipped central tail feathers, purple to crimson air sacs, and white spotting on wings and upper back; white underparts show clearly in flight.

Range
Southern Alberta and Saskatchewan, British Columbia (extirpated), Washington, Oregon, eastern California, Idaho, Montana, Nevada, Wyoming, southwestern North Dakota, extreme western South Dakota, to western and central Utah, Colorado, and New Mexico (extirpated). At one time, Sage Grouse extended to extreme western Nebraska and Oklahoma. In general, their distribution follows that of big sagebrush.   *Clait E. Braun*

Displaying male
1. *Black bib above air sacs.*
2. *Inflated white air sacs.*
3. *Spread tail with pointed tail feathers.*

Breeding male
1. *Black bib.*
2. *White breast.*
3. *Black filoplumes on side of neck.*
4. *Black belly.*
5. *Pointed tail.*

Large size.

Breeding female
1. *Mottled gray-brown plumage.*
2. *Black belly.*
3. *Pale base to lower mandible.*

Greater Prairie-Chicken

Tympanuchus cupido
Males of both the Greater and Lesser prairie-chickens have
elongated feathers, or pinnae, that can be erected to form earlike
structures. However, except during spring display this is not as
useful a field mark as the barred body pattern. The prairie-chickens
are fairly rare and local species that are associated with natural
grasslands; the Greater prefers prairie habitat, while the Lesser is
usually found in more arid or sandy grasslands.

Description
17–18″ (43–45.5 cm). This species has strong vertical bars of dark
brown and buff-white in a zebralike pattern over the mantle, flanks,
and underparts. The tail is short, rounded, and dark brown,
inconspicuously barred with buff in females. During display, the
male erects the earlike pinnae, engorges the yellow combs above the
eyes, and inflates the neck sacs, which are bright orange, shading to
red near the head. This display occurs only on traditional display
grounds, or leks, usually at dawn but sometimes also at dusk. The
bird's takeoff is explosive, and in flight the birds exhibit white wing
linings and a profile almost identical to that of the Sharp-tailed
Grouse. In flight, the best field marks are the short, rounded dark
brown tail and an absence of white on the flanks. Greater and Lesser
prairie-chickens in flight cannot be distinguished with certainty.

Voice
During display, male utters a far-carrying cooing sound, *old mul-
doon*, lasting about a second and distinctly 3-parted; cackles and
whines. Females usually silent.

Similar Species
See Lesser Prairie-Chicken and Sharp-tailed Grouse.

Range
Local and limited to native grassland areas from Dakotas,
Nebraska, and northeastern Colorado south to northeastern
Oklahoma, east in remnant pockets in Minnesota, Wisconsin,
Missouri, and Illinois; also isolated population ("Attwater's" Prairie-
Chicken) on Texas Coast. Colorado, Kansas, and Oklahoma support
isolated populations of both prairie-chickens; observers there should
take special care in identification.   *Paul A. Johnsgard*

Lesser Prairie-Chicken

Tympanuchus pallidicinctus
The Lesser Prairie-Chicken is a very close relative—some believe a
subspecies—of the Greater Prairie Chicken. It occurs to the
southwest of the Greater's range and favors more arid and sandy
grasslands. The male Lesser also has air sacs of a different color and
a different call. At present, the ranges of the 2 prairie-chickens do
not overlap, simplifying identification.

Description
16″ (40.5 cm). The strong vertical barring on this species is very
slightly paler than in the Greater Prairie-Chicken, producing a
slightly more washed-out appearance. As in the Greater, the tail is
rounded, short, and dark brown, and is distinctly darker than the
rest of the bird. The most distinctive field marks for separating the 2
species are visible only during display, when the male erects the
long pinnae, exposes the reddish-purple air sacs (which are smaller
and more rounded than in the Greater), and engorges the chrome-
yellow combs, which are as large or even larger than the Greater's.

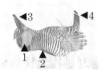

Displaying male
1. *Orange or reddish air sacs.*
2. *Bold, zebralike pattern.*
3. *Elongated pinnae.*
4. *Brown, rounded tail.*

Displays in groups. Cooing display call.

Female
1. *Bold, zebralike pattern.*
2. *Brown, rounded tail.*

Inhabits prairie grasslands.

Female
1. *Finely barred pattern.*
2. *Short, rounded tail.*

Inhabits sandy sage grasslands.

Voice
A yodelling series of 5 or more bubbling notes, emitted in continuous series. Also various chickenlike cackling notes and squeaking sounds. Female calls of 2 species not distinguishable; consist in part of high-pitched cackling notes, similar to those of male.

Similar Species
Greater Prairie-Chicken slightly larger and darker, associated with prairie; air sacs larger, bright orange to red; booming *old-muldoon* call. See Sharp-tailed Grouse.

Range
Limited to extreme southeastern Colorado (Prowers and Baca counties), western and southwestern Kansas (Arkansas and Cimarron valleys), Panhandles of Oklahoma and Texas, and New Mexico east of the Pecos River. Only in central Kansas and central Oklahoma is there the possibility of confusion with Greater Prairie-Chicken, but even there the 2 species are ecologically and geographically isolated from each other.   *Paul A. Johnsgard*

Sharp-tailed Grouse

Tympanuchus phasianellus
Like most other Galliformes, the Sharp-tailed Grouse is a local, nonmigratory bird that can be difficult to find. It is primarily northern in its range and is found in a wide variety of habitats, such as brushy prairies, open bogs, abandoned or recently cleared farmland, and boreal forest edges. Like the prairie-chickens and Sage Grouse, male Sharp-taileds gather at dawn in spring at traditional booming grounds to "dance" in courtship display. When flushed, the Sharp-tailed flies quite fast—for a bird of its size—on rapid wingbeats alternating with short glides.

Description
15–20″ (38–51 cm). A typical large, brownish grouse, the Sharp-tailed is characterized by its white outer tail feathers and pointed tail with square-tipped central feathers that project only a short distance. The best mark of this species, especially in flight, is the pale, frosty appearance of the wings, which are heavily spotted with white. Sharp-taileds are also relatively pale below, being only lightly barred beneath. Displaying males also show purple neck sacs and a yellow comb over the eye.

Voice
On booming grounds, males give dovelike *hoo* or *hoo hoo*, like Mourning Dove's call; higher-pitched than Greater Prairie-Chicken's. Also muffled cackling or gobbling notes. Otherwise usually silent.

Similar Species
Greater and Lesser prairie-chickens, only other grouse associated with prairies, have short, rounded, dark brown tails. Ruffed Grouse and Spruce Grouse also have different tail pattern. No other grouse has Sharp-tailed's frosty-looking wings.

Range
Resident from north-central Alaska, Yukon, western Mackenzie, Saskatchewan, Manitoba, and Ontario, south to eastern Oregon, northern Nevada, Utah, northeastern New Mexico, western Nebraska, central South Dakota, northern Minnesota, northern Wisconsin, and northern Michigan.   *Kim R. Eckert*

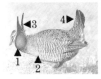

Displaying male
. *Reddish-purple air sacs.*
. *Finely barred pattern.*
. *Elongated pinnae.*
. *Brown, rounded tail.*

Displays in groups. Bubbling display call.

Displaying male
. *Short, pointed tail with white outer tail feathers.*
. *White spots on wings.*
. *Purple neck patch.*
. *Yellow comb over eye.*

Female
. *White outer tail feathers.*
. *White spots on wing.*
. *Finely marked underparts.*

Wild Turkey

Meleagris gallopavo
The Wild Turkey is a very large, long-legged fowl with a naked
head and neck, iridescent plumage, and a long, broad tail. It has
disappeared from much of its original range but is locally common in
open forests and forest edges, especially in the South. The male and
some females have a black "beard" on the breast. The male is
considerably larger than the female; it erects its tail in courtship
display. This wary species is a weak flyer; it runs to avoid danger,
and feeds on the ground on acorns, nuts, seeds, fruits, and insects.
It roosts in trees.

Description
Male: 48–50″ (122–127 cm); female: 35–37″ (89–94 cm). The male has
a bluish head and red wattles on the throat and foreneck. The body
is iridescent bronze, the primaries and secondaries are barred, and
tail is rust-colored to brown and finely barred, with a narrow black
subterminal band and a pale rust tip. The female, which seldom has
a beard, has a smaller head, a slimmer body, and less iridescent
plumage.

Voice
Male gobbles; female clucks. Also gives a *pit* or *put-put* alarm call
and *keow-keow* flock call.

Range
Resident locally from Arizona to New England south to Florida and
southern Mexico. Reintroduced in much of its former range;
introduced elsewhere.   *Paul W. Sykes, Jr.*

Montezuma Quail

Cyrtonyx montezumae
This stout bird of grassy oak and pine woodlands is probably the
most difficult North American quail to see well. It is most frequently
observed huddled at the side of the road or bursting out of the grass
at one's feet and flying low to the ground in a whirl of wingbeats,
only to land, crouch, and become invisible again. The defense of
crouching rather than running or flying leads to the common name
"fool quail." If one does get a good view, the harlequin black-and-
white face pattern, heavily spotted underparts of the male, and
bushy, helmetlike crest of both sexes identify this species.
Monetzuma Quail are usually detected by their calls.

Description
8½–8¾″ (21.5–22 cm). The Montezuma is a stocky, robust quail with
a complex pattern of black-and-white facial markings and a buff-
colored, rounded crest that is bushy toward the rear. A black-and-
white collar separates the head from the underparts, which are
slate-gray and heavily spotted with white except for a narrow

Female
1. *Iridescent bronze plumage.*
2. *Naked head and neck.*

Large size.

Displaying male
1. *Large, fan-shaped tail.*
2. *Naked head and neck.*
3. *Drooping, barred wing feathers.*

Large size.
Gobbling call.

Male
1. *Black-and-white face pattern.*
2. *Buff, rounded crest.*
3. *Black flanks with bold white spots.*

Stocky build.
Inhabits pine-oak grasslands.

chestnut midline down the breast that widens and turns to black on the midbelly and undertail coverts. The upperparts are heavily barred with blackish on a cinnamon, buff, and brown background that is broken by long, white to buff pinstriping. The wings and tail have a ground color similar to the back, but the wings are spotted and the tail is barred with blackish. The gray legs and feet are quite stocky. Females resemble males, but the facial pattern is an obscure buff-and-brownish version of the male's. The upperparts are buff to pinkish-brown, barred with blackish and with elongated pinstripes of dull buff, and the underparts are pale cinnamon-brown to pale buff, lightly speckled with blackish.

Voice
A mellow, soft, single *whooo* note, owl-like in quality; also a descending tremolo simlar to Eastern Screech-Owl's.

Range
Fairly common but local resident in central and southeastern Arizona, in central and southern New Mexico; in small numbers in extreme southwestern Texas (Davis Mountains). Also in Mexico.
Scott B. Terrill

Northern Bobwhite

Colinus virginianus
The Northern Bobwhite is a medium-size bird with a short tail. It is found in open woodland around fields and in country with scattered brush. It spends by far the largest part of its life on the ground. The only exceptions are in summer, when a male may call from a low perch, and in winter, after a covey has been flushed, when a few individuals may alight in a tree. When frightened, Bobwhites usually run for a short distance into thicker cover, then freeze in a group before flushing with a rather loud whir of wings. As nights become cooler, individuals form coveys of 8 to 25 birds and spend most of their time in cover.

Description
10″ (25 cm). The adult Bobwhite is reddish-brown above, with irregular chestnut streaks on the sides and a white breast and belly mottled with black. The male has a white throat and a white line from the upper mandible over the eye and down the side of the neck. There is a contrasting black stripe that extends from the back of the eye to the side of the neck. The female is nearly identical, but the white on the head and throat is replaced by buff. Soon after hatching, chicks start growing primary coverts that are retained until the first postbreeding molt. The prebreeding and postbreeding molt of adults is so gradual that the different plumages are difficult to distinguish.

Voice
A clear, whistled *bobwhite* or *ah bobwhite* by males from spring to fall; also calls in winter at daybreak, dusk, or when flushed. Both sexes give a *wa-lo-he-he* whistle, repeated 3–4 times.

Similar Species
No other quail in present range of Bobwhite. Gray Partridge has bright rusty tail, occurs in open agricultural land.

Range
Permanent resident throughout Southeast. Stable populations as far west as eastern portions of Kansas, Oklahoma, and Texas, and as far north as southern Iowa, central portions of Illinois, Indiana, Ohio, and southern Pennsylvania; in Northeast to Cape Cod. Beyond these limits numbers fluctuate depending on severity of winter in north and amount of rainfall in west.   *Walter Rosene*

Male
1. *Black-and-white face pattern.*
2. *Buff upperparts with long stripes.*

Male
1. *Black-and-white face pattern.*
2. *Reddish-brown upperparts.*
3. *Irregular streaking on sides.*

Female
1. *Black-and-buff face pattern.*
2. *Reddish-brown upperparts.*
3. *Irregular streaking on sides.*

Scaled Quail

Callipepla squamata
This quail, common in southwestern desert grasslands and desert scrub, can often be detected by its loud 2-syllable call.

Description
10–12″ (25–30.5 cm). Adults blue-gray on nape, upper back, and breast, gray-brown elsewhere above; cream to buff below (chestnut in some males in southern Texas) with heavy blackish scaling. Crest and throat buff-white, face and head gray-brown. Juveniles gray-brown above with black and brown spots, buff below with brown bars and whitish spots, with short brown-and-buff crest.

Voice
A low, nasal *pe-cos*, a loud, harsh *puck-hornk*, and a single *oonk*.

Range
South-central Arizona, southeast Colorado, southwest Kansas, and western Texas south into central Mexico.   *Scott B. Terrill*

Gambel's Quail

Callipepla gambelii
This species, abundant over much of its range, inhabits desert scrub, cacti, mesquite, and riparian areas. Gambel's Quail are often seen in large coveys that include several family groups in the summer months. The males call conspicuously from exposed perches, but the sound of the numerous, soft clucking notes of a flock concealed in the brush is often the only clue to this bird's presence. When flushed, these birds often fly in noisy bursts of whirring wings, uttering explosive alarm calls. The buff belly (with a bold black circle in the male) instantly distinguishes Gambel's.

Description
10–11½″ (25–29 cm). The male is primarily grayish on the upperparts and slightly washed with brown on the mantle, with a bright rust-brown crown bordered in front and on the sides by black and white lines; the white line curves around behind the eye, and there is a conspicuous black curved head plume. The forehead and throat are black, also outlined by white. The sides and upper breast are gray, contrasting with a buff belly and undertail coverts, with a central large, blackish spot in the midbelly. The flanks are rust with buff-colored diagonal barring. The female is similar but paler, and lacks the black area on the belly.

Voice
Loud *chi-kar-ke-ke-cut-cut* (accent on second syllable) and *kee-err* (accent on first syllable); more often 3 syllables, a *ha-haah-haaa* or *puk-kwaw-ca*, with second syllable accented and highest-pitched. Also gives various flocking notes.

Similar Species
In southern California, occurs sympatrically with California and Mountain quails. California Quail lacks buff belly and dark central spot; instead, belly appears scaled. Mountain Quail has chestnut throat and very long plume; lacks buff belly with central spot.

Range
Resident in deserts of southeastern California, southern Nevada, southwestern Utah, western and south-central Arizona, western Colorado, western New Mexico, and extreme western Texas south into northern Mexico. Introduced in Idaho and western New Mexico.
Scott B. Terrill

Adult
1. *Blue-gray, scaly plumage.*
2. *Buff-white crest.*

   Inhabits desert grassland and scrub.

Male
1. *Bold face pattern, black forehead, curved head plume.*
2. *Gray upperparts.*
3. *Rusty sides with diagonal stripes.*
4. *Buff belly with black central spot.*

   Inhabits deserts.

Female
1. *Reduced face pattern and head plume.*
2. *Duller upperparts.*
3. *Pale belly without black spot.*

   Often found in coveys.

California Quail

Callipepla californica
The California Quail is common over most of its range. It tolerates a relatively broad variety of climates, from arid desert to cool, wet coast. Shrub cover and woodlands with patches of open ground—including suburban gardens, chaparral, and river bottoms below areas of snowfall—are its favored haunts. It ranges into the western edges of desert where Gambel's Quail is absent, but contacts and sometimes hybridizes with this species near San Gorgonio Pass in Southern California. Pairs and medium-size coveys stay close to the shadows of brushy cover, and scattered groups communicate using a variety of clucking notes. California Quails roost low in trees or bushes and may form very large coveys during the winter.

Description
9½–10½″ (24–27 cm). The upperparts are blue-gray with brownish wings, and the belly has a dark, scaly appearance. The body is plump and stocky. Males have a short, curved, black plume, the feathers of which may become separated. The throat is black and framed with white; the forehead is usually buff; the crown is dark brown. Females lack the black throat, have paler faces, and have a shorter plume. Juveniles are similar to females.

Voice
Three-syllable *ca-cah-co;* accent varies, but typically on second syllable. Unpaired males give a single *cah* in spring. Also clucking notes, *whit-whit* and *tek-tek.*

Similar Species
Male Gambel's Quail has plain buff-white belly with dark spot; richer, rusty brown crown; black forehead; paler above. Female Gambel's has chestnut on flanks; buff-white belly with fine streaks. Mountain Quail has chestnut throat, black-and-white bars on chestnut flanks, and long, straight plume (spike).

Range
Native resident from southern counties in Oregon to tip of Baja California and east barely into western Nevada. Also on Catalina Island off Southern California. Introduced and established from southern British Columbia south, including western Idaho, Nevada, Utah, and Santa Cruz and Santa Rosa islands off southern California.   *Louis R. Bevier*

Mountain Quail

Oreortyx pictus
These fairly common quail are fond of cover and difficult to observe; their temperate range is mainly along the Pacific mountain system.

Description
10–11½″ (25–29 cm). Head and breast dark blue-gray, throat chestnut with white border. Long, slender, straight black plume on head, held swept back or erect. Flanks chestnut with broad white bars bordered with black. Upperparts plain olive-brown.

Voice
In spring a loud, resonant *kyork*, or fast series of short whistles.

Similar Species
See Gambel's and California quails.

Range
Southwestern Washington to northern Baja California and western Nevada; birds in western Idaho and western Nevada may be introduced. Introduced in Pacific Northwest.   *Louis R. Bevier*

Female
1. *Reduced face pattern and head plume.*
2. *Scaly belly.*

Generally found in moister habitats than Gambel's Quail.

Male
1. *Bold face pattern with buff forehead and curved head plume.*
2. *Blue-gray upperparts.*
3. *Rusty sides with diagonal stripes.*
4. *Scaly belly.*

Adult
1. *Long, straight head plume.*
2. *Chestnut throat.*
3. *Chestnut flanks with bold white bars.*

Loud call.

Rails

(Family Rallidae)
These are small to medium-size marsh and water birds with short, rounded wings and long legs and toes. Most rails have laterally compressed bodies and small tails; from the side, many resemble chickens. They usually escape danger by running through cover or swimming rather than flying. When these birds do fly, the short wings beat rapidly and weakly, and the legs dangle behind. Rails, gallinules, and coots are often detected by their loud vocalizations. Many species call frequently at night. (World: 142 species. North America: 14 species.)   *Scott B. Terrill*

Yellow Rail

Coturnicops noveboracensis
Local and sometimes surprisingly common, the tiny Yellow Rail breeds in northern grassy marshes and wet meadows. Usually easy to hear but quite difficult to see, it is primarily active at night, when its rhythmic pattern of ticking notes can go on endlessly. With careful stalking, a group of observers can see this rail by surrounding a calling bird; unless the bird falls silent or sneaks mouselike through the reeds, it will freeze or flutter off weakly, looking like a buff blur. During migration and in winter, the Yellow Rail can be flushed from upland grasslands and grainfields.

Description
6–7½″ (15–19 cm). The Yellow Rail is mostly buff-colored or yellowish below but darker above with a checkered pattern of very dark brown on buff. In flight, it has distinct broad white tips on the secondaries; at night these patches are hard to see since the entire bird appears pale in a flashlight's beam. The short bill and legs are greenish-yellow.

Voice
At night, a long series of rhythmic ticking in alternating groups of 2 and 3: *tic-tic, tic-tic-tic, tic-tic, tic-tic-tic.* Easily imitated by hitting 2 stones together.

Similar Species
Immature Sora larger, darker, with solid brown back and white patch under tail; lacks white wing patch.

Range
Breeds from Great Slave Lake, northern Saskatchewan, Manitoba, northern Ontario, southern Quebec and New Brunswick, south to central Alberta, southern Saskatchewan, central North Dakota, northern Minnesota, northern Wisconsin, northern Michigan, and southern Ontario. Winters in coastal central California (rare) and from coastal North Carolina to Texas. Formerly bred in northeastern California.   *Kim R. Eckert*

Front view
1. *Buff underparts and face.*

   Small size.
   Ticking call.

Side view
1. *Checkered buff-and-brown upperparts.*
2. *White wing patch.*

Black Rail

Laterallus jamaicensis
This rare, local, and secretive bird nests in coastal marshes, inland freshwater marshes, and wet meadows.

Description
5–6″ (13–15 cm). Black above with chestnut nape, white speckling on back; slate-gray below, barred and finely spotted with white posteriorly. Bill black; eye red; legs greenish. Juvenile paler.

Voice
Male: *kee-kee-keer;* female: *who-whoo;* often heard on still nights.

Similar Species
Chicks of other rails have glossy black down, lack bars on flanks.

Range
South of Great Lakes; Connecticut to Gulf Coast; California coast and lower Colorado River. Winters in southern part of range. Also in Central and South America.   *Dan Clark Holliman*

Clapper Rail

Rallus longirostris
The Clapper Rail is the common "marsh hen" of coastal salt marshes. Its raucous calls have a derisive quality, as if the bird were mocking the frustrated birder straining for a glimpse of this elusive species. But patience can be rewarded, particularly at dawn and dusk, when Clapper Rails may emerge from the marsh grass and feed on open mud flats. The rather chickenlike shape, with a long, slightly drooping bill and an often upturned tail, is distinctive. Despite their unwebbed, long, slender toes, these birds swim well and often do so. Though abundant in the east, Clapper Rails are local in California, where many populations are endangered by habitat destruction.

Description
14–16″ (35.5–40.5 cm). Clapper Rails are mostly olive-brown or gray-brown, with dark streaks above, gray cheeks, white undertail coverts, bold vertical gray-and-white bars on the flanks, and buff or rust-colored breasts. Birds on the Atlantic Coast look very washed out compared with the more richly colored Gulf Coast and western populations, some of which closely resemble King Rails. The Clapper's olive-brown—not rust-colored—shoulders are diagnostic. The downy chicks are all black and have often been misidentified as Black Rails.

Voice
A loud, harsh, chattering *he-e-eh-heh-heh-heh*, in a series of 20–25 notes; slows down near end.

Similar Species
King Rail larger, more richly colored, with rust-colored shoulders and cheeks; usually found in freshwater or brackish habitats. Virginia Rail much smaller, with strongly contrasting gray cheeks, rust breast. See Black Rail.

Range
Coastal areas from Massachusetts to Texas, locally along coast of central and southern California, and inland at Salton Sea and in lower Colorado River valley. Rare in central Arizona. Extends south into Mexico on both coasts, and into West Indies and South America.   *H. Douglas Pratt*

Adult
1. *Black face and breast.*
2. *Chestnut nape.*
3. *Black and white barred flanks.*
4. *Black back with fine white spots.*

   Small size.
   Very secretive.

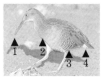

Atlantic Coast form
1. *Long, slightly drooped bill.*
2. *Gray-brown breast.*
3. *Barred flanks.*
4. *White undertail coverts.*

   Inhabits salt marshes.

Gulf Coast form
1. *Long, slightly drooped bill.*
2. *Rust-colored breast.*
3. *Barred flanks.*
4. *White undertail coverts.*

   Inhabits salt marshes.

King Rail

Rallus elegans
This is a more richly colored version of the Clapper Rail; along the
northern Gulf Coast, differences between the 2 are subtle.

Description
15–19″ (38–48 cm). Like Clapper Rail but olive-brown replaced by
rust-cinnamon; shoulders always rust-colored; breast bright rust; no
contrast between cheek and side of neck.

Voice
Harsh, chattering *he-e-eh-heh-heh-heh*, almost identical to Clapper's;
also a *kik-kik-kik-kik-krrrrrr* call.

Similar Species
See Clapper and Virginia rails.

Range
Breeds from North Dakota and western New York to Gulf Coast,
and from Massachusetts to Florida and Cuba. Winters along coast
from Connecticut to Florida and Texas; in Mississippi valley north to
southern Illinois.   *H. Douglas Pratt*

Virginia Rail

Rallus limicola
Much more widespread than its larger relatives, the Virginia Rail is
a miniature version of the King Rail. It is the only small rail in
North America with a long bill. Found mostly in freshwater and
brackish marshes, it also inhabits salt marshes in winter. A very
local breeder, the Virginia Rail is more familiar to most birders on
its wintering grounds.

Description
9″ (23 cm). The Virginia Rail is only about half the size of the King
Rail, but the coloration of the 2 birds is almost identical. It has a
rusty breast, strongly barred black-and-white flanks, a streaked,
olive back, and white undertail coverts. The Virginia Rail can be
distinguished from the King by its strongly contrasting, clear gray
cheeks. Juveniles in late summer are mostly black below.

Voice
A metallic *ti-dick*, *ti-dick* and a descending laugh: *wack-wack-wack*.
Also other *kick* notes and grunts.

Similar Species
Other small rails have short bills. King Rail much larger, with less
boldly contrasting gray cheeks. Clapper Rail larger, usually paler,
with olive-brown shoulders.

Range
Breeds locally from British Columbia to Maritime Provinces, south
to southern California, Arizona, Oklahoma, Ohio, northern Virginia,
along coast to North Carolina, and sporadically in Gulf States.
Winters near both coasts from southern British Columbia and North
Carolina south. Also in Mexico and South America.
H. Douglas Pratt

Adult
1. *Rich cinnamon-rust breast.*

   Shoulders rusty. Inhabits freshwater or brackish marshes.

Adult
1. *Rust-colored breast.*
2. *Gray cheeks.*
3. *Long bill.*
4. *Barred flanks.*

   Smaller than King and Clapper rails.

Juvenile
1. *Blackish underparts.*
2. *Long bill.*

Sora

Porzana carolina
This small, short-billed rail is widely distributed in North America.
It inhabits densely vegetated freshwater and salt marshes as well as
damp meadows. It is the most common of the rails and the easiest to
see, flushing readily and often feeding at the edge of openings in the
marsh or along watercourses. It responds by calling when hands are
clapped or car doors slammed, and when other loud noises are made.
Like other members of its family, it flicks its short tail when walking
and swims when necessary.

Description
8–10″ (20.5–25.5 cm). The Sora has a plump body and a yellow bill.
The adult is mostly brown on the upperparts and wings, with
heavily barred flanks. The sides of the head and foreneck are gray;
the face is black. The juvenile is buff-brown below and lacks the
adult's black chin and throat.

Voice
Plaintive, rising *ker-wee;* a sharp *keek;* also a descending whinny.

Similar Species
Yellow Rail smaller, has buff back streaked and checkered with very
dark markings; in flight shows white patches on secondaries.
Virginia Rail has brighter plumage and long, thin bill. See Corn
Crake*

Range
Breeds from British Columbia and Mackenzie east to Maritime
Provinces and south to central California, central Arizona, New
Mexico, Kansas, and Maryland. Winters in California, Arizona, New
Mexico (uncommon), and extreme western Texas, and from coastal
Texas east along Gulf Coast to Florida; on coastal plain from
Virginia (occasionally southern New England) south to Florida.
Paul W. Sykes, Jr.

Purple Gallinule

Porphyrula martinica
The Purple Gallinule is an uncommon, brightly colored, and heavy-
bodied bird of freshwater marshes. It has long toes that allow it to
walk on floating plants, such as the leaves of water lilies. It tends to
occur in wetlands where there is an abundance of pickerelweed, and
during migration it often turns up in odd places outside of its usual
habitat. This bird swims, walks, wades, and climbs in bushes; in
flight its long legs and feet dangle. The Purple Gallinule associates
freely with American Coots and Common Moorhens, but is more apt
to stay in cover than these species.

Description
12–14″ (30.5–35.5 cm). The adult has a bronze-green back and
wings, a deep blue head and underparts, pure white undertail
coverts, a red bill with a yellow tip, a pale blue frontal shield, and
bright yellow legs. The immature has a dark brown back and wings,
a white throat, a buff head and underparts, white undertail coverts,
and a dark bill.

Immature
1. Lacks black face of adult.
2. Buff-brown breast.
3. Barred flanks.

Adult
1. Black face and short yellow bill.
2. Gray neck and breast.
3. Barred flanks.

Immature
1. Dark bill.
2. Buff head.
3. Copper-colored upperparts.
4. White undertail coverts.
5. Yellow legs.

Voice
Repeated *kr-r-ruk*, *kek*, *kek*, *kek*, *kek;* similar to Common
Moorhen's call but higher-pitched; also chucks.

Similar Species
Adult and immature Common Moorhens have brown back, white
side stripe, greenish legs, and black central division of white
undertail coverts. Immature American Coot has grayish back, white
or grayish-white bill, gray legs, and black central division of white
undertail coverts.

Range
Breeds from southern Texas to eastern Arkansas and western
Tennessee, along Gulf Coast to Florida, and north along Atlantic
Coast to South Carolina. Wanders to Arizona and Utah, and from
Colorado to southeastern Canada. Winters along Gulf Coast of
Texas, Louisiana, and Florida. Also in West Indies and Central and
South America.   *Paul W. Sykes, Jr.*

Common Moorhen

Gallinuia chloropus
The Common Moorhen (formerly called the Common Gallinule) is a
plump, chickenlike bird of freshwater marshes, ponds, and lake
edges. It is often seen together with American Coots in open water
near cover. When frightened, the bird flies clumsily or dashes into
vegetation. It is generally quite active; on the water, it bobs its head
when swimming.

Description
12–15″ (30.5–38 cm). The adult is brown above with a slate-black
head, neck, and underparts, a white horizontal stripe on the side, a
red bill with a yellow tip, and a red frontal shield. The immature is
similar to the adult but paler, with a grayish head, neck, and
underparts, and a dark bill.

Voice
Repeated *kr-r-ruk*, *kek*, *kek*, *kek*, *kek*, sharper and higher pitched
than American Coot's; also henlike clucks.

Similar Species
See Purple Gallinule and American Coot.

Range
Breeds in California, southern Nevada, Arizona, and New Mexico,
and from Minnesota, Michigan, southern Ontario, Quebec, Vermont,
and New Brunswick south to Texas, Florida, and Gulf Coast.
Winters in California, Arizona, Texas, east along Gulf Coast to
Florida and north along Atlantic Coast to Virginia and, occasionally,
New England. Also in West Indies, Central and South America, and
Hawaii; widespread in Eurasia.   *Paul W. Sykes, Jr.*

Adult
. Pale blue frontal shield and red bill with yellow tip.
. Green upperparts.
. Blue head and underparts.
. Yellow legs and long toes.

Adult
. Red frontal shield and red bill with yellow tip.
. Slate-black head, neck, and underparts.
. White stripe on side.

Plump build.

Immature
. Dull bill.
. Grayish head, neck, and underparts.
. White stripe on side.
. White undertail coverts.

American Coot

Fulica americana

The American Coot is a very common, wide-ranging species found
on fresh water, and in winter on both fresh and salt water. It has a
plump body and resembles the Common Moorhen. Like that species
it bobs its head when it swims, but it is slightly larger and has lobed
toes. The American Coot feeds by dipping from the surface, or
sometimes by diving. It patters across the water with its feet as it
takes flight; the wingbeats are labored, and the feet extend beyond
the short tail. In winter, American Coots often congregate in large
rafts on open water.

Description
13–16″ (33–40.5 cm). The adult has a black head and neck and a
slate-black body. The sides of the undertail coverts are white and
the white bill has a red ring near the tip. A red swelling at the upper
edge of the white frontal shield is visible at close range. The legs are
greenish or grayish. The immature is similar but much paler and has
a duller bill.

Voice
Grating *kuk-kuk-kuk-kuk* and various other short rough notes,
cackles, clucks, and croaks.

Similar Species
In Florida, see Caribbean Coot. See Eurasian Coot*, Purple
Gallinule, and Common Moorhen.

Range
Breeds across most of central Canada south to New York, and
throughout California, Arizona, New Mexico, Illinois, Louisiana,
southern Texas, and southern Florida. Winters from British
Columbia south to California and eastward across Arizona, New
Mexico, Texas, Kansas, Illinois, and Massachusetts, south to Florida
and Gulf Coast. Also in Mexico, Central America, West Indies,
northern South America, and Hawaii.   *Paul W. Sykes, Jr.*

Caribbean Coot

Fulica caribaea

This West Indian bird just barely reaches Florida, where it is an
uncommon visitor and associates with American Coots.

Description
13–16″ (33–40.5 cm). This species is similar to the American Coot,
but has a large, bulbous white frontal shield that extends onto the
crown; this shield lacks the red swelling present in the American
Coot and has a yellow wash or yellow to red streaks on the upper
portion. Because some American Coots show variation in the size
and shape of the frontal shield, birds with intermediate bill
characteristics cannot reliably be identified in the field.

Voice
Similar to American Coot's.

Range
Resident in West Indies and northern South America; a few winter
in peninsular Florida.   *Paul W. Sykes, Jr.*

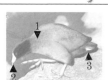

Adult
- *Blackish plumage.*
- *White bill and frontal shield with reddish swelling at upper edge.*
- *White undertail coverts.*

Plump build.
Lobed toes.

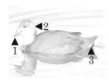

Immature
- *Duller bill than adult's.*
- *Paler head and body than adult's.*
- *White undertail coverts.*

Adult
- *Bulbous white frontal shield extending onto forehead and lacking reddish swelling.*

Limpkins

(Family Aramidae)
Limpkins are brownish, cranelike wading birds with long, slender necks, long, laterally compressed, slightly drooping bills, elongated bodies, and long, sturdy legs. They are often seen singly, wading or swimming in shallow water, perched upon the shore, or in adjacent vegetation. (World: 1 species. North America: 1 species.)
Scott B. Terrill

Limpkin

Aramus guarauna
The Limpkin is a locally common, medium-size wader of southeastern freshwater swamps and marshes that feeds on various species of mollusks. This bird is similar to a heron in shape, has the habits of a rail, and is closely related to the cranes. It usually flies low with its neck extended; the wingbeat is slow and steady, with a quick upward jerk of the wings like that of a crane. When walking, the Limpkin often pumps its tail. Its loud, distinctive call is most often heard on cloudy days and at dawn, dusk, and during the night. The call of one bird often stimulates others.

Description
25–27″ (63.5–68.5 cm). The Limpkin is dull brown and heavily spotted and streaked with white. The long, slender bill is pale at the base, dark toward the tip, and slightly decurved; the neck and legs are long.

Voice
A loud, wailing *kur-r-ee-ow, kur-r-ee-ow, kra-ow, kra-ow.*

Similar Species
Immature night-herons have much shorter legs and necks, and shorter, stouter, straight bills. Immature Glossy Ibis and White Ibis lack white spots and streaks in brown plumage, have more strongly decurved bills.

Range
Resident from southeastern Georgia and northern Florida (east of Apalachicola River) south through peninsular Florida. Recorded in South Carolina. Also in West Indies.   *Paul W. Sykes, Jr.*

Limpkin

Adult with snail
1. *Brown plumage with whitish spots and streaks.*
2. *Long legs.*

Adult
1. *Decurved bill.*
2. *Long neck.*

Cranes

(Family Gruidae)
Cranes are large, long-necked, long-legged wading birds that
resemble the taller herons. In flight, cranes hold their necks straight
out in front of the body, while herons fold the neck in close to the
body. North American cranes have naked red foreheads and
extremely long tertials, which give the rear a tufted appearance.
(World: 15 species. North America: 3 species.)   *Scott B. Terrill*

Sandhill Crane

Grus canadensis
These gray cranes rest in shallow, open wetlands, and also frequent
open dry uplands. The 3 northern subspecies are migratory and
abundant, while the 3 tropical, nonmigratory subspecies are fewer
and restricted in range to the southeastern United States and Cuba.
The guttural, loud, broken call of this crane is unmistakable.

Description
"Greater" Sandhill: 40–50″ (102–127 cm); "Lesser" and "Cuban"
sandhills: 20–30″ (51–76 cm). The sexes look identical; however the
females are usually smaller than the males. Adult Sandhills are pale
gray; the nonmigratory tropical subspecies are darker than the
migrating subspecies. The bill is dark green, the iris yellow, and the
crown is covered by bare red skin; the legs are black. In spring,
adults paint iron-carrying mud on their feathers; the iron oxidizes
and blends with the feather pigments, rendering the cranes a
reddish-brown. This color is lost with molting in summer. Juveniles
are the same color as the painted adults, but the feathers are
genetically brown; the crown is covered by brown feathers.

Voice
Loud call a long, rolling, hollow rattle, *garooooooooooo;* can carry
more than 1 mile. Call lower and more broken than Whooper's. Male
and female can be distinguished by voice when emitting unison call
—a synchronized duet of mated pair during which male emits a
series of long, low calls for each 2–3 shriller calls of female. Female's
bill usually horizontal in unison call, male's vertical.

Similar Species
See Whooping Crane.

Range
Breeds from eastern Siberia to Hudson Bay and south through
Canada east of Rockies to western Ontario. Rocky Mountain and
Lake States flocks constitute migratory and nesting population in
lower United States, ranging into southwest British Columbia,
southern Manitoba, and southwest Ontario, and wintering in
California (principally in Central Valley), New Mexico, Arizona,
Texas, and Mexico. Resident population from Mississippi to Georgia,
in southern Florida, and in Cuba.   *George Archibald*

Sandhill Crane
Common Crane
Whooping Crane

Adult
1. *Long, straight neck.*
2. *Gray plumage.*
3. *Naked red crown.*

Large size.
Travels in large,
noisy flocks.
Flies with neck
extended.

Juvenile
1. *Long, straight neck.*
2. *Reddish-brown*
   plumage.
3. *Feathered crown.*

Whooping Crane

Grus americana
The Whooping Crane is North America's tallest flying bird, standing
4 to 5 feet tall and inhabiting shallow wetlands that provide visibility
over a wide area. It is an extremely rare bird, numbering fewer
than 80 individuals in the traditional wild flock, about 15 in a new
Rocky Mountain flock, and about 30 in captivity. The Rocky
Mountain flock, which was initiated in 1976, is the result of an
experiment in placing Whooping Crane eggs in the nests of Sandhill
Cranes.

Description
50–60″ (127–151 cm). Although the sexes are alike, the males are
usually slightly larger than the females. The bare red skin on the
chin and crown appears in adults and subadults when the birds are
more than 10 months old. The bill is greenish, the eyes are yellow,
and the legs and primaries are black. Juveniles are cinnamon-brown
with a white belly and secondaries; they acquire the white adult
plumage by the time they are 1 year old. Adult Whoopers are
readily distinguished from Sandhill Cranes by their brilliant white
plumage, while brownish juvenile Sandhills lack white on the belly
and secondaries. The flight posture, with long neck and legs fully
extended, distinguishes a flying Whooping Crane from the short-
legged White Pelican and the smaller Snow Goose.

Voice
Like all cranes, Whooping Cranes have loud calls that can carry
more than a mile. Whooper's call higher-pitched and more
continuous than that of Sandhill. They often call while flying or when
disturbed by man or by other cranes. Male and female readily
distinguished during unison call—a long duet often given in
territorial defense by mated pairs. Male emits sequence of long, low
calls for each 2–3 shorter, shriller calls of female.

Similar Species
Sandhill Crane has similar flight profile, with neck and legs fully
extended; however, gray Sandhill easily distinguished from white
Whooper in good light.

Range
Nesting grounds lie in impenetrable muskeg wilderness of Wood
Buffalo National Park on Alberta-Yukon border, Canada. Winter
migration approximately 3,700 miles along central flyway south to
salt marshes of Aransas National Wildlife Refuge on Gulf Coast of
Texas. Early autumn birds often found in small flocks on prairie
marshlands and agricultural fields in southern Saskatchewan. One
new Whooping Crane flock established in Rocky Mountains at Grays
Lake National Wildlife Refuge, Idaho, and can be observed in
migration at Monte Vista National Wildlife Refuge, Colorado, and in
wintering grounds at Bosque del Apache National Wildlife Refuge,
New Mexico.   *George Archibald*

Adult with wings spread
1. *White plumage.*
2. *Black wing tips.*
3. *Neck held out straight in flight.*

Adult
1. *Long, straight neck.*
2. *White plumage.*
3. *Naked red crown and cheeks.*

Large size.
Loud calls.

Juvenile
1. *Cinnamon-brown plumage.*
2. *White belly and secondaries.*
3. *Black wing tips.*

Usually associates with adults.

Plovers

(Family Charadriidae)
The typical plover is a plump shorebird with a large head and eyes, a short neck, and a dovelike bill. Plovers are found along shores as well as in grassland and agricultural fields; they tend to run in swift spurts, stopping abruptly. Worldwide, the many species of ringed plover have complete or partial breastbands and upperparts that match the color of their favored habitats; these birds often have a diagnostic bill shape and distinctively patterned head, breast, and tail. Most North American plovers have long, sharply pointed wings with bold whitish wing stripes. The tails are relatively short and rounded, generally marked with contrasting blacks, whites, or shades of brown. Plovers often hold the posterior body horizontally or at an upward angle when running. (World: 64 species. North America: 14 species.)   *Scott B. Terrill and Claudia Wilds*

Northern Lapwing

Vanellus vanellus
This distinctive European plover has been recorded very rarely in North America, mainly from November through January.

Description
12″ (30.5 cm). This species has a black crown, crest, throat, and breast, a white face crossed by a black line, and dark metallic green upperparts. The belly is white; the undertail coverts are cinnamon. The rounded wings have white wing linings and black flight feathers; the white tail has a black terminal band. Winter adults have a white throat and buff face with more black lines; the juvenile is similar but has a shorter crest.

Voice
A unique high, thin, almost nasal *pee-wit;* accent on first syllable.

Range
Recorded in eastern North America from Baffin Island to South Carolina. Breeds in Eurasia.   *Stuart Keith*

Immature

Black-bellied Plover

Breeding

Pluvialis squatarola
The Black-bellied Plover and the golden-plovers (genus *Pluvialis*) are medium-size shorebirds with heavy builds and short, stout bills. Their plumage always exhibits a barred tail and spotted upperparts. They feed very deliberately, standing in a motionless, erect position, running forward a few feet, then resuming their stance or picking at food. The Black-bellied Plover is usually associated with salt marshes, tidal flats, and seacoasts, but also frequents plowed fields and wet, grassy pastures in migration and winter. Thousands of birds may be seen at favored migration stops along the coast, and many estuaries harbor hundreds during the winter. This species' plaintive, whistling flight call is one of the most haunting seaside sounds and may be heard day or night.

Winter

Description
10½–13½″ (26.5–34.5 cm). In flight, birds in all plumages exhibit a white rump, a conspicuous white wing stripe, and white wing linings with sharply contrasting black axillars. In breeding plumage, the

Winter adult
1. *Long crest.*
2. *Green upperparts.*
3. *Black breast.*
4. *Rounded wings.*

   Loud, thin call.

Winter adult
1. *Gray upperparts with pale spots and feather edges.*
2. *Dull white eyebrow.*
3. *White underparts.*
4. *White wing linings.*
5. *White rump.*
6. *Black axillars.*

upperparts are marbled silvery white, the underparts are black to
the belly, and the undertail coverts are white. Winter-plumage birds
are gray above, with pale white spots and feather edges, dull white
eyebrows, and predominantly white underparts. Fresh-plumage
juveniles are boldly spotted golden-yellow above, but this color
rapidly fades to white; the underparts are coarsely streaked with
brown to the midbelly. The legs and feet are dark gray or black,
with a rudimentary hind toe; the bill is black.

Voice
Flight call a plaintive, whistled *quee-u-eee* or *pee-u-wee;* when
flushed, a harsh *kee.*

Similar Species
Nonbreeding Lesser Golden-Plover shows more contrast between
pale eyebrow and dark crown, and has proportionately smaller bill;
in breeding plumage, Lesser Golden-Plover has underparts wholly
black, upperparts spotted with golden-yellow. In flight, Lesser
Golden-Plover shows no white wing stripe, pale axillars, and dark
rump; Black-bellied has prominent white wing stripe, black axillars,
and white rump. Nonbreeding Red Knot smaller, with
proportionately longer and more slender bill, uniform grayish
upperparts; holds body more horizontally, not in erect posture
typical of plovers.

Range
Breeds in Arctic tundra from Alaska to Baffin Island. Winters along
coasts from British Columbia and Massachusetts south to South
America. Widespread inland during migration. Also in Old World.
Thomas H. Davis

Lesser Golden-Plover

Pluvialis dominica
The Lesser Golden-Plover favors plowed fields and short-grass
pastures in migration, but there is some overlap with the Black-
bellied, especially in coastal areas.

Description
9½–11″ (24–28 cm). In flight, all plumages of the Lesser Golden-
Plover exhibit a dark rump, an indistinct wing stripe, and pale
grayish wing linings and axillars. In breeding plumage, the
upperparts are splotched and spotted with golden-yellow; the
underparts are wholly black. Birds in winter plumage appear similar
to winter-plumage Black-bellied Plovers but are slightly darker
above, especially on the crown, and have white eyebrows. A
subspecies found only on the West Coast, *P. d. fulva,* is slimmer and
smaller, with longer legs; the adult in breeding plumage has
narrower white sides to the breast and in winter it is yellower
overall with a buff-yellow eyebrow. Juveniles of both races are
heavily spotted with golden-yellow on the upperparts; below, the

Breeding

Winter

Juvenile
1. *Boldly spotted, golden-yellow upperparts.*
2. *Streaked breast and belly.*

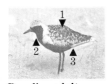

Breeding adult
1. *Marbled upperparts.*
2. *Black face and breast.*
3. *White belly.*

In flight, shows white rump, black axillars.

Breeding adult
1. *Marbled golden-yellow upperparts.*
2. *Wholly black underparts.*

In flight, shows dark rump, no wing stripe, and pale axillars.

neck is coarsely streaked with brown, and the breast and belly are
marked with broad pale brown bars. The juvenile *fulva* is brighter
above, more golden on the upper breast, and also has a buff-yellow
eyebrow. The legs and feet are dull gray or black; the bill is black.

Voice
Flight call a sickly, whistled *kleep* or *queedle*, shorter and harsher
than that of Black-bellied Plover.

Similar Species
Nonbreeding Black-bellied shows less contrast between crown and
eyebrow, has proportionately larger bill; underparts of fresh juvenile
have different pattern. All plumages easily distinguished in flight.

Range
Breeds in Arctic and subarctic tundra from Alaska to Baffin Island.
Spring migration mainly up Mississippi Valley; in autumn, large
numbers fly to eastern Canada (and smaller numbers south along
Atlantic Coast), then over Atlantic Ocean to South America, while a
few pass south along Pacific Coast. Winters in southern South
America; rare but regular to California.   *Thomas H. Davis*

Mongolian Plover

Charadrius mongolus
A migrant from Asia, the Mongolian Plover is rare in spring and fall
in the western Aleutian Islands. There, members of this species
appear singly or in small groups, feeding at the storm tide line, in
the intertidal zone, or on open beaches, rarely at freshwater
margins.

Description
8″ (20.5 cm). Larger than a Semipalmated Plover, the Mongolian
Plover in spring is warm brown above with a short, inconspicuous
wing stripe. The crown, collar, and broad breastband are cinnamon-
rufous; the throat is white and contrasts strongly with the breast. A
black mask from the bill to the ear coverts and a black line across
the forehead between the eyes contrast with a white patch below
the forehead line and between the eyes. The bill is black, the legs
blackish or dark gray. The tail, back, and rump are brown; the outer
third of the tail is slightly darker. The outer tail feathers are
whitish, and all tail feathers have narrow white tips. The sexes look
generally similar, but the male is more brightly colored, more
cleanly marked, and has a blacker head pattern than that of the
female. Juveniles are also distinctive; like adults, they are brown
above, but they are subtly scaled with buff throughout the
upperparts, including the wing coverts. A warm brown breastband,
complete or mostly complete, is washed with bright buff, as are the
lores and ear coverts. The entire breast and flanks are washed with
paler buff; the belly, undertail coverts, and throat are pure white.
The juvenile's bill is blackish or dark gray, and the feet are dark
gray-green.

Voice
One or 2 notes, short and soft: *crrik* or *crrik-crrik*, rather low-
pitched.

Similar Species
Other banded plovers have black or dark brown breastbands.

Range
In North America, annual in western Aleutian Islands. Casual
farther east in Aleutians, on Alaska islands of Bering Sea, and on
Alaska mainland (where it has occasionally bred). Accidental
elsewhere in North America. Native to Asia.   *Daniel D. Gibson*

Juvenile
1. Dark crown and contrasting pale eyebrow.
2. Marbled golden-yellow upperparts, with no white rump or wing stripe.
3. Streaked and barred underparts.

Breeding adult
1. Broad rufous chest band.
2. Black-and-white head pattern.
3. Brown upperparts.

Juvenile
1. Scaled brown upperparts, including wing coverts.
2. Brown breastband, tinged with buff.
3. Black bill.
4. Black legs.

Snowy Plover

Charadrius alexandrinus
Like its larger, paler relative the Piping Plover, the Snowy Plover is
an uncommon bird that inhabits sandy coastal beaches and the
shores of salt ponds and alkaline lakes; its numbers decrease
wherever man usurps its habitat for industry or recreation. Both
species feed at the water's edge or among scattered debris on the
upper beach. They avoid thick vegetation and narrow beaches
littered with driftwood or backed by bluffs where they may be
trapped by high water.

Description
6½″ (16.5 cm). Smallest of the North American plovers, the Snowy
has light gray-brown upperparts (including the rump), a conspicuous
patch on either side of the breast, a white eyebrow extending back
from the white forehead, a long, thin, black bill, and slate-colored
legs. Adults have dark ear coverts and breast patches, blackish in
breeding plumage, gray-brown in winter; breeding birds have a
black bar across the forecrown as well. The juvenile has paler ear
coverts and breast patches, the same color as that of the upperparts.
Like all juveniles of the ringed plover group, the juvenile Snowy has
buff-edged feathers on the back and on the wing coverts.

Voice
A low *grr-grr* and a soft *ca-wee*.

Similar Species
Piping Plover larger and paler, with shorter, orange legs (often very
dull in winter), and much shorter bill, orange-based in breeding
birds; it has pale ear coverts and a white rump. In breeding
plumage, dark bar behind forehead separates forehead from
eyebrow.

Range
Found worldwide. In North America, resident on Pacific Coast from
southern Washington south to Baja California (both sides) and on
Gulf Coast from Mexico to Florida panhandle. Breeds locally and
sporadically in interior of Oregon, California, Nevada, Utah, New
Mexico, Kansas, Oklahoma, and Texas.   *Claudia Wilds*

Wilson's Plover

Charadrius wilsonia
Wilson's Plover almost never strays from ocean beaches or the sand,
mud, and saltwort flats among coastal dunes or just behind them.
This species is an especially solitary member of the family; it is slow-
moving and approachable when it is not vigorously seeking to
distract the observer from a nearby nest or young.

Description
7–8″ (18–20.5 cm). The upperparts of Wilson's Plover are the color
of the wet sand it lives on. Its most distinctive feature is its heavy
black bill, more than half as long as its head. The short eyebrow
extends back from the white forehead, which is separated from the
crown on breeding males by a dark bar. The broad breastband,
sometimes narrowed at the center, is black in breeding males,
brown in all other plumages, and often incomplete in juveniles. The
legs are flesh-colored. On the Pacific Coast, the breeding male has a
rufous hindcrown, nape, and ear coverts, while the female has a
rufous breastband.

Breeding adult
1. *Thin black bill.*
2. *Dark ear coverts.*
3. *Light gray-brown upperparts.*
4. *Blackish breast patches.*
5. *Slaty legs.*

Juvenile
1. *Thin black bill.*
2. *Pale ear coverts.*
3. *Pale breast patches.*
4. *Buff-edged feathers on back and wing coverts.*

Female
1. *Long, heavy black bill.*
2. *Broad brown breastband.*

Voice
A shrill *wheet*, rarely *quit-quit-keet*. Typically silent except when
very alarmed.

Similar Species
See Semipalmated Plover and Killdeer.

Range
Breeds on Pacific Coast from Baja California to Peru, along Atlantic
and Caribbean coasts from Maryland to Guyana. In winter, rare
north of Florida. Several records for southern California; casual
north of breeding range to Maritimes. Accidental inland.
Claudia Wilds

Common Ringed Plover

Charadrius hiaticula
This rare plover, very similar to the Semipalmated, is best identified
by its mellow call.

Description
7½″ (19 cm). Small, with single black breastband (often widest at
center); black bridle pattern on forehead and face; large white spot
behind eye. Bill yellow, dark-tipped; legs yellowish.

Voice
A soft, mellow *tooli* or *tooeep*, with slightly rising inflection.

Similar Species
See Semipalmated Plover.

Range
Breeds in Bering Strait area, Alaska (St. Lawrence Island), and
islands in eastern Canadian Arctic. Also in northern Eurasia.
Winters in Old World.   *Daniel D. Gibson*

Semipalmated Plover

Charadrius semipalmatus
This species is the most widespread and well known of the small
plovers. It is found on mud flats, beaches, freshly plowed fields, and
peat banks. It travels in large flocks, often with sandpipers, and its
flight is swift and acrobatic. After landing, these birds spread out to
feed; like other plovers, they may shiver their feet or pat the
ground, perhaps to stir up prey.

Description
6½–7½″ (16.5–19 cm). This plover can be recognized year-round by
its stubby bill and its upperparts, which are the color of dark mud.
In breeding plumage, the short legs and the base of the bill are
bright orange. The head is marked by a white forehead with a black
bar above it; another bar extends from bill to cheek, with a whitish
spot above it. The breastband is blackish. Winter birds have duller
legs, mostly black bills, and brown breastbands; the head is wholly
brown except for the white forehead and a connecting narrow white
eyebrow. The juvenile has a black bill and a brown breastband,

Adult male
1. *Long, heavy black bill.*
2. *Broad black breastband.*
3. *Upperparts colored like wet sand.*

Shrill wheet *call*

Breeding adult
1. *Broad black breastband.*
2. *Large white spot behind eye.*
3. *Dark brown upperparts.*
4. *Short bill with orange base.*

Mellow call.

Breeding adult
1. *Mud-brown upperparts.*
2. *White wing stripe.*
3. *Narrow breastband.*
4. *Stubby bill with orange base.*
5. *Orange legs.*

Rising tu-wee *call.*

which is narrower at the ends and in the center. The webbing between the bases of the toes is rarely visible in the field.

Voice
Clear, rising *tu-wee;* during spring migration and on breeding grounds, a distinctive, liquid, accelerating rattle.

Similar Species
Piping Plover much paler above, with white rump. Wilson's Plover somewhat paler above, with longer, flesh-colored legs, much longer, heavier, black bill, and broad breastband. Killdeer much larger, with longer legs, 2 breastbands (except when very young), long black bill, and long tail with rusty base. Common Ringed Plover usually has breastband wider overall, widest at center; white spot behind eye larger and usually more clearly defined.

Range
Breeds from Alaska across northern Canada to Newfoundland and Nova Scotia, migrating throughout continent. Winters along coast from South Carolina and California (rarely north to Washington) to Chile and southern Argentina.   *Claudia Wilds*

Piping Plover

Charadrius melodus
The Piping Plover, an uncommon species of decreasing numbers, is found only on sandy beaches, where it nests above the high-water line or on sandy flats among the dunes, where vegetation is sparse. Its constant piping attracts the observer's attention, although its pale plumage provides perfect camouflage as it scurries away from the water's edge or crouches in the bare sand. Oversand vehicles, pets, foxes, and crows are among the most serious threats to its survival.

Description
7¼″ (18.5 cm). The Piping Plover has upperparts the color of dry sand and a white rump. In breeding plumage, the adult has an orange-based bill, bright orange legs, a black bar across the forecrown, and a narrow blackish breastband that is often incomplete. Winter birds and juveniles have blackish bills and dull orange legs; the black bands on the head and breast are absent, and instead of a breastband there is a sandy patch on each side of the breast.

Voice
A repeated, melodious plaintive *peep* or *peep-lo,* a *pee-a-weet,* and a flat *per-wee.*

Similar Species
See Semipalmated and Snowy plovers.

Range
Breeds from Quebec and Newfoundland south to North Carolina and locally from central Alberta to Minnesota and around Great Lakes. Casual in California. Winters on coast from Texas to North Carolina, sparsely in Bahamas and Greater Antilles. *Claudia Wilds*

Juvenile
1. *Mud-brown upperparts.*
2. *Reduced brown breastband.*
3. *Stubby black bill.*

Juvenile
1. *Sandy upperparts.*
2. *Stubby black bill.*
3. *Dull orange legs.*
4. *Gray patch at side of breast.*

Shows white rump in flight.

Breeding adult
1. *Sandy upperparts.*
2. *White rump.*
3. *Stubby bill with orange base.*
4. *Bright orange legs.*
5. *Black head band.*
6. *Narrow black breastband.*

Killdeer

Charadrius vociferus
Conspicuous, noisy, and highly adaptable, the Killdeer is found throughout the continent in all kinds of open habitats: lawns, pastures, plowed fields, prairies, mud flats, and shorelines— anywhere not too far from water. Patches of gravel are preferred nesting sites. The Killdeer is gregarious except when nesting, and flocks may be active around the clock, calling all night long. This species is easily alarmed, and its ready flight and warning cries often panic every other bird in sight.

Description
9–11″ (23–28 cm). Largest of the ringed plovers in North America, the Killdeer is the only one that has 2 breastbands and a tail that extends well beyond the wing tips. The rufous rump and uppertail coverts are conspicuous in display and in flight. The black band across the forecrown separates the white forehead from the eyebrow. The bill is fairly thin and black, the legs long and flesh- colored, and the eye-ring bright red. The downy young has a single breastband and may be identified incorrectly if the absence of feathering on the wing and tail is overlooked; its white collar is bordered by 2 black collars, and its stumpy wing is black at the base and white at the tip.

Voice
Ringing *kill-dee* and repeated cries of *dee-dee-dee*, both readily used alarm notes. Also a single, rising *dee*.

Similar Species
Wilson's Plover smaller, has proportionately longer, heavier bill, 1 broad breastband; its short white eyebrow extends back from forehead. See Semipalmated Plover.

Range
Breeds throughout North America south of line running from central Alaska to Newfoundland. Outside breeding season, northern population withdraws to region where southern population resides year-round: on West Coast from southwest British Columbia south across southern tier of states north to Oklahoma, and in lowlands from Oklahoma northeast to Massachusetts. Also in coastal Peru and Chile.   *Claudia Wilds*

Mountain Plover

Charadrius montanus
This plover is poorly named, since it generally avoids mountainous areas. It favors instead arid plains and short-grass prairies of western valleys and hills, usually far from water. In winter, flocks occur in a variety of open arid habitats, as well as in fields.

Description
8–8¾″ (20.5–22 cm). The large, long-legged Mountain Plover is the plainest of the North American plovers, sandy-brown above and creamy-white below; the breast is washed with gray-buff. The breeding adult has a white forehead, a black forecrown, and a thin black line through the lores. All plumages show a whitish wing stripe, whitish wing linings, and a broad black band near the tail tip that contrasts with the gray-white outer rectrices. In nonbreeding birds, the dark eye stands out conspicuously on the plain face.

Voice
Birds in winter flocks give harsh, low *krrip* note. Various harsh notes and whistles given on breeding grounds.

Adult
1. *Two black bands on breast.*
2. *Long tail.*
3. *Long, flesh-colored legs.*
4. *Brown upperparts.*

Larger than other banded plovers.

Displaying adult
1. *Rusty uppertail coverts and rump.*
2. *White wing stripe.*

Juvenile
1. *Plain face with large, dark eye.*

Similar Species
Winter-plumage and juvenile Black-bellied Plovers larger and grayer, with mottled or spotted upperparts and much white in rump, tail, and wings; always show black axillars in flight. Lesser Golden-Plover spotted with buff or gold above, has spotted or finely streaked breast, lacks prominent wing stripe, and lacks overall sandy color of Mountain Plover. Other plovers in same range have distinct breast and head markings.

Range
Breeds from Great Basin east to western Great Plains, from Montana (and formerly North Dakota) to New Mexico and Texas Panhandle. Winters in flocks in central and south-coastal California, east locally to southwestern deserts. Also in south to central Mexico. Vagrant in Pacific Northwest and Texas Gulf Coast.
Kimball L. Garrett

Eurasian Dotterel

Charadrius morinellus
A distinctively patterned Old World plover, the Eurasian Dotterel breeds in small numbers in the mountains of western Alaska. It nests on alpine tundra; in Alaska it rarely occurs at sea level, since most migrants in spring arrive in the Alaska mountains via direct flight across the Bering Strait from the Siberian coastal mountains. A tame bird, it often stands quietly when approached and is easily overlooked in its frequently cloud-shrouded habitat.

Description
8½" (21.5 cm). Smaller than the Lesser Golden-Plover, the Eurasian Dotterel is readily distinguished from other plovers in summer by a combination of bold white eyebrows that meet at the nape, and a bold white band across the middle of the breast separating the brownish-gray upper breast from the coppery lower breast and sides. The belly is black, the throat white. The upperparts are brown, the crown blackish, and the wing and back feathers are edged with pale rufous. The tail is mostly brownish-gray, with the outer third darker, and the outer 3 pairs of tail feathers have bold white tips. The bill is black, and the legs are yellowish or greenish. Juveniles superficially resemble golden-plovers, but, like adults, have bolder, buff eyelines that meet at the nape; there is also a suggestion of a white breastband and of a belly patch. The tail pattern is distinctive: the basal two-thirds of the feathers are gray, the outer third black, and all the tail feathers are broadly tipped with buff-white.

Voice
A soft *pip-pip*, often trebled and accelerated.

Similar Species
Juvenile Lesser Golden-Plover has less distinct eye stripes that do not meet at nape, lacks breastband; tips as well as sides of all tail feathers marked in beige; voice different.

Range
In North America, rare breeder on mountains in vicinity of Bering Strait, Alaska (St. Lawrence Island and Seward Peninsula). Rare autumn migrant in western Aleutian Islands. Accidental on Pacific Coast east and south of Aleutian Islands. Widespread in Eurasia. Winters in Old World.   *Daniel D. Gibson*

Breeding adult
1. *Black forecrown.*
2. *White forehead.*
3. *Thin black eyeline.*
4. *Sandy upperparts.*
5. *Long legs.*
6. *Whitish wing stripe.*
7. *Dark band near tail tip.*

Breeding adult
1. *Bold white eyebrow.*
2. *Bold white band across mid-breast.*
3. *Coppery lower breast and sides.*

Juvenile
1. *Bold buff eyebrows that meet at nape.*
2. *Faint breast band.*

Oystercatchers

(Family Haematopodidae)
Oystercatchers are large, chunky, and boldly patterned with black
and white or entirely black; they have bright reddish or orange bills
and legs. All members of this family are in a single genus,
Haematopus. The long, heavy, laterally compressed bill is unique.
The legs and feet are stout and there is no hind toe. The tail and
neck are short and broad. Oystercatchers are found primarily in
marine habitats, including sandy, rocky shores and rocky intertidal
areas. The 2 North American species have bright yellow eyes and
orange eye-rings that contrast sharply with the blackish heads.
Oystercatchers are known for their elaborate courtship rituals.
(World: 14 species. North America: 2 species.)   *Scott B. Terrill*

American Oystercatcher

Haematopus palliatus
One of the most striking of the North American shorebirds, the
American Oystercatcher is a characteristic resident of uninhabited
barrier islands and coastal marshes, where it nests on the sand
above the high-tide line and probes for food in the intertidal mud.
Wherever there are beds of oysters or other mollusks, these birds
move in to feed as soon as the falling tide exposes their prey gaping
to release water. At high tide, Oystercatchers gather in flocks to
roost on the drier stretches of marsh and beach; several dozen at a
time may be seen in winter. In spring and summer, adult pairs
attract attention with their loud piping, as they fly off on flashing
wings or pace slowly away from their nest or young.

Description
17–21″ (43–53.5 cm). An unmistakable species with its long, heavy,
chisel-tipped, orange-red bill, thick pale pink legs, and red-ringed
yellow eyes, the American Oystercatcher has a black hood, brown
back, and white belly. When it flies, its bold white wing stripe and
white uppertail coverts contrast strongly with the rest of the dark
upper surface. In some lights, the darker males may appear black-
backed. Juveniles have orange-based, dusky bills and dark eyes.

Voice
Ringing, repeated *wheep* or *cleep*, creaky *crik-crik-crik*, and rattling
cle-ar, like the call of a plover.

Similar Species
American Black Oystercatcher has entirely dark plumage.

Range
Breeds from Baja California to northern Chile and from
Massachusetts to east coast of Argentina; winters north as far as
Delaware. Casual as far north as central California and Maine.
Claudia Wilds

American Oystercatcher
American Black Oystercatcher

In flight
Dark back and head.
White wing stripe.
White uppertail
coverts.

Ringing wheep *call.*

Adult
Long orange-red
bill.
Black hood.
Brown back.
White belly.
Pink legs.

American Black Oystercatcher

Haematopus bachmani
A very distinctive, large, and stocky shorebird, the American Black
Oystercatcher is an inhabitant of rocky shores and islands along the
Pacific Coast of North America. It is encountered only very rarely
on sandy beaches or mud flats. It is usually found singly or in small
groups, and is very often heard before it is seen, because its
uniformly blackish-brown coloration blends in with its dark, rocky
surroundings.

Description
17–19″ (43–48 cm). This stocky shorebird is unmistakable. The
entire plumage is blackish-brown, without a white wingstripe. The
bill is long, stout, and bright orange-red. The stocky legs and feet
are dull pink, and the eyes are yellow. Juveniles are somewhat
browner than adults and have dusky bills that are orange at the
base.

Voice
A loud, sharp, piping *wheep;* typically given in a series but also
given singly.

Similar Species
American Oystercatcher occurs in Baja California and casually north
to southern California; has white underparts and broad white wing
stripe; prefers sandy beaches. Other rock-inhabiting shorebirds are
much smaller, have paler upperparts and light underparts, and most
have conspicuous wing stripes or a white rump.

Range
Permanent resident along Pacific Coast from western Aleutian
Islands south to islands off central Baja California. Casual on
Pribilof Islands and in Yukon.   *Paul Lehman*

Adult
. *Black plumage.*
*. Long, orange-red
   bill.*
. *Pink legs and feet.*

Juvenile
. *Brownish plumage.*
*. Orange bill with
   dusky tip.*

Stilts and Avocets

(Family Recurvirostridae)
Stilts and avocets are slim, elegant shorebirds with extremely long
legs, long slender necks, and plumage that is boldly patterned,
primarily in black and white. The long bills are very slender and are
either curved gently upward, as in the avocets, or straight, as in the
stilts. The heads are relatively small and rounded. Members of this
group usually feed in shallow water, constantly probing with the bill
partially submerged. They are excellent swimmers and are
occasionally seen in deeper waters. (World: 10 species. North
America: 2 species.)   *Scott B. Terrill*

Black-necked Stilt

Himantopus mexicanus
The graceful Black-necked Stilt is a conspicuous resident of shallow
freshwater and brackish ponds, open marshes, and flooded fields and
pastures. It strides along muddy shores or wades out into open
water, sometimes up to its belly, neatly picking insects from the
surface; on land, it must bend its legs in order to reach the ground
with its bill. In its strong, steady flight, the bird holds the bill
straight out while the legs dangle behind. The Stilt builds its nest
along the shore or on little islands, often under a clump of
vegetation. Initially, the nest may be quite shallow, but a rise in
water level stimulates more elaborate construction, which results in
a deep, well-built floating platform. Flocks of Stilts defend their
territories by screeching vigorously and, like fighter-pilots, buzzing
invaders; if only 1 or 2 pairs are present, they are much more timid
and self-effacing. Distraction displays include an effective broken-
wing performance and an unequaled broken-leg act.

Description
13½–15½″ (34.5–39.5 cm). The Black-necked Stilt is readily
identified by its black upperparts (brownish-black in females and
juveniles) and white underparts, its needlelike, straight black bill,
and its very long pinkish-red legs. In flight, the black back and the
wings, which are black above and white below, contrast with the
whitish tail. The eye is dark red.

Voice
A yelping *yip-yip-yip.*

Range
Breeds locally along coast from Oregon and Delaware south to Chile
and Argentina, and in scattered locations in interior of all western
states east to Idaho, Wyoming, Kansas, and Texas. Winters from
coast of southern Oregon, Gulf Coast, and southern Florida south.
Casual north to British Columbia.   *Claudia Wilds*

Black-necked Stilt
American Avocet

In flight
1. *Needlelike black bill.*
2. *Black upperparts.*
3. *White underparts.*
4. *Very long pinkish-red legs.*
5. *White tail.*

Yelping call.

Adult male
1. *Needlelike black bill.*
2. *Black upperparts.*
3. *White underparts.*
4. *Very long pinkish-red legs.*

Slim build.

American Avocet

Recurvirostra americana
A large, handsome, and engaging shorebird, the gregarious
American Avocet commonly feeds and rests in flocks of up to several
hundred strong. Although it may be found foraging in saltwater,
brackish, and freshwater ponds and marshes, this species
particularly favors shallow alkaline lakes, wet meadows, and
pastures with scattered open pools. In a distinctive feeding
technique, the bird moves briskly forward, turning its head rapidly
from side to side and sweeping its conspicuously recurved bill across
the soft mud or muddy water as it searches for seeds, aquatic
insects, and small crustaceans. A long line of American Avocets may
advance abreast, entirely submerging their heads and necks as they
enter deeper water and readily swimming, often with their wings
held high, across the stretches where their webbed toes can no
longer touch the bottom.

Description
17–18½″ (43.5–47 cm). The American Avocet's distinctive black-and-
white plumage pattern is easily recognized even at a great distance.
When the bird is at rest, the whiteness of the body contrasts with
the broad black stripes along the back and on the folded wing. In
flight, the entire outer half of the wing is black, and the white inner
wing is crossed by a broad black panel on the greater and median
wing coverts. The wing linings are white. In breeding plumage, the
head and neck are a rich buff-cinnamon; in juveniles and birds in
winter plumage, the head and neck are grayish-white. The shape of
the fine, clearly upturned black bill is diagnostic; the degree of
curvature is noticeably greater in females than in males. The feet
and long legs are gray-blue.

Voice
Alarm note a noisy *pleek* or *plee-eek;* also a softer *whuck.*

Similar Species
In distant flight possibly confused with Willet, winter Hudsonian
and Black-tailed godwits, but these lack black stripes down back and
across inner wing; Black-tailed extremely rare in range of American
Avocet. Both godwits have a black tail band; Hudsonian has black
wing linings.

Range
Breeds locally on coast of California; in interior of western states
and provinces from central Saskatchewan east to western Minnesota
and south to northern Baja California, Utah, Colorado, New
Mexico, and Texas. Winters in California, both at Salton Sea and
along Pacific Coast south Guatemala; on Atlantic Coast in North
Carolina, Georgia, and Florida; also winters on Gulf Coast at least as
far south as Mexico. Nonbreeding birds are seen in summer from
coastal New Jersey south to South Carolina. Rare fall migrant along
Atlantic Coast from Massachusetts south to New York.
Claudia Wilds

In flight
. *Thin, upturned bill.*
. *Black-and-white wing pattern.*
. *Long gray-blue legs.*

Breeding adult
. *Thin, upturned bill.*
. *Cinnamon head and neck.*
. *Black-and-white pattern on back.*
. *Long gray-blue legs.*

Large size.

Winter adult
. *Thin, upturned bill.*
. *Whitish head and neck.*
. *Black-and-white pattern on back.*
. *Long gray-blue legs.*

Jacanas

(Family Jacanidae)
The jacanas are a small family of tropical marsh birds characterized
by extremely long toes that enable the birds to walk with ease
across floating vegetation (hence the nicknames "lily-trotter" and
"water-walker"). The small bill and head, longish neck, short
rounded body, and long legs give jacanas a general appearance
somewhere between that of a plover and a rail. (World: 8 species.
North America: 1 species.)   *Kenn Kaufman*

Northern Jacana

Jacana spinosa
The Northern Jacana is an irregular and mostly rare visitor to
southern Texas. Individuals or small groups turn up unpredictably
at marshy ponds, sometimes remaining for months. It is less retiring
than most marsh birds and may be observed foraging in the open.
Its flight is weak and rail-like, with the feet trailing behind the
stubby tail. The bright yellow flight feathers in the short, rounded
wings are very conspicuous when the bird flies or raises its wings
above its back, as it frequently does for a moment upon alighting.

Description
8–9″ (20.5–23 cm). The adult is unmistakable, with a blackish head
and neck, shading into deep chestnut on the body and wing coverts.
The flight feathers are lemon-yellow, dark at the tips and on some of
the outer edges; the yellow is somewhat concealed when the wings
are folded; the tertials are chestnut, like the wing coverts. The bill,
frontal shield, and eyes are yellow; the legs and long toes are usually
greenish. The immature is quite different: brown above and white
below, with a dark crown, white forehead and eyebrow, and dark
line behind the eye. It lacks the frontal shield but has the yellow
wing pattern of the adult.

Voice
Hoarse *wheek-wheek-wheek-wheek*, often given in flight; might be
confused with descending call of Virginia Rail.

Similar Species
White-bellied immature might momentarily be mistaken for Wilson's
Phalarope or similar shorebird.

Range
A rare wanderer and occasional breeder in southern Texas, north as
far as Angleton (where a colony persisted for several years).
Accidental in Florida. Also in West Indies, Mexico, and Central
America.   *Kenn Kaufman*

Northern Jaçana

Adult
1. *Yellow frontal shield.*
2. *Black head.*
3. *Chestnut body.*
4. *Very long toes.*
5. *Large yellow patches in wings.*

   Stocky build.

Immature
1. *White eyebrow.*
2. *White underparts.*
3. *Very long toes.*

Sandpipers

(Family Scolopacidae)
This is a large and diverse family of wading and upland birds. The
majority feed by probing soft mud or moist earth with a bill that
lacks the distal swelling seen in the plovers. In most species, the bill
is rather long, narrow, and straight, but in some it is upturned,
downturned, or even spatula-shaped. Most members of this family
have long, slender legs. The necks vary from very short and stocky
to very long and slender. The wings are generally long and pointed
or rounded; the flight is rapid and usually direct. Except during the
breeding season, most species are highly gregarious. The majority
breed at high latitudes and some are famous for their very long
migrations. Most have distinctive breeding, nonbreeding, and
juvenal plumages, and the sexes are usually similar. A detailed
knowledge of molt, plumage wear, and aging criteria is often a
prerequisite to identifying similar closely related species. Juveniles
often show conspicuously pale, often buff edges to the feathers of
the upperparts, and the primaries are generally paler than those of
adults. Many species molt during migration. The family can be
divided into clusters of species; distinguishing species within these
clusters can be quite difficult. The tringines—the yellowlegs and
their allies—are medium-size, long-legged, slender shorebirds. The
bills are long and slender, straight or only slightly upturned or
decurved; the Willet and tattlers have stockier proportions, with
thicker necks, more rotund bodies, and sturdier legs. Common and
Spotted sandpipers are small birds with relatively stout legs and
bills and dark-tipped tails; they teeter almost constantly and fly with
erratic wingbeats on stiff wings. The curlews are medium-size to
large shorebirds with long, usually decurved bills; the head is small
and the neck and legs are long. The related Upland Sandpiper is
similar but has a shorter, nearly straight bill. The godwits are
similar in proportions to the curlews, but their long bills are curved
upward or straight; generally the bill is dark at the tip and pale at
the base. Turnstones are fairly small shorebirds of sandy and rocky
shorelines; the bill tapers abruptly to a point and appears slightly
upturned. The calidridines—the 20 species of *Calidris* and a few
related birds—are mostly small, rotund birds with stocky necks,
short legs, and short, usually straight bills. The sexes are similar in
plumage, but bill length may vary and is an important aspect of
identification. These birds have rather long, pointed wings, usually
with wing stripes. Included here are the "peeps" (the Semipalmated,
Western, and Least sandpipers and the stints)—small, stubby,
sparrow-size birds with short bills, legs, and necks, and wings that
do not extend beyond the tail when at rest. Distinguishing the peeps
is quite challenging, but with practice and a good view, the birder
can recognize them by differences in plumage, the size and shape of
the bill, and voice. Dowitchers are medium-size shorebirds with
deep-based, long, rather straight bills. The lower back and upper
rump are white, the lower rump and tail barred with dark and light.
The 2 species are very similar in plumage, but have different calls.
Snipes are similar in shape to dowitchers, but are primarily upland
and wetland birds and have dark stripes on or bordering the crown
and a dark eyeline. Woodcocks are very stocky, terrestrial birds
with short, thick legs and long, slightly tapered bills with a
noticeable droop to the upper mandible. The eyes are large and set
far back on the large head. The wings and tail are broad and
rounded; when flushed, woodcocks fly off with twittering wings. The
phalaropes are highly aquatic, with lobed toes, and swim easily; 2
species are often found far at sea. Females are more brightly colored
in breeding plumage than males. (World: 86 species. North America:
61 species.)   *Scott B. Terrill and Thomas H. Davis*

Common Greenshank
Greater Yellowlegs
Lesser Yellowlegs
Marsh Sandpiper
Spotted Redshank
Wood Sandpiper
Green Sandpiper
Solitary Sandpiper
Willet
Wandering Tattler
Gray-tailed Tattler
Common Sandpiper
Spotted Sandpiper
Terek Sandpiper
Upland Sandpiper
Eskimo Curlew
Whimbrel
Bristle-thighed Curlew
Slender-billed Curlew
Far Eastern Curlew
Eurasian Curlew
Long-billed Curlew
Black-tailed Godwit
Hudsonian Godwit
Bar-tailed Godwit
Marbled Godwit
Ruddy Turnstone
Black Turnstone
Surfbird
Great Knot
Red Knot
Sanderling
Semipalmated Sandpiper
Western Sandpiper
Rufous-necked Stint
Little Stint
Temminck's Stint
Long-toed Stint
Least Sandpiper
White-rumped Sandpiper
Baird's Sandpiper
Pectoral Sandpiper
Sharp-tailed Sandpiper
Purple Sandpiper
Rock Sandpiper
Dunlin
Curlew Sandpiper
Stilt Sandpiper
Spoonbill Sandpiper
Broad-billed Sandpiper
Buff-breasted Sandpiper
Ruff
Short-billed Dowitcher
Long-billed Dowitcher
Jack Snipe
Common Snipe
Eurasian Woodcock
American Woodcock
Wilson's Phalarope
Red-necked Phalarope
Red Phalarope

Common Greenshank

Tringa nebularia
This Old World sandpiper is very similar to the Greater Yellowlegs.

Description
12″ (30.5 cm). Lower back and rump white; tail barred with gray.
Mostly white below; neck, upper breast, and flanks streaked. In
flight, looks almost completely white from shoulders to tail. Blackish
wrist on folded wing; legs dull olive.

Voice
Sharp 3- to 5-note whistle.

Similar Species
Greater Yellowlegs darker above and below, with bright yellow
legs; white confined to rump, lower belly, and undertail coverts.

Range
In North America, a rare annual spring migrant in western Aleutian
Islands. Native to Northern Eurasia.   *Daniel D. Gibson*

Greater Yellowlegs

Tringa melanoleuca
The *Tringa* group of shorebirds are rangy, medium-size to large
sandpipers with slim bodies and rather long bills, necks, and legs.
The bills are usually straight or only slightly curved up or down.
The Greater Yellowlegs is the largest North American *Tringa;*
south of its breeding grounds, it is normally seen singly or in loose
flocks of fewer than a dozen birds feeding in shallow pools, lakes,
and impoundments, or along the edges of tidal creeks and marshes.
On occasion, this species attacks schools of minnows with rapid
sideward sweeps of the bill, and large groups may join flocks of
egrets and ibis in a feeding frenzy. Like other *Tringa* species, this
species bobs its head and tail and readily takes flight when it is
alarmed; as it flies, its long legs extend well beyond the tail.

Description
12½–15″ (32–38 cm). Both the Greater and Lesser yellowlegs have
long, bright yellow to orange legs, dark wings, white rumps, and
finely barred tails. In direct comparison, the Greater Yellowlegs is
clearly the larger species; its proportionately longer bill is 48 to
61 mm long, obviously longer than the head, and angled slightly
upward, at least along the lower mandible. The bill is 2-toned, pale
at the base and black at the tip. In breeding plumage, the
upperparts are checkered black, gray, and white; the throat and
upper breast are heavily streaked; the lower breast, sides and
flanks, and usually the belly are coarsely barred and spotted. Belly
markings when present are diagnostic; they are often retained by
adults until late September. In winter plumage, the Greater and
Lesser yellowlegs are virtually identical; the mantle is brownish-
gray, the feather edges notched with black and white; the throat and
upper breast are finely streaked with gray, and the remainder of the
underparts are white. Juveniles, seen south of the breeding grounds
from August to November, are blackish-brown above, densely
marked with fine whitish spots. The throat and upper breast are
finely streaked with brownish-black, and the sides are often lightly
barred.

Voice
A clear, ringing *whew-whew-whew*, usually 3–5 notes; sometimes
single, loud cry. In spring, a yodeling, repeated *tu-wee* or *whee-
oodle*.

Breeding adult
1. *Dull olive-green legs.*
2. *White belly.*
3. *Blackish shoulder in folded wing.*

In flight, shows white lower back and rump.

Breeding adult
1. *Long yellow legs*
2. *Long, slightly upturned, 2-toned bill.*
3. *Dark upperparts.*
4. *Streaks and bars on breast and belly.*

Winter plumage
. *Long yellow legs.*
. *Long, slightly upturned, 2-toned bill.*
. *Finely streaked throat and breast.*
. *White belly.*
. *White rump.*

Similar Species
Lesser Yellowlegs smaller, has fine, straight, shorter black bill,
proportionately longer legs, white belly in breeding plumage, gray
breast in juvenal plumage, different call. Willet has blue-gray legs,
heavier bill, bold black-and-white pattern to wings.

Range
Breeds from south-central Alaska across prairie provinces of Canada
to Labrador. Fairly common migrant throughout most of United
States. Winters near coast from central Washington and New York
and inland across states along Mexican border as far south as
southernmost South America. In summer, nonbreeders found
throughout winter range.   *Claudia Wilds*

Lesser Yellowlegs

Tringa flavipes
The smaller of the 2 yellowlegs shares most of the habits of its
larger relative but is considerably more gregarious, often feeding in
large, loose flocks of several dozen or even hundreds of birds. Both
species pick and snatch at their food, but the Lesser lacks the
sweeping technique for catching fish. The Lesser is more apt than
the Greater to avoid open beaches and typically more approachable.

Description
9½–11″ (24–28 cm). The Lesser Yellowlegs is so similar to the
Greater Yellowlegs that identification of a solitary, silent bird is
often difficult. The single most useful feature is the thin, straight,
black bill, which is 33 to 40 mm long and approximately equal to the
head in length or slightly longer. When the legs are fully visible
(that is, out of the water), their greater length relative to bill length
makes the Lesser appear to be a much longer-legged species. The
Lesser also appears distinctively short-billed in flight. In breeding
plumage, the belly is immaculately white and sharply set off from
the streaked breast and the fine, sometimes concealed barring on
the sides and flanks. In juvenal plumage, the breast is washed and
finely streaked with gray, thus appearing solidly gray at a distance;
juveniles are browner above than adults.

6

Winter

Voice
A high, flat, soft *tew* or *tew-tew*. Under stress may emit a very long,
loud, evenly spaced series of sharp *cuw* notes, bobbing head and tail
on every note.

Similar Species
See Greater Yellowlegs. Solitary Sandpiper smaller, dark brown
above with brown rump and largely dark tail and much shorter, dull
green legs.

Range
Breeds from Alaska (except along Arctic Ocean) and northwest
Mackenzie south to central prairie provinces and east to James Bay.
Migrates primarily along Mississippi Valley and, in fall, along
Atlantic Coast. Less common west of Rockies. Winters on coast
from southern California and Virginia south to southern South
America. In summer, nonbreeders found throughout winter
range.   *Claudia Wilds*

Juvenile
1. *Blackish-brown upperparts, densely marked with fine white spots.*
2. *Finely streaked throat and breast.*
3. *Lightly barred sides.*

Juvenile
1. *Long yellow legs.*
2. *Fine, straight, black bill.*
3. *Finely streaked breast.*

Smaller than Greater Yellowlegs. Shows white rump in flight.

Breeding adult
1. *Long yellow legs.*
2. *Fine, straight, black bill.*
3. *Streaked breast.*
4. *Sparse barring on flanks.*
5. *Dark upperparts.*
6. *White rump.*

Spotted Redshank

Tringa erythropus
The Spotted Redshank is a large *Tringa* from Asia that occurs as a rare spring and fall migrant in the western Aleutian Islands. It appears singly or in small groups, feeding at pond margins and in the storm tide line.

Description
12″ (30.5 cm). In breeding plumage, Spotted Redshanks are unique: black except for the white back and upper rump, with red legs, and a red base on the lower mandible of the otherwise dark bill. The white upperparts are finely dotted; there is a white trailing edge to the wings. Winter-plumage birds are uniformly gray above, with whitish edges on the wing coverts and whitish underparts. The bill is long and straight with a distinctive down-curved kink at the very tip. Juveniles have the white back and rump pattern of adults but are dull gray-brown above and barred ventrally with warm brownish-gray.

Voice
A distinctive, clear *chew-whit*, with rising inflection.

Similar Species
Unique in spring plumage. In fall, distinguishable from other *Tringa* species in Alaska by size, orange or red base of straight bill, white back and rump, and deep red or orange-red legs. Greater Yellowlegs nearly same size; in fall appears darker above, shorter-billed. Ruff smaller, stockier, with shorter bill; lacks white rump.

Range
In North America, rare migrant through western Aleutian Islands. Casual farther east in Aleutians and on Alaska islands of Bering Sea. Accidental in North America outside Alaska. Native to northern Eurasia.   *Daniel D. Gibson*

Wood Sandpiper

Tringa glareola
This small *Tringa* occurs in the western and central Aleutian Islands as an uncommon to common migrant. It appears singly or in flocks.

Description
8–9″ (20.5–23 cm). Upperparts gray-brown spangled with white. Rump white; underwings whitish. Legs yellowish.

Voice
Calls are loud *fee-fee-fee-fee-fee* and *chip-ip-ip-ip*.

Similar Species
Solitary Sandpiper and Lesser Yellowlegs similar; rarely overlap.

Range
Migrates through and has bred in western and central Aleutian Islands of Alaska; much more numerous in spring than in fall. Rare on Alaska islands of Bering Sea and casual on Alaska mainland coast. Accidental elsewhere in North America. Native to northern Eurasia.   *Daniel D. Gibson*

Sandpipers

Juvenile
1. *Straight bill with orange or red base.*
2. *Red legs.*
3. *Dull gray upperparts.*
4. *Brownish-gray barring on underparts.*

Large size. Shows white lower back and rump in flight.

Breeding adult
1. *Blackish plumage.*
2. *Straight bill with orange or red base.*
3. *Red legs.*

Large size. Shows white lower back and rump in flight.

Breeding adult
1. *Warm brown upperparts.*
2. *Yellowish legs.*

Shows white rump, whitish wing linings in flight.

Solitary Sandpiper

Tringa solitaria
Smallest common North American *Tringa*, the Solitary Sandpiper is
typically seen alone, more rarely in groups of 3 or 4. It stalks the
shores or wades in the shallow edges of slow-moving woodland
streams, stagnant ponds, and freshwater and brackish marshes,
constantly bobbing its head and tail. It has a distinctive swooping,
swallowlike flight.

Description
7½–9″ (19–23 cm). The Solitary Sandpiper has a prominent white
eye-ring, dark olive-brown upperparts and wings speckled with
white or buff, a dark rump, and a dark-centered tail with barred
brown-and-white outer tail feathers. The olive-green legs and
straight, rather heavy, olive-brown bill are both shorter than those
of the Lesser Yellowlegs. In breeding plumage, the upperparts are
strongly spotted white, the upper throat and belly are white, the
foreneck and breast heavily streaked with black. In winter and
juvenal plumage, the throat and upper breast are washed and subtly
streaked with brown; winter adults are grayer and faintly spotted
white above, juveniles more olive and faintly spotted buff.

Voice
Peet-weet or *peet-weet-weet*, higher and sharper than call of Spotted
Sandpiper; usually heard in flight, especially when flushed.

Similar Species
See Lesser Yellowlegs. Wood Sandpiper similar but ranges overlap
only minutely. Spotted Sandpiper has white wing stripe and trailing
edge, unspotted upperparts, heavily spotted underparts in breeding
plumage, and rapid, stiff, shallow wingbeats.

Range
Breeds from west-central Alaska across central Canada east to
central Quebec and Labrador and south to northeastern Minnesota.
Migrates across most of North America but is rare on Pacific Coast
north of California. Rare in winter in lower Rio Grande valley and
southeastern Florida; most winter south of United States to Peru
and Argentina.   *Claudia Wilds*

Willet

Catoptrophorus semipalmatus
This is a large shorebird that spends much time dozing in hunched
postures or feeding deliberately in sloughs and marshes or at the
edge of incoming tides. It is drab at rest, but its bold black-and-
white wings and noisy cries make it very conspicuous in flight.
Western birds nest on moist plains and prairies, eastern birds on
coastal marshes and nearby grassy areas. Willets are usually seen
singly or in pairs when nesting, but even before the young are fully
grown, adults mass in large flocks to migrate south. The western
race moves to all 3 coasts in late summer.

Description
14–16¼″ (36–41 cm). Easily recognized in flight by strongly
patterned black-and-white wings, gray-tipped white tail. Drab at
rest, with rather long, heavy, straight bill (longer and slimmer in
western birds) and rather long blue-gray legs. In breeding plumage,
eastern race gray-brown above; upperparts, breast, and flanks finely
barred and spotted with black (may look quite dark when worn).

Breeding adult
1. *Short olive bill and white eye-ring.*
2. *Olive-brown, speckled upperparts.*
3. *Heavily streaked breast.*
4. *Short olive legs.*

Floppy, swallowlike flight.

Winter plumage
1. *Gray-brown, faintly spotted upperparts.*
2. *Throat and upper breast washed and obscurely streaked with brown.*
3. *Dark rump.*

Winter plumage
1. *Drab, gray-brown plumage.*
2. *Long, straight, heavy bill.*
3. *Black-and-white wing pattern.*
4. *White rump.*

Large size.

Western race larger, much paler, grayer, often with pinkish wash on breast. Winter adults uniform pale brownish-gray above and on breast, fading to white on belly. Juveniles similar below, gray-brown above with contrasting buff edgings. Bill color varies with age, race, and season from all-black to black with flesh-colored base, or blue-gray with black tip.

Voice
Loud, shrill *pillo-willo-willet*, *kip-kip-kip*, and *beat-it.*

Similar Species
Winter-plumage Hudsonian Godwit has longer, tapered, upturned bill, always pink at base; less white on wing; broad black tail band. See Greater Yellowlegs.

Range
Western race breeds from central Saskatchewan to northeastern California and Nevada, Nebraska, and Minnesota; eastern race from Nova Scotia south to Mexico and Caribbean. Winters on coasts from Oregon and North Carolina south.   *Claudia Wilds*

Wandering Tattler

Heteroscelus incanus
Breeding along cold mountain streams, the Wandering Tattler frequents rocky shores along the Pacific Coast for much of the year. It is seen only rarely on sandy beaches and mud flats. A medium-size shorebird, this species is immediately distinguished by its uniform dark gray upperparts, which have no white markings whatsoever. It has relatively long wings and pumps the rear part of its body when it walks. Usually seen singly or in small groups, it is regularly found among flocks of other rocky shorebirds.

Description
11″ (28 cm). All plumages of the Wandering Tattler show uniform slate-gray upperparts and a white eyebrow. Adults in breeding plumage are heavily barred below with dark gray, except for the white lower belly. Nonbreeding adults and juveniles are unbarred but washed with gray across the breast and on the flanks. The bill is of medium length and straight; the legs and feet are greenish-yellow.

Voice
Call a distinctive, rapid series of hollow whistles given on 1 pitch.

Similar Species
Gray-tailed Tattler slightly paler above; barring on underparts limited to breast, sides, and flanks, and narrower, paler, especially on flanks; adults may have broader white eyebrow. Juveniles and non-breeding adults distinguishable only by call. Other shorebirds lack combination of uniform slate-gray upperparts and straight, medium-length bill.

2

Range
Breeds in interior from western Alaska east to Yukon and northwestern British Columbia. Winters along coast from northern California south to Ecuador and on islands in Pacific. Casual inland and in East.   *Paul Lehman*

Breeding plumage

1. *Gray-brown plumage, finely spotted and barred with black.*
2. *Long, straight, heavy bill.*
3. *Long blue-gray legs.*

Breeding adult

1. *Slate-gray upperparts.*
2. *Whitish eyebrow.*
3. *Heavily barred underparts.*
4. *Greenish-yellow legs.*

Winter adult

1. *Slate-gray upperparts.*
2. *Dark rump and tail.*
3. *Whitish eyebrow.*
4. *Gray wash on breast and flanks.*

Gray-tailed Tattler

Heteroscelus brevipes
This Asiatic sandpiper is found singly or in small parties along the
seacoast, sometimes with the Wandering Tattler.

Description
10″ (25.5 cm). Spring birds slate-gray above, with fine, pale gray
barring below confined to breast and flanks. Midbreast, belly, and
undertail coverts almost pure white; eyebrow white.

Voice
Mellow, 2-note, up-slurred whistle; also call like Wandering Tattler's.

Similar Species
See Wandering Tattler.

Range
Annual migrant in western Aleutians; casual farther east in
Aleutians, on Alaska islands of Bering Sea, and on Alaska coast
north to Point Barrow. Native to eastern Asia.   *Daniel D. Gibson*

Common Sandpiper

Actitis hypoleucos
This bird migrates annually to the beaches and reefs of the western
Aleutians. It is also found on the margins of lakes and ponds.

Description
8″ (20.5 cm). In spring, bronze-green above with fine dark bars;
white below with streaks across upper breast and lower throat.
Legs and bill green-gray; lower mandible paler. Juvenile almost
identical to juvenile Spotted Sandpiper.

Voice
A shrill piping.

Similar Species
See Spotted Sandpiper.

Range
Migrates through western Aleutians. Casual in eastern Aleutians
and on Alaska islands of Bering Sea. Native to Eurasia.
Daniel D. Gibson

Spotted Sandpiper

Actitis macularia
The Spotted Sandpiper may be found wherever there is water, from
a damp patch in a meadow to a forest stream or pool or the edge of
the ocean surf. As it feeds, it teeters back and forth, tipping up its
tail with nearly every step. The Spotted Sandpiper is usually a
loner. Its flight is distinctive: between quick, shallow wingbeats, it
sails low over the water on stiffly bowed, quivering wings.

Winter

Description
7–8″ (18–20.5 cm). This fairly small sandpiper has a trim build,
rather short legs, a stout, often slightly drooping bill, and a tail that
extends a little beyond the wing tips. Entirely gray-brown above, in
flight it displays a conspicuous white wing stripe, a narrow, white
trailing edge to the secondaries, and a round-tipped tail with black-
barred white outer feathers. A whitish eyebrow runs above a black
line through the eye. Breeding-plumage birds have boldly spotted
underparts; the dark-tipped bill and the legs are bright flesh-pink to
yellow. In winter and juvenal plumages, the underparts are white

Breeding adult
1. *Barring on underparts finer than in Wandering Tattler, and confined to breast and flanks.*

Breeding adult
1. *Finely streaked neck and breast.*
2. *Gray-brown upperparts.*
3. *Greenish legs.*

Teeters like Spotted Sandpiper.

Breeding adult
. *Gray-brown upperparts.*
. *White wing stripe.*
. *Spotted underparts.*
. *Pink to yellow bill.*

Teeters constantly. Stiff-winged flight.

interrupted only by brown patches on the sides of the foreneck and breast. A prominent wedge of white separates the back edge of the breast patch from the dark bend of the wing. The wing coverts are narrowly barred brown and buff, conspicuously so in juveniles. The bill and legs are much duller and quite variable.

Voice
A loud *weet* or *peet-weet*, often extended to several notes.

Similar Species
See Solitary Sandpiper. Common Sandpiper has longer tail, longer, more prominent wing stripe and trailing edge, streaked breast patches, pale-based, dark-brown bill, and pale greenish legs all year; lacks spots in breeding plumage. Winter birds and juveniles browner, less gray, with less conspicuous barring on wing coverts.

Range
Breeds throughout North America south to southern California, east across northern portions of Gulf States to North Carolina. Winters along Pacific Coast from southern British Columbia to Chile; from southern California east to South Carolina and south to Argentina. Nonbreeders summer throughout winter range.   *Claudia Wilds*

Upland Sandpiper

Bartramia longicauda
The Upland Sandpiper is a rather solitary, uncommon bird of prairies, meadows, rank sloughs, and hay and alfalfa fields. Ploverlike in much of its behavior, it runs in spurts and stops abruptly, often perching on rocks or stumps to gain a vantage point above the tall grass. Its stiff, bowed-winged flight is reminiscent of the Spotted Sandpiper's. After alighting, it often holds its wings upraised for a few seconds, displaying the barred wing linings.

Description
11–12½″ (28–32 cm). The Upland Sandpiper is closely related to the curlews and resembles them in plumage. It has a bony little head on a long, very thin neck; its heavy body terminates in a tail that extends well beyond the wing tips. The eyes are large and dark; the straw-colored bill is short and straight or slightly drooped, and the long legs are also straw-colored. The upperparts appear scaly, the black feathers narrowly edged with bright buff. The underparts are buff; the upper breast is streaked with brown, and the lower breast and flanks are barred. In flight, the wings are long, dark, and pointed, the tail long and wedge-shaped. The wing linings are heavily barred with brown and white, but appear brownish at a distance.

Voice
Loud, liquid, mournful trills and whistles; in migration, often rich *hoo-lee-lee*. Alarm note, *quip-ip-ip-ip*.

Similar Species
Buff-breasted Sandpiper smaller, with proportionately larger head, thicker neck, and shorter tail; lacks strong bars or streaks on buff underparts.

Range
Breeds from north-central Alaska east to southern New Brunswick and south to northeastern Oregon, northern Oklahoma, and Virginia. Migrates throughout continent, but rare along Pacific and southern Atlantic coasts. Winters in southern South America.
Claudia Wilds

Juvenile
1. *Gray-brown uparts.*
2. *Buff bars on wing coverts.*
3. *White underparts with gray-brown patch at sides of breast.*

   Peet-weet *call*

Adult
1. *Small head.*
2. *Long, thin neck.*
3. *Scaly upperparts.*
4. *Streaked and barred underparts.*
5. *Long straw-colored legs.*

In flight
1. *Small head.*
2. *Long wedge-shaped tail.*
3. *Long, dark, pointed wings.*

   Flight bowed-winged, like Spotted Sandpiper's.

Eskimo Curlew

Numenius borealis
This species was once extremely abundant, but was slaughtered by
the thousands both along its migration routes in North America and
on its wintering grounds in South America. Since the end of the 19th
century it has hovered near extinction. Recently, however, there
has been evidence of birds nesting in the Northwest Territories, and
well-documented sightings every few years along the traditional
migration routes, especially on the Texas coast in spring and on the
Atlantic Coast in summer and fall. Eskimo Curlews associate with
Lesser Golden-Plovers in fields, pastures, and the drier parts of salt
and brackish marshes; occasionally they have been found on coastal
beaches and among vegetated dunes. They are reportedly sluggish
and slow to take flight. On alighting they stretch their wings above
their backs, displaying the cinnamon-colored wing linings.

Description
12–14″ (30–36 cm). The Eskimo Curlew is appreciably smaller than
the smallest Whimbrel, with a more delicate build and a bill that is
markedly shorter (42–58 mm), thinner, and less decurved. A narrow
stripe divides the dark brown crown, but is often indistinct; the
eyebrow is buff and does not contrast strongly with the dark crown
and eyeline. There are buff spots and narrow buff edges on the dark
upperparts, giving the bird a rich brown look in flight. The dark
primaries lack the barring found in the Whimbrel. The streaked
lower throat and breast are warm buff, shading to rich cinnamon on
the barred axillars and wing linings, and contrasting strongly with
the dark upperparts. The sides and flanks are marked with dark
chevrons. The bill is mostly dark brown or reddish-black; the legs
are dark green to blue-gray.

Voice
A soft, melodious whistle: *tee-tee-tee.*

Similar Species
See Whimbrel.

Range
Breeds in northern Mackenzie, migrating south and east to coasts of
Labrador and Newfoundland and offshore to South American
wintering grounds. Spring migration route more westerly, through
Texas and prairie states and provinces.   *Claudia Wilds*

Whimbrel

Numenius phaeopus
The Whimbrel is a beautiful, large brown shorebird with a long,
decurved bill and a quite conspicuously striped head. It forms small
flocks and is often seen flying in small lines or V-shaped wedges. The
Whimbrel nests on the tundra, and is most often seen in migration,
especially as it heads north in May and returns south in July or
August; the first birds head south very early in July. It frequents a
variety of habitats, especially exposed mud flats, sandbars, lake
shores, beaches, moorlands, and occasionally plowed fields. Listen
for its exciting, clear call.

Description
15–18″ (38–45.5 cm). This curlew is a large brown shorebird with a
long, decurved bill (2¾–4″ long) and conspicuous striping on the
crown. The brown plumage is mostly mottled; the bill is somewhat
thick. The legs are a dark blue-gray.

Voice
Loud, clear, rapid, whistled notes, given singly or repeated 4–7

Adult
1. *Thin, slightly decurved bill.*
2. *Vague buff eyebrow.*
3. *Rich brown upperparts.*
4. *Buff underparts.*

Small size.

In flight
1. *Short, thin, slightly decurved bill.*
2. *Cinnamon-colored axillars and wing linings.*

Small size.

In flight
1. *Long, decurved bill.*
2. *Uniform brown or gray-brown upperparts without pattern or buff tone.*

Large size.

times on same pitch, *pip, pip, pip.* On breeding ground, long, drawn-out *poor-weee;* also long series of many rapidly repeated clear, bubbling notes similar to first call.

Similar Species
Long-billed Curlew usually has much longer bill (5–7″), lacks head stripes, and is much warmer brown, with bright cinnamon wing linings. Bristle-thighed Curlew (restricted to Alaska and Hawaii) warmer brown with light reddish-brown tail and rump. Extremely rare Eskimo Curlew smaller, has shorter, more slender, less decurved bill, pale cinnamon wing linings. Godwits' bills also very long but slightly upturned.

Range
Breeds in Alaska, western Yukon, northern Mackenzie, southern Keewatin, northern Manitoba, and northern Ontario. Migrates primarily along coasts, less commonly inland but through prairie states in spring. Winters from California, Texas, Louisiana, Virginia (Eastern Shore—uncommon but regular), and southern North Carolina south to Florida, Mexico, and South America. Casual migrant in Southwest. Also in Eurasia.   *Henry T. Armistead*

Bristle-thighed Curlew

Numenius tahitiensis
This curlew is much better known in the South Pacific islands, where it winters, than on its Alaska breeding grounds. The bristlelike feathers on the thighs are usually not visible.

Description
17″ (43 cm). This bird is similar to the Whimbrel, with prominent head stripes, but has a rust tinge, a pale base to the downcurved bill, and a pale rufous rump and tail. The breast has dark streaks.

Voice
A slurred, ploverlike whistle, *too-lee* or *wee-o*, repeated 2–3 times.

Similar Species
Whimbrel much grayer brown, lacks rufous rump and tail; call differs.

Range
Breeds only in western Alaska; migrates directly southward to islands of tropical Pacific.   *H. Douglas Pratt*

Long-billed Curlew

Numenius americanus
The largest of shorebirds, the Long-billed Curlew is best known for its exceptionally long, decurved bill. In breeding season, it is seen primarily in the Great Plains grasslands. In migration and winter, it frequents wetlands such as marshes, mud flats, sandbars, and shorelines. The cinnamon wing linings are conspicuous in flight.

Description
20–26″ (51–66 cm). This is an extremely large shorebird with a spectacular, sickle-shaped bill 5–7″ long (in adults). The warm brownish plumage is mottled on the wings and back; the belly is unmarked buff, the wing linings cinnamon. The neck is rather long, and the crown is unstriped. The remarkable bill, when fully developed in adults, can be almost as long as the bird's body, and may be twice the length of a Whimbrel's bill. (Young "sicklebills" may have bills as short as those of Whimbrels.)

Voice
A loud, clear, rising *cur-lee*, often repeated 3–4 times; and a loud,

Adult
1. *Long, decurved bill.*
2. *Bold head stripes.*
3. *Brown or gray-brown upperparts.*

   Large size.

Adult
1. *Long, decurved bill.*
2. *Bold head stripes.*
3. *Warm brown upperparts.*
4. *Salmon-colored tail.*

In flight
1. *Very long, decurved bill.*
2. *Cinnamon wing linings.*

   Larger than Whimbrel.

emphatic *wit-wit, wit-wit, wit, wit, wit, wit.* Also long, rolling, whistled calls like those of Upland Sandpiper, but shorter and clearer: *cuurrleeeeeuuu.*

Similar Species
Whimbrel has prominent crown stripes, lacks bright cinnamon wing linings, usually has much shorter bill; plumage not as warm in tone. Godwits' bills very long but slightly upturned. Marbled Godwit very similar; differing bill shape may not be discernible at a distance.

Range
Breeds from southern parts of British Columbia east to Manitoba and south to northeastern California, Nevada, Utah, northern New Mexico, and northern and coastal Texas. Winters from northern California, southern Arizona, southern New Mexico, northern Texas, and Louisiana, south into Mexico, and from South Carolina to Florida. Uncommon migrant along northern Gulf Coast. Once regular migrant in Northeast: now casual there; also bred farther east; range now greatly constricted. Occasional in coastal Virginia and North Carolina.   *Henry T. Armistead*

Black-tailed Godwit

Limosa limosa
This rare spring migrant to the western Aleutians is casual on the East Coast; it feeds on pond margins, beaches, or wrack lines.

Description
12–15″ (32.5–38 cm). Bill long, straight, with black outer half, flesh-colored base. Head, neck, and breast orange; belly white. Tail bold black and white. White wing stripe and wing linings. Male has much barring on flanks; female almost none.

Voice
A loud *quee-quee-quee;* often silent.

Similar Species
See Hudsonian Godwit; no other shorebird has similar tail pattern.

Range
Spring migrant in western Aleutians; casual farther east in Aleutians and Bering Sea islands, and on Atlantic Coast. Breeds in northern Eurasia.   *Daniel D. Gibson*

Hudsonian Godwit

Limosa haemastica
The Hudsonian Godwit is locally common within the United States only in the brief period of spring migration, when it progresses along its narrow flyway from the Texas coast through the Great Lakes to its nesting grounds in the bogs, marshes, and tundra at the edge of the boreal forest. En route, this species stops on sandy beaches, mud flats, shallow ponds, and flooded fields, where tight flocks rest or quickly spread out to feed. Like all godwits, it feeds comfortably standing in water up to its belly (too deep for most shorebirds) or plunges its bill in mud up to its eyes. The hunched posture and deliberate gait of the Hudsonian Godwit, in addition to its very long bill, give this bird an awkward air. Its powerful, direct flight and strong swimming ability may account for the scarcity of sightings during fall migration. The thousands of Hudsonian Godwits that mass together in late summer on staging areas in eastern Canada take off on an immense offshore flight to South America. Juveniles travel later and quite independently of adults. Generally, only a small number of birds makes a stopover along the

Adult
1. *Very long, decurved bill.*
2. *No stripes on head.*
3. *Warm brown upperparts.*
4. *Buff underparts.*

Breeding adult
1. *Long, straight bill with black outer half.*
2. *Black bars on white belly.*
3. *Salmon-colored head and breast.*

   Shows white wing linings in flight.

Breeding adult
1. *Long, slightly upturned bill.*
2. *Barred chestnut underparts.*

Atlantic seaboard, although their ranks are occasionally increased
by the pressures of a tropical storm.

Description
14–16″ (35.5–40.5 cm). The Hudsonian Godwit is like other godwits
in its large size and very long, tapered, slightly upturned bill. It is
instantly identifiable in flight by the black axillars and wing linings,
the narrow white wing stripe, and the broad black band across the
white-based tail. In breeding plumage, this species has a whitish
eyebrow, a streaked gray face, mottled brownish-black upperparts,
and deep chestnut underparts, barred with dark brown and some
white. Winter adults at rest are uniformly brownish-gray on the
upperparts, neck, and upper breast, whitish on the lower breast and
belly. Juveniles, rarely seen south of the breeding grounds, have
brownish-black upperparts, edged and barred with cinnamon, and
buff-gray underparts. Adults have 2-toned bills, salmon-pink at the
base, dark at the tip; juveniles' bills are flesh-colored with a purplish
cast. Leg color varies from blue-gray to black.

Voice
Rarely heard south of breeding grounds: *ta-it; qua-qua* or *quee-quip*,
loud and repeated.

Similar Species
Black-tailed Godwit (rare) has white axillars and wing linings,
longer, wider wing stripe, straight bill. Marbled Godwit larger,
tawny below, lacks wing stripe and contrasting tail pattern, has
cinnamon wing linings. Rare Bar-tailed Godwit has barred tail,
brownish wing linings, shorter legs. See Willet.

Range
Breeds in south-central and western Alaska, Mackenzie,
northwestern British Columbia, and around Hudson Bay. Winters in
southern South America. Migrates north through center of North
America from Texas and Louisiana through Great Lakes and prairie
provinces; migrates from James Bay to South America; may pass
through Maritime provinces and New England. Casual to rare in
rest of United States and Canada; no fully documented North
American winter record.　　*Claudia Wilds*

Bar-tailed Godwit

Limosa lapponica
A common Old World species, the Bar-tailed Godwit is likely to be
seen in North America only on its breeding grounds, although the
handful of records on either coast and the 1 sighting from Texas
make it worth searching for. Like the other godwits, it is
conspicuous and noisy near its nest site on the tundra, where flocks
engage in graceful aerial displays. At low tide, the birds feed
together on exposed mud flats, wriggling their long bills from side to
side to penetrate deep into the muck. As the water rises, they roost
in flocks on the high ground nearby.

baueri

Description
14–17″ (35.5–43 cm). The Bar-tailed Godwit is short-legged for a
godwit; its toes are barely visible beyond the tail when it flies.
Alaska breeders (*L. l. baueri*) are larger than the Hudsonian and
Black-tailed godwits; vagrants occurring along the Atlantic (*L. l.
lapponica*) are about the same size as the Hudsonian. The Pacific
race has brown wing linings inconspicuously barred with white; its

lapponica

Adult with wings raised

1. *Black axillars and wing linings.*
2. *White wing stripe.*

Winter plumage

1. *Grayish-brown upperparts.*
2. *Grayish-brown upper breast.*
3. *Whitish lower breast and belly.*
4. *White wing stripe.*
5. *Black-and-white tail.*

Juvenile

1. *Long, upturned, pink-based bill.*
2. *Streaked breast.*

    In flight, baueri *has brown rump and wing linings;* lapponica *has white rump, light wing linings.*

white rump and uppertail coverts are heavily spotted and barred
with brown and do not contrast dramatically with the dull back or
prominently barred tail. The Atlantic race has whitish wing linings
more narrowly barred with brown; its white lower back, rump, and
uppertail coverts have few dark markings and contrast strongly
with the mantle and barred tail. Breeding males of both races have
entirely warm rust-brown underparts and dark upperparts edged
with rust. Breeding females are pale pinkish-buff below, fading on
the belly, with streaks on the breast and sparse bars on the flanks;
the upperparts are duller and browner. Winter adults are pale buff-
gray above and on the breast, fading to white on the belly, with few
or no markings on the underparts. Juveniles have brown upperparts
edged with buff, a streaked buff breast, and whitish belly.

Voice
On breeding grounds, many vocalizations, including a repeated *ker-
reck*, and a whistled *cu-wew* from the males.

Similar Species
Marbled Godwit much larger, with proportionately longer bill and
legs; has cinnamon wing linings and much cinnamon in wings and
tail. Hudsonian and Black-tailed godwits smaller (than Pacific race),
have proportionately longer legs, bold wing stripe, white-and-black
tail, black or white wing linings.

Range
L. l. baueri breeds in western Alaska and northeastern U.S.S.R.,
winters from Pacific islands and coast of southeast Asia to Australia
and New Zealand; casual visitor to the Pacific Coast south of Alaska.
L. l. lapponica casual visitor to Atlantic Coast of North America;
breeds from northern Scandinavia to western U.S.S.R., winters in
Europe, Africa, and Asia east through India.   *Claudia Wilds*

Marbled Godwit

Limosa fedoa
The Marbled Godwit is the largest of the 4 godwits and the most
widespread south of Alaska. A noisy, aggressive, and conspicuous
nester, it breeds in the wet meadows of the northern prairies. In
late summer it heads for its wintering grounds along the seashore,
where it is found on tidal flats in sheltered bays, next to inlets, and
on open beaches. In migration it also frequents lake shores and open
coastal beaches, where it chases the waves like a huge, ponderous
Sanderling. In shallow lagoons and brackish ponds it feeds well out
from the edges and flats frequented by smaller shorebirds, as well as
deep in the exposed soft mud.

Description
16–20″ (40.5–51 cm). Remarkably similar to Long-billed Curlew, but
slightly smaller, with upturned, long, salmon-pink bill with dark tip.
Distinguished from other godwits by cinnamon wing linings, inner
primaries, and secondaries. Outer wing dark toward tip; blackish
primary coverts form dark patch. Dark pattern of marbled mantle

Breeding female
1. *Long, upturned, pink-based bill.*
2. *Streaked, pinkish-buff breast.*
3. *Dull brown upperparts.*

Breeding male
1. *Long, upturned, pink-based bill.*
2. *Entirely reddish-brown underparts.*
3. *Dark upperparts edged with rust.*

Breeding adult
1. *Very long, upturned pink bill with dark tip.*
2. *Dark, mottled upperparts.*
3. *Barring on cinnamon-buff underparts.*

and rump continues on tail, which is finely barred black and buff to
cinnamon. Cinnamon-buff underparts marked by dark bars on breast
and flanks in breeding birds, largely unmarked on winter birds and
juveniles (which often look paler and grayer). Dark legs vary from
brown to blue-gray or slate.

Voice
Noisy cries on breeding grounds include repeated *god-wit* or *ker-rek*,
with emphasis on second syllable.

Similar Species
See Black-tailed, Hudsonian, and Bar-tailed godwits. Long-billed
Curlew larger, has very long decurved bill.

Range
Breeds from central Saskatchewan to western Ontario, south to
Montana, South Dakota, Minnesota. Has nested around James Bay;
seen very rarely in summer in western Alaska. Winters commonly
on Pacific Coast from California to Mexico and in much smaller
numbers on Atlantic and Gulf coasts from Virginia to Mexico,
irregularly as far south as Chile. Rare fall migrant to northeast
coast. Nonbreeders summer in winter range.   *Claudia Wilds*

Ruddy Turnstone

Arenaria interpres
The Ruddy Turnstone is a plump, pugnacious, versatile shorebird
with a stout, wedge-shaped bill with which it flips aside stones,
shells, and seaweed, opens barnacles, and excavates holes in pursuit
of small invertebrates. Although it is typically associated with
coastal rocks and jetties and migrates abundantly along sandy
beaches, it is often seen with Black-bellied Plovers in bare fields
after a spring rain, or briskly chasing insects on grassy flats among
barrier dunes and marshes. When food is scarce, Ruddy Turnstones
defend their feeding territories, vigorously chasing off all intruders.

Description
7¾–9¼″ (19.5–23.5 cm). This chunky, almost neckless species has a
short, wedged-shaped bill and short sturdy legs. In breeding
plumage it has rusty upperparts, a black-and-white head, black bib
and white belly, and orange-red legs. In flight, the upper surface has
bold blocks, stripes, and bands of rust, black, and white. Winter
adults are much duller, largely brown, but the pattern of the
upperparts in flight remains unmistakable. The head is mostly
brown, and the brown bib is often divided, or nearly so, by a white
line up the center. Juveniles are similar but paler around the head,
and have tawny feather edges on the upperparts. The legs are
tinged brownish-yellow and may appear quite dark.

Voice
Usually a low, harsh rattle; also an abrupt *cut-a-cut*, similar to
tudulu flight call of Short-billed Dowitcher.

Similar Species
Black Turnstone lacks rust in any plumage, is black and white in
summer, somewhat more slate-colored in winter. The head and
breast are almost entirely black, the legs dark reddish-brown.

Range
Breeds from northwestern Alaska across Canadian Arctic islands to
southern Greenland. Winters on coast from Oregon and Connecticut
south to South America. Abundant migrant on Atlantic Coast, fairly
common on Pacific Coast, rare inland. Nonbreeders summer in
winter range. Also in Old World.   *Claudia Wilds*

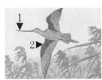

In flight
1. *Very long, upturned bill.*
2. *Cinnamon wing linings.*

Large size.

Winter adult
1. *Mostly brown head.*
2. *Brown upperparts.*
3. *Brown bib.*
4. *Short orange-red legs.*

Chunky build. Shows bold pattern in flight.

Breeding plumage
1. *Black-and-white head.*
2. *Rusty back.*
3. *Bold flight pattern.*
4. *Black bib.*
5. *White belly.*
6. *Orange-red legs.*

Rattling call.

Black Turnstone

Arenaria melanocephala
The Black Turnstone is a common, medium-size, stocky, short-legged shorebird found primarily along rocky shores of the Pacific Coast. It also occurs somewhat regularly on sandy beaches and mud flats, particularly where deposits of rotting kelp are found. It is usually found in small or medium-size flocks, often with other shorebirds that frequent rocky shores. At rest, the Black Turnstone appears quite dark and blends with its rocky surroundings, but upon taking flight, it exhibits a bold black-and-white pattern on the upperparts.

Description
9″ (23 cm). All plumages in flight show a striking pattern on the upperparts of black with white shoulder patches, a broad white line across the secondaries and inner primaries, and white lower back and tail base. Breeding adults have a black head and breast, a distinct white loral spot, white flecking to the forehead, nape, and sides of the breast, and a white belly. Nonbreeding adults and juveniles show a solidly black head and breast and white belly; nonbreeding plumage is overall somewhat grayer than the plumage of breeding birds. The short bill is dark and slightly upturned. The legs are usually dark, although some Black Turnstones have dark red legs.

Voice
A grating rattle similar to that of Ruddy Turnstone but higher-pitched.

Similar Species
Nonbreeding Ruddy Turnstone browner overall, with paler cheek and throat, patchier dark coloration to breast, and bright orange legs; some dark juvenile Ruddies almost as dark as Blacks. Surfbird larger; grayer overall in winter, with dark lower back, less white in wing, yellow or orange-yellow base to bill, and greenish-yellow legs.

Range
Breeds along coast of western and southern Alaska. Winters from southeastern Alaska south to northwestern Mexico. Casual inland.
Paul Lehman

Surfbird

Aphriza virgata
The Surfbird is a medium-size, stocky, short-legged shorebird found most of the year on rocky shores along the Pacific Coast. Only rarely —primarily during migration—does it occur on sandy beaches. It breeds in rocky alpine areas in Alaska. This species is found in small or medium-size flocks during the nonbreeding season, often in mixed flocks with tattlers and turnstones. Its short, thick-based bill is almost ploverlike.

Description
10″ (25.5 cm). All plumages in flight show a prominent white wing stripe and a white rump and tail base, which contrast with a black triangular patch on the outer half of the tail. Breeding adults have a whitish head and neck, both streaked with gray; the back is grayish-black with distinct white-and-chestnut feathering that creates a spangled look (the chestnut coloration is most extensive on the scapulars); the breast and flanks are heavily marked with grayish-black spotting and chevrons, and the belly is white. Nonbreeding

Breeding plumage
1. *Black head with white spot on lores.*
2. *Black upperparts.*
3. *Bold flight pattern.*
4. *Black breast.*
5. *Dark legs.*

Chunky build.

Winter plumage
1. *Dark head and breast.*
2. *Dark upperparts.*
3. *White belly.*
4. *Dark legs.*

Winter plumage
1. *Dark gray head and breast.*
2. *Dark gray back.*
3. *White wing stripe.*
4. *White rump and base of tail.*

Stocky build.

adults and juveniles have a uniformly dark gray head, upperparts, and breast; there is dark spotting along the flanks, and the belly is white. The bill is dark with an orange-yellow or yellow base to the lower mandible. The legs are greenish-yellow.

Voice
A low, 2- or 3-syllable *kee-wee* or *ke-wee-ek*, given in flight. Much less vocal than turnstones.

Similar Species
Wandering Tattler uniformly dark gray above with no white markings, has longer bill. Black Turnstone smaller, blacker, and has more white in upperparts visible in flight on lower back and wing. Rock Sandpiper smaller, longer-billed, and has vertical black bar across rump.

Range
Breeds in interior of western and central Alaska. Winters along coast from southeastern Alaska south to southern South America. Casual inland. Accidental in East.   *Paul Lehman*

Red Knot

Calidris canutus
The Red Knot is chunky and ploverlike, but its proportionately longer, thinner bill makes it obvious in the field that the bird is a sandpiper. During migration from its Arctic breeding grounds, it appears mainly along the coasts (generally in greater numbers along the Atlantic), foraging on exposed mudflats at low tide and roosting in flocks on sand spits, beaches, or matted salt marshes at high tide. Tens of thousands of northbound Red Knots gather at the shores of Delaware Bay in late May; elsewhere, and in the fall, the birds are not as abundant and numbers in the low thousands are exceptional. The species is present along the coast during the winter only in small numbers, except in southern California and southern Florida, where it is more abundant.

Description
10–11″ (25–28 cm). All plumages of the Red Knot in flight exhibit a pale grayish-white rump, a gray tail, a faint wing stripe, and white wing linings. The breeding plumage is distinctive and easily recognized; the face and underparts are rich rufous-red, and the upperparts are dark brown with rufous or white edges to the feathers. Birds in winter plumage are dusky gray above and whitish below. Juveniles resemble winter adults, but the feathers of the scapulars and wing coverts are edged white and have narrow, dark subterminal bands, which give the upperparts a scalloped appearance. The legs and feet are dark green or black; the bill, which is from 31–35 mm long, is black, straight, and slightly tapered.

Voice
Flight call a soft, musical *ker ek*, with accent on second syllable. Also a soft *k-nut*.

Similar Species
Nonbreeding Black-bellied Plovers somewhat similar to winter and juvenile Red Knot, but larger, with short, stout bill, spotted upperparts, and more erect posture; the 2 species are often found together. Breeding-plumage Curlew Sandpiper smaller, darker rufous, with bolder wing stripe and drooped or decurved bill.

Range
Breeds locally in high Arctic tundra of north-central Canada eastward

Sandpipers *373*

Breeding plumage
1. *Grayish-black back, spangled with white and chestnut.*
2. *Spots and bars on breast and flanks.*
3. *Greenish-yellow legs.*

Breeding plumage
1. *Rufous face and underparts.*
2. *Dark brown upperparts with white and rufous feather edges.*

Winter plumage
1. *Gray upperparts.*
2. *Faint wing stripe.*
3. *White underparts.*
4. *Black, straight, slightly tapered bill.*

Chunky, ploverlike build.

through Arctic islands to Ellesmere and Southampton islands.
Winters from California and New York south along both Atlantic
and Pacific coasts to southern South America. Found mainly along
coasts in migration, with larger numbers on Atlantic Coast
(especially from Cape Cod south to Chesapeake Bay); occurrences
are more sporadic inland. Also breeds in Greenland and Eurasia,
and winters in Africa and New Zealand.   *Thomas H. Davis*

Sanderling

Calidris alba
When many people think of a sandpiper, they probably have in mind
this small, pale gray bird that can often be seen chasing waves back
and forth along sandy beaches during most months of the year.
Sanderlings also frequent tidal flats, and inland migrants are
encountered on lake beaches and on sandbars along rivers.
Sanderlings sometimes associate with other shorebirds, particularly
when they gather at roosting places, but they are rather clannish
and are often observed in pure foraging flocks of up to a few dozen
birds.

Description
7–8½″ (18–22 cm). In flight, all plumages of the Sanderling exhibit a
conspicuous white wing stripe and a white rump divided by a broad
black median line. The breeding plumage is distinctive, with the
head and upper breast rust-colored and spotted with black; the rest
of the underparts are white and the back is black with rufous feather
edgings. Summer adults in fading breeding plumage have the rufous
confined to the face and neck, and the feathers of the upperparts are
edged with white. Birds in winter plumage are pale gray on the
upperparts, with white eyebrows and underparts, and the bend of
the wing is often conspicuously black. Juveniles look like winter-
plumage adults, but have a black-and-white checkered pattern on
the upperparts; they too have the bend of the wing conspicuously
black. In both adults and young birds throughout the year, the bill
(22–27 mm long) is black, straight, and slightly tapered, and the legs
and feet are black. The Sanderling is the only member of the family
Scolopacidae that lacks a hind toe.

Voice
Flight call a distinctive, sharp *kip* or *quit*.

Similar Species
Rufous-necked Stint similar to fading adult Sanderling, but Rufous-
necked and other peeps smaller, browner, with proportionately
slimmer bills; peeps lack bold white wing stripe. Winter-plumage
Sanderling paler gray than any sandpiper of similar size. Sanderling
in breeding plumage sometimes mistaken for Baird's Sandpiper, but
Baird's slimmer, longer-winged, with thinner bill and no conspicuous
wing stripe.

Juvenile
1. *Scalloped edges on scapulars and wing coverts.*

Similar to winter adult.

Juvenile
1. *Black-and-white checkered upperparts.*
2. *Bold white wing stripe.*
3. *White rump divided by broad black median line.*
4. *Black bend of wing.*

Winter plumage
1. *Pale gray upperparts.*
2. *Bold white wing stripes.*
3. *White rump divided by broad black median line.*
4. *Black bend of wing.*

Range

In North America, breeds in high Arctic tundra from Alaska
eastward to Baffin Island. Winters from British Columbia and
Massachusetts south along Atlantic and Pacific coasts to South
America. Occurs inland on lake beaches and sand bars of rivers;
rare in interior Southwest. Also found in Old World: breeds in
Greenland and northern Eurasia and winters from Africa to New
Zealand.   *Thomas H. Davis*

Semipalmated Sandpiper

Calidris pusilla

In migration, both the Semipalmated Sandpiper and the very closely
related Western Sandpiper favor the vicinity of water on tidal flats,
lagoons, and ponds. The Semipalmated is the predominant peep
throughout the eastern United States in the spring, but only occurs
north of the mid-Atlantic states in the fall. Favored coastal areas
attract thousands of birds, sometimes more.

Male

Description

5½–7″ (14–18 cm). In flight, all plumages exhibit a narrow white
wing stripe and a white rump divided by a broad black median line.
Birds in breeding plumage have rufous-edged scapulars, a rufous
tinge to the ear coverts and nape, and white underparts with a band
of dark brown streaks across the upper breast and a few thin
streaks on the sides. Fading midsummer adults are largely gray-
brown above, unevenly blotched with remnant black feathers.
Winter-plumage birds are uniformly gray-brown above, with broad
whitish eyebrows and a dusky suffusion to the sides of the breast.
Juveniles have a scaled back pattern of black feathers narrowly
edged with pale buff or white; the shoulder scapulars are dull
chestnut- or rufous-edged, and the wing coverts are edged with pale
buff or white. Birds in extremely fresh plumage have a buff band
across the upper breast, with a few thin, dark streaks along the
sides. The legs and feet are black, and the front toes have very small
webs between the bases. The black bill (15–23 mm long) is blunt-
tipped in shorter-billed males and slightly tapered and drooped in
longer-billed females.

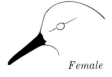

Female

Voice

Most frequently heard flight call a harsh *cherk;* foraging birds also
utter various chipping and twittering notes and a short whinny.

Similar Species

Western Sandpiper's longer, drooped bill often cited as best field
mark to distinguish Western and Semipalmated, but Semipalmateds
show increasing bill length from west to east. Many female
Semipalmateds from eastern Canada have bills overlapping in size
with those of male Westerns. Where these species mix in migration,
only birds with very short or very long bills can be identified by bill
length alone. Breeding-plumage birds distinctive; more rapidly

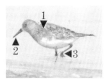

Breeding plumage
1. *Orange-rufous foreparts and upperparts.*
2. *Black, straight, slightly tapered bill.*
3. *Black legs and feet.*

Breeding plumage
1. *Grayish-brown and black upperparts with light rufous edges.*
2. *Band of streaks across upper breast.*

Juvenile
1. *Chestnut-edged scapulars.*
2. *Grayish-brown upperparts with buff edges.*
3. *Narrow white wing stripe.*
4. *White rump divided by broad black median line.*

molting adult Westerns show some rusty scapular feathers and
streaks on flanks into August. Juvenile Westerns have brighter,
more rusty-edged scapulars and tertials than juvenile
Semipalmateds, but also molt earlier. Best characteristic for
distinguishing these species is voice, but recognizing different calls
takes practice, and individual calls often difficult to pick out. Also
see Rufous-necked Stint and Least and Baird's sandpipers.

Range
Breeds in Arctic and subarctic tundra from Alaska to Labrador,
south to James Bay. Winters in South America, rarely to southern
tip of Florida. In spring migration, common along Atlantic Coast
and inland up Mississippi Valley; in fall most birds fly to
southeastern Canada and northeastern United States, then south
over Atlantic to South America. Rare but regular in West,
especially fall juveniles along Pacific Coast.   *Thomas H. Davis*

Western Sandpiper

Calidris mauri
The Western Sandpiper usually exhibits a slightly longer, more
drooped bill than its close relative, the Semipalmated Sandpiper.
This difference is correlated with the Western's preference for
foraging in deeper water than the Semipalmated, but much overlap
exists between the 2, and both species probe and pick for food.
During migration and in winter, the Western Sandpiper is the
predominant peep of the Pacific Coast, and along the middle Atlantic
Coast southward in fall and winter.

Description
6–7″ (15–18 cm). In flight, the Western Sandpiper resembles the
Semipalmated Sandpiper in all plumages. In breeding plumage, the
Western differs in having bright rusty-edged scapulars, a rusty
tinge to the crown, ear coverts, and back, and streaking across the
upper breast that extends in a double row of V-shaped marks to the
flanks. Summer adults in fading breeding plumage molt their rust-
colored scapulars last, and the color remains visible in most birds
until mid-August or September. Winter-plumage birds are
indistinguishable from Semipalmated Sandpipers except by voice
and, in some birds, by bill length. The length of the bill is not always
a reliable characteristic because there is much overlap; males have
shorter bills than females, and a short-billed male Western may
have a bill similar in length to that of a long-billed female
Semipalmated. Juvenile Western Sandpipers resemble
Semipalmated Sandpipers but have bright, rusty-edged scapulars;
they also molt rapidly, and most attain winter plumage by late
September. The legs and feet are black, and the front toes have
very small webs between the bases. The bill is black (21–30 mm
long), and slightly tapered and drooped, especially in longer-billed
females.

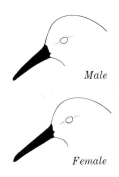

Male

Female

Voice
Flight call a rather high-pitched *cheep*, like a cross between calls of
White-rumped Sandpiper and Dunlin. Other twittering, chirping
calls similar to Semipalmated's but squeakier.

Similar Species
See Semipalmated, Least, and White-rumped sandpipers, Rufous-
necked Stint, and Dunlin.

Winter plumage
1. *Uniform grayish-
   brown upperparts.*
2. *Whitish eyebrow.*
3. *Dark legs.*

   Harsh cherk *flight
   call.
   Tends to have
   shorter bill than
   Western Sandpiper.*

Juvenile
1. *Bright, rust-edged
   scapulars.*

Winter plumage
1. *Uniform grayish-
   brown upperparts.*
2. *Whitish eyebrow.*
3. *Dark legs.*

   Cheep *flight call.
   Tends to have longer
   bill than
   Semipalmated
   Sandpiper.*

Range
Breeds in North America in Arctic tundra along western and
northern coasts of Alaska. Winters from California and Virginia
south along Atlantic and Pacific coasts as far south as South
America. Spring migration mainly along Pacific Coast; during fall
migration, small numbers pass through northeastern United States
and Canada. Rare inland. Some nonbreeders summer throughout
winter range.   *Thomas H. Davis*

Rufous-necked Stint

Calidris ruficollis
This bird is an uncommon migrant of Bering Sea coasts and islands,
where it occurs on open beaches and other places near water.

Description
6–6½″ (15–16.5 cm). In spring and summer, washed with rufous on
face, throat, and breast; dark streaks on lower breast. Chin whitish;
rufous edges on crown, back, and tertials. Bill short, black; legs
very short and dark. Juvenile like juvenile Semipalmated Sandpiper
but has slender bill, unwebbed toes.

Voice
Call a short *chit*, often doubled or trebled.

Similar Species
See Sanderling and Semipalmated Sandpiper.

Range
Migrant on Bering Sea coasts and islands. Casual in Alaska east of
Aleutians. Breeds in northeastern Asia.   *Daniel D. Gibson*

Long-toed Stint

Calidris subminuta
A migrant from Asia, the Long-toed Stint usually occurs near cover,
in the grassy margins of ponds, or in the wrack line.

Description
6¼″ (16 cm). Like Least Sandpiper but brighter in spring; back,
scapulars, and crown have dark centers and rufous edges. Ear
coverts and breast rufous; upper breast has fine streaks. Throat
white. Legs pale greenish; toes long. Bill olive; base of lower
mandible usually paler.

Voice
A low *chrrrp.*

Similar Species
See Least Sandpiper.

Range
Migrant in western Aleutians; casual farther east. Native to
northeastern Asia.   *Daniel D. Gibson*

Breeding plumage

1. *Bright rust tinge on crown.*
2. *Rust tinge on ear coverts.*
3. *Rust-edged scapulars.*
4. *V-shaped marks on flanks.*

Breeding adult

1. *Short black bill.*
2. *White chin spot.*
3. *Rufous face, throat, and upper breast.*

Breeding adult

1. *Contrasting dark feather centers and bright rufous edges above.*
2. *White throat.*
3. *Finely streaked breast washed with rufous.*
4. *Pale legs and long toes.*

Least Sandpiper

Calidris minutilla
The smallest peep is the Least Sandpiper. It favors wet, muddy, or
grassy areas and salt marshes, where it forages with its head
lowered, picking for food. It also frequents tidal flats and sometimes
wades into shallow water to probe for food. In flight, Least
Sandpipers hold their wings closer to the body than other peeps do,
often flushing with a snipelike, zigzag course. Both along the coasts
and inland, favored migration stops attract hundreds of birds,
sometimes more.

Description
5–6½″ (13–15 cm). In flight, all plumages resemble Semipalmated
Sandpiper but are darker-backed and have somewhat less obvious
wing stripes. The black bill, always a reliable fieldmark, is rather
long (16–21 mm); the tip is fine and slightly drooped. Least
Sandpipers in breeding plumage are extensively sooty brown on the
upperparts, with narrow chestnut and buff edges also on the
upperparts. The foreneck and upper breast are pale buff with coarse
dark brown streaking; in fading adults the colorful edges to the
upperparts become worn, producing an overall sooty brown
appearance. Least Sandpipers in winter plumage are like the
Semipalmated and Western sandpipers, but shaded dusky gray
above. Fresh-plumage juveniles are remarkably different from
midsummer adults, with an almost orange tone caused by the bright
rufous edges to the feathers of the crown and upperparts, and a
creamy white incomplete V pattern on the sides of the back; this
plumage rapidly wears and fades, and most birds molt into winter
plumage by the end of October. In all plumages, the legs and feet
are dull yellow or greenish; the legs and feet of juveniles are usually
the darkest.

Voice
Flight call a *kreet* or *kreep*, sometimes drawn out.

Similar Species
Other peeps larger with paler mantles, less finely tapered bill,
distinctly different voice, and black legs and feet (but beware birds
foraging in dark mud or viewed in midday sunlight). Semipalmated
and Western not as warmly colored, appear larger-headed; crouch
much less often. Long-toed Stint has more contrast above, white
throat; upper breast finely streaked; perfectly straight bill has finer
tip; appears rounder-headed.

Range
Breeds in subarctic from Alaska to Newfoundland south to James
Bay and Nova Scotia. Winters from Oregon and North Carolina
south along both Atlantic and Pacific coasts to northern South
America. Widespread inland in migration; local inland in winter.
Some nonbreeders summer throughout winter range.
Thomas H. Davis

Winter plumage
1. *Shorter bill than Western or Semipalmated sandpipers'.*
2. *Duskier upperparts than Western or Semipalmated sandpipers'.*
3. *Yellowish legs.*

Breeding plumage
1. *Sooty-brown upperparts with narrow chestnut and buff edges.*
2. *Yellowish legs.*

High-pitched kreet *flight call.*

Juvenile
1. *Rufous-fringed upperparts.*
2. *Incomplete, creamy white V on back.*
3. *Yellowish legs.*
4. *Narrow wing stripe.*

White-rumped Sandpiper

Calidris fuscicollis
The White-rumped and Baird's sandpipers are sometimes included
with the peeps, but they are perceptibly larger and longer-winged.
At rest, their wing tips extend beyond the end of the tail, giving
them a slimmer, attenuated appearance. In migration, White-
rumpeds favor the borders of ponds and coastal lagoons; they are
seldom encountered in numbers exceeding a few dozen birds,
although in some places—notably Labrador and Newfoundland—
they are often seen in groups of hundreds. The White-rumped's
presence among large mixed flocks of shorebirds is often revealed by
its very distinctive call.

Description
7–8″ (18–20.5 cm). In flight, all plumages exhibit a narrow white
wing stripe and white rump. Breeding-plumage birds have chestnut-
tinged crown and ear coverts, and the mantle feathers are edged
with chestnut and buff; the underparts are white with a pattern of
dark brown streaks on the neck and upper breast, extending in a
double row to the flanks. Molting adults in late summer exhibit long,
narrow, whitish eyebrows that contrast with the dusky gray
foreparts, including the crown, nape, back, and face; there is blurry
streaking on the foreneck and upper breast. Winter-plumage birds
are uniformly brownish-gray above. Fresh-plumage juveniles are
like bright breeding-plumage birds above, but with a buff-white
incomplete V pattern on the sides of the back; the foreneck and
upper breast are buff with thin brown streaks. In all plumages, the
legs and feet are black. The black bill (21–26 mm long) is reddish or
yellowish at the base of the lower mandible, tapering to a slightly
drooped tip.

Voice
Distinctive flight call a very high-pitched, thin, mouselike *tzeet;* also
a high-pitched, insectlike trill.

Similar Species
Standing White-rumpeds usually exhibit their rumps only when
preening. Breeding Western Sandpiper far more colorful above.
Winter-plumage Semipalmated and Western sandpipers quite
similar, have broader whitish eyebrows and largely white foreparts;
wing tips do not extend beyond end of tail. Baird's in fresh plumage
has bright buff foreneck and upper breast, but also has clearly
defined scaled pattern to the back; different flight call. Curlew and
Stilt sandpipers also white-rumped but larger, with proportionately
longer bills, necks, and legs.

Range
Breeds in Arctic tundra from Alaska (rarely) to Baffin Island.
Winters in southern South America. Spring migration is mainly up
Mississippi Valley; in fall migrates to northeastern United States
and Canada, then over Atlantic Ocean to South America. Occurs
casually in migration in Far West.   *Thomas H. Davis*

Juvenile
1. *Wing tips extend beyond end of tail.*
2. *Narrow white eyebrow.*
3. *Chestnut-fringed upperparts.*

   Incomplete buff-white V on back.

Breeding plumage
1. *Wing tips extend beyond end of tail.*
2. *Rust tinge on crown and ear coverts.*
3. *Dark brown streaks on breast and flanks.*

Winter plumage
1. *Wing tips extend beyond end of tail.*
2. *Narrow, whitish eyebrow.*
3. *Dusky gray foreparts.*
4. *White rump.*
5. *Faint wing stripe.*

   Thin tzeet *call.*

Baird's Sandpiper

Calidris bairdii
Built like a White-rumped Sandpiper, this species prefers muddy, sandy, or grassy areas in migration; it is often seen far from water and is seldom encountered in numbers exceeding a few dozen birds.

Description
7–7½″ (18–19 cm). In flight, all plumages exhibit a faint white wing stripe and buff-white rump divided by a broad black median line. Birds in breeding plumage have a buff tinge to the face, a splotchy pattern of buff-edged black and gray-brown feathers on the back and scapulars, and the foreneck and upper breast are buff with thin dark brown streaks. The remainder of the underparts is unmarked bright white. Winter-plumage birds resemble the White-rumped Sandpiper, but have a dark rump. Juvenile birds resemble breeding adults, but with a scaly rather than a splotchy pattern to the back and scapulars, formed by white or pale buff edges to the feathers. In all plumages, the legs and feet are black; the legs appear short. The black bill (21–25 mm long) is straight and slightly tapered.

Voice
Flight call a low, soft *krrrit*, often doubled and similar to flight call of Pectoral Sandpiper.

Similar Species
See White-rumped Sandpiper. Juvenile Semipalmated Sandpiper in fresh plumage noticeably smaller, with scaled pattern on back; upper breast buff with thin dark streaks, but face and foreneck white; wing tips do not extend beyond end of the tail at rest.

Range
Breeds in high Arctic tundra from Alaska to Baffin Island and Greenland. Winters in southern South America. Migrates mainly through plains; in fall, along Pacific Coast, more sparingly along Atlantic. Casual on both coasts in spring. Also in northeastern Siberia.   *Thomas H. Davis*

Pectoral Sandpiper

Calidris melanotos
The Pectoral Sandpiper is a large member of the genus *Calidris*, and usually presents a plump and big-chested appearance. Considerable variation in size may be observed within a single flock of these birds because the males are appreciably larger than the females. During migration, Pectoral Sandpipers tend to favor wet, grassy areas, usually bordering water or salt marshes, and are only rarely found on open mud flats,where many other species of *Calidris* feed. They often forage singly, in loose association with other shorebirds, but flocks numbering a few dozen or a few hundred are sometimes encountered. In many respects, this species looks and behaves like an overgrown Least Sandpiper, but it has a proportionately longer neck, which is evident when the bird is alarmed and raises its head.

Description
Male: 9–9½″ (23–24 cm); female: 8–8½″ (20–22 cm). In flight, all plumages of the Pectoral Sandpiper exhibit a faint white wing stripe

Breeding plumage
1. *Wing tips extend beyond end of tail.*
2. *Buff tinge on face.*
3. *Splotchy pattern on upperparts.*

Juvenile
1. *Wing tips extend beyond end of tail.*
2. *Buff foreparts.*
3. *Scaly back pattern.*
4. *Faint wing stripe.*
5. *Buff-white rump divided by broad median line.*

   Dry kritt *call.*

Adult
1. *Streaks on underparts end evenly across lower breast.*
2. *Dark upperparts with chestnut and buff edges.*
3. *Yellowish legs.*

and a white rump that is divided by a broad, black median line.
Birds in breeding-plumage have largely sooty brown upperparts,
with chestnut and buff edges to the feathers; the dense, dark brown
streaking on the throat and upper breast terminates abruptly in a
clean-cut line across the lower breast, contrasting with the white
belly, flanks, and undertail coverts. Birds in winter plumage are
similar to breeding-plumage adults but are duller. Juveniles also
resemble breeding-plumage adults, but are brighter above, with a
buff-white, incomplete V pattern on the sides of the back; the
streaking on the underparts is suffused with pale buff. The legs and
feet are yellow and are often tinged with green or brown. The bill
(27–29 mm long) is black with a flesh-colored base and is slightly
decurved.

Voice
Flight call a low, guttural *krrick*.

Similar Species
Sharp-tailed Sandpiper in breeding plumage resembles juvenile
Pectoral but lacks incomplete V mark on back; in flight, all plumages
of Sharp-tailed show different pattern of streaking on underparts.
Least Sandpiper somewhat similar in all plumages, but much
smaller.

Range
Breeds in Arctic and subarctic tundra from Alaska east to
Southampton Island and south along west shore of Hudson Bay.
Winters in southern South America. Spring migration mainly up
Mississippi Valley; widespread in fall on both coasts. Casual in Far
West in spring; 1 midwinter record for California. Also breeds in
eastern Siberia. Winters also in Australia and New Zealand.
Thomas H. Davis

Sharp-tailed Sandpiper

Calidris acuminata
The Sharp-tailed Sandpiper replaces the Pectoral Sandpiper as a
breeding species in Siberia. Its plumages tend to be brighter than
the Pectoral's, but its habits are much the same; in North America it
has often been found in association with the Pectoral. Most
occurrences of the Sharp-tailed outside of Alaska involve single
birds.

Description
Male: 8½–9″ (21.5–23 cm); female: 8–8½″ (20.5–21.5 cm). In flight,
all plumages are much like the Pectoral Sandpiper, except for a
difference in the pattern of streaking on the underparts. Birds in
breeding plumage are rusty to sooty brown above, with chestnut
and buff edges on the feathers; they resemble the juvenile Pectoral,
but lack the incomplete V mark on the back. The cap is rust with no
dark streaking; there is a low-contrast buff eyebrow. The
underparts are white, coarsely streaked with dark brown on the
throat and upper breast; on the lower breast the streaks splay

Fading juvenile
1. *Buff-white, incomplete V pattern on back.*
2. *Streaks on underparts end evenly across lower breast.*

Fresh juvenile
1. *Bright buff edges on upperparts.*
2. *Faint wing stripe.*
3. *White rump divided by broad black median line.*

Low krrick *flight call.*

Juvenile
1. *Contrasting reddish cap and white eyebrow.*
2. *Bright buff breast, finely streaked at sides.*
3. *Black bill shorter than Pectoral Sandpiper's.*

outward and turn to bold chevrons that continue along the flanks.
The undertail coverts are white with thin, dark streaks that form a
V. Birds in winter plumage are largely brownish-gray above, with
white underparts and a pale buff or grayish breast thinly streaked at
the sides. Fresh-plumage juveniles are remarkably different from
adults, with a contrasting bright chestnut cap and white eyebrow
that is broader behind the eye than in front of it. The upperparts are
largely rufous with an incomplete buff V pattern on the sides of the
back. The underparts are white, with a bright buff foreneck and
breast, thinly streaked with dark brown along the sides. Adults
have dark green legs and feet; those of juveniles are strongly tinged
with yellow. The black bill (24–26 mm long) is shorter and straighter
than the Pectoral's, with a trace of flesh-color or yellow-brown at the
base of the lower mandible.

Voice
Flight call a reedy *reet-reet.*

Similar Species
Pectoral Sandpiper always has breast streaking terminating in well-
defined line across lower breast. Juvenile Ruff has noncontrasting
buff eyebrow and dark brown cap, longer legs. Juvenile Dunlin
much smaller, with decurved bill.

Range
In North America, small numbers occur irregularly in fall from
western Alaska along coast to California; scattered records to
Atlantic Coast. Spring records from Alaska, Alberta, and California.
Almost all fall birds are juveniles; most seen from mid-September
through early November, a few to mid-December. One winter
record from California. Breeds in Arctic tundra of Siberia; winters
in Australia and New Zealand.   *Thomas H. Davis*

Purple Sandpiper

Calidris maritima
The Purple Sandpiper, once limited in winter to the rocky coasts of
eastern Canada and New England, now occurs far to the south on
stone jetties and breakwaters along the shore. These birds forage
among slippery, seaweed-coated rocks exposed by the falling tide,
searching for crustaceans, mollusks, and insects.

Description
8–9½" (20.5–24 cm). The darkest of the eastern sandpipers, this
species is short-legged and plump, with a rather long, thin bill
slightly drooped at the tip. The legs and the base of the bill are dull
yellow or orange. The narrow white wing bar and trailing edge to
the secondaries are evident in flight. In breeding plumage, the
crown has a rusty tinge and the head and neck are finely streaked;
there is a whitish eyebrow and eye-ring and dusky ear coverts. The
dark back and scapulars are edged with buff and rust, the throat is
streaked dark gray, the breast is washed with gray and heavily
spotted; the belly is white, and the flanks and undertail coverts are

Breeding plumage
1. *Streaks not sharply defined on breast.*
2. *Chevrons on flanks.*
3. *Streaks on undertail coverts.*
4. *Black bill shorter than Pectoral Sandpiper's.*

Winter plumage
1. *Brownish-gray upperparts.*
2. *Buff or grayish breast finely streaked at sides.*

Breeding plumage
1. *Finely streaked head and neck.*
2. *Heavily spotted breast.*
3. *Coarse streaks on flanks and undertail coverts.*
4. *Yellowish legs.*

   Chunky build.

coarsely streaked. Winter birds have a uniformly slate-gray head, neck, and upper breast, broken only by a white eye-ring (not always complete), a small white spot before the eye, and a whitish throat. The belly is white and the lower breast, flanks, and undertail coverts are streaked with brown. The dark gray mantle is often glossed with purple. Juvenal plumage is marked by broad buff edges on the outer wing coverts, chestnut edges on the inner ones, a gray-brown neck, and a streaked and mottled breast.

Voice
Twitters all year-round; takes flight with a soft *prrt-prrt*. On breeding grounds, a noisy trill.

Similar Species
See Rock Sandpiper and winter Dunlin.

Range
Breeds on Arctic islands of North America from Melville Island in northwestern Canada to Greenland. Winters on Atlantic Coast from Newfoundland to Virginia, rarely to Florida. Rare but regular in recent years on Great Lakes; scattered records inland and from Gulf Coast. Also in Eurasia and northern Europe.   *Claudia Wilds*

Rock Sandpiper

Calidris ptilocnemis
Similar to the Purple Sandpiper in size, shape, and winter habitat, the Rock Sandpiper is found, except during the breeding season, primarily on rocky shores along the Pacific Coast. This is the most northerly of the western shorebirds, remaining well to the north in winter; small numbers normally occur only as far south as northern California. It is usually found in flocks of Black Turnstones and Surfbirds. It blends in with its surroundings in winter because of its dark coloration. Birds breeding on the Pribilof Islands are the palest and have reduced redness in the mantle.

Description
9″ (23 cm). All plumages in flight show a conspicuous white wing stripe, a vertical dark bar across the rump, and a dark tail. Breeding adults have rusty upperparts, a pale head and neck, a dark smudge on the ear coverts, and a variable amount of dark grayish-black on the sides of the upper breast and on the middle of the lower breast. The more often encountered nonbreeding plumage is characterized by uniform dark brownish-gray upperparts, head, and upper breast; the lower breast and flanks are paler and streaked with dusky gray. There is a grayish-white eyebrow. All birds have a dark bill of medium length with a yellow or orange base and a slight droop to the tip. The short legs are greenish-yellow.

Voice
On breeding grounds, a curious series of decelerating bleating notes; also a short series of low, flickerlike whistles, occasionally heard in winter as well.

Similar Species
Dunlin in breeding plumage (found occasionally on rocky shores) has blacker patch on belly (not lower breast) and dark legs. Probably indistinguishable from Purple Sandpiper in winter, but ranges of these 2 species do not overlap. Surfbird larger; Surfbird and Black Turnstone have shorter, stouter bill and white rump and tail base.

Range
Breeds from western Alaska south to Aleutian Islands. Winters along coast from Aleutians south to Washington and, sparingly, northern and central California. Also from northwestern Siberia to Kurile Islands of Asia.   *Paul Lehman*

Winter plumage
1. *Whitish spot in front of eye.*
2. *Uniform dark gray head, breast, and upperparts.*
3. *Streaked lower breast and flanks.*
4. *Yellowish legs.*

Winter plumage
1. *Dark brownish-gray upperparts.*
2. *Brownish-gray breast.*
3. *Streaks on flanks.*
4. *Dark bill with pale base.*

Breeding plumage
1. *Rusty upperparts.*
2. *Pale head with dark ear patch.*
3. *Black patch on lower breast (not belly).*
4. *Greenish-yellow legs.*

Dunlin

Calidris alpina
The Dunlin is a medium-size *Calidris* with a long, thick, decurved
bill. Dunlins favor coastal tidal flats, lagoons, and beaches, and
inland mud flats in migration, where they forage slowly and
deliberately, both picking and probing for food. They are most
abundant on both coasts from the late fall through the winter
months, occurring in flocks numbering into the thousands, and often
in association with Sanderlings.

Description
7½–9″ (19–23 cm). In flight, all plumages exhibit a bold white wing
stripe and white rump divided by a broad black median line.
Breeding plumage is distinctive: the crown, back, and scapulars are
largely chestnut- to rust-red; the underparts are white with a black
belly. Winter-plumage birds are brownish-gray above; there is
blurry gray-brown streaking on the neck and breast. Fresh-plumage
juveniles are nearly as bright above as adults in breeding plumage;
below they are bronze-buff on the neck and upper breast with pale
brown streaks; the white belly is splotched with dark brown spots.
This plumage is rapidly molted, and by late October most are
distinguishable from adults only by the buff-edged wing coverts that
they have retained. The legs and feet are black. The bill, black and
stout, appears drooped in shorter-billed individuals and decurved in
longer-billed individuals. The bill length varies from 32–42 mm; this
wide range reflects the different geographic origins of individuals.

Voice
Flight call a distinctive, harsh, grating *gzeep* or *jeerp;* also a soft *chu*
when flushed.

Similar Species
Rock Sandpiper in breeding plumage has smudge on underparts
usually less solidly black and on lower breast rather than belly.
Sanderling much paler than winter-plumaged Dunlin, with shorter,
straight bill. Winter-plumage Purple Sandpiper slightly darker
above and below, with shorter, orange-yellow legs, feet, and base of
bill; has streaked flanks and undertail coverts. Winter-plumage
Western Sandpiper smaller, paler in winter, lacks black belly patch
in summer. Curlew Sandpiper in winter plumage has paler streaking
below; best distinguished from winter Dunlin by white rump with no
median line. Differing proportions are only apparent in direct
comparison.

Range
Breeds in Arctic and subarctic tundra from Alaska to Southampton
Island, south along west shore of Hudson Bay. Winters from
southern Alaska and Massachusetts south along coasts to Mexico.
Widespread inland in migration. Also breeds in Greenland and
northern Eurasia; winters in southern Eurasia.
Thomas H. Davis

Breeding plumage
1. *Rusty upperparts.*
2. *Black patch on belly (not lower breast).*
3. *Black legs.*
4. *Drooped bill.*

Juvenile
1. *Rusty upperparts.*
2. *Dark brown spots on white belly.*
3. *Drooped bill.*

Winter plumage
1. *Brownish-gray upperparts.*
2. *Light underparts with blurry brown streaking on neck and upper breast.*
3. *Drooped bill.*

Curlew Sandpiper

Calidris ferruginea
The Curlew Sandpiper is often likened to the Dunlin, a species it sometimes associates with, but it is longer-necked and longer-legged, with a more finely tapered bill. The Curlew Sandpiper usually forages belly-deep in water, probing for food in the manner of a Stilt Sandpiper, and associating with that species at times, although the Curlew Sandpiper usually feeds on tidal flats and roosts on matted salt marshes or sandy beaches. It tends to "salute" with its wings upon landing, holding them vertically over the back for a moment and flashing the conspicuous white wing linings. Nearly all occurrences within North America involve single birds, rarely 2 or more.

Description
7–9″ (18–23 cm). In flight, all plumages of the Curlew Sandpiper exhibit a bold white wing stripe, white rump (partially obscured with barring in breeding plumage) and sooty gray tail. Breeding plumage is distinctive, with rich chestnut-red underparts and chestnut-red edges to the sooty-brown upperparts. Winter-plumage birds are gray-brown above with a whitish eyebrow and white underparts, lightly streaked on the upper breast. The juvenile Curlew Sandpiper resembles the juvenile Stilt Sandpiper, but juvenile birds in fresh plumage exhibit brighter buff on the foreneck and breast, and rounded rather than pointed back feathers. The legs and feet are black. The bill is black and from 33–43 mm long; it appears drooped in shorter-billed males, decurved in longer-billed females, and tapers to a fine tip.

Voice
Flight call a soft, whistled *chirrup*.

Similar Species
Dunlin in winter plumage has darker streaking below; best distinguished from winter Curlew by dark rump. Differing proportions are only apparent in direct comparison. Juvenile Stilt Sandpiper quite similar to juvenile Curlew Sandpiper, but has blunt-tipped bill; legs much longer; legs and feet grayish-green or yellowish, white wing stripe short and narrow, tail grayish-white; flight call dissimilar. Fall White-rumped Sandpiper smaller than Curlew Sandpiper and more heavily marked below; bill nearly straight.

Range
Breeds very rarely in northern Alaska. Occurs in North America primarily as a rare but regular migrant along Atlantic Coast, especially from Massachusetts to Delmarva Peninsula; less frequent occurrences along Pacific Coast and inland. Breeds in Arctic tundra of Siberia; winters in southern Eurasia and Africa to New Zealand; some nonbreeders summer throughout winter range.
Thomas H. Davis

Juvenile
1. *Long, decurved bill.*
2. *Bright buff breast.*
3. *Upperparts with buff and chestnut feather edges.*

Breeding adult
1. *Rich chestnut-red underparts.*
2. *Long, decurved bill.*

Winter plumage
1. *Long, decurved bill.*
2. *Gray-brown upperparts.*
3. *White rump.*
4. *Lightly streaked underparts.*
5. *Black legs.*

Stilt Sandpiper

Calidris himantopus
Slim-bodied and long-legged, the Stilt Sandpiper habitually wades into deep water, probing for food with a rapid dowitcherlike stitching motion. In migration, Stilt Sandpipers prefer ponds, pools, and lagoons, shunning tidal flats and beaches. They are often found roosting in shallow pools with dowitchers and yellowlegs. Groups of a few dozen to a few hundred—occasionally thousands—are found at favored migration stops.

Description
7½–9¼″ (19–23.5 cm). In flight, adults exhibit a white rump, a non-contrasting whitish tail, and no wing stripe. Juveniles show a white rump, contrasting grayish-white tail and a short, narrow white wing stripe. Breeding plumage is distinctive: the mantle feathers are black with pale fringes, the ear coverts and nape are tinged with chestnut, and the underparts are white with heavy black or dark brown barring, a pattern unique among North American shorebirds. Winter-plumage birds are brownish-gray above with a whitish eyebrow and indistinct white edges to the wing coverts and white underparts. Juveniles are blackish-brown above with conspicuous buff edges, especially on the wing coverts. The foreneck and breast are pale buff, indistinctly streaked with brown; birds in very fresh plumage also have chestnut-edged scapulars and a faint chestnut tinge to the ear coverts. The legs and feet are dull yellow to grayish-green; those of juveniles tend to be darkest. The bill is black and 38–43 mm long; it is usually drooped along the outer one-third and is sometimes decurved along its length, but always has a blunt tip rather than a tapered one.

Voice
Flight call a monosyllabic squawk *querp.*

Similar Species
Winter-plumage small dowitchers and Lesser Yellowlegs similar to winter-plumage Stilt Sandpiper. Dowitchers much heavier-bodied, longer-billed, distinctly different in flight, with white lower backs. Lesser Yellowlegs slightly larger with straight bill, bright yellow legs, indistinct whitish eyebrow, and different manner of feeding. Juvenile Curlew Sandpiper quite similar to juvenile Stilt Sandpiper, but has bill tapering to fine tip; legs much shorter; legs and feet black; bold white wing stripe visible in flight. Curlew Sandpiper also has sooty gray tail and gives different flight call.

Range
Breeds in Arctic and subarctic tundra from northern Alaska to west shore of Hudson Bay. Winters in South America, with small numbers at Salton Sea of California, along Texas coast, and in southern Florida. Migrates mainly through plains; in fall, uncommon along Atlantic Coast except in ideal habitat; casual to rare along Pacific.   *Thomas H. Davis*

Breeding plumage
1. Long, drooped bill.
2. Chestnut ear coverts.
3. Barred underparts.
4. Grayish-green to dull yellow legs.

Querp *flight call.*

Juvenile
1. Long, drooped bill.
2. Whitish eyebrow.
3. Buff-edged upperparts.

Querp *flight call.*
Resembles Lesser Yellowlegs in flight.

Winter plumage
1. Long, drooped bill.
2. Whitish eyebrow.
3. Plain brownish-gray upperparts.

Buff-breasted Sandpiper

Tryngites subruficollis
Away from its tundra breeding grounds, the Buff-breasted
Sandpiper is very much a "grasspiper," frequenting grassy areas.
Easily approached, it usually prefers to walk or run away. In spring
migration, it gives samples of its courtship display, raising one or
both wings to reveal the snowy linings.

Description
7½–8½″ (19–21.5 cm). Somewhat similar to the much larger Upland
Sandpiper, the Buff-breasted Sandpiper has more typical sandpiper
proportions: a larger head, a thicker neck, and a tail extending no
farther than the folded wing tips. Like the Upland, the Buff-
breasted has large eyes set off by a pale eye-ring in an unpatterned
buff-colored face, scaly upperparts, buffy underparts, and yellow
legs. The crown is speckled; the feathering extends far down the
bill. Its underparts are brownish-buff, fading to whitish toward the
belly on juveniles, and marked only by small spots on the sides of
the breast. In flight, the buff body contrasts strongly with the white
underwing; from above, the bird appears quite brownish, with no
wing stripe. The upperparts have a crisply defined pattern of scales
formed by brownish-black feather centers cleanly edged buff on
adults, white on juveniles. The short, straight, tapered bill is pale at
the base, darkening to black at the tip.

Voice
A thin *tik-tik-tik* and a soft trill.

Similar Species
Larger Upland Sandpiper has small, bony head, very thin neck, long
tail; face finely streaked, underparts streaked and barred,
underwing barred. See juvenile Baird's Sandpiper.

Range
Breeds from Barrow, Alaska, along Arctic coast to northwest
Mackenzie and on Arctic islands to King William Island, Canada.
Common migrant through the interior of North America; uncommon
to rare in fall on Atlantic Coast; mostly juveniles. Casual on Pacific
Coast. Winters in Paraguay, Uruguay, and northern Argentina.
Claudia Wilds

Ruff

Breeding males

Philomachus pugnax
Built like a potbellied yellowlegs—and often associating with them
—this bird has a proportionately shorter bill and legs that are rarely
yellow. In migration, Ruffs frequent muddy borders of ponds and
lagoons, short-grass marshes, and tidal flats.

Description
Males: 10–11½″ (25.5–29 cm); females: 8½–9½″ (21.5–24 cm). In
flight, all plumages exhibit a narrow white wing stripe and a dark
median line on the rump bordered by oval white patches. Breeding
males have elongated facial tufts and breast feathers that vary from
white or orange through brown to black. These feathers are erectile
but often flattened. Breeding females have black-and-brown
upperparts; the underparts are white with a scaly pattern of black-
and-brown tips to the feathers of the foreneck and breast. Winter-
plumage birds are gray-brown above with white around the base of
the bill. The underparts are white with a scaly, gray-brown wash to
the breast. Juveniles have dark brown upperparts with rufous edges

Adult with wing raised
1. *Buff underparts contrasting with white underwing.*
2. *Larger head and thicker neck than Upland Sandpiper.*
3. *Shorter tail than Upland Sandpiper.*

Juvenile
1. *Buff face and underparts.*
2. *Scaly upperparts.*
3. *Spots on sides of breast.*
4. *Short, dark, tapered bill.*
5. *Dull orange-yellow legs.*

Juvenile
1. *Short, tapered bill.*
2. *Rufous-fringed upperparts.*
3. *Buff breast with dark streaks.*

to the mantle feathers and wing coverts. The underparts are white, with a bright buff foreneck and breast streaked with dark brown at the sides. The legs and feet are orange, red, yellowish-brown, or greenish (darkest in juveniles). The bill (30–36 mm long) is black, paler at the base of the lower mandible; tapers to a slightly drooped tip.

Female

Voice
Flight call: short, whistled *tu-whit* (rarely heard).

Similar Species
Smaller Pectoral Sandpiper always has breast streaks terminating evenly across lower breast. Both yellowlegs slimmer-bodied with streaked breasts, bright yellow legs, and show dark, unstriped wings in flight. Winter-plumage Red Knot shorter-legged, white-breasted, with dark lores; shows soft wing stripe, grayish-white rump and tail in flight. See Sharp-tailed Sandpiper.

Range
Rare migrant along Pacific Coast, Great Lakes, and Atlantic Coast; casual elsewhere. Breeds in northern Eurasia. Winters in southern Eurasia south to Africa and Borneo.   *Thomas H. Davis*

Short-billed Dowitcher

Limnodromus griseus
Dowitchers are medium-size shorebirds with chunky bodies, very long, straight, heavy bills, a wedge of white up the rump and back, and barred tails. Distinguishing the 2 dowitchers is very difficult, especially in winter. Plumage variations among different populations of the Short-billed are as great as the differences between Short-billed Dowitchers and Long-billed Dowitchers—causing considerable difficulty in field identification. Both species are normally found on shallow ponds and open marshes; the Short-billed strongly prefers salt or brackish water to fresh when it has the choice. Coastal migrants are heavy patrons of tidal creeks and flats; they are also abundant in brackish impoundments at Atlantic refuges. Dowitchers typically feed in silent flocks; with their heads underwater, they stab the bottom with rapid movements.

Description
10½–12″ (27–30.5 cm). Most Short-billed Dowitchers have light and dark brown on the tail feathers; the light bars are as wide as or wider than the black ones. However, this barring is very difficult to see unless the bird is preening or otherwise spreading the tail. On standing birds, the closed tail is usually concealed by the barred uppertail coverts. *L.g. hendersoni* is the most widespread form of Short-billed Dowitcher, and the only one seen between the Rockies and the Appalachians. In breeding plumage (May to mid-August), it has largely or entirely orange-red to brownish-red underparts, usually with some white on the belly or the vent. Most *hendersoni* are lightly spotted with black from throat to undertail coverts and have moderate to dense spotting on the sides of the upper breast; in fresh plumage, the feathers of the upperparts are broadly edged with reddish-buff. Other forms, *griseus*, and *caurinus*, are seen on both coasts, especially in the Northeast; these have a white belly, with a densely spotted breast, often including scalloped bars, and narrower, rusty edging on the upperparts. All forms have barred flanks; the white-bellied forms often are more densely barred. In winter plumage both types of dowitchers have gray upperparts, throats, and breasts and white bellies and eyebrows. At close range, the breast of the Short-billed is paler and less extensively gray than that of the Long-billed (a useful feature only in a mixed flock) and may show fine dark speckles. Juveniles are brightly marked:

Winter plumage
1. *Short, tapered bill.*
2. *Whitish area at base of bill.*
3. *Scaly gray-brown wash on breast.*
4. *Conspicuous white oval patches at sides of rump.*

Breeding plumage
L. g. griseus
1. *Long, straight, heavy bill.*
2. *Reddish underparts with dense spotting on breast.*
3. *Barred flanks.*
4. *Narrow edging on upperparts.*

Breeding plumage
L. g. hendersoni
1. *Long, straight, heavy bill.*
2. *Reddish underparts with light spotting.*
3. *Lightly barred flanks.*
4. *Broad reddish edges on upperparts.*

the back feathers, scapulars, inner wing coverts, and tertials are broadly edged with rust or buff and have conspicuous internal patterns. The tertials are barred, striped or both. In fresh plumage, the sides of the head and neck are buff. The underparts are strongly washed with rust and the breast is speckled or streaked.

Voice
Flight and alarm call a mellow *tudulu;* may be extended, accelerated, or abbreviated to 1–2 abrupt notes, but never as high, thin, shrill, or strident as Long-billed Dowitcher's calls.

Similar Species
See Long-billed Dowitcher, Stilt Sandpiper. Common Snipe has shorter legs, median crown stripe, and facial and back stripes; lacks white wedge up back and barred tail.

Range
Three breeding populations: on southern Alaska coast (*caurinus*), in western Canada from southern Yukon across Prairie Provinces to Hudson Bay (*hendersoni*), and in northern Quebec and Labrador (*griseus*). Winters on coast from North Carolina (rarely Virginia) and California to South America.   *Claudia Wilds*

Long-billed Dowitcher

Limnodromus scolopaceus
The Long-billed Dowitcher is a common migrant in spring and fall west of the Mississippi, becoming much less common farther east. Along the Atlantic Coast, it is rarely seen in spring or early summer; the first flocks of adults usually appear in mid-August, although some are seen as early as late July. Throughout the continent, migrating juveniles first appear in September. Long-billeds have a strong predelicion for fresh and brackish ponds and marshes, but are still common in saltwater habitats. Feeding flocks keep up a desultory, high-pitched chatter.

Description
11–12½″ (28–32 cm). Only a very small proportion of Long-billed Dowitchers have bills longer than all Short-billeds. The length of the bill ranges from 54–81 mm, while the length in Short-billeds ranges from 51–67 mm. In all plumages, this species' tail feathers are black, with narrow bars that are usually light cinnamon in breeding plumages and white in winter. Birds in breeding plumage (April or May to August) have entirely deep salmon-red underparts. The throat is densely spotted with black; the upper breast, especially along the sides, is marked by short, thin, black bars. As on many Short-billeds, the flanks are finely barred with black. The lower breast and belly are an immaculate red, although the white tips of newly molted feathers may briefly form pale bars in spring. The upperparts are usually darker, narrowly edged with rust and sometimes white-tipped. By midsummer, most of the dark markings have worn away and the underparts have faded, making sight identification difficult. In winter plumage (September to April), Long-billeds are almost impossible to identify visually, though in direct, close comparison with Short-billeds the gray on the breast is seen to be darker and more extensive. Juvenile Long-billeds have gray sides to the head and neck. The upperparts are diagnostic: the scapulars and inner wing coverts are black with narrow, scalloped, reddish-buff edges. The tertials are blackish, edged narrowly with reddish-buff; many have no internal markings, but others have a faint mark just inside the tip. The juvenile's upperparts can be used as field marks on some birds until the end of the year; the underparts are like the adult's in winter but washed with buff through September; the breast has no speckles or streaks.

Juvenile
1. *Upperparts with broad rust edges.*
2. *Scapulars and tertials with internal pattern of bars and stripes.*
3. *Underparts washed with rust.*
4. *Breast speckled or streaked.*

Juvenile
1. *Upperparts with narrow buff edges.*
2. *Scapulars and tertials without internal markings.*
3. *Sides of head and neck gray.*
4. *Underparts washed with buff.*

Winter plumage
1. *Gray upperparts.*
2. *Gray throat and breast.*
3. *Barred flanks.*
4. *White belly.*

In flight shows broad white wedge up back.

Voice
Alarm note a shrill, sharp *keek*, much more strident than Short-billed Dowitcher's *tu*. Feeding note and flight call a high, thin *kee* or *kee-kee-kee*, sometimes in drawn-out series.

Similar Species
Breeding Short-billed Dowitcher either has white belly or lacks densely spotted throat and bars on sides of upper breast. Light bars on tail feathers usually broader. Juvenile upperparts broadly edged rust or buff with conspicuous internal markings; breast speckled or streaked. Difference in call diagnostic. Common Snipe has shorter legs, median crown stripe, and facial and back stripes; lacks white wedge up back and barred tail.

Range
Breeds from northeast Siberia along coast of west and north Alaska to extreme northwest Canada. Winters from Washington and Virginia south to Panama; rare north of California and Georgia and south of Guatemala. Mostly found near coast.   *Claudia Wilds*

Common Snipe

Gallinago gallinago
This is a secretive bird of peat bogs, marshes, and sodden fields. When flushed, it zigzags away on long, pointed wings, often uttering a rasping call. On the breeding grounds, it is famous for its remarkable courtship flight that includes a power dive in which the vibrating outer tail feathers produce a series of rapid, hollow notes, known as "winnowing."

Description
10½–11½″ (27–29 cm). This heavy-bodied, large-headed shorebird has a very long, straight, substantial bill. The head and the dark, mottled upperparts are marked by prominent buff-colored stripes. In flight, the wings are long, dark, and pointed; the short, fanned tail shows a brown rump, a rusty base, an ill-defined dark subterminal band, and whitish sides and tip. The buff breast and flanks are heavily spotted and barred; the belly is clear white. The bill is dark with a pale base and the legs are light dull green.

Voice
Alarm note a grating *scaip*. On breeding grounds, a shrill *wheet-wheet-wheet-wheet*. Winnowing often transcribed as *huhuhuhuhu*.

Similar Species
Dowitchers lack stripes on head, have white wedge up back, barred tail; rusty below in breeding plumage, grayish in winter plumage.

Range
Breeds from northern Alaska to Labrador and south over most of United States to central California, eastern Arizona, northern New Mexico, and northern New Jersey. Winters north to British Columbia and Virginia in suitable unfrozen habitat. Also in South America; widespread in Old World.   *Claudia Wilds*

Breeding plumage
1. *Reddish underparts.*
2. *Heavily spotted throat.*
3. *Barred sides to upper breast.*
4. *Unmarked, reddish belly.*

Adult
1. *Very long, heavy, straight bill.*
2. *Striped head.*
3. *Striped upperparts.*
4. *Buff breast with dark spots and bars.*

*Zigzag escape flight.
Scaip call.*

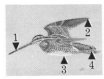

In flight
1. *Very long, heavy, straight bill.*
2. *Long, dark, pointed wings.*
3. *White belly.*
4. *Rust in tail.*

*Zigzag escape flight.
Grating scaip call.*

American Woodcock

Scolopax minor
The American Woodcock is a shy, short-legged, upland shorebird
that is most at home in wet thickets and moist woodlands, especially
alder swales. It probes with its long bill for earthworms, and relies
upon its cryptic coloration for protection. It is most often observed
in grassy meadows in early spring, performing a crepuscular
courtship flight. When flushed, it flies away on rounded wings that
make a twittering sound.

Description
10–12″ (25–30.5 cm). This plump species is quite unlike any other
North American shorebird. The upperparts are mottled with rust,
black, brown, and gray, very much like the color of dead leaves. The
underparts are an unmarked, bright cinnamon-rufous. The crown is
black and crossed with 4 rusty bars; the large, dark eyes are set
high in the head.

Voice
Ground call a nasal *peent* or *bzeep!* Aerial courtship call a series of
trills produced by wings during ascent; during descent low whistled
notes with a liquid, "kissing" quality, normally in groups of 3: *chew-
chew-chew*, *chip-chip-chip*, *chew-chew-chew*, *chip-chip-chip*. Song
ends abruptly just before bird alights. Often heard at dusk,
occasionally at night or dawn in spring.

Similar Species
Common Snipe has striped head and back, pointed wings; usually
calls when flushed.

Range
Breeds from southeastern Manitoba east to southern Quebec and
southern Newfoundland, south to eastern Texas, Gulf Coast, and
central Florida. Winters in southeastern United States, occasionally
north to New England.   *Wayne R. Petersen*

Wilson's Phalarope

Phalaropus tricolor
The females of all 3 species of phalarope are more brightly plumaged
than the males and are the aggressors in courtship. After laying the
eggs, the females take no further responsibility for them, leaving
the males to incubate them and look after the chicks. Unlike the 2
pelagic phalaropes, Wilson's migrates primarily over land; it winters
in freshwater and saltwater marshes, lakes, and coastal bays similar
to those it frequents in summer. Graceful and energetic, this species
often dashes to and fro along the margins of ponds, frequently in a
crouched position; it wades through the shallows searching for
insects and seeds, or swims buoyantly, often spinning around and
around, stabbing at insects on the water's surface.

Description
8½–9½″ (21.5–24 cm). Wilson's is the slimmest of the phalaropes; it
is the only one without a wing stripe and with a white rump and
whitish tail. Its very fine, straight, black bill is clearly longer than
the head, when the head is measured from the back of the skull to

In flight
1. *Very long bill.*
2. *Rounded wings.*

   Stocky build.
   Wings make
   twittering sound
   in flight.

Adult
1. *Very long bill.*
2. *Bars on crown.*
3. *Rust-colored*
   underparts.

   Stocky build.
   Found in moist
   thickets.

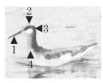

Breeding female
1. *Fine, straight, black*
   bill.
2. *Pale crown and*
   nape.
3. *Dark stripe through*
   eye and down neck.
4. *Chestnut wash*
   across breast.

the base of the bill. The legs are black in breeding birds and straw-yellow in winter birds and juveniles; they are longer than those of the other 2 phalaropes. The female in breeding plumage has a pale gray crown fading to white on the nape and a black stripe running through the eye down the side of the neck; this stripe is bordered with chestnut on the lower neck and fades to a bright chestnut wash across the upper breast. The back of the breeding female is dark gray with chestnut stripes. The breeding male has a brown crown and brown-and-chestnut back; the eye and neck stripe is brown fading to chestnut, with a much paler wash across the breast. Winter adults of both sexes are a uniform pale gray above and pure white below; the forehead, face, and sides of the neck are white with a pale hint of a mask. Juveniles have browner upperparts with buff feather edges, and a buff wash on the sides of the breast.

Winter

Voice
Largely silent except on breeding grounds, where it utters soft, low, nasal notes.

Similar Species
Both other phalaropes have shorter bill and legs, white wing stripe, dark-centered rump, dark crown and nape in breeding plumage, black mask in winter plumage. Lesser Yellowlegs has finely spotted upperparts and dark streaks or gray wash on throat and upper breast. Stilt Sandpiper has longer, heavier bill, drooping near tip.

Range
Breeds from southern Yukon south to central California and across to Manitoba, Minnesota, and Kansas; around southern and eastern Great Lakes; locally in New Mexico and Massachusetts. Winters in southern South America, with a few found sporadically in California and Texas. Migrates across North America; much less common east of Mississippi.   *Claudia Wilds*

Red-necked Phalarope

Phalaropus lobatus
Male and female Red-necked Phalaropes are unmistakable in breeding plumage; winter-plumage birds, on the other hand, are much more nondescript and less easy to identify. During migration and in winter, Red-necked and Red phalaropes occur on the ocean, where they are sometimes seen in large flocks. This species' flight is erratic and darting.

Winter

Description
7″ (18 cm). The Red-necked Phalarope has a thin bill that appears no longer than the head. Breeding-plumage adults have streaked backs, chestnut patches on the sides of the face, and generally white underparts and wing linings. The breeding female is more brightly colored than the male. Winter birds are medium gray above and white below, with a dark mark behind the eye. Winter adults retain their back streaking, which generally stands out against the darker upperparts; a dark cap extends to the nape and neck, sometimes onto the back. Juveniles show buff-rust streaks on the back.

Bird molting into winter plumage
. *White forehead and face.*
. *Dark line through eye.*
. *White belly.*
. *Straw-yellow legs.*

Breeding male
. *Brown crown.*
. *Brown and chestnut line from eye down neck.*
. *Brown and chestnut upperparts.*
. *Chestnut wash on breast.*
. *Black legs.*

Breeding female
. *Thin bill.*
. *White throat.*
. *Chestnut patch on sides of face and neck.*
. *Streaked back.*

Voice
Flight call a soft *prip* or *krit*.

Similar Species
Red Phalarope larger, with stouter bill and more robust appearance, less contrasting white wing stripe; streaks on back less obvious in breeding plumage and absent in winter. Wilson's Phalarope has longer, thinner bill, no white wing stripe. Winter-plumage Sanderling has less erratic flight, lacks head pattern and streaks on back.

Range
Breeds in Alaska and across northern Canada; common transient on both coasts during migration; much more common in West, where it also occurs in interior. Very few winter records off both coasts. Along Pacific, Red-necked appears earlier than Red Phalarope in spring. In western North Atlantic, Red-necked more common in migration than Red Phalarope, appearing later in spring and earlier in fall than its relative. Also breeds in Eurasia; winters mainly at sea in Southern Hemisphere.   *Ron Naveen*

Red Phalarope

Phalaropus fulicaria
Chunkier in appearance than the Red-necked Phalarope, the Red Phalarope can be distinguished in winter plumage by its gray back with little or no streaking. Like the Red-necked Phalarope, this species breeds in the Arctic tundra and is found at sea during migration and in winter.

Description
8″ (20.5 cm). This species is larger than the Red-necked Phalarope and has a stockier, heavier bill. The bill is yellow with a black tip during breeding season, and virtually all-black in winter. Breeding adults are distinguished by their deep reddish underparts and white faces; the males are paler than females. In flight they appear very dark with highly contrasting white wing linings. In winter plumage, the Red Phalarope is pale gray and unstreaked above and white below, with a black stripe behind eye, and a dark cap that generally does not extend to the back.

Voice
Flight call a high-pitched *creep*.

Similar Species
See Wilson's and Red-necked phalaropes. Winter-plumage Sanderling has less erratic flight, darker wing with more contrasting white wing stripe, and shows no patterning on head.

Range
Breeds in Alaska and northern Canada; regular migrant off both coasts. Irregular but sometimes in sizeable numbers along Pacific Coast; a few winter records from Atlantic Coast. In western North Atlantic, Red Phalarope less common than Red-necked; generally appears earlier in spring and later in fall. Very rare to casual inland. Also breeds in Eurasia. Winters mainly at sea in Southern Hemisphere.   *Ron Naveen*

Juvenile
. *Thin bill.*
. *Dark eyeline.*
. *Dark crown and hindneck, often extending to back.*
. *Dark, streaked back.*

Winter plumage
. *Thick bill.*
. *Dark eyeline.*
. *Dark cap usually restricted to head and nape.*
. *Gray, unstreaked back.*

Breeding female
. *Thick bill.*
. *White face.*
. *Reddish underparts.*

Part Three

Accidental Species

Accidental species are those that have strayed from their normal ranges and have been recorded only a handful of times on the North American continent.

Wandering Albatross
Diomedea exulans. 44–48″ (112–122 cm); wingspan 114–130″ (284.5–330 cm). Larger and longer-winged than Short-tailed Albatross, with pink bill at all ages. Full adult has white upperwing except at tip, no yellow on head, and narrower, dark tail tip. Juvenile mainly brown, like juvenile Short-tailed, but has white face, upper throat, and white underwing (underwing of Short-tailed not white until body is white). Subadults do not have black-throated or black-hooded stages of Short-tailed. Throat becomes pale before breast and belly; crown and hindneck become pale at same time as back; hindneck often white while crown and back retain dark mottling. Upperwings develop as in Short-tailed, starting with small white patches. Underparts retain much brown until fairly late, when upperparts largely white (underside of Short-tailed becomes white at earlier age, while upperparts mainly brown). Common in southern oceans but extremely rare north of Equator. One record from Sonoma County, California.   *Stuart Keith*

Albatrosses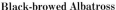

Black-browed Albatross
Diomedea melanophris. 32–37″ (81.5–94 cm); wingspan 84–96″ (213.5–244 cm). Differs from Yellow-nosed Albatross as follows: Adults have broad, dark edges to underwing with broader leading edge; juveniles have mostly brown underwing with narrow, pale stripe up center. Adults have no gray on head; juveniles have gray top and back of head and hindneck, extending as collar around lower throat and not quite meeting in center. Bill stouter; dark gray-brown with blackish tip in juveniles; tip stays dark but remainder lightens with age through light brown and horn to pale yellow. Dark tip then disappears; in mature adults, bill is orange-yellow with pink tip. At least 4 sightings—3 from Massachusetts, 1 from Newfoundland—and other possible occurrences reported. The Black-browed Albatross is the most common albatross in South Atlantic.   *Stuart Keith*

Shy Albatross
Diomedea cauta. 35–39″ (89–99 cm); wingspan 96″ (244 cm). All races and ages immediately distinguishable from Laysan Albatross by entirely white underwing with very narrow, dark leading and trailing edges. In white-headed race (*D. c. cauta;* only race so far found in our waters), adult has gray wash on face below eye like some Laysans, but has gray-green bill with yellow tip. Subadult has gray bill with dark tip like some Laysans, but also much gray on head and hindneck. Other races (all ages) have mainly gray head and neck (*D. c. salvini* has white cap). Found in southern oceans. One record from Washington.   *Stuart Keith*

Cape Petrel
Daption capense. 14–16″ (35.5–40.5 cm). Similar to Northern Fulmar in shape. Flight very stiff-winged, with a few rapid wingbeats interspersed. Upperparts and upperwings dark brown with variable pattern of white spots, bars, and patches, producing unique checkered effect. Viewed from side, head entirely dark (some have white center of throat). Tail white with dark terminal band; underparts white; underwing white with dark borders. Follows ships and often alights on water. Abundant in southern oceans, very rare in northern hemisphere. One possible sight record from California; 1 specimen from Maine of doubtful origin.
Stuart Keith

Shearwaters and Petrels

Cahow
Pterodroma cahow. 15" (38 cm). Typical birds distinguished from very similar Black-capped Petrel by dark nape (no white collar) and indistinct white rump patch. Intermediates in western North Atlantic with smudgy napes and rumps cannot be assigned to either species. Also known as the "Bermuda Petrel." Native to Bermuda. No definite Cahow records in our area.   *Ron Naveen*

Murphy's Petrel
Pterodroma ultima. 16" (40.5 cm). Large, little-known, dark gadfly petrel. Entirely dark underwings distinguish it from Great-winged and Providence petrels, which have some degree of paleness under primaries. Pale-phase Providence Petrels also have white bellies. Native to central South Pacific Ocean. One beached specimen from Oregon.   *Ron Naveen*

Cook's Petrel
Pterodroma cookii. 10–11" (25.5–28 cm). Small, pale-headed gadfly petrel, easily confused with Stejneger's Petrel. Pale above with dark M across wings and mantle; dark tail with whitish outer tail feathers; light underwing with no prominent black bar across underwing coverts. Native to New Zealand waters. Accidental in eastern Pacific Ocean.   *Ron Naveen*

Stejneger's Petrel
Pterodroma longirostris. 10" (25.5 cm). Small gadfly petrel, sharing with Cook's pale underwings; has dark M mark, which may be less distinct than Cook's. Stejneger's has more distinctly capped appearance, darker back, and entirely dark tail; marked contrast between cap and mantle may greatly diminish with wear. Native to western South America. One record off West Coast.
Ron Naveen

Streaked Shearwater
Calonectris leucomelas. 19" (48.5 cm). Same size as Pink-footed Shearwater, but with whitish face and streaking on rear portion of crown and nape. Upperparts appear scaly, and underwings are very white from axillars to dark tips. Native to Japan, northern China, and Korea. Accidental to California.   *Ron Naveen*

Little Shearwater
Puffinus assimilis. 10–11" (25.5–28 cm). Smaller than Audubon's Shearwater, much smaller than Manx Shearwater, with different flight. Rises from water like small alcid, with rapidly whirring, short wings; flight a mixture of gliding and fluttering, like that of auklet trying to fly like shearwater. Generally stays very close to surface of water; does not soar like Manx. Bill smaller and shorter than Manx's or Audubon's, but plumage pattern very similar and distinguishable only at close range; extra caution needed because of extensive racial variation, including 2 races in North Atlantic. Two records for North America (Nova Scotia and South Carolina) both *P. a. baroli* (native to Azores, Madeira, Salvage, and Canary islands); *baroli* differs from Manx and Audubon's in having more white on face, extending above eye and onto ear coverts. Undertail coverts white, as in Atlantic race of Manx; upperparts entirely black, as in Manx (brownish-black in Audubon's). Race *P. a. boydi* from Cape Verde Islands may occur; more like Audubon's, with somewhat browner upperparts and dark undertail coverts.   *Stuart Keith*

Storm-Petrels

British Storm-Petrel
Hydrobates pelagicus. 6" (15 cm). Smaller than Wilson's Storm-Petrel, with whitish bar across underwing coverts. Has rounded wings and very weak, fluttery flight. Feet do not extend beyond short, squarish tail; does not patter feet extensively. Beware of considerable underwing paleness shown by many Wilson's. Native to

eastern North Atlantic and Mediterranean. One confirmed record
from Cape Sable, Nova Scotia.   *Ron Naveen*

Wedge-rumped Storm-Petrel
Oceanodroma tethys. 7–8″ (18–20.5 cm). Possesses largest white
rump patch of all storm-petrels; this patch triangular and so large
that tail appears short and black-tipped. Flight direct on relatively
pointed wings. Native to Galápagos Islands and Peru. Two have
reached Monterey Bay, California.   *Ron Naveen*

Red-tailed Tropicbird

Tropicbirds

Phaeton rubricauda. 18″ (45.5 cm) not including tail streamers.
Adults readily identified by red bill, red tail streamers, and very
white upperparts that lack Red-billed's barring on back and White-
tailed's large, black patches across tertials. Juvenile lacks collar of
juvenile Red-billed; adults and juveniles have less black on outer
primaries than juvenile Red-billeds and White-taileds. Native to
tropical Pacific. Accidental off California.   *Ron Naveen*

Lesser Frigatebird

Frigatebirds

Fregata ariel. 30″ (76 cm). Entirely dark adult male readily
identified from below by white axillary patches. Black-throated
female resembles female Great Frigatebird, but also has white
axillary patches. Juveniles have less white on belly than Great
Frigatebird juveniles and possess Lesser's characteristic axillary
patches. Native to tropical Indian and Pacific oceans; 2 breeding
colonies in South Atlantic. Accidental in Maine.   *Ron Naveen*

Chinese Egret

Herons

Egretta eulophotes. 27″ (68.5 cm). Most similar to Snowy Egret,
with black legs, yellow feet, and entirely white plumage. In
breeding plumage, has thicker yellow bill, bright blue lores, and
short, bushy crest. Rare and local throughout limited range in east-
central Asia. One spring record from western Aleutian Islands,
Alaska.   *Theodore G. Tobish Jr.*

Little Egret
Egretta garzetta. 22″ (56 cm). Very similar to Snowy Egret. In
breeding plumage has 2 very long, narrow breeding plumes instead
of Snowy Egret's long, light, filamentous plumes. Snowy's lores
bright yellow; Little Egret's greenish or greenish-yellow. Other
subtle overlapping differences exist, making the 2 species difficult or
impossible to identify outside breeding period. Native to Old World.
One specimen and 1 photograph from eastern Canada; also 1 record
from Trinidad.   *Scott B. Terrill*

*Ibises and
Spoonbills*

Scarlet Ibis
Eudocimus ruber. 23″ (58.5 cm). Adults distinctive: scarlet with
black wing tips. Immature similar to immature White Ibis, but
tinged pink on rump. Native to South America. Accidental in
southern Florida and along Texas coast.   *Thomas H. Davis*

Jabiru
Jabiru mycteria. 48–57″ (122–145 cm). Superficially resembles Wood
Stork, but identified in all plumages by very large size and very
heavy, deep, noticeably recurved bill. Adult entirely white with no
black on wings; has red on neck that is absent in Wood Stork.

Storks

Immature less white but shares characteristic large size and bill
shape. Rare and local throughout Neotropical range. Casual
straggler to Texas; 1 record from Oklahoma. These extralimital
reports may, at least in part, be of escaped aviary birds.
Scott B. Terrill

Pink-footed Goose
Anser brachyrhynchus. 23½–29½″ (60–75 cm). Similar to adult
Greater White-fronted Goose but slightly smaller, stouter, and lacks

Swans, Geese, and Ducks

extensive white area around bill and dark speckling on belly. More difficult to distinguish from juvenile Greater White-fronted Goose. In adult and juvenile, bill has more black (more than one-half black) than any age group of Greater White-fronted. Bean Goose larger with bright orange soft parts. One photograph of likely wild individual from Newfoundland. Breeds primarily in Iceland and Greenland; most winter in British Isles.   *Scott B. Terrill*

Baikal Teal
Anas formosa. 16" (40.5 cm). Male unmistakable, with striking, colorful yellow and green head feathering, and white vertical stripe at shoulder. Female very difficult to identify; most similar to female Green-winged Teal and Garganey, but usually shows bold white spot at base of bill and diffuse pale eyebrow that includes lores. Often has warm rust wash to breast and sides. Native to eastern Eurasia. Casual migrant to Bering Sea islands of western Alaska, mainly in spring. Straggler in western Alaska and accidental elsewhere along Pacific Coast and in North Carolina.   *Theodore G. Tobish Jr.*

Spot-billed Duck
Anas poecilorhyncha. 24" (61 cm). Slightly larger than American Black Duck, with similar plumage. Shows distinct dark cap and pale, dusky-gray face with black eyeline and mustache. Entirely black bill with bright yellow band at tip and completely white tertials are further distinguishing field marks. Upperwing and underwing patterns like Mallard's, but tail feathers dark brown, not white. Native to eastern and southern Asia. Two records from Alaska.   *Theodore G. Tobish Jr.*

White-cheeked Pintail
Anas bahamensis. 16" (40.5 cm). Small brown teal with striking white cheeks and throat and red base to dark bill. Native to West Indies and South America. Noted sporadically in southern Florida, casually along Gulf Coast, and north to Delaware; some extralimital reports are probably escaped aviary birds.   *Thomas H. Davis*

Hawks and Eagles

White-tailed Eagle
Haliaeetus albicilla. 27–36" (68.5–91.5 cm). Similar to Bald Eagle, but with broader wings and dark undertail coverts. Head rarely pure white, usually pale buff to medium brown. Very short wedge-shaped tail gives different flight silhouette. Immature mostly dark brown, with small white patches and lines in underwing, and dark, fringed tail feathers with pale centers. Native to northern Eurasia. Regular visitor and probably resident on Attu Island where it has bred; casual in western Alaska; accidental off northeast Atlantic Coast.   *Theodore G. Tobish Jr.*

Steller's Sea-Eagle
Haliaeetus pelagicus. 34–36" (86.5–91.5 cm). Adult larger than Bald or White-tailed eagles, with conspicuous white shoulder patches, white thighs, and massive orange-yellow bill. Further differs from White-tailed by longer, wedge-shaped white tail and white undertail coverts. Immature plumage similar to White-tailed's, but has broad, white, squarish patches on underwing extending from inner primaries to bases of outer primaries. Native to northeastern Asia. Casual in western Alaska; only 1 recent record.
Theodore G. Tobish Jr.

Roadside Hawk
Buteo magnirostris. 14" (35.5 cm). Adults dusky-gray above and on breast; lower breast and belly closely barred with cinnamon-brown and white; best identified by contrasting rufous bases of primaries. Immatures distinguished by combination of streaked breast and coarsely barred belly. Native to Central and South America. Two records from southern Texas.   *Thomas H. Davis*

Eurasian Kestrel

Falco tinnunculus. 13½" (34.5 cm). Obviously larger, longer-winged, and longer-tailed than American Kestrel. Tail feathers blue-gray in male and rust in female; adult male has rust wing coverts. Upperparts of adults more spotted than barred. Shows only 1 vertical bar on face. Immatures, like females, have broad subterminal band on tail and completely rust crown. Native to Eurasia and Africa. Accidental in Alaska, Massachusetts, and New Jersey.   *Theodore G. Tobish Jr.*

Corn Crake

Crex crex. 10" (25.5 cm). Short-billed rail larger than native North American rails with short bills. Unique plumage: buff-gray with extensive blackish streaking on upperparts, chestnut wing coverts, and chestnut bars on flanks. Native to Old World. Formerly a straggler to East Coast; now accidental.   *Scott B. Terrill*

Paint-billed Crake

Neocrex erythrops. 8" (20.5 cm). Superficially similar to Sora, but adults have uniformly olive-brown upperparts without Sora's dark spotting or light edgings. Legs and base of bill orange-red in Crake; in Sora, legs greenish and bill lacks red. Crake lacks Sora's black around bill. Undertail coverts of Crake barred black and white; Sora's white. Native to American tropics. One specimen from Texas and 1 from Virginia, both in winter.   *Scott B. Terrill*

Spotted Rail

Pardirallus maculatus. 10" (25.5 cm). Similar in shape and size to Virginia Rail. Unlike any North American rail, heavily spotted with black and white on head, back, neck, and breast; barred on lower underparts. Legs and feet red. Juvenile brownish rather than black; underparts uniformly drab with indistinct barring. Native to Neotropical freshwater marshes. One record from Pennsylvania and 1 from Texas.   *Scott B. Terrill*

Eurasian Coot

Fulica atra. 16" (40.5 cm). Plumage resembles American Coot's but with essentially dark undertail coverts. Bill and entire frontal shield on forehead pure white. Native to Eurasia. Accidental on Pribilof Islands, Alaska.   *Theodore G. Tobish Jr.*

Common Crane

Grus grus. 45" (114.5 cm). Most resembles Sandhill Crane. Head pattern different, with red cap and black throat, neck, and rear crown; conspicuous, curving white stripe extends from eye to base of neck. Primaries and secondaries fully black and contrast more than Sandhill Crane's with wing coverts. Bill pale. Native to Eurasia. Accidental in central Alaska, prairie provinces, New Mexico, and Nebraska.   *Theodore G. Tobish Jr.*

Double-striped Thick-knee

Burhinus bistriatus. 18" (45.5 cm). Member of family Burhinidae, a group of mostly terrestrial, ploverlike birds. Thick-knees have long, sturdy legs with conspicuous joints, large yellow eyes, and characteristic striped pattern on head. In flight, wings have striking black-and-white pattern. Family contains 9 species worldwide. The 1 North American species is large, brown inhabitant of tropical grasslands. Largely nocturnal; seldom flies by day. Characterized by long legs, large eyes, striking white eyebrow, and white wing stripe. Native to Central and South America; recorded December 1961 in southern Texas.   *Thomas H. Davis and Scott B. Terrill*

Greater Golden-Plover

Pluvialis apricaria. 11" (28 cm). Similar to but slightly larger than Lesser Golden-Plover. In breeding plumage, differs in possessing white undertail coverts and some white on flanks visible at rest; juvenal and winter plumages more golden-tinged above and on breast; all plumages distinguished by entirely white wing linings and axillars. Native to Western Europe. Small flocks noted on 3 occasions in Newfoundland in April and May.   *Thomas H. Davis*

Little Ringed Plover
Charadrius dubius. 7″ (18 cm). Smaller, slimmer, and longer-legged than similar Common Ringed or Semipalmated plovers. In breeding plumage, shows complete yellow eye-ring, thin breastband, and full white line separating crown from black forehead and auricular. Bill mostly dark brown to blackish; legs dull flesh-colored to dusky-green. No wing stripe. Call whistled and descending. Native to Eurasia. Accidental in western Aleutians, Alaska.
Theodore G. Tobish Jr.

Sandpipers

Marsh Sandpiper
Tringa stagnatilis. 10″ (25.5 cm). Same size as Lesser Yellowlegs, with quite long, spindly, dull green legs, and long, needlelike bill like that of Wilson's Phalarope. Back spotted light and dark gray in breeding plumage; unmarked pale gray in juvenal and winter plumages. In all seasons, dark-barred, white tail and white wedge up center of back. Native to Eurasia. Accidental in western Aleutians.   *Theodore G. Tobish Jr.*

Green Sandpiper
Tringa ocrophus. 9½″ (24 cm). Closely resembles Solitary Sandpiper in plumage and behavior, but slightly larger, with blackish underwing, white tail with black bars across center and trailing edge, and white rump. Darker above with darker legs; has more white in tail and rump and less prominent eyebrow than Wood Sandpiper. Native to Eurasia. Three records from Attu Island, Alaska.   *Theodore G. Tobish Jr.*

Terek Sandpiper
Xenus cinereus. 10″ (25.5 cm). Unmistakable, with long, upturned, pale-based, dark bill. Medium-size shorebird with short orange legs and cool gray-brown upperparts outlined with black scapular lines. Blackish primaries set off white trailing edge of secondaries. Rolling call reminiscent of Short-billed Dowitcher's. Native to central and eastern Eurasia. Casual, perhaps annual, migrant to Bering Sea islands of western Alaska; 3 mainland Alaska records from Anchorage.   *Theodore G. Tobish Jr.*

Slender-billed Curlew
Numenius tenuirostris. 16″ (40.5 cm). Similar to Whimbrel, but lacks crown stripes and has white lower back and rump; in breeding plumage, exhibits distinctive heart-shaped brown spots on flanks. Native to central Asia. Known from specimen taken in early 1900s in Ontario.   *Thomas H. Davis*

Far Eastern Curlew
Numenius madagascariensis. 23″ (58.5 cm). Eurasian counterpart of Long-billed Curlew. Differs in having heavily barred, whitish underwings and underparts conspicuously marked with dark streaks and chevrons. Lacks Long-billed Curlew's strong, warm buff tones. Very rare late-spring or early-summer migrant in central and western Aleutian Islands, Alaska.   *Theodore G. Tobish Jr.*

Eurasian Curlew
Numenius arquata. 22″ (56 cm). Similar to Long-billed Curlew, but pale brown overall with white lower back and rump. Differs from much smaller Whimbrel in lacking crown stripes. Native to Eurasia. Known from 4 seasonally scattered records in Nova Scotia, Ontario, and Massachusetts.   *Thomas H. Davis*

Great Knot
Calidris tenuirostris. 12" (30.5 cm). Largest *Calidris* sandpiper; plump, long-billed, and distinctly larger than Red Knot or Ruddy Turnstone. In breeding plumage, upperparts are mottled black and gray with conspicuous chestnut-centered scapulars. Conglomerate of black scales on breast extends onto flanks. Rump mostly unmarked, paler than Red Knot's. Native to eastern Eurasia. Casual in spring on Bering Sea islands.   *Theodore G. Tobish Jr.*

Little Stint
Calidris minuta. 6" (15 cm). In all plumages very closely resembles Rufous-necked Stint. In breeding plumage, has mostly whitish throat surrounded by dark brown spots, and wing coverts and tertials tinged with rust. Bill short and fine. Autumn juveniles most difficult to distinguish from young Rufous-necked Stints, with only subtle differences discernible. Native to Eurasia. Casual in spring, accidental in fall in Bering Sea region of western Alaska; also accidental in New Brunswick, Delaware, and Massachusetts. *Theodore G. Tobish Jr.*

Temminck's Stint
Calidris temminckii. 6" (15 cm). Gleaming white outer tail feathers and soft, twittering call distinguish this species from all other peeps. Shows sandy-buff tone on finely streaked breast and random spotting on upperparts. Has short, straight bill. Lacks rufous tones of other Asiatic stints. Juveniles have dull grayish-brown, unmarked back with only a few pale feather edgings. Native to Eurasia. Rare, regular spring migrant in western Aleutian Islands; casual farther north; casual in fall; accidental in British Columbia. *Theodore G. Tobish Jr.*

Spoonbill Sandpiper
Eurynorhynchus pygmeus. 6" (15 cm). Unique, spatulate-tipped bill immediately sets this rare Asiatic species apart. Plumage otherwise like Rufous-necked Stint's. Native to eastern Eurasia. Rare and local in restricted range in northeast Asia; casual migrant in western Alaska; accidental in British Columbia.   *Theodore G. Tobish Jr.*

Broad-billed Sandpiper
Limicola falcinellus. 7" (18 cm). Short-legged Dunlinlike wader with conspicuous, long, thick-based bill, slightly decurved at tip. In all seasons, shows forked, double, creamy eyebrow. Often stands in hunched posture at rest. Breeding plumage dark brown above with rust fringes. Two V's, like those of snipes, outline back. Call soft, rolling trill. Native to northern Eurasia. Casual in fall in western Aleutian Islands, Alaska.   *Theodore G. Tobish Jr.*

Jack Snipe
Lymnocryptes minimus. 8" (20.5 cm). Similar in size to Rock Sandpiper, with short, unsnipelike stubby bill and unmarked, wedge-shaped tail. Dark crown shows no pale central stripe, and pale streaks on upperparts, typical of snipes, brighter than in Common Snipe. Usually silent, and an extreme skulker; difficult to find once flushed. Native to Eurasia. Accidental in Alaska, California, and Labrador.   *Theodore G. Tobish Jr.*

Eurasian Woodcock
Scolopax rusticola. 14" (35.5 cm). Similar to but larger than American Woodcock, with heavily barred underparts; American's unbarred. Native to Eurasia. In 19th century records primarily from East Coast; only 1 record this century: Ohio, November 6, 1935.   *Scott B. Terrill*

Classification and Nomenclature

Like all other organisms, birds are classified according to estimates of the closeness of their relationships. These estimates are based on anatomy, behavior (including vocalizations), biochemistry, and other data. Relationship is often expressed in terms of common ancestry; the more recently two kinds of birds shared an ancestor, the more closely related they are said to be. For example, the Herring Gull and the Great Black-backed Gull shared an ancestor not long ago in geological time. At some unknown point, obviously much earlier, gulls and terns shared an ancestor. According to current ideas about bird relationships, an ancestral kind existed even earlier that eventually gave rise not only to gulls and to terns, but also to auks and to shorebirds.

Taxonomy

Each level of relationship is expressed as a taxonomic rank in the classification hierarchy. Thus the Herring and Great Black-backed gulls are species (this word is both singular and plural, and should never be spelled specie). Because they are closely related, they are placed in the same genus, along with many other species. All gulls and terns, constituting several genera (the plural of genus), belong to a single family. This family, plus the family of auks and several families of shorebirds, are collectively placed in an order. Every kind of animal belongs to a species, a genus, a family, an order, and a class. All birds, living and extinct, belong to a single class, Aves. For convenience in grouping related birds together, intermediate categories are available; unlike the ones already mentioned, these are not mandatory. For instance, the family to which the gulls and terns belong is divided into four subfamilies: gulls, terns, skuas, and skimmers. Some other large families, however, are so uniform that they usually are not subdivided. This is true, for example, of the family of fulmars, petrels, and shearwaters.

Scientific Names

Every species has a scientific name, which is sometimes called a Latin name even though the words used may be derived from Greek or other languages. This name always consists of two words, the generic name and the specific name. Technically, both words constitute the name of the species, but in common usage the second word is usually called the specific name. The scientific name of the Herring Gull is *Larus argentatus;* that of the Great Black-backed Gull is *Larus marinus.* Among the members of a genus, such as the gull genus *Larus,* only one species can bear a specific name. That specific name can be used for other birds (or other animals of any kind) in other genera; thus there are many organisms that bear the specific name *marinus,* but the combination *Larus marinus* is unique to the Great Black-backed Gull.

The formation and application of scientific names are governed by the *International Code of Zoological Nomenclature,* formulated by a commission of the International Congress of Zoology. This code has several important provisions. The Law of Priority dictates that the earliest specific name ever published for any animal is the correct one, if the publication included an adequate description of the animal. Priority also governs generic and family names. The code standardizes the formation of the names of families and other categories. Family names are formed by taking the root of one of the family's generic names and adding the suffix -idae. The root of the generic name *Larus* is Lar-, and the family name thus becomes Laridae. For the optional but frequently used category of subfamily, the standard suffix is -inae; thus the subfamily of gulls, within the family Laridae, is Larinae, and that of the terns is Sterninae, from the tern genus *Sterna.* In the class Aves (birds), the name formation for orders is also standardized, although this is not true for all groups of animals. All names of bird orders end in -iformes. The order to which gulls belong is Charadriiformes, based on the root of the generic name *Charadrius,* the typical plovers.

All group names are capitalized. Only the names of genera and species are italicized, and in the two-part scientific name of a species, only the generic name is capitalized.

Changes in Names

Scientific names (as opposed to common or vernacular names) have the advantage of being international; for example, the German name for the Great Black-backed Gull is *Mantelmöwe,* but books in German and all other languages use the name *Larus marinus.* It is often stated, in addition, that scientific names are stable. However, comparison of several reference works will readily show that different scientific names have been used for the same species. Changes in scientific name are made for nomenclatural or taxonomic reasons. Nomenclatural changes are objective and usually based on the Law of Priority. For many years, the White Ibis was known as *Guara alba;* the generic name *Guara* was coined for these ibises in 1853. In 1951, it was discovered that the name *Eudocimus,* published in 1832, referred to the same ibises. The Law of Priority dictated that the correct name for the White Ibis become *Eudocimus albus* (note that the specific name changed its feminine ending -*a* to the masculine ending -*us* to agree with the gender of the generic name). Similarly, Franklin's Gull was long known as *Larus franklini,* a name first applied to this species in 1832. A century later, it was discovered that another name for this species had been published in 1831, so it is now called *Larus pipixcan.* Fortunately, such nomenclatural changes seldom occur today. There are few old publications that have not been scoured for bird names, and there is a provision in the code that permits an author who discovers an old name that has priority over a currently used name to declare the old name a *nomen oblitum,* or forgotten name, if it has not appeared in the literature for the past fifty years.

Changes in Taxonomy

Although it has often been said that birds are the best-known group of animals, this is true in only one sense. A higher proportion (probably about 99 percent) of the species of living birds is known to science than of any other class of animals. However, the classification of birds remains highly controversial, and is being re-examined in the late 20th century more intensely than at any other time in the past hundred years. The classification followed in this book is widely used, but may be altered, even radically, as new data and new interpretations are published in future years.

Because taxonomy remains as much an art as a science, in spite of many attempts to provide ways of making taxonomic decisions less subjective, there will always be name changes for taxonomic reasons. Sometimes the changes are based on new research. In other cases, changes coincide with shifting fashions in taxonomic philosophy. The two extreme schools in taxonomy are often called the lumpers and the splitters. The lumpers prefer to emphasize resemblances and therefore combine presumably related kinds into larger and larger assemblages. The splitters stress differences and tend to separate groups that can be shown consistently to differ, no matter how trivially, from other groups. After a long period during which the splitters dominated American ornithology, the lumping school, heavily influenced by European taxonomists, gained ascendancy after World War II. To a large extent, this philosophy still dominates; thus the family Emberizidae in this book includes birds that were separated into five families in the 1957 edition of the American Ornithologists' Union *Checklist of North American Birds.*

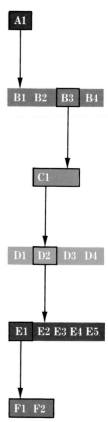

A Order
1. Charadriiformes

B Suborders
1. Charadrii
2. Scolopaci
3. Lari
4. Alcae

C Family
1. Laridae

D Subfamilies
1. Stercorariinae
2. Larinae
3. Sterninae
4. Rynchopinae

E Genera
1. *Larus*
2. *Rissa*
3. *Rhodostethia*
4. *Xema*
5. *Pagophila*

F Species
1. *Larus marinus*, Great Black-backed Gull
2. *Larus argentatus*, Herring Gull

The genus is perhaps the most subjective of the taxonomic categories and thus heavily affected by the debates between the lumpers and the splitters. It would be difficult indeed to find any group of taxonomists who could agree completely about the correct scope of all avian genera, but it is possible at least to approach a consensus, and this has been attempted by committees responsible for official checklists all over the world.

Subspecies

So far, no mention has been made of subspecies, or races. These consist of populations that belong to the same biological species but differ consistently from one another in size or color or both; these characteristics are assumed to be genetically based. Subspecies occupy a particular portion of the species' entire geographic range; however, as members of the same species, they normally interbreed, and hence show intergradation of characteristics where their ranges meet. If populations are not in contact, a subjective decision must be made as to whether they could interbreed. Subspecific status is indicated by the use of a third word, or trinomial, in the scientific name. Thus the North American population of the Herring Gull, which has numerous named races around the world, is *Larus argentatus smithsonianus*. This population differs in various size and color characteristics from other populations of Herring Gulls. Most subspecific differences are relatively subtle and noticeable only with the birds in hand. In some instances, however, populations are so distinctive that they were for many years considered to be separate species. The discovery that such populations freely interbreed, with no apparent detriment to the intermediate offspring, led to the change in taxonomic status whereby all are considered members of a single biological (and hence nomenclatural) species. Perhaps the best-known example in North America is the species now called the Northern Oriole. Long thought to be two species, the Baltimore (*Icterus galbula*) and Bullock's (*Icterus bullockii*) orioles, both easily identifiable in the field, these two kinds of orioles are now known to interbreed freely in parts of the Great Plains where the eastern and western populations meet. Baltimore and Bullock's orioles are therefore now considered to be subspecies of a single species. The Law of Priority determined that the scientific name for the combined species must be *Icterus galbula*, which is older than the name *Icterus bullockii*. Bullock's Oriole thus became *Icterus galbula bullockii;* the Baltimore Oriole became *Icterus galbula galbula*. The subspecies whose trinomial is the same as the specific name, as in the Baltimore Oriole, is called the nominate subspecies. This is only a nomenclatural matter, however, and the Baltimore Oriole is not a more important component of the combined species than the Bullock's. The often heard statement that "the Bullock's Oriole has been made a subspecies of the Baltimore Oriole" is utterly erroneous; *both* kinds of oriole have been combined into a single species, for which the official English name is Northern Oriole. Although only a single subspecies of a species breeds in any locality, members of several subspecies may be found together in winter or during migration. Identifying these wintering or migrating subspecies can be extremely difficult. Obviously, however, some birds now recognized as subspecies can easily be identified in the field; the orioles mentioned above are good examples. In general, only subspecies that are so distinctive as to have been considered separate species before their interbreeding was discovered should be identified in the field. These can be referred to by using the current broad English species name, with the English name of the identifiable component in parentheses—for example, Northern ("Bullock's") Oriole.   *Kenneth C. Parkes*

Glossary

This glossary was prepared by Peter F. Cannell.

Accidental A species that has appeared in a given area a very few times only and whose normal range is in another area.

Air sac A membranous extension of the lung that provides interior ventilation; in some groups, such as certain grouse, air sacs are inflated and used for display, and in some water birds they contribute to buoyancy.

Allopatric Occupying separate, nonoverlapping geographic ranges. *Cf.* Sympatric.

Auriculars *See* Ear coverts.

Axillars The long, innermost feathers of the underwing, covering the area where the wing joins the body. *Cf.* Scapulars.

Back The portion of the upperparts located behind the nape and between the wings.

Belly The portion of the underparts between the breast and the undertail coverts.

Bib An area of contrasting color on the chin, throat, upper breast, or all three of these.

Breast The area of the underparts between the foreneck and the belly.

Breeding plumage A coat of feathers worn by an adult bird during the breeding season, usually acquired by partial spring molt, feather wear, or both; the male's breeding plumage is often more brightly colored than its winter plumage or than the adult female's breeding plumage.

Cap An area of contrasting color on the top of the head.

Carpal bar A band of contrasting color in some gulls on the upper surface of the wing near the wrist, formed by the ends of the primary coverts.

Carpal joint *See* Wrist.

Casual Occurring infrequently in a given geographic area but more often than an accidental.

Cere A bare, fleshy area at the base of the upper mandible that surrounds the nostrils; swollen and distinctively colored in some birds.

Cheek The side of the face.

Chin The area immediately below the base of the lower mandible.

Collar A band of contrasting color that runs across the foreneck, hindneck, or both.

Color morph or Color phase One of two or more distinct color types within a species, occurring independently of age, sex, or season.

Conspecific Belonging to the same species.

Cosmopolitan Occurring on all continents except Antarctica; worldwide.

Coverts Small feathers that cover the bases of other, usually larger, feathers, and provide a smooth, aerodynamic surface.

Crown The upper surface of the head, between the eyebrows.

Culmen The midline ridge along the top of a bird's upper mandible.

Dimorphic Having two distinct forms within a population, differing in size, form, or color.

Dorsal Pertaining to the upper surface of the body.

Ear coverts	Small, loose-webbed feathers on the side of the face behind and below the eye, covering the ear region.
Ear tuft	A group of elongated feathers above the eyes that resemble ears; characteristic of some owl and grebe species and the Horned Lark.
Eclipse plumage	A dull-colored coat of feathers acquired by most male ducks and certain other birds immediately after mating, but worn for only a few weeks or months before being replaced again by the brighter breeding plumage.
Escape	A bird that has escaped from captivity rather than arriving in an area by natural means.
Eyebrow	A stripe on the side of the head immediately above the eye.
Eyeline	A straight, thin, horizontal stripe on the side of the face, running through the eye.
Eye plate	A small, horny plate adjacent to the eye.
Eye-ring	A fleshy or feathered ring around the eye, often distinctively colored.
Eye stripe	A stripe that runs horizontally from the base of the bill through the eye; usually broader than an eyeline.
Facial disk	The feathers that encircle the eyes of some birds, especially owls.
Flank	The rear portion of the side of a bird's body.
Flight feathers	The long, firm feathers of the wings and tail used during flight. The flight feathers of the wings are the primaries, secondaries, and tertials; those of the tail are called rectrices.
Forehead	The area of the head just above the base of the upper mandible.
Foreneck	The front or underside of the neck.
Frontal shield	A fleshy, featherless, and often brightly colored area on the forehead.
Gape	The angle between the upper and lower mandibles when the bill is open; the opening between the upper and lower mandibles.
Gonys	The prominent midline ridge along the lower surface of the lower mandible.
Greater wing coverts	A row of short feathers that covers the bases of the secondaries; also called greater secondary coverts.
Gular pouch	*See* Throat pouch.
Hallux	The innermost toe of a bird's foot; it usually extends backward, is sometimes reduced or absent, and sometimes raised above the level of other toes.
Hindneck	The rear or upper surface of the neck; the nape.
Hood	A distinctively colored area usually covering most or all of the head.
Introduced	Established by humans in an area outside the natural range.
Juvenal plumage	The first covering of true feathers, usually of a somewhat looser texture than later plumages; the juvenal plumage, often brown and streaked, is usually replaced during the bird's first summer or fall.
Juvenile	A bird in juvenal plumage.
Lek	A place where males of some species gather and perform courtship displays in a group; females visit the lek to mate, but generally build their nests elsewhere.
Lesser wing coverts	The short feathers on the shoulder that are arranged in several irregular rows and cover the base of the median wing coverts.

Local   Of restricted occurrence within a larger, discontinuous range; birds with local distributions are often dependent on some uncommon habitat type.

Lore   The area between the eye and the base of the bill; sometimes distinctively colored.

Lower mandible   The lower of the two parts of a bird's bill.

Malar streak   *See* Mustache.

Mantle   The upper back and occasionally the scapulars and upperwing coverts when these are the same color as the upper back.

Mask   An area of contrasting color on the front of the face and around the eyes.

Median crown stripe   A stripe of contrasting color along the center of the crown.

Median wing coverts   The row of short feathers that covers the bases of the greater wing coverts.

Mirror   A translucent area on the extended wing of some birds, usually at the base of the primaries; in gulls, small white spots at or near the tips of the dark primaries.

Molt   The periodic loss and replacement of feathers; most species have regular patterns and schedules of molt.

Morph   *See* Color morph.

Mustache   A colored streak running from the base of the bill back along the side of the throat.

Nail   A horny plate at the tip of the upper or lower mandible.

Nape   The back of the head, including the hindneck.

Patagium   A membrane extending from the body to the wrist along the front of the wing, supporting many of the wing coverts.

Phase   *See* Color morph.

Pinnae   *See* Ear tuft.

Plumage   Generally, the feathers worn by a bird at any given time. Specifically, all the feathers grown during a single molt; in this sense, a bird may have elements of more than one plumage at a time.

Polyandrous   Mating with more than one male.

Polymorphic   Having two or more distinct types within a population, usually differing in size, form, or color.

Primaries   The outermost and longest flight feathers on a bird's wing, forming the wing tip and part of the outer trailing edge; there are usually nine to twelve primaries on each wing, attached to the wing distal to the wrist.

Primary coverts   The small feathers of the wing that overlie the bases of the primaries.

Race   *See* Subspecies.

Rectrices   The long flight feathers of the tail; singular rectrix.

Resident   Remaining in one place all year; nonmigratory.

Rump   The lower back just above the tail; may also include the uppertail coverts.

Scapulars   The feathers of the upperparts at the side of the back that cover the area where the wing joins the body.

Secondaries	The large flight feathers of the inner wing, attached to the inner wing proximal to the wrist.
Sexual dimorphism	A difference between the sexes in size, form, or color.
Shaft	The stiff central axis of a feather.
Side	The lateral part of the breast and belly.
Spectacles	A color pattern formed by the lores and eye-rings.
Speculum	A distinctively colored area on the upper surface of the secondaries, especially the iridescent patch of some ducks.
Subadult	A bird that has not yet acquired adult plumage.
Subspecies	A geographical subdivision of a species differing from other subdivisions in size, form, color, song, or several of these in combination; also called a race.
Summer resident	A bird that remains in an area during the summer but winters elsewhere.
Sympatric	Having overlapping ranges. *Cf.* Allopatric.
Tarsus	The lower, usually featherless, part of a bird's leg, often called simply the "leg."
Tertials	The innermost secondaries (usually three), often with a different shape, pattern, and molt schedule from the other secondaries, and sometimes considered distinct from them; also called tertiaries.
Throat	The area of the underparts between the chin and the breast.
Throat pouch	A bare patch of skin on the throat that may differ in color from the rest of the throat; in some birds the throat pouch can be inflated.
Transient	A bird that occurs at a location only during migration between its winter and breeding ranges.
Underparts	The lower surface of the body, including the chin, throat, breast, belly, sides and flanks, and undertail coverts, and sometimes including the underwing surface and the under surface of the tail.
Undertail coverts	The small feathers that lie beneath and cover the bases of the tail feathers; sometimes referred to as the crissum.
Upper mandible	The uppermost of the two parts of a bird's bill; also called the maxilla.
Upperparts	The upper surface of the body, including the crown, nape, back, scapulars, rump, and uppertail coverts, and sometimes including the upperwing surface and the upper surface of the tail.
Uppertail coverts	The small feathers that lie over the bases of the tail feathers.
Vagrant	A bird occurring outside of its normal range, usually during or following migration.
Ventral	Pertaining to the lower surface of the body.
Vermiculated	Marked by fine lines.
Window	A translucent area on the wing of certain birds that is visible from below on a bird in flight.
Wing lining	A collective term for the coverts of the underwing.
Wing stripe	A conspicuous lengthwise stripe on the upper surface of the extended wing, often formed by the pale bases of the primaries and secondaries.
Wrist	The forward-projecting angle or bend of the wing; also called the carpal joint.

The Authors

Davis Finch and Paul Lehman each reviewed some or all of the species accounts; Paul Lehman also read and commented on some of the special essays.

Robert Arbib
is the editor of *American Birds*. He has served as president of the Linnaean Society of New York and the Federation of New York State Bird Clubs, and has written several books, including the Burroughs Medal winner, *The Lord's Woods*. He helped found and is currently the secretary of the Hawk Migration Association of North America. He has birded extensively in North and Central America, Europe, and Africa, and has a life list of over 2,400 species.

George Archibald
received his doctorate from Cornell University in 1971 for research on the behavior of cranes. He is director and co-founder of the International Crane Foundation in Baraboo, Wisconsin, where 13 of the world's 15 crane species, including the Sandhill and Whooping cranes, have been bred in captivity, some for the first time.

Henry T. Armistead,
a Philadelphia librarian, became interested in birds in 1949 when he was nine. He is a regional editor of *American Birds*, book review editor of *Birding*, and compiles the Cape Charles, Virginia, Christmas bird count. His special interests include birds of the Delmarva Peninsula, colonial water birds of the Chesapeake Bay, mist-netting fall land birds, and May birding marathons. On his family's farm in Bellevue, Maryland, he has seen 240 species of birds.

Frank C. Bellrose
has worked for the Illinois Natural History Survey for 44 years as a waterfowl research biologist stationed at Havana, in the Illinois River valley. He has written almost 100 technical papers on the migration and ecology of waterfowl, and is the author of the book *Ducks, Geese, and Swans of North America*.

Louis R. Bevier
has been actively watching birds in California for 14 years. During the past five years, he has served as a field assistant and consultant for research projects, environmental impact reports, and publications about birds. Currently, he is an undergraduate in environmental biology at the University of California at Santa Barbara.

Clait E. Braun
is a wildlife research leader for the Colorado Division of Wildlife and a faculty affiliate in the department of fishery and wildlife biology at Colorado State University at Fort Collins. He has 17 years of field experience in western North America with grouse and native columbids. Braun is an officer of the Wilson Ornithological Society and was editor of the *Journal of Wildlife Management* from 1981 to 1983. He is also a member of the American Ornithologists' Union, the Cooper Ornithological Society, and the American Association for the Advancement of Science.

Peter F. Cannell
has worked at the Manomet Bird Observatory and is currently enrolled in a doctoral program at the American Museum of Natural History and the City University of New York. Cannell's doctoral work has concentrated on the systematics of the "pre-passerines," based on the anatomy of the syrinx. During 1979 and 1980 he served as acting director of Bowdoin's Kent Island ornithological research station in the Bay of Fundy.

Thomas H. Davis,
a lifelong resident of New York City, is especially interested in the
field identification and distribution of the birds of New York State
and the Neotropics. He has served as president and fellow of the
Linnaean Society of New York. He is also an honorary
associate of the Cornell University Laboratory of Ornithology,
and a licensed bird bander.

Kim R. Eckert
lives in Duluth, Minnesota, where he has done extensive field
work. The author of numerous articles in *The Loon, Birding,* and
American Birds, he has also written *A Birder's Guide to Minnesota.*
Eckert has served as a regional editor of *American Birds* magazine,
and is currently a member of the Minnesota Ornithological Records
Committee, and a naturalist of the Hawk Ridge Nature Reserve in
Duluth. In addition, he has led bird tours in Minnesota and the
Dakotas and taught bird identification classes.

David L. Evans
is deeply involved in the study of raptor migration in Duluth,
Minnesota, and in long-term field studies of Bald Eagles in
Wisconsin and wintering Snowy Owls in the Duluth harbor.
He has also participated in research projects on the Red-tailed,
Ferruginous, Swainson's, and Marsh hawks, and the Bald Eagle,
Osprey, and Prairie Falcon.

John Farrand, Jr.,
is natural science editor at Chanticleer Press and an associate in the
department of ornithology at the American Museum of Natural
History. Co-author of *The Audubon Society Field Guide to North
American Birds (Eastern Region)* and a past president of the
Linnaean Society of New York, he has watched birds in most of
North America, as well as in Central and South America, Europe,
and East Africa.

Davis Finch
lives in East Kingston, New Hampshire. Interested in birds since
childhood, he has studied them in virtually all parts of North
America, as well as in Europe and Central and South America. He is
a founder and director of WINGS, Inc., a company that conducts
birdwatching tours in many parts of the world.

Kimball L. Garrett,
an ornithologist with the Los Angeles County Museum of Natural
History, has had extensive field experience in western North
America. He teaches bird identification workshops at the University
of California at Los Angeles. With Jon Dunn, he has written
numerous papers on bird identification for the Los Angeles Audubon
Society newsletter, *The Western Tanager,* as well as *Birds of
Southern California: Status and Distribution.*

Daniel D. Gibson
works at the University of Alaska Museum in Fairbanks, Alaska.
He has studied the status and distribution of Alaska's birds for
almost 20 years. Gibson's particular interests are the Palearctic and
Aleutian components of Alaska's avifauna, their routes of
migration, and their geographic variation.

Joseph A. Grzybowski
received his doctorate in zoology from the University of Oklahoma in
1980. Currently, he is an assistant professor at Central State
University in Edmond, Oklahoma. His publications include papers
on bird distribution, ecology, behavior, and wildlife management,
and a bibliography of Oklahoma ornithology (in press). His primary
research is on the winter ecology of grassland birds in Oklahoma
and Texas.

Gordon W. Gullion

is a professor of wildlife management at the University of
Minnesota. Stationed at the Cloquet Forestry Center near Duluth,
since 1958 he has studied the impact of forest management on the
Ruffed Grouse. Prior to that, he studied the Sage Grouse and
Gambel's Quail in Nevada, and completed a graduate research study
of American Coots at the University of California, Berkeley. Since
1947, Gullion has written more than 120 papers and articles.

Harold J. Harju

received his bachelor's and master's degrees from Northern
Michigan University in Marquette. He was awarded his doctorate in
1974 by the University of Wyoming in Laramie. His master's
research concerned acoustical communication of Spruce Grouse, and
for his doctorate he researched the ecology of Blue Grouse in
southeastern Wyoming. He has also studied Ruffed Grouse and Sage
Grouse. Currently, he is supervisor of biological services for the
Wyoming Game and Fish Department in Cheyenne.

Dan Clark Holliman,

a professor of biology at Birmingham-Southern College in Alabama,
teaches coastal ornithology at the Dauphin Island Sea Lab in Mobile,
where he is involved in research on Alabama wetlands. Holliman
contributed data on rails and gallinules in *Management of Migratory
Shore and Upland Game Birds in North America*, published in 1977
by the U.S. Department of the Interior.

Paul A. Johnsgard

is a Foundation Professor of Life Sciences in the school of life
sciences at the University of Nebraska, Lincoln. His special
interests are waterfowl, gallinaceous birds, and cranes, and how
their behavior has been shaped by evolution. He currently has 19
books in print; three more are in preparation.

Kenn Kaufman

spent his teens birding throughout North America and Mexico. Now
living in Tucson, Arizona, he continues to travel extensively as a
leader of birding tours. He has served as editor of *Continental
Birdlife*, and has been a regional editor for *American Birds* and a
field identification consultant for *Birding*.

Stuart Keith

is a scientific assistant in the department of ornithology at the
American Museum of Natural History in New York City. He is
co-author of the *Collins Bird Guide*, and served as chairman of the
American Birding Association committee that drew up the second
edition of the association's checklist. In 1980, Keith spent two
months studying seabirds in the South Atlantic. Currently he is
co-authoring and editing a five-volume work, *The Birds of Africa*.

Paul Lehman

is a resident of Santa Barbara, California. His major interests are
bird distribution and field identification. He received a master's
degree in physical geography in 1982, and is currently a part-time
instructor of geography and environmental studies. He also teaches
bird classes to adults. Lehman spends most of his time birding.

Ron Naveen

is editor of *Birding*, the journal of the American Birding
Association, and the author of *Storm-Petrels of the World: An
Introductory Guide to Their Field Identification*. Through his
organization, Whales and Seabirds, he leads tours year-round to the
outer continental shelf of the western North Atlantic and to the
Galapagos Islands. He also leads Antarctic tours and lectures on
seabird identification and the conservation of marine mammals.

John C. Ogden
is a senior staff scientist for the National Audubon Society and co-director of the California Condor Research Program. Prior to his current position, he directed research on colonial wading birds and raptorial birds in the southeastern states for the Audubon Society and the National Park Service. He lives in Ojai, California.

Kenneth C. Parkes
is Curator of Birds at the Carnegie Museum of Natural History in Pittsburgh. Parkes has traveled extensively in North America and elsewhere on birding trips; his professional field work has also taken him to Mexico, the West Indies, Argentina, the Canary Islands, and the Philippines. His research interests include taxonomy, molts, and plumages, with a special focus on the plumage characteristics used in determining the age and sex of birds.

Wayne R. Petersen
is a resident of Massachusetts who has traveled from Arctic Canada to South America and the West Indies. An active bird bander, Petersen is affiliated with the Manomet Bird Observatory and has worked in James Bay with the Canadian Wildlife Service, and as an Earthwatch investigator in Belize. In addition to his biology classes, he teaches bird identification courses, lectures extensively, and has published many papers on various aspects of ornithology.

H. Douglas Pratt
is a freelance wildlife artist and a research associate at the Museum of Zoology at Louisiana State University. For his master's thesis, he studied grackles in southwest Louisiana, and for his doctoral dissertation in zoology he researched the systematics of birds native to Hawaii. He has studied birds throughout Polynesia and Micronesia, as well as in Hawaii, and is preparing a field guide to birds of that region. His work has been widely published.

John T. Ratti
is a professor of wildlife biology at Washington State University. Previously, Ratti was a professor of ornithology and wildlife management at South Dakota State University. His research and publications have focused on the Western Grebe, Canada Goose, Black Brant, Gray Partridge, and Spruce Grouse. Ratti is senior editor of the recent book *Waterfowl Ecology and Management: Selected Readings*, published by the Wildlife Society.

William L. Robinson
received his doctorate from the University of Toronto in 1963. He is author of a monograph about the Spruce Grouse titled *Fool Hen, the Spruce Grouse on the Yellow Dog Plains* (1980) and co-author of the textbook *Wildlife Ecology and Management* (in press). He is a professor of biology at Northern Michigan University in Marquette.

Walter Rosene
received his bachelor's degree from Iowa State University and his master's degree in wildlife biology from Auburn University in Alabama. He spent 25 years with the United States Fish and Wildlife Service, and for the past 20 years has worked as a wildlife consultant on problems of game management. The author of *The Bobwhite Quail–Its Life and Management*, he has published numerous articles and reports.

Richard W. Stallcup
has studied the birds of Point Reyes for more than 25 years, as well as those of San Francisco Bay. As a partner of WINGS, Inc., he has led hundreds of people on North American birding tours. Stallcup has served as president of Western Field Ornithologists and on the California Bird Records Committee; he is the author of *Pelagic Birds of Monterey Bay*. He was instrumental as Steward of the

Farallon Islands in establishing the Point Reyes Bird Observatory, and has been on its staff for 12 years.

Paul W. Sykes, Jr.,
is a wildlife research biologist with the Patuxent Wildlife Research Center of the U.S. Fish and Wildlife Service in Maryland. He is a member of the American Birding Association checklist committee, and Christmas count compiler for Back Bay National Wildlife Refuge and Little Creek, Virginia, and Bodie-Pea Island, North Carolina. He is also a cooperator for three U.S. Fish and Wildlife Service Cooperative Breeding Bird Survey routes in Florida, and serves as a technical and scientific consultant to federal agencies and several conservation organizations. He has seen 746 species to date in North America.

Scott B. Terrill
has been birding since he was ten years old. Terrill is enrolled in the doctoral program at the State University of New York at Albany. His research concerns the behavioral and ecological factors involved in bird migration. He shares his birding enthusiasm with his wife, Linda, with whom he has made birding trips as far south as the Guatemalan border.

Theodore G. Tobish Jr.
was born and raised in eastern Pennsylvania. Since 1973, he has lived in Alaska, where he received a bachelor's degree in biology from the University of Alaska. He has spent several field seasons in the Aleutian Islands and throughout Alaska, working for the U.S. Fish and Wildlife Service and leading bird tours.

Peter D. Vickery
is on the staff of the Natural History Tour Services of the Massachusetts Audubon Society, and has traveled throughout North America, Mexico, and Costa Rica. For six years, he was regional editor of the northeastern Maritime region for *American Birds.* Vickery is the author of the *Annotated Checklist of Maine Birds* and continues to investigate Maine's avifauna.

Terence Wahl
is a research associate in biology at Western Washington University in Bellingham, where he is studying the associations of seabirds with oceanography in the North Pacific. He has served as a consultant on marine birds in Washington, and has led pelagic bird survey trips. His survey experience includes several research cruises in the Pacific and in the Bering Sea.

Robert B. Weeden
holds degrees in wildlife conservation from the universities of Massachusetts and Maine, and has a doctorate in zoology from the University of British Columbia. For 13 years, he studied the ecology and population dynamics of Rock and Willow ptarmigans in northern British Columbia and Alaska. Currently, Weeden is a professor of resource management at the University of Alaska, where he teaches advanced courses in wildlife and natural resource management.

Claudia Wilds
is a research collaborator in the division of birds at the National Museum of Natural History; she is also the field identification editor of *Birding* magazine. Wilds lives in Washington, D.C., and has recently published a guide to finding birds in and around the nation's capital. Most of her field work during the past decade has been at Chincoteague National Wildlife Refuge on the Virginia coast where she has made an intensive study of shorebird migration.

The Artists

As art editor, Al Gilbert selected the artists who were called upon to provide color portraits and black-and-white illustrations. After assigning the pictures, he supervised their accuracy and production until completion.

Guy Tudor served as art consultant, making his knowledge of bird art and photographic sources available to the artists.

James E. Coe
has exhibited his bird paintings at the Leigh Yawkey Woodson Art Museum in Wausau, Wisconsin, and at the Cleveland Museum of Natural History in Ohio. His drawings have appeared in *The Living Bird* and *American Birds* magazines. Coe majored in biology at Harvard University, and is currently a graduate student in painting at Parsons School of Design in New York. His field work has been concentrated in New York and southern New England, with occasional forays into the Neotropics. Most recently, he completed illustrations for a guide to the birds of New Guinea.

Michael DiGiorgio
is a freelance artist living in Potsdam, New York. He enjoys field sketching and painting from life. His illustrations have been published by the National Wildlife Federation, the New York State *Conservationist*, the Cornell Laboratory of Ornithology, the Massachusetts Audubon Society, and the Nature Conservancy. He also illustrated the book *A Life Outdoors*.

Georges Dremeaux
is a wildlife artist and photographer who specializes in birds. He received his bachelor's degree from the University of Miami, where he studied ornithology and avian illustration. For the past five years, he has worked for the Linnaean Society and the Queens County Bird Club in New York City. He is also a jewelry designer.

Al Gilbert
began drawing birds and animals when he was a child. In his teens, he received advice and guidance from George M. Sutton and Don Eckelberry, who helped launch his career as a wildlife artist. Working closely with Dean Amadon of the American Museum of Natural History in New York City, he has illustrated many books, among them *Eagles, Hawks and Falcons of the World* and *Currassows and Related Birds*. His field work has taken him to Africa, Madagascar, Mexico, and South America. In 1978, Gilbert won the Federal Duck Stamp Competition. His paintings have been exhibited in museums and galleries throughout the United States, and he is currently president of the Society of Animal Artists.

Robert Gillmor
is a British freelance artist who received his training at the Fine Art Department of Reading University in England. He is currently chairman of the Society of Wildlife Artists, which he helped to found. His illustrations have appeared in 70 books, as well as numerous journals, and he has exhibited work in the United States, Kenya, France, and the United Kingdom. Gillmor is art editor of *Birds of the Western Palaearctic*, and a vice president of the British Ornithologists' Union. His travels have taken him to Spitsbergen, Iceland, the United States, and East Africa.

H. Jon Janosik
attended Oberlin College, where he studied zoology and anatomy. His ornithological illustrations have appeared in such publications as the *Encyclopaedia Britannica* and the *Florida Naturalist*. In addition, he has worked for the National Geographic Society, the Carnegie Museum in Pittsburgh, and the Saunders Company in

Philadelphia. Janosik's work has been exhibited at numerous institutions, including the British Museum in London and the Los Angeles County Museum. His special interests lie in North American warblers and sea and shore birds.

Michel Kleinbaum

is an amateur illustrator who lives in New York City. His illustrations have appeared in books on the birds of Venezuela, Colombia, and China. Kleinbaum has traveled to Mexico, Costa Rica, Panama, Guatemala, Venezuela, and Colombia; since 1978, he has helped in organizing bird tours to Senegal.

Lawrence B. McQueen

first became interested in birds in his native town in central Pennsylvania. He received his bachelor's degree in wildlife studies from Idaho State University in 1961, and went on to conduct field work on the birds of Idaho. He later attended art school at the University of Oregon, Eugene, where he now lives and specializes in ornithological paintings. His work has been exhibited at the Smithsonian Institution, and in England and Scotland. Currently he is doing field work in Peru.

Paul Singer

is a graphic designer who lives in Brooklyn. A graduate of the Philadelphia College of Art, he has designed exhibits for the Bronx Zoo, the New York Aquarium, the Franklin Park Zoo, the American Numismatic Society, and the Little League Baseball Museum. His work appears in more than 30 books, including the *Audubon Society Encyclopedia of North American Birds*.

Guy Tudor

is a resident of Forest Hills, New York, and has been a freelance wildlife illustrator for 25 years. With extensive field experience in 11 Neotropical countries, he has contributed illustrations to guides on the birds of Venezuela and Colombia. He is currently co-authoring a *Field Guide to South American Birds: Passerines*. His work has appeared in a variety of publications and has been exhibited at the Chicago Field Museum and the National Collection of Fine Arts. Tudor has co-authored articles for *American Birds*, *Birding*, and the *Wilson Bulletin*, and currently serves as a trustee of R.A.R.E., Inc., and as an elective member of the American Ornithologists' Union and the American Birding Association.

John C. Yrizarry

is a lifelong resident of Brooklyn, New York. He is a graduate of the Yale School of Fine Arts and a member of the Society of Animal Artists. His work appears in private collections and has been published in numerous books and magazines, including many nature guides. Yrizarry is an enthusiastic leader of birding tours in the United States, Central America, and the Caribbean.

Dale A. Zimmerman

teaches ornithology at Western New Mexico University in Silver City and serves as an elective member of the American Ornithologists' Union and as a fellow of the Explorers' Club. He travels frequently to his favorite African haunts, and has made birding visits to tropical Asia, Australasia, and the Neotropics. A former student of the late George M. Sutton, Zimmerman is chief artist and co-author of a forthcoming field guide to New Guinea birds. He is currently illustrating Ben King's comprehensive handbook to the birds of the Indian region.

Credits

Photo Credits
The letter immediately following each page number refers to the position of the color photographs on the page; A represents the picture at the top, B, the middle, and C, the bottom.

Ardea London: Jack A. Bailey, 363B; Ian Beames, 173A; J. B. & S. Bottomley, 331C; G. K. Brown, 321C, 349A; C. R. Knights, 269C; Ake Lindau, 349B.

Ron Austing: 227B, 229B, 229C, 231A, 251B, 253B, 259B, 265C, 329A, 409B.

Stephen F. Bailey: 63C, 119B, 255A, 277A, 353B, 359C, 361C.

Don Bleitz/Bleitz Wildlife Foundation: 359A.

William J. Bolte: 309C.

L. Page Brown: 77C.

Fred Bruemmer: 265A, 387A.

P. A. and F. G. Buckley: 381A, 381B, 383C.

S. R. Cannings: 229A.

Ken Carmichael: 155C, 231B.

Robert P. Carr: 291C.

Roger B. Clapp: 53A, 61C, 81C, 361B.

Herbert Clarke: 37A, 47A, 95C, 97C, 111C, 135C, 147B, 195B, 215B, 303B, 327B, 329C, 371A, 409C.

Bruce Coleman, Inc.: Larry R. Ditto, 41B.

Cornell Laboratory of Ornithology: J. Hangle, 367A; Michael Hopiak, 125A; Anthony Losapio, 127B; Paul A. Pemberton, 77B; Caulion Singletary, 305B; Mary M. Tremaine, 319C.

Kent and Donna Dannen: 281A, 281C.

Harry N. Darrow: 121B, 193A, 211B, 219C, 227A, 237A, 237B, 239C, 257B, 307C, 333B, 351B, 355C, 377A, 385C.

Thomas H. Davis: 63A, 65A, 195A, 319A, 321A, 347A, 347B, 365B, 375A, 377C, 379B, 385A, 385B, 387C, 389B, 393A, 395B, 395C, 397B, 399B, 399C, 403C, 405A, 405B.

R. H. Day: 101C, 389C.

Jack Dermid: 109B, 109C, 111B, 129B, 129C, 153A, 299C, 301B, 333C.

Larry R. Ditto: 167C, 207C, 273A, 273B, 297C, 305A, 313C.

Georges Dremeaux: 51A, 275C.

DRK Photo: Stephen J. Krasemann, 35B, 89C; Wayne Lankinen, 239B, 279B, 363C, 383B.

Harry Engels: 125C, 169A, 199B, 217C.

Jacob Faust: 223C, 237C, 247A.

Kenneth W. Fink: 37B, 39C, 43A, 55C, 105C, 113C, 125B, 139A, 141A, 145A, 147C, 149B, 149C, 151C, 155A, 155B, 157A, 157B, 157C, 161B, 165A, 165B, 167A, 169B, 187B, 191A, 191B, 201C, 207B, 211C, 251C, 267B, 271A, 275A, 287C, 289A, 289B, 291A, 307A, 323B, 325B, 339B, 351C, 357B, 363A, 371C, 373B, 379C, 395A, 399A.

Jeff Foott: 85A, 103C, 225A, 255B, 285A, 285B, 285C, 311C, 313B, 319B.

Dick Forsman: 355B.

Thomas W. French: 217B.

D. A. Gill: 277B, 279C.

James M. Greaves: 137B.

William D. Griffin: 107C, 115C, 121A, 127C.

Velma Harris: 305C.

Hiroshi Hasegawa: 49B, 49C.

James Hawkings: 185C, 371B, 391C.

Dale R. Herter: 107B.

F. Eugene Hester: 159C.

Warren Jacobi: 95A, 135B.

Gord James: 93C.

Joseph R. Jehl, Jr.: 83C, 197C.

Isidor Jeklin: 199C, 203B, 203C.

Paul Johnsgard: 163A, 163B, 169C, 171A, 265B, 393C.

David B. Johnson: 367C.

R. Y. Kaufman/Yogi, Inc.: 119C, 151C, 183C, 185A, 369B.

Steven C. Kaufman: 115A, 275B.

Stuart Keith: 53C.

G. C. Kelley: 41C, 47B, 123B, 123C, 213C, 267C, 295A, 295B, 325C, 327A, 327C, 339C.

Wayne Lankinen: 37C, 43C, 89B, 141C, 247B, 273C, 283C, 329B, 351A, 365A, 369C, 377B.

Frans Lanting: 253C.

Calvin Larsen: 91A, 213A.

Tom and Pat Leeson: 171C, 191C, 283B.

Linnea Associates: Sue Quinlan, 353C, 375A.

Thomas W. Martin: 389A.

Joe McDonald: 263C.

Albert D. McGrew: 241C.

David P. McNicholas: 181A.

Anthony Mercieca: 113B, 137C, 153C, 163C, 167B, 177C, 179C, 181B, 205B, 221B, 247C, 259A, 261C, 263B, 289C, 297A, 297B, 301C, 307B, 365C, 403A.

C. Allan Morgan: 243B, 245C, 287B, 293A, 309A, 315A, 315B, 341B, 379A.

Stephen H. Morrell: 335B.

National Audubon Society Collection/Photo Researchers, Inc.: Tom Bledsoe, 339A; John Bova, 93B; Philip Boyer, 245A; William R. Curtsinger, 165C; Jerry L. Ferrara, 337B; M. P. Kahl, 261B; William Ray, 239A, 347C; Gail Rubin, 317B; Bill Wilson, 59A.

Naturfotograferna Bildbyra: Bjorn Eyvind Swahn, 331B.

J. Oldenettel: 59C, 103B, 115B, 149A.

Arthur Panzer: 69B, 81B, 143A, 205A, 227C.

Dennis R. Paulson: 45A, 61B, 83A, 99B, 145B, 233C.

Jan Erik Pierson: 95B, 293C.

John C. Pitcher: 45B, 179A, 349C, 393B.

Rod Planck: 147A, 153B, 159A, 345B.

H. Douglas Pratt: 109A, 259C, 271B.

John T. Ratti: 47C, 271C, 303A.

C. Gable Ray: 407B.

J. V. Remsen: 223B, 397A.

Laura Riley: 105B.

Lynn Rogers: 161A.

Root Resources: Ben Goldstein, 311B.

Leonard Lee Rue, III: 175A, 177A, 189A, 189C, 201A, 209A, 317C.

Ervio Sian: 99C, 161C, 187A, 201B, 203A, 235B, 257C, 283A, 375B, 401C, 403B.

Arnold Small: 39A, 39B, 43B, 45C, 59B, 63B, 87A, 97B, 101A, 113A, 117A, 117B, 117C, 121C, 131C, 145C, 151A, 171B, 173C, 175B, 181C, 183B, 193C, 195C, 199A, 213B, 215A, 235C, 243A, 337C, 373C, 375C, 405C, 407A, 411A, 411B.

Bruce A. Sorrie: 51B, 57C, 65B, 65C, 85C, 91B, 97A, 99A, 175C, 233B, 235A, 323C, 325A, 353A, 387B, 401B, 413A.

Barbara Spencer: 57A.

Tom Stack and Associates: Keith H. Murakami, 301A.

Alvin E. Staffan: 299B.

Lynn M. Stone: 111A.

Paul W. Sykes, Jr.: 85B, 87B, 209B, 209C, 221C, 223A.

Frank S. Todd/ Sea World, Inc.: 71B, 131B, 139B, 141B, 143B, 143C, 159B, 173B, 177B, 193B, 197A, 197B, 215C, 291B, 293B.

R. Van Nostrand: 119A.

Peter D. Vickery: 251A, 277C.

VIREO (Academy of Natural Sciences of Philadelphia): P. G. Connors, 413B; J. P. Myers, 401A; Don Roby, 279A, 373A.

Black-and-white Drawings

The letter immediately following each page number refers to the position of an illustration: A indicates the drawing at the top of a page, B, the second drawing, C, the third, and so forth.

Color Portraits

The letter following each page number refers to the position of the color portrait: A represents the portrait at the top of a page, B, the middle, and C, the bottom.

Index

In this index, the names of orders are preceded by red dots; family names are preceded by blue dots.

Chanticleer Staff

Publisher: Paul Steiner
Editor-in-Chief: Gudrun Buettner
Managing Editor: Susan Costello
Natural Science Editor: John Farrand, Jr.
Project Editor: Ann Whitman
Senior Editor: Mary Beth Brewer
Editorial Assistants: Karel Birnbaum, Katherine Booz
Production: Helga Lose, Amy Roche
Art Director: Carol Nehring
Art Assistants: Ayn Svoboda, Karen Wollman
Picture Library: Edward Douglas, Dana Pomfret
Range Maps: Paul Singer
Design: Massimo Vignelli